PUBLIC COMMUNICATION CAMPAIGNS

THIRD EDITION

We dedicate this volume to our wives,
who have shown remarkable
patience during this project,
as during most other aspects of our lives:
Claire Brown Johnson and Sandi Walker Smith.

RONALD E. RICE | CHARLES K. ATKIN

Editors

PUBLIC COMMUNICATION CAMPAIGNS

THIRD EDITION

Sage Publications, Inc.
International Educational and Professional Publisher
Thousand Oaks ▪ London ▪ New Delhi

For information:

Sage Publications, Inc.
2455 Teller Road
Thousand Oaks, California 91320
E-mail: order@sagepub.com

Sage Publications Ltd.
6 Bonhill Street
London EC2A 4PU
United Kingdom

Sage Publications India Pvt. Ltd.
M-32 Market
Greater Kailash I
New Delhi 110 048 India

Printed in the United States of America

Library of Congress Cataloging-in-Publication Data

Public communication campaigns / edited by Ronald E. Rice and Charles K. Atkin.— 3rd ed.
    p. cm.
Includes bibliographical references and index.
ISBN 0-7619-2205-9 (cloth) — ISBN 0-7619-2206-7 (pbk.)
1. Publicity. 2. Public relations. 3. Advocacy advertising.
I. Rice, Ronald E. II. Atkin, Charles K.
HM1226 .P83 2000
659—dc21

00-011070

06 07 7 6 5 4

Acquiring Editor:	Margaret H. Seawell
Editorial Assistant:	Heidi Van Middlesworth
Production Editor:	Claudia A. Hoffman
Editorial Assistant:	Cindy Bear
Typesetter/Designer:	Tina Hill and Janelle LeMaster
Indexer:	Molly Hall

Contents

Preface

The first edition of *Public Communication Campaigns* in 1981, with William Paisley as coeditor, broke new ground in publishing about theory, research, and practice in nonprofit communication campaigns. The second edition, with Charles Atkin as coeditor, benefited from feedback about the uses and needs of the first edition. In both editions, the book has been widely adopted for classes, and used for research and training, in communication, journalism, public relations, mass media, advertising, and public health programs in undergraduate, master's, and PhD classes. More than 13,000 copies of the two editions have been sold. Clearly, this book has an established presence, broad scope, and rigorous reputation.

The third edition will continue in the tradition of ongoing improvement and expansion into new areas. Most chapters are entirely new, reflecting up-to-date theory, research, experience, and campaigns. We keep a few, significantly revised, central chapters and campaign samplers from the second edition.

Part I, Historical and Theoretical Foundations, begins with Paisley's overview of the conceptual and historical foundations of public communication campaigns. Part I continues with McGuire's comprehensive review of the social-psychological research on persuasive communication with specific practical implications, Atkin's integrative summary of the theoretic foundations of and practical guidelines for the design of health messages and campaigns, Dervin and Frenette's theoretical overview and summary of experiences from campaigns using the Sense-Making approach, and Stephenson and Witte's review and analysis of the use of fear appeals (grounded in a recent theoretic model for message design).

Part II, Campaign Design and Evaluation, includes Valente's tutorial on campaign evaluation, Atkin and Freimuth's much-revised overview of forma-

tive evaluation emphasizing message design, Rice and Foote's updated expli-
cation and application of a systems approach to campaign evaluation, Salmon
and Murray-Johnson's theoretic and pragmatic analysis of the distinctions between campaign effects and effectiveness, and Snyder's brief but comprehensive meta-analysis of the effectiveness of large-scale-mediated campaigns.

Part III, Lessons From the Field, provides Flora's review of the famous
Stanford community health projects; Cappella, Fishbein, and Hornik's integration of theoretical foundations (especially media priming) for health campaigns as applied to the current national antidrug campaign; Dozier, Grunig,
and Grunig's analysis of the potential for public relations to be two-way symmetric communication campaigns; and Piotrow and Kincaid's discussion of a
strategic communication approach toward family health and reproductive
planning in international settings.

Part IV, A Campaign Sampler, covers a wide range of short "lessons from
the field," with many new, intriguing, and controversial campaigns ranging
from bears, cows, and rats to drinking, littering, and sensation-seeking.

Part V, New Approaches and Current Challenges, introduces a variety of recent developments in communication campaigns: Bracht's overview of community partnership strategies, Singhal and Rogers's review and analysis of the
entertainment-education approach, Buller and colleagues' case study of using
World Wide Web-based messages and resources for smoking cessation and
prevention, Lieberman's conceptual and empirical introduction to the use of
interactive compact disk and computer games for children's health campaigns,
and Wallack and Dorfman's review and suggestions for using media advocacy
as a policy component of health communication.

We decided not to include political campaigns in this edition. From a practical standpoint, we cannot do justice to this complex and heavily researched domain in just a couple of chapters. Philosophically, political campaigns are
somewhat distinct from "public communication" campaigns. The latter are
public service oriented in the sense that the purpose is to benefit society, although the philosophy of what is "good for the public" can be rather biased and
self-serving for certain campaign sponsors. A private communication campaign, in contrast, is exemplified by a candidate attempting to get elected, a
political party attempting to bend public opinion in an advantageous partisan
direction, a company trying to sell its product or service (or to enhance its reputation), and an advocacy group attempting to advance its own particular cause
(or enhance its organization's condition).

We acknowledge and thank all our contributors. They have been creative,
thoughtful, rigorous, timely, and downright pleasant, despite the first editor's
continued revisions to their drafts, gentle but possibly intrusive inquiries about
the status of chapters, constant warnings about page lengths, and requests
for differently formatted word processing files, and the second editor's
straight-to-the-point questions about theoretical and research details. It has
been a great honor, and social and academic pleasure, to work with them all—

although they may or may not feel the same way. The Internet has definitely made a major improvement with regard to keeping in touch with, and exchanging draft chapters among, a diverse, busy, and variously located group of contributors and collaborators. We also thank Margaret Seawell from Sage, who encouraged us to take on the revision, Leticia Gutierrez from Sage, who managed all the legal and financial details, and Claudia Hoffman from Sage, who managed the editing and proofreading process.

PART I

Historical and Theoretical Foundations

Public Communication Campaigns

The American Experience

William J. Paisley

Public communication campaigns are a familiar and essential part of American civic culture. Campaign topics range from personal issues such as health to social issues such as equal opportunity, energy conservation, and environmental protection. Campaigns are regarded as public service programs if their goals are widely supported by the public and policymakers. If their goals are controversial, however, then campaigns are regarded as advocacy strategies. As societal values change, some campaign topics (e.g., race and gender equality) move from the second category to the first. Some topics (e.g., the traditional American diet now regarded as unhealthy) move from the first category to the second.

CAMPAIGN STAKEHOLDERS

This volume, written by social scientists, discusses how public communication campaigns have matured in recent decades, in part as a result of the contributions of social science to campaign planning and implementation. Social scientists are only the latest group of stakeholders to be involved in public communication campaigns, however. Prior to World War II, the principal stakeholders were voluntary associations, the mass media, and the federal government. These stakeholders are as active as ever. Three other stakeholders—foundations, trade unions, and corporations—became increasingly involved in public communication campaigns following World War II.

Voluntary associations—professional, service oriented, religious, and social—are often the lead organizations in public communication campaigns. In the public's view, associations possess entitlement to address particular issues.

The mass media publish and broadcast an agenda of issues that are thought to be important to the public. Via editorials and investigative reporting, publishers and broadcasters advocate action with respect to certain issues. "One editorial does not a campaign make," but with tenacity and courage (in the face of possible revenue losses), the media have conducted effective campaigns for more than a century.

Government agencies also conduct and sponsor public communication campaigns. Direct government involvement in campaigns was once rare. Beginning with the expansion of federal social programs in FDR's New Deal, however, it became common for agencies to use communication campaigns to foster public awareness and favorable attitudes toward federal social programs.

Foundations, including endowments and charitable trusts, are similar to government agencies in their methods of sponsoring public communication campaigns. Foundations tend to be less politicized than government agencies and more able to undertake controversial campaigns, support innovative methods, and address issues continuously across political cycles. The officers of large foundations, however, tend to be more conservative than their counterparts in government. As a result of these contrasting tendencies, a groundbreaking campaign may make its surprising debut in either sector.

Trade unions owe much of their success and, in some cases, their very existence to communication campaigns that persuade the public to support their goals. The leverage of public support is important when workers are less skilled and therefore more replaceable by management. In such cases, public action such as a consumer boycott may be needed to balance the negotiating power of management and labor. This scenario, guided by the Gandhian principles of labor organizer César Chávez, led to the "grape boycott" and the subsequent recognition of the United Farm Workers union in California's agricultural valleys in 1970.

Corporations and industry councils promote awareness of activities that have public benefits (e.g., Chevron's "People Care" campaign). There are also campaigns of greater depth on issues about which industry is expected to be concerned. One example is Shell Oil's campaign of driver safety booklets, such as "Alone Behind the Wheel," prepared in cooperation with the National Safety Council.

Social scientists' main contribution to campaigns is their theory-grounded approach to planning and conducting campaigns. This approach sometimes conflicts with the intuitive approach of other stakeholders, but social scientists are the catalysts of a new era of cooperation among the stakeholders of campaigns. Their research confirms the roles played by other stakeholders.

This chapter is largely devoted to campaigners who came before the social scientists. During three centuries of American public communication campaigns, there are more similarities than differences in the objectives and methods of campaigners. The chapter discusses some defining characteristics of public communication campaigns and then summarizes some major reform movements and campaigns in the colonial, national, and modern eras. The final section explores three challenges to public communication campaigns that arose between the postwar years and the beginning of the 21st century.

DEFINING CHARACTERISTICS OF PUBLIC COMMUNICATION CAMPAIGNS

Two different but complementary definitions of public communication campaigns are in use. Definition in terms of *objectives* focuses on one group's intention to change another group's beliefs or behavior. This definition comes to the fore when intentions are controversial, such as campaigns about abortion. Its most important implication is that the change objectives may be accomplished through a communication campaign or through noncommunication strategies such as behavioral engineering.

Public communication campaigns are also defined in terms of the *methods* they employ. This definition comes to the fore when campaigns employ innovative or controversial methods, such as guerrilla theater in the Vietnam era or the confrontational tactics of antiabortion groups today. Its most important implication is that a public communication campaign may involve a conventional mix of brochures, posters, advertisements, and commercials or a different array of communication methods. In industrialized nations, the crowded communication environment favors unusual methods that draw attention to themselves, such as large billboards and murals, issue mascots, issue icons, and messages that appear in unexpected places. In nations with fewer media, innovative methods have ranged from acting troupes to birth-control slogans painted on elephants and key chains bearing plastic-encased condoms.

Reform, defined as action that makes society or the lives of individuals better, is a unifying principle of public communication campaigns. *Better* is defined by emerging values in a society during each period in its history. Public consciousness of a social issue generally increases over time. Today's definition of better may have been too extreme yesterday and may be too moderate tomorrow. In addition, when an issue involves contending interests, the negotiated settlement of those interests is adjusted through experience—that is, over time.

Thus, the definition of public communication campaigns can focus on objectives (Are they strategies of social control insofar as one group intends to influence the beliefs or behavior of another group?) or methods (Are they a genre of communication that could be called noncommercial advertising?).

Implications of the Social Control Definition

If campaigns are defined as strategies of social control, then their relationship to other social control strategies is thought-provoking. One government agency, the U.S. Forest Service, has developed a paradigm of the "three E's" to protect the forests from public misuse: education, engineering, and enforcement. Public communication campaigns concerned with wildfires, vandalism, pollution, and so on comprise the education part of this triad. Foresters also try to make the forest "people proof" without limiting access. They engineer campsites that are fire safe and install durable fixtures such as steel trail signs. If the public persists in damaging the forests, then enforcement takes over. Foresters can limit access, require fire permits, and prosecute vandals.

Each society in each era of its development has an ideology that guides its use of education, engineering, and enforcement to promote change. In the United States, if engineering promises a quick solution, as was often the case in the 19th and 20th centuries, then education and enforcement may not be tried until engineering has had its chance. The first hope is that a miracle drug or equivalent technology will be developed. Education is often the second strategy to be tried. Enforcement is the third, and usually unpopular, strategy.

It is important to note that the social control definition is only a heuristic for planning campaigns and not a judgment of campaign planners' motives. In fact, it is assumed that campaign planners do intend to influence the beliefs and behavior of others. Most public communication campaigns are regarded as prosocial and are overseen by responsible advisers. Even so, many campaign issues are two-sided (e.g., abortion, nuclear power, and lumbering in national forests), and each side will claim prosocial benefits.

In all five postwar decades—a period of rapid social change in the United States—the intertwined strategies of education, engineering, and enforcement could be seen in operation. In the 1950s, civil rights activists innovated new forms of protest that exploited the mass media coverage of their movement. The fledgling medium of television provided a national showcase for the principles of nonviolence and "the dignity of the oppressed" that were borrowed from Gandhi's Indian independence movement and the nonviolent disruptions and hunger strikes of British and American suffragists. The 1950s saw a burst of engineering creativity ranging from antibiotics, polio vaccine, and the oral contraceptive to highway and automobile safety, housing, community planning, and the first social uses of computing. Also in the 1950s, enforcement in the form of a U.S. Supreme Court decision struck down the doctrine of "separate but equal" services for African Americans.

The early 1960s were marked by an eager faith in engineering solutions. Buoyed by successes in medicine that were linked metaphorically to social ills,

John Kennedy's and Lyndon Johnson's social engineers drafted programs to combat poverty, illiteracy, inequality, and so on. Some of the programs benefited some people, but it was obvious by 1970 that social engineering was quite different from medical engineering.

The favored solution in the 1970s was enforcement. Harmful or wasteful conditions were targeted for regulation. Richard Nixon signed a bill banning cigarette advertising on television and radio. With the blessing of the Supreme Court, the Federal Trade Commission expanded its antitrust powers to ban deceptive advertising. The Occupational Safety and Health Administration, the Equal Employment Opportunity Commission, and even the Federal Communications Commission took their turns as "enforcers" in the 1970s.

Dissatisfaction with both the engineering and the enforcement strategies became evident in the 1980s. Engineering often fails because of a faulty analysis of the problem. Engineering also fails when available knowledge cannot produce a solution. Enforcement fails when policies are difficult to enforce and when the policies overreach the problem (e.g., some policies that are lampooned for "political correctness").

The 1990s restored a promising balance in the three social change strategies. Engineering improvements ranged from new drugs (e.g., for HIV remission) to safer environments (e.g., automobile airbags). New laws significantly reduced the amount of smoking in workplaces and public sites. New policies of inclusiveness increased the participation of many groups in the social mainstream.

The most dramatic developments of the 1990s, however, involved communication technology. The prior edition of this book, published in 1989, did not anticipate the Internet revolution, the ubiquity of personal computers, or the proliferation of cable and satellite television channels. Future historians may regard the Internet as the most significant paradigm-shifting development of the 1990s. (For specific treatment of new media, see Chapters 14, 29, and 30, this volume.)

Hundreds of Internet web sites are devoted to campaign issues. For example, the two-sided issues mentioned previously (abortion, nuclear power, and lumbering) are well represented on the Internet. One popular search engine lists 333 web sites for abortion, 134 web sites for nuclear power, and 79 web sites for lumbering. The search engine classifies many abortion web sites as prochoice or prolife by their own descriptions. It is clear that the Internet is now one of the venues of public debate and that other competing points of view are only "a click away."

Implications of the Process Definition

When engineering and enforcement are less feasible and education is the only strategy that is worth pursuing, attention shifts to the process of communicating. Modern campaigns draw on the techniques of journalists, media producers, educators, small group specialists, and others. Campaign planners synthesize these techniques into a variety of approaches designed for different target audiences, because each audience lives in its own communication environment that filters the messages that reach it. Each audience responds in its own way to appeals based on altruism, self-interest, desire, fear, and so on.

The process-based discipline of planning campaigns leads to conceptual frameworks for understanding what a campaign should accomplish in terms of objectives, messages, contexts, and audiences. These frameworks enable the planner to (a) clarify the objectives and roles of the campaign's stakeholders, (b) choose and adapt approaches according to audience differences, (c) sequence and coordinate campaign activities, (d) monitor the campaign's possible failure points, (e) improve the campaign on the basis of field trials, and (f) transfer the successes of one campaign in one setting to other campaigns in other settings.

THE ESSENTIAL CONCEPTS OF AGENDA AND ENTITLEMENT

The success of a campaign depends on public perception that the campaign issue is an important one, according to its position on the ever-changing public agenda of issues, and that the campaigners have an entitlement to be involved with the issue.

The concepts of agenda and entitlement originate in a society's social contract. Limits on authority in early America, combined with the diverse goals and customs of American settlers, created a primary role for persuasion and consensus in the American social contract. The first "negotiated settlements" in America were just that—places where people agreed to live together. Disagreement had a novel geographical dimension. If dissenters could move on to the next valley, then those who remained were agreeing to build a community together.

Enclaves of like-minded people, dotted along the rivers and trails of westward expansion, were a feature of early America. No one community was exceptional, but the juxtaposition of so many different communities was exceptional. We can never forget the two dark forces of American settlement—slavery and the suppression of native cultures—nor the bloodshed sometimes caused by uncompromising convictions. Simultaneously, a remarkable social experiment, based on persuasion and consensus, was beginning.

The public agenda, when measured by pollsters, always contains some "gut issues," such as disease, and some "pocketbook issues," such as taxes. Few issues, however, are truly universal. At any time, issues rise on the public agenda because the problem has gotten worse (e.g., pollution), because changes in the society have made the problem relevant to more people (e.g., heart disease), because public consciousness has caught up with the problem (e.g., rights of disabled persons), or because a solution for the problem has become more feasible (e.g., pollution-reducing technologies).

We come now to the question of entitlement to be the advocate of an issue. Is entitlement mainly a question of law, public policy, or public acceptance? Constitutional entitlement is a given in the United States. Within the modern era, however, Margaret Sanger was indicted for sending birth-control tracts through the mail. Authorities and citizens still harass unpopular campaigns, but the courts affirm the First Amendment right of the campaigns to proceed.

Public policy affects entitlement when there is a jurisdictional or "ownership" debate over issues. For example, a recently formed agency or association may have a more activist charter and more funds for its cause than an established agency or association. (This chapter in the second edition briefly described the rivalry and eventual cooperation between the older American Cancer Society and the newer National Cancer Institute.)

Public acceptance is the final test of entitlement. The public is ready with the American comeback, "This is none of your business," unless the communicator is clearly a stakeholder in the issue. Aggrieved groups have first-party entitlement to communicate in their own interest. Second-party entitlement is suspect; we wonder why a group wants to be involved in someone else's grievance.

Some issues, however, have no first-party group to claim entitlement. Whales, seal pups, and future generations of Americans are the first parties of campaigns, but they are not their own advocates. In such cases, second-party groups step forward to serve as advocates, sometimes putting themselves at risk as surrogate first parties. For example, the "save the whales" and "save the seals" groups increased their entitlement when the public saw them risking harm on the ocean and ice floes. Even when first parties are their own advocates, other groups, such as white civil rights workers in the South during the 1960s, Vietnam draft protesters who were beyond draft age, and straight supporters of gay and lesbian causes, gain entitlement according to the personal risk or cost of their actions.

Frederick Douglass, regarded as the most effective black abolitionist of the 19th century, had an unusual entitlement problem. His self-taught public speaking was so forceful that audiences doubted his origins in slavery and his fugitive status. He felt compelled to write his autobiography, *Life and Times of Frederick Douglass* (1845), giving the name of his former owner. He then spent 2 years on a speaking tour in England to avoid recapture but returned with enough funds to purchase his freedom and to launch an abolition newspaper, *The North Star,* in Rochester, New York.

Entitlement based on expertise is subject to public acceptance as well. Expert entitlement is a limited license that can be used up if experts publicize too many issues or issues outside their area of expertise. In the late 1980s, Surgeon General C. Everett Koop was perhaps the most effective expert communicator in America. He skillfully spent his entitlement on only the major issues of smoking and AIDS prevention, resisting the temptation to use his "bully pulpit" on behalf of all health issues.

THREE CENTURIES OF AMERICAN
PUBLIC COMMUNICATION CAMPAIGNS

The history of the United States is interwoven with communication campaigns from the colonial era to the present day. The communication campaign is only one means of influencing public knowledge, attitudes, and behavior. The limited authority of American governments, both colonial and national, created an early reliance on the communication campaign as an instrument of social change.

The French writer Alexis de Tocqueville was one of the first to describe how communication informs and mobilizes public action in America. In his notes on traveling throughout the United States (translated as *Democracy in America*, 1835/1961), he described "the skill with which the inhabitants of the United States succeed in proposing a common object to the exertions of a great many men, and in getting them voluntarily to pursue it" (p. 129).

Reform was accomplished differently in America than in England or France, according to de Tocqueville (1835/1961):

> Wherever, at the head of some new undertaking, you see the Government of France or a man of rank in England, in the United States you will be sure to find an association. . . . If it be proposed to advance some truth or foster some feeling by the encouragement of a great example, [Americans] form a society. (pp. 128-129)

In his American travels, de Tocqueville witnessed the flowering of the abolition, temperance, and women's rights movements as well as the ferment of Jacksonian democracy and westward expansion. The public agenda was crowded with other issues as well: treatment of the insane; reform of prisons; education of children; education and other opportunities for the deaf and blind; better housing for workers and particularly the "mill girls" of New England; control of gambling and prostitution in the cities; construction of libraries; and always the latest news on utopian communities and their experiments with property, labor, marriage, child rearing, nutrition, and so on.

Individual Reformers in the 18th Century

Prior to 1800, American public communication campaigns were often conducted by strong-willed individuals who reached the public through the pulpit or the printing press. One of the earliest and best examples in the colonial era was Reverend Cotton Mather's campaign to promote inoculation during Boston's smallpox epidemic of 1721-1722. Mather was able to show that death from smallpox was nine times more prevalent among the uninoculated than among the inoculated. Mather's pamphlets and personal appeals were opposed by the city's physicians and the *New England Courant,* published by James and Benjamin Franklin. In November 1721, at the height of the controversy, a bomb was thrown into Mather's home.

For a time, Philadelphia was the headquarters of many types of campaigns. In 1775, the first abolition society in America, the Society for the Relief of Free Negroes Unlawfully Held in Bondage, was founded there by Benjamin Franklin and Benjamin Rush. In the same year in Philadelphia, Thomas Paine published the first American defense of women's rights in his *Pennsylvania Magazine*. In 1776, Thomas Paine's *Common Sense,* the rallying call of American independence, sold 100,000 copies. Because the population of the 13 colonies was approximately 1% of today's national population, a comparable bestseller today would sell 10 million copies.

In 1784, the first important temperance tract, *Inquiry Into the Effects of Spiritous Liquors on the Human Body and Mind,* was written by Benjamin Rush. In 1787, Rush wrote *Thoughts on Female Education,* which argued that the education of women was necessary to ensure that children would be instructed properly in citizenship. Three intertwined issues of American social reform in the 19th century—abolition, women's rights, and temperance—were thus brushed by the 18th century quill of the Philadelphia physician Benjamin Rush. In 1812, Rush also published *Medical Inquiries and Observations Upon the Diseases of the Mind.* Actual reform in the treatment of the mentally ill, however, did not begin until Dorothea Dix's crusade in the 1840s.

Dix is a transitional figure in American reform. She was a lone crusader in a century that saw increasing reliance on associations and mass media to move voters and legislators toward unavoidable decisions on abolition and suffrage.

Dix, a New England schoolteacher and single woman of modest means, was probably not seeking a life of exhaustion and sacrifice when she volunteered to teach Sunday school at a Cambridge, Massachusetts, jail. On that visit in 1841, however, she witnessed treatment of mentally ill persons that stunned her, and she spent more than 1 year visiting other jails and prisons throughout Massachusetts, gathering facts for a deposition to the Massachusetts legislature. Her goal was humane treatment of the mentally ill in new institutions created for them. In Massachusetts and later in many other states and countries, she worked effectively behind the scenes, seldom speaking in public. Subsequently, her cause broadened to prison reform, particularly the need to establish separate facilities for women.

Associations and Reform in the 19th Century

Issues that are entrenched in law or custom may require decades of lobbying, campaigning, and confronting the opposition. The numeric strength and continuity of associations have proved to be invaluable in achieving reform over the long term.

Abolition associations were the first to adopt the modern form of local chapters coordinated by a headquarters office. The American Anti-Slavery Society was founded in 1833. Its membership increased with each act of violence against the movement, such as the mob beating of abolitionist publisher

William Lloyd Garrison in Boston in 1835 and the murder of another abolitionist publisher, Elijah Lovejoy, in Alton, Illinois, in 1837. Mobs demolished the printing press at Lovejoy's *Alton Observer* three times during 1836 and 1837. He was killed defending the fourth press. By 1838, the American Anti-Slavery Society had 1,350 chapters and 250,000 members. Adjusted for population growth, an association of comparable size today would have more than 4 million members.

When Lucretia Mott and Elizabeth Cady Stanton were rebuffed because of their gender as delegates to the 1840 World Anti-Slavery Conference in London, they realized that their loyalties were divided between Negro rights and women's rights. Several years of increasingly public protest led to the Seneca Falls (New York) Convention on Women's Rights in 1848, where 68 women and 32 men signed a Declaration of Principles for women's suffrage. Frederick Douglass, the black abolitionist and publisher of *The North Star* in Rochester, spoke in support of the declaration.

The intertwined character of 19th-century reform movements is also evident in the lifelong temperance campaigning of feminists. Mott, Stanton, Lucy Stone, Susan B. Anthony, and Frances Willard spoke on suffrage one day and on temperance the next. The "evil" of alcohol was not primarily a moral issue for the feminists but an economic issue. Not until legislatures began to pass property reform laws, led by Vermont in 1847, could married women retain title even to real estate they had owned prior to marriage. Nor were women guaranteed a share even of their own earnings. A drunkard husband could bring economic disaster to the household.

The Women's Christian Temperance Union was founded in 1874. By 1878, after Frances Willard took control from more conservative leadership, it was sponsoring "Home Protection Drives" to petition state legislatures for local option on the manufacture and sale of alcoholic beverages.

The coalition against women's suffrage drew its oratory from southern politicians and its funds from the liquor lobby. The politicians were determined to deny the vote to black women, whereas the liquor manufacturers were determined to keep protemperance women away from the polls (Flexner, 1975, p. 307).

The suffragists' communication strategy was multifaceted. Susan B. Anthony's New York campaign of 1854 was the first to use county "captains" to gather petition signatures. In the same New York campaign, Stanton testified before the state legislature.

Mass communication was another strategy of the suffragists. Several suffrage newspapers were published after the Civil War, notably Anthony's *The Revolution,* the masthead of which proclaimed, "Men, their rights and nothing more; women, their rights and nothing less."

A book is not regarded as a public communication campaign in itself. A few books, however, became the texts of campaigns in America. The importance of Harriet Beecher Stowe's tract, *Uncle Tom's Cabin* (1852), was such that

Abraham Lincoln, it is said, greeted her 10 years later as "the little woman who wrote the book that started this great war." With sales of 300,000 copies in the first year, *Uncle Tom's Cabin* was known everywhere in the nonslave states. Later critics charged that Stowe portrayed black people as childlike, but in the 1850s, she brought the issue of slavery back to a moral foundation when it had become a pawn of sectional rivalry.

In addition to grassroots organizing, legislative testimony, and mass communication, a fourth strategy of the reformers was confrontation, which brought publicity in newspapers that ignored their peaceful efforts. In the general election of 1872, Anthony led a party of 16 women to the polls in Rochester, New York, where they registered and voted illegally. The Grant administration chose to make an example of Anthony; she was tried and convicted in 1873.

Confrontation was a strategy of other 19th-century movements as well. The abolitionists did not need to seek confrontation, which awaited them in many northern cities. Neither did they avoid confrontation by meeting only in safe settings such as churches. The temperance movement did not have an official confrontation policy, but Carry Nation made headlines in Kansas and New York. Her saloon-bashing hatchet was a newspaper cartoonist's delight. Saloon owners and patrons dreaded the sight of her 6-foot, 175-pound frame at the door. She was repeatedly beaten during her forays, and she was arrested at least 30 times.

The increasing power of the mass media to shape public opinion after the Civil War is illustrated by cartoonist Thomas Nast's campaign to unseat William Marcy "Boss" Tweed and the Tammany Hall political machine in New York. Nast enjoyed high credibility among New York readers because of his prounion and antislavery cartoons in *Harper's Weekly* during the Civil War.

Tweed was only one in a long line of corrupt New York politicians. As late as 1932, Tammany leader and New York mayor Jimmy Walker was forced to resign. Tweed was the target at hand, however, when Nast turned his attention to local politics. Nast's famous cartoons "Tammany Tiger Loose" and "Group of Vultures Waiting for the Storm to Blow Over," both published in 1871, led to probes that toppled Tweed. After a brief prison sentence, Tweed fled to Spain to evade arrest on other charges. He was recognized from his likeness in Nast's cartoons, extradited, and convicted.

Throughout the continent, a one-person campaign to preserve wilderness areas was evolving into a major national organization. Scottish-born John Muir came to California in 1868, imbued with a transcendental respect for wilderness. In the 1870s, Muir began to gather public and government support for national parks in the Sierra Nevada mountains. This was a hard sell because almost no one in the eastern establishment had seen the wonders of the Yosemite Valley or the sequoia groves of the Sierra Nevada. Muir's strategy was to describe in articles and books what others had not seen. Some of Muir's books, such as *The Mountains of California* (1894) and *The Yosemite* (1912), rank among the finest American nature writing.

Yosemite and Sequoia National Parks were established by Congress in 1890, followed within a few years by other national parks and national forests adjacent to them. During the 1890s, business interests were partly successful in delaying congressional implementation of these land protection measures. Conservationists, led by Muir, countered by establishing the Sierra Club in 1892. With Muir as its president until his death in 1914, the Sierra Club became an effective voice for conservation.

Mass Media and Reform in the 20th Century

The role that mass media would play in America's increasingly pluralistic society was anticipated by de Tocqueville's (1835/1961) observation:

> When men are no longer united amongst themselves by firm and lasting ties, it is impossible to obtain the concurrence of any great number of them, unless you can persuade every man whose concurrence you require that his private interest obliges him voluntarily to unite his exertions to the exertions of all the rest. This can only be habitually and conveniently effected by means of a newspaper; nothing but a newspaper can drop the same thought into a thousand minds at the same moment. (p. 134)

At the end of the 19th century, the initiative for reforming many social problems shifted from associations to the mass media. Many of the problems, by their very nature, were not the rallying causes of organized activity. The muckrakers writing for *McClure's, Cosmopolitan, Collier's, Hampton's, Pearson's, Everybody's,* and other magazines first had to convince the public that impure food, price collusion, child labor, tenement squalor, and unavailable health care for the poor were social evils.

New printing technologies, the rise of literacy, and momentous national events combined to put more publications in the public's hands than ever before in history. Newspaper circulation increased from one newspaper for every five households in 1850 to more than one for one in 1910. To sustain the rapid growth in circulation, newspapers and magazines began to create news on causes of their own choosing.

Muckrakers such as Lincoln Steffens, Ida Tarbell, Upton Sinclair, David Graham Phillips, Ray Stannard Baker, and Samuel Hopkins Adams made new enemies with each story. The publications risked economic sanctions; their strategy for survival was to build readerships too large for advertisers to boycott them.

The muckrakers' issues comprised a new century's agenda for social reform. The main issues of 19th-century reform—slavery, women's lack of franchise, and the threat of alcohol to the family—were recognized as evils in light of America's original social contract. Issues of 20th-century reform entailed a new interpretation of social responsibility: Food producers should not adulterate their products; corporations should not collude to fix prices; children should be in schools, not in factories; and so on.

Another difference between 19th- and 20th-century reform is apparent now as we acknowledge that many reforms begun in the 20th century were left incomplete at its end. The 19th-century reformers believed that an issue was resolved when legislative or judicial action was taken. The abolitionists' accomplishments consisted of the Thirteenth, Fourteenth, and Fifteenth Amendments (abolition of slavery, equal protection under the law, and suffrage for former slaves). The suffragists first achieved reform in state property laws, then secured suffrage in a few western states, and capped their struggle with the Nineteenth Amendment (suffrage for women). Temperance advocates won local prohibition referenda and then swept the country with the Eighteenth Amendment (prohibition of intoxicating liquors). Many abolitionists, suffragists, and temperance advocates "retired" when their amendments were ratified. The freed slave, the enfranchised woman, and the family of the former drunkard could now work out their own fortunes.

It was soon apparent that legislative and judicial actions were necessary but not sufficient conditions for the changes that 20th-century reformers wanted to achieve. In the new century, reformers came to know the ambiguity of a "solution." First, a solution might be nullified, as in the repeal of the Eighteenth Amendment by the Twenty-First. Second, the solution might not be implemented substantively for years after it was decided on. Third, the opposition's legal staff might find loopholes, and compliance would be token and evasive. Fourth, the solution to one problem might generate another problem.

The muckrakers savored few victories; there was a limit to how far they could carry their reforms. They were journalists, not administrators. They could conceive a reform and even attend its birth, but they could not rear it. Ironically, they investigated government corruption and ineptitude, but their writings played a major role in building today's bureaucracy. Inadequate health care required a board of health, impure food required a pure food agency, labor abuses required a department of labor, and so on. Most of the reforms conceived by the muckrakers had to be reared by government officials. In this way, 20th-century reform passed into the hands of the civil service.

Enter the Federal Government

Responding to pressure from reformers, muckrakers, and public opinion at the beginning of the 20th century, the federal government was drawn into causes that were far removed from its original charter. After passage of the Interstate Commerce Act in 1887, the federal government's right to regulate interstate commerce became the slim thread for tying the 1906 Pure Food and Drug Act, the 1910 "White Slave Traffic Act," the 1916 Child Labor Act, and many other social reform laws to the Constitution. The Supreme Court struck down some of these laws but sustained others.

The two other watersheds of reform legislation in the 20th century occurred during the early years of Franklin Roosevelt's New Deal and Lyndon Johnson's Great Society administrations. These completed the pattern of federal involvement in almost every issue that formerly occupied the associations and mass media as well as a new 20th-century emphasis on issues such as pollution, environmental protection, and health care.

A NEW CENTURY OF
PUBLIC COMMUNICATION CAMPAIGNS

Amazingly, public communication campaigns are entering their fourth century in America. They are adapting, as always, to new social forces. Three challenges for today's campaigns are public distrust, episodic issues, and the rise of issue literacies.

Public Distrust

The last third of the 20th century in the United States saw a crisis in public trust that threatened to undermine public communication campaigns. Within a period of a few years, criticism of public officials, public agencies, corporations, and other powerful entities such as labor unions and agricultural interests found its postwar voice.

One timeline of distrust begins with the publication of Vance Packard's *The Hidden Persuaders* in 1957, followed by *The Status Seekers* in 1959 and *The Waste Makers* in 1960. Packard reached a large audience through his books and articles precisely because he was not an urban intellectual but a small-town moralist (Horowitz, 1994). He was offended not by the capitalist system but by those who abused it.

Rachel Carson's *The Silent Spring,* published in 1962, warned the public that the pesticide DDT was being used in agriculture without regard for its effect on other living things. In 1963, Jessica Mitford described practices of the funeral industry that prey on bereaved families in *The American Way of Death.* Victor Lasky's exposé of John Kennedy, *JFK: The Man and the Myth,* published in 1963, was noteworthy at the time although tame by today's standards.

Betty Friedan's *The Feminine Mystique,* published in 1963, continued the theme of manipulation. Ralph Nader's indictment of the automobile industry, *Unsafe at Any Speed,* was published in 1965. Mark Lane's critique of the Warren Commission report on the Kennedy assassination, *Rush to Judgment,* appeared in 1966.

The ultimate cynicism is a lack of surprise, and the instant history of Richard Nixon's victory over Hubert Humphrey, *The Selling of the President—1968,* written by Joe McGinnis and published in 1969, evoked no public outcry over the methods by which Nixon was packaged and sold to the voters. Nor was there much surprise when David Halberstam's *The Best and the Brightest,* published in 1973, indicated that U.S. leaders during the Vietnam conflict were neither.

By the time that Carl Bernstein and Bob Woodward reported the Watergate scandal as a detective mystery in *All the President's Men* (1974), there was little that the public could not imagine happening in corporate or political America.

The national conscience had to reflect on past wrongs when Dee Brown wrote *Bury My Heart at Wounded Knee,* which was the number one best-seller for 25 weeks in 1971. This book, together with the activism of Native American leaders such as Russell Means, focused the public's attention on the continuing injustices that Native Americans have endured.

Notwithstanding the wrongs revealed in this "second era of American muckraking," many negative events after World War II had positive consequences. The political terror of McCarthyism brought courageous journalists such as Edward R. Murrow to the fore. The flaws in John F. Kennedy's character did not deter American youth from social activism that flourishes to this day. The criminality of the Nixon administration ultimately proved that the rule of law extends to the highest office. Civil rights strife from Selma to Stonewall showed that the main legacy of discrimination was not hatred or separatism but a desire to move forward in the mainstream.

Under the media microscope, the flaws of individuals and institutions were enormous but not monstrous. At century's end, it was not the idealist but the cynic who was being told to "Get over it."

Episodic Issues

Issues rise and fall on the national agenda according to external factors, such as crises, incidents, and the appearance of effective advocates on the national scene. Some issues are solved by actions or events; they drop off the national agenda until they become unsolved again. Many persisting issues are subject to issue fatigue; they leave the national agenda for a time and then return with new advocates or proposals.

Table 1.1 shows the amount of coverage received by representative public issues in U.S. magazines during four decades. Only a few issues were at their highest levels at the beginning or end of this time period. Other issues rose and fell during one decade more or less, such as Vietnam in the 1960s, desegregation in the 1960s, energy in the 1970s, apartheid in the 1980s, drug abuse in the 1980s, sexual harassment in the 1990s, and gay/lesbian issues in the 1990s. The decline in coverage is dramatic among issues that are regarded as "over," such as Vietnam or apartheid. Communism and disarmament did not remain high on the agenda after the political rebirth of Russia.

"An issue by any other name" is a different issue. For example, the desegregation issue of the 1960s became the busing issue of the early 1970s and the affirmative action issue of the late 1970s. Similarly, the smoking issue of past decades is evolving into the issue of the tobacco industry, complete with corporate wrongdoing and cover-ups.

It may be true that "episodic" applies only to issues that are "over" or receive less attention when issue fatigue sets in. It is evident in Table 1.1 that some issues, such as cancer and heart disease, rise more or less continuously even over four decades.

Many issues reached their highest recent levels of attention in the 1991-1995 time period and then declined at the end of the decade. This trend reminds us that some time periods are ideological in the best sense—that is, they are periods in which ideas are put forward and debated. The end of the Bush presidency and the beginning of the Clinton presidency, up to and including the Republican "Contract With America" that dominated congressional debate in 1995, brought many major issues to the fore. It seemed that the time had arrived for debate on the post-Cold War role of the United States overseas; the role of gays and lesbians in the military and, by extension, in the mainstream of American society; the intransigence of racism and sexism; the best way to manage health care reform; the haves and have-nots of the booming economy and the Information Society; the concerns of America workers and social activists as free trade agreements sent U.S. jobs to other countries; and the diminished role of the federal government in an era of "Think globally, act locally." As mysteriously as this ideological period arrived in approximately 1990, it departed after the elections of 1996.

The Rise of Issue Literacies

The problem of "too many issues, too little time" has led to a creative strategy to reclaim our attention. Many advocates now contend that their concern is not an issue but a literacy. In recent years, the public has been urged to attain scientific literacy (first noted in 1960; Paisley, 1998), technological literacy (1982), ethnic literacy (1983), legislative literacy (1983), environmental literacy (1988), legal literacy (1988), sexual literacy (1990), multicultural literacy (1991), ecological literacy (1992), and health literacy (1995), among many others, such as cultural literacy and computer literacy.

At one level, the redefinition of issues as literacies is only a strategy to regain attention in the crowded marketplace of issues. At another level, this trend acknowledges the complexity of issues such as cancer prevention and treatment. From wartime posters and slogans half a century ago, public communication campaigns have matured into many differentiated forms. A few issues, such as forest fire prevention, can still be addressed by posters and slogans. At the other extreme, the potentially relevant knowledge about breast cancer, for

Table 1.1 Number of U.S. Magazine Articles on Representative Public Issues in Half-Decades From 1961 to 1998, Weighted by Total Number of Articles Indexed per Time Period

	Time Period							
Issue	*1961-1965*	*1966-1970*	*1971-1975*	*1976-1980*	*1981-1985*	*1986-1990*	*1991-1995*	*1996-1998*
Energy								
Energy conservation	0	0	190	162	75	37	29	13
Nuclear power	11	24	137	309	159	120	55	40
Solar power	2	1	44	125	59	23	32	22
Environment								
Acid rain	0	0	2	13	50	53	16	4
Earth Day	0	0	0	5	0	33	8	4
Global warming	0	0	0	1	11	100	134	151
Ozone layer	0	0	0	3	0	56	75	25
Pollution	118	316	252	300	236	365	308	210
Recycling	0	1	104	60	35	81	138	84
Wildlife								
Endangered species	0	1	29	32	25	86	103	59
Greenpeace	0	0	0	5	18	7	14	6
Whales	35	42	33	69	72	66	80	73
Health								
Alzheimer's disease	0	0	0	2	23	48	86	79
Cancer	155	178	258	427	453	531	998	1,002
Breast cancer	7	2	60	59	44	88	257	265
Mammography	0	0	4	8	2	16	52	47
Heart disease	69	65	90	88	127	179	234	254
HIV/AIDS	0	0	0	0	24	106	250	191
Osteoporosis	0	0	0	3	26	52	54	81
Calcium	0	1	0	23	33	54	73	103
Estrogen	7	10	4	26	20	27	83	117
Smoking	100	76	62	80	80	135	252	318
Tobacco	61	45	22	104	114	151	190	347
International issues								
Apartheid	20	21	18	24	74	205	82	46
Communism	1,380	864	351	260	289	426	449	296
Disarmament	184	112	99	290	517	364	113	78
Nuclear freeze	0	0	0	1	16	1	0	1
Vietnam	1,444	4,417	927	267	303	231	342	180
Famine	26	32	66	23	59	37	65	29
Social issues								
Abortion	28	78	141	131	154	229	362	233
Prochoice	0	0	0	2	7	56	88	52
Prolife	0	0	0	1	22	63	112	69
Affirmative action	0	1	33	43	44	55	163	183
Civil rights	640	357	146	315	422	325	322	199
Racism	18	25	20	13	41	118	306	181
Busing	3	12	161	36	12	3	4	10
Desegregation	260	258	9	11	8	5	9	11
Voting rights	19	10	2	3	16	5	19	9

(Continued)

Table 1.1 Continued

Issue	\multicolumn{8}{c}{Time Period}							
	1961- 1965	1966- 1970	1971- 1975	1976- 1980	1981- 1985	1986- 1990	1991- 1995	1996- 1998
Sexism	0	1	49	20	25	35	92	34
Sexual harassment	0	0	0	23	23	36	249	232
Women's rights	3	6	249	226	238	171	433	237
Safe sex	0	0	0	0	1	40	49	21
Condoms	0	2	2	4	5	45	68	31
Teenage pregnancy	1	2	4	4	7	27	32	26
Gay/lesbian	46	68	97	143	150	160	554	371
Privacy	42	91	88	80	54	66	153	185
Obscenity	23	57	55	19	16	46	42	36
Pornography	12	24	88	43	43	51	85	100
Drug abuse	12	26	77	104	112	262	143	138
Alcohol abuse	22	29	64	45	58	74	87	55
Drunk driving	0	0	2	3	51	29	33	35
Air bags	0	1	18	6	13	11	25	53
Disabled	24	7	15	56	76	159	217	181
Elderly	9	7	31	39	40	56	124	148
Child care	4	21	35	36	76	201	179	149
Child abuse	1	4	24	28	81	81	151	83
School violence	0	0	9	2	2	7	9	14
School prayer	14	2	0	2	12	1	20	10
Information highway	0	0	0	0	0	0	139	26

NOTE: The number of articles per topic per time period is weighted by the total number of articles per time period indexed in the Magazine Index database. It is then expressed as a standardized number of articles per 100,000 articles indexed in the database. Thus, for example, the highest number in the table (4,417 articles on Vietnam in 1966-1970) means that 4.4% of all articles indexed in the Magazine Index for the 1966-1970 time period concerned Vietnam. The annual number of articles indexed in the Magazine Index fluctuates—hence the need for weighting the raw frequencies—but averaged approximately 165,000 in the late 1990s. The weighting allows numbers to be compared across topics and time periods. Thus, in the rows immediately above this note, it can be seen that information highway briefly reached almost the same level of discussion as child abuse (139 articles per 100,000 versus 151 per 100,000), but the "trendy" issue then receded to a low level of discussion (26 articles per 100,000).

example, is very extensive and conditional with respect to individual factors. It is reasonable to refer to familiarity with this knowledge as a literacy.

Furthermore, relationships between knowledge gain and behavior change as the goals of a campaign are altered when the most appropriate behavior for any member of the target audience must be determined by weighing individual factors, many of which are known only to him or her. At this historic juncture, a public communication campaign no longer exhorts. Instead, it informs and advises.

CONCLUSION

Public communication campaigners may wish that the organizing skill of a Susan B. Anthony, the charisma of a William Lloyd Garrison, or the appalling disclosures of an Upton Sinclair could be as effective now as in the past. The world of cancer, AIDS, drug abuse, the toxic environment, bioengineered food, tobacco control, domestic violence, and a host of other issues has moved beyond these appealing simplicities.

The world of modern campaigns, however, contains solutions as well as problems. Campaigns learn from the successes and failures of other campaigns. As a result of the relatively detached perspective of social science, campaigns can be documented, compared, and evaluated for the new concepts and techniques they offer.

At the beginning of this century, the science of public communication campaigns has come to the fore and generates its own excitement. As the agenda of social issues changes, so too will campaigns continue to change in adaptive ways to meet the new challenges.

REFERENCES

de Tocqueville, A. (1961). *Democracy in America.* New York: Schocken. (Original work published 1835)

Flexner, E. (1975). *Century of struggle: The women's rights movement in the United States.* Cambridge, MA: Harvard University Press.

Horowitz, D. (1994). *Vance Packard and American social criticism.* Chapel Hill: University of North Carolina Press.

Paisley, W. (1998). Scientific literacy and the competition for public attention and understanding. *Science Communication, 20,* 70-80.

2

Input and Output Variables Currently Promising for Constructing Persuasive Communications[1]

William J. McGuire

A pervasive error in evaluating a program or agency is to judge it by the effort expended rather than by the effect produced. Shakespeare referred to this hazard in *Henry IV*, Part I, when Glendower brags, "I can call spirits from the vasty deep," only to be deflated by Hotspur's reply, "So can I, or so can any man; but will they come when you do call for them?" This chapter will keep Hotspur's question in mind by reporting not what variables are currently used in persuasion campaigns but rather which variables should be used if one's public persuasion campaign is to have impact.

This chapter first briefly sketches a general procedure for developing a persuasion campaign (e.g., one designed to induce the public to adopt a more healthful lifestyle). Then the following sections identify promising input and output variables for use in such persuasion campaigns.

A SEVEN-STEP PROCEDURE FOR DEVELOPING HEALTH CAMPAIGNS

A general procedure for constructing a persuasion campaign (McGuire, 1984a) is called acronymically the "RASMICE" procedure after its seven steps:

1. Reviewing the realities involves picking as a target a serious (health) problem that has a solution that can be cost-effectively achieved through a persuasion campaign.

2. Axiological analysis involves examining the ethics of the campaign to ensure that its ends and means, direct and indirect, are sufficiently in accord with one's moral principles and sense of good taste sufficiently so that one can think creatively about the campaign.

3. Surveying the sociocultural situation involves identifying high-risk groups and factors in the social environment that instigate or interfere with the healthier lifestyle that is being urged, information obtainable by interviews, participant observation, focus group techniques, or analyzing data from social data archives (see Chapter 8, this volume).

4. Mapping the mental matrix calls for obtaining information about thoughts, feelings, and values that the public perceives as associated with the health risk, for example, by contrasting criterion groups on these characteristics.

5. Teasing out the target themes calls for reviewing the information yielded by the previous four steps that identified the high-risk, high-yield subpopulations on whom the persuasion campaign should focus and culling out the health-promoting behavior that should be urged and the persuasive material that would enhance campaign effectiveness.

6. Constructing the communication involves selecting the source, message, channel, audience, and target variables (discussed later) that have the greatest potential for eliciting the output steps (described later) that are needed to achieve the desired health behavior.

7. Evaluating the effectiveness should be built into the campaign in the form of immediate and delayed measures of the health behavior of the groups exposed to the various health campaigns. In addition to these postcampaign effectiveness checks, there should be ongoing evaluation of the campaign construction at each of the six preceding steps to maximize the contribution of each step to the total process.

PROMISING INPUT TOPICS ON HOW
COMMUNICATIONS CAN BE MADE MORE PERSUASIVE

Here and in the next section, the focus is on Step 6, constructing the communication. The two sections review in turn the input variables from which persuasive communications can be constructed and the mediational output behaviors that must be elicited if the public's behavior is to be channeled as intended (e.g., into adopting a more healthful lifestyle). The persuasive communication's promising input variables can conveniently be divided into five classes: source, message, channel, audience, and destination; that is, who says what, via which media, to whom, regarding what. More detailed discussions of these and other variables are available elsewhere (Eagly & Chaiken, 1993; McGuire, 1985).

Source Variables That Increase Persuasive Impact

Conventional Analysis of Source Variables

When choosing a source to deliver the influence message, designers of persuasion campaigns conventionally search for three obvious source characteristics: credibility, attractiveness, and power. This conventional approach to choosing communicators to maximize persuasive impact will be considered first, and then less obvious alternative source-selection criteria will be described.

Credibility, attractiveness, and power are conventionally assumed to enhance persuasive impact via three processes—internalization, identification, and compliance, respectively. *Credibility* derives from the source's perceived expertise and trustworthiness—that is, the source's appearing to know the facts on the issue and to be reporting them honestly. Perceived source expertise, in turn, derives from characteristics such as the source's general education level, familiarity with the subject matter, and speaking in an authoritative tone. Perceived trustworthiness derives from the source's general reputation for honesty, being in a trustworthy profession, not standing to profit personally from convincing the audience, emitting nonverbal cues perceived as indicating honesty, and so forth. Perceived *attractiveness* (likeableness) derives from qualities such as the source's pleasantness, beauty, familiarity, and similarity. Perceived *power* is a positive function of the source's control over the listener's rewards and punishments, desire for the audience's compliance, and ability to monitor the extent of this compliance.

This conventional approach tends to yield valid but rather obvious hypotheses, such as that sources are more persuasive if the audience perceives them as honest or more similar to themselves. Elsewhere (McGuire, 1983, 1989b, 1997), I described how to go beyond demonstrating such banalities by the use of a variety of discovery techniques that will be illustrated briefly here. For example, an obvious independent variable such as source similarity can be elaborated by division into subvariables, as in Rokeach's and Triandis's work on whether ideological or demographic similarity between source and recipient enhances persuasive impact more.

Source's Physical Appearance and Persuasiveness

Patzer (1985) and Hatfield and Sprecher (1986) provide useful reviews of the research on perceived beauty and its effects. The perception of what is facial attractiveness may be innate, detectable even by infants (Langlois, Roggman, & Rieser-Danner, 1990), although preferred physique may vary over time and place (Rothblum, 1990). Surprisingly, faces appear beautiful to the extent that they approximate the average human face, even mixing male and female faces (Langlois & Roggman, 1990). Perceived attractiveness increases with formality of costume, perhaps more for female than for male observers

(Townsend & Levy, 1990); it also increases with females' use of cosmetics, although cosmetics may affect males' judgments more than those of females (Cash, Dawson, Davis, Bowen, & Galumbeck, 1989). Flashing a smile appears to be a cheaper and surer way of appearing attractive (Reis et al., 1990). The source's beauty does tend to enhance his or her persuasive impact (DeBono & Telesca, 1990), partly due to beauty per se and partly to the tendency to view beautiful sources as having other desirable persuasiveness-enhancing characteristics, such as intelligence (Chaiken, 1979). Beautiful sources in TV ads might suffer from contextual contrast in appearing less attractive if the ads are embedded in a program in which the actors are even more attractive (Kenrick & Gutierres, 1980).

Source's Group Characteristics and Persuasiveness

The fact that source-audience similarity tends to increase persuasive impact (although reversals occur in some contexts) leads to the hypothesis that the source's persuasiveness increases when his or her demographics match the audience's with regard to age, sex, religion, and ethnicity. McGuire's (1984b) distinctiveness theory of perception predicts on purely cognitive grounds that as a society becomes more integrated (e.g., including people of multiple ethnicities), the salience of ethnicity in the members' sense of self will increase. This "us-them" distinctiveness is likely to become an "us-versus-them" divisiveness (Campbell, 1965). The source's ethnicity has little effect on majority white males but may have more effect on those in the minority, low-power groups (Ramirez, 1977). Sidanius's (1993) social dominance theory, Tajfel's (1982) social identity theory, and Turner's social categorization theory (Turner & Oakes, 1989) have further implications regarding how the in-group versus out-group status of the source will affect persuasive impact (Abrams & Hogg, 1990).

Sex effects in persuasion have been studied more than ethnic effects, but studies have focused more on the persuadability of male versus female audiences than on the persuasiveness of male versus female sources (Eagly, 1983; Eagly & Carli, 1981). Male sources may have more persuasive impact than female sources, even on female audiences (Dion & Stein, 1978; Lincoln, 1977), due in part to the tendency to use "male" topics in persuasion research.

Message Variables That Increase Persuasive Impact

Message variables constitute the most interesting and heavily investigated category of input factors, with subcategories including structure and type of arguments, type of appeals, message style, humor, repetition, and so on.

The Structure of Argument

Attitude structure, a variable of increasing interest (Pratkanis, Breckler, & Greenwald, 1989), assumes that attitudes are organized into interconnected systems so that a persuasive communication that deals explicitly with one issue is likely also to have remote ramifications on unmentioned related issues. Thus, a persuasive communication arguing for the truth of a given proposition (e.g., that parents should bring their preschoolers in for inoculations) is likely also to affect unmentioned but related propositions (such as that parents bring their preschoolers in for dental exams and that parents should get themselves inoculated). Related attitudes are affected to the extent that they are concurrently "salient," suggesting that attitudes can be changed not only by presenting new information from an outside source but also by increasing the salience of information already within the audience's own belief system by means of a directed thinking task or by Socratic questioning (McGuire, 1960; McGuire & McGuire, 1992).

Types of Arguments

The ancients were highly interested in the comparative persuasive power of various types of arguments, but contemporary researchers have tended to neglect the topic. Aristotle's *Rhetoric* lists 38 tropes or types of arguments in just one category, and Cicero and Quintilian list many additional ones. Practitioners and researchers can review lists of argument types and theorize about their different modes of operation, deriving testable hypotheses about their main and interaction effects on persuasive impact. The empirical work so far has been confined largely to Aristotle's three types of proof—pathos, ethos, and logos (Edwards, 1990; Millar & Millar, 1990). In recent years, progress has been made on a related issue—the relative merits of various compliance-gaining tactics, such as foot-in-the-door, door-in-the-face, lowballing, and click-whirr (Cialdini, 1993).

Types of Appeals

Elsewhere (McGuire, 1989d, 1991), I identified 16 types of human needs to which health persuasion campaigns can appeal. The 16 divide into four classes: *cognitive stability* needs (such as the need for consistency and herme-neutic/attributional needs), *cognitive growth* needs (such as the need for stimulation and for felt competence), *affective stability* needs (such as tension reduction and ego defense), and *affective growth* needs (such as affiliative and identity needs). Research is needed on the comparative persuasive efficacy of the 16 types of appeals; the relative effectiveness of threat versus reassurance appeals has been well studied (Covello, von Winterfeldt, & Slovic, 1990; see also Chapter 5, this volume). The public health educator may be too narrow in using only appeals to the obvious needs (feeling of well-being, vigor, risk avoidance, freedom from morbidity and mortality, etc.), when appeals to other motives (beauty, altruism, and independence) may be more effective, at least in some high-risk groups. For example, campaigns to induce use of sun block might appeal to preventing not only skin cancer but also premature skin aging.

Message Style Variables

Another set of message variables rich in persuasive potential involves the style in which the persuasive material is communicated—for example, the message's clarity, forcefulness, literalness, or humorousness. Classical rhetoricians distinguished among three styles differing in forcefulness—low, middle, and grand, also known as Attic, Rhodian, and Asian—theorizing that each may be the most persuasive depending on the situation, a view confirmed in modern speech research (Pearce & Brommel, 1972). Psychologists have revived interest in this topic under the rubric of "vividness" (Taylor & Thompson, 1982). One partial definition of vividness, arguing by factual examples versus by abstract principles, has had particularly rich implications (Reyes, Thompson, & Bower, 1980). Literal versus figurative language constitutes another style variable that deserves more investigation (McGuire, 2000). Classical rhetoricians agreed that figurative language adds to persuasive impact but debated whether the mechanism was source credibility, positive mood, enhanced attention, or some other mechanism. Empirical research has indicated that similes and especially sustained metaphors enhance persuasive impact (Bowers & Osborn, 1966).

Effects on Persuasion of Amount of Material

Many variables having to do with quantitative aspects of persuasive communication are of considerable practical importance. Advertising costs increase sharply with the amount of material (length of commercials, number of showings, etc.), and if one goes beyond repetition of identical material to increasing the amount of material, there are the added costs of production. These practically important amount-of-exposure variables tend to be neglected by basic researchers because they are of low theoretical relevance. Empirical work indicates that when a given audience is subjected to repetitions of an ad (even in varied form), diminishing returns set in quite early, by three to five repetitions (Calder & Sternthal, 1980), perhaps because beyond the first few receptions, repetitive presentations of the ads tend to evoke increasing numbers of negative thoughts about the product (McCullough & Ostrom, 1974). "Wearout" may also be involved. The elaboration-likelihood model (Petty & Cacioppo, 1986b) indicates that repetition can, under certain conditions such as weak arguments, reduce persuasion.

Channel Variables That Increase Persuasive Impact

Most persuasion campaigns (political, public health, commercial, etc.) are transmitted via the mass media, usually the electronic media, in the form of ads, public service announcements (PSAs), news, documentaries, or interview programs. Because many public health campaigns involve prevention by establishment of lifetime habits best laid down in childhood and adolescence, school-based educational programs may be more cost-effective than those via the mass media. Among the mass media, radio stations directed at youth groups may be more cost-effective than prime-time network television. Direct mail advertising addressed specifically to high-risk groups may deserve greater usage, as might word-of-mouth agitation through community groups such as churches and workplaces and through posters placed at congregation places of high-risk groups.

Television is generally assumed to have massive effects on viewers for a variety of reasons. First, a great deal of money is spent on advertising, and big spenders are assumed to know what they are doing. Also, people spend a deplorable percentage of their waking hours in front of television sets, presumably with proportional effects. In addition, the proliferation of television at midcentury was accompanied by other social trends ascribable to television, such as a trend toward violence, a materialistic consumerist society, the sexual revolution, changing family situations, and increasing drug abuse. Also supporting the belief in massive impacts is that all the contentious constituencies in the media debates, both supporters and critics of the industry, share a vested interest in agreeing that the media do have massive impacts (McGuire, 1986). Nevertheless, the assumption of massive media effects, however plausible, has received only weak support.

Evidence for Intended Television Effects

McGuire (1986) reviewed in detail evidence for massive television effects in six areas in which there is a deliberate attempt to influence the viewers—for example, the effects of commercial advertising on purchasing, the effects of political campaigning on voting, and the impact of public service health ads on changing audiences' lifestyles. The studies rarely show massive effects, as can be illustrated in what is probably the best studied of the intended mass media effect, namely, the effect of commercial advertising on purchasing behavior (or even on weaker criteria such as brand recognition or preference). Effects tend to be surprisingly small, even when the evaluations are done by the advertising agencies' own study groups, which would be highly motivated to find large effects of ads (Albion & Farris, 1981).

Good examples of "macro, econometric" studies are time-lagged product-class studies of fluctuations in total cigarette advertisements in relation to total cigarette sales; these show little effect of the industrywide level of cigarette advertising (or of the level of anticigarette health PSAs) on total cigarette sales (Murphy, 1980). Brand-share macro studies have likewise found only modest effects. "Micro, behavioral" evaluation studies use individual persons as the unit of sampling (rather than the product or brand units used in the macro-econometric studies) in either field or laboratory settings. The effects of "field" studies tend to be weak, for example, regarding the relation between exposure to over-the-counter drug ads and use of legal or illegal drugs (Milavsky, Pekowsky, & Stipp, 1975; Rossiter & Robertson, 1980). The "laboratory" subtype of behavioral studies involves exposing people in a controlled situation to advertisements of various types and then measuring their attitudes or behavior toward the products advertised. Significant effects are sometimes found, but the artificiality of these laboratory situations makes generalization to the natural world hazardous. Thus, the empirical evidence for massive effects is remarkably weak for commercial ads and even weaker for the other domains of intended television impact, such as the effect of televised political ads on voting behavior.

Evidence for Unintended Television Effects

The intended effects of the media reviewed previously are communicated primarily through advertisements, PSAs, and so on inserted in brief interruptions (it seems longer) in the programs. The unintended effects that I discuss here tend to involve material presented in the programs themselves. The most heavily investigated effect is the extent to which depiction of violence in programs affects viewers' antisocial aggression. Laboratory studies yield an effect that often reaches the conventionally accepted levels of significance, at least in preangered viewers and with somewhat ambiguous measures of aggression (Comstock, 1982). In natural world studies, the effects tend to be small, accounting at most for only a few percent of the individual-difference variance in violence (Milavsky, Kessler, Stipp, & Rubens, 1982). Similarly unimpressive effect sizes tend to be found for television programs' other unintended effects, such as whether underrepresentation and biased representation of certain demographic groups (especially the elderly) causes them to become socially "invisible" or to be perceived as stereotypes (Gunter & Wober, 1983). Such modest effects as are found tend to be reduced when extraneous factors are controlled (Hirsch, 1981; Hughes, 1980).

Excuses Used to Salvage Belief in Massive Media Effects

I am not arguing that no media effects have been demonstrated, but only that the attained effect sizes suggest that the media account for no more than a few percent of the variance in the behaviors they are purported to be greatly influencing. Five classes of excuses have been used to explain away the weakness of the evidence and to keep the faith in massive media effects.

A first class of excuses is the poor methodology in the evaluation, such as flaws in measurement of media exposure and dependent variable effects, poor measurement of relations between them (e.g., due to lack of control of extraneous variables), and experimenter bias. However, it seems that the better the measures, the less the obtained relation. A second class of excuses is that there would be massive media impacts except for some specified accidental circumstances regarding media exposure, such as conflicting or competing messages, selective avoidance of belief-discrepant material, and distractions from mass media clutter. A third, more modest, class of excuses is the claim that searching for large overall effects obscures circumscribed effects that the media do have, such as reinforcing prior preferences, bringing attention to new products or candidates, or the occasional large effects of "media events." A fourth class of excuses is that the media may not have massive effects on the general population but do have sizable effects on especially susceptible subgroups—for example, the effect of TV violence on 15- to 30-year-old males, effect of commercial advertising on children, or effects on the influential elite or on susceptible personality types. A fifth class of excuses is that the mass media do have sizable effects but they occur only indirectly and so are missed in evaluation studies that seek only direct impacts. Examples include the two-step flow theory, the "agenda-setting" hypothesis (Iyengar, 1991), the "spiral of silence" notion, the perception of what is normative in society, and the "self-realizing prophesy" that the general belief in massive media effects, even if false, may produce its own truth. Many of these and other excuses are tenable, although some can be shown (McGuire, 1986) to be implausible on the basis of available research results. Currently, it is not valid to argue that the available research results support the widespread belief in pervasive and massive media effects.

Context Effects

Information overload research (Pool, 1983) raises a "more is less" possibility that the vast number of messages impinging on the public may reduce meaningful reception (Malhotra, 1984). Other context effects arise when health PSAs are presented within the context of entertainment and information programs. For example, when attractive sources used in the ads are less attractive than the actors in the program, there may result a contrast effect such that the ad sources appear less attractive (Kenrick & Gutierres, 1980) or an opposite assimilation effect such that the ad sources are perceived as more attractive in the context of the even more attractive actors in the program (Geiselman, Haight, & Kimata, 1984). The program's content may also influence the audience's moods or cognitions about people in ways that affect the persuasive impact of the inserted PSA (Krugman, 1983). Indeed, health educators might more effectively present their messages within the program itself rather than confining them to the commercial breaks.

Another context consideration is the distracting situational clutter of life situations in which health messages tend to be presented, which might either enhance or reduce the message's persuasive impact. For example, if the person is engaged in some pleasant concurrent activity, the persuasive impact of a communication tends to be enhanced (Janis, Kaye, & Kirschner, 1965), whereas being put in a negative mood can decrease persuasive impact. Incidental factors in the persuasion situation, such as ambient temperature or background music, may affect impact (Gorn, 1982; Kellaris & Cox, 1989). Research is needed on whether such effects are mediated by cognitive or affective processes (e.g., via the audience's perceptions of the characteristics of people and of societies or by the audience's emotional mood). Conversely, such background factors can under some conditions serve as distractions, which could either enhance persuasive impact (by reducing audience ability to counterargue) or reduce persuasive impact (by interfering with message reception) (Bless, Bohner, Schwarz, & Strack, 1990).

Audience Variables That Affect Persuasive Impact

A persuasion campaign aimed at the general public should be able to influence all types of people, if necessary, by including variant forms of the campaign to reach different high-risk subgroups who differ in susceptibility to various modes of influence.

A Mediational Theory of Susceptibility to Social Influence

McGuire's (1989a) general theory uses seven postulates to predict and explain how people's individual differences in personality, abilities, and motivations affect their susceptibility to social influence by mass communication persuasion and conformity pressures, suggestion, and face-to-face discussion.

The first, multiple mediator, principle asserts that how peoples' position on individual-difference variables (e.g., their anxiety levels) will affect their ultimate compliance (e.g., with a blood donation campaign) will depend on how anxiety affects each of the dozen-plus output mediators—attention, comprehension, agreement, and so on—shown in Table 2.1. Because each step is evoked only probabilistically by the preceding step, the ultimate payoff is a multiplication of probabilities well below 1.00, so that any one campaign will have only an attenuated impact.

The second, compensatory, principle is that individual-difference variables such as anxiety tend to have opposite effects via different mediators. For example, anxiety would tend to lower persuasive impact by interfering with comprehension of the communication contents, but it would tend to increase persuasive impact by enhancing yielding to such arguments as are comprehended. A third, nonmonotonic, principle states that because of this compensatory tendency, people with intermediate levels of anxiety (or any other individual-

Table 2.1 The Communication-Persuasion Matrix: Input Communication Variables and Output Mediational Steps That Comprise the Process of Being Persuaded[a]

Input communication factors
1. Source (number, unanimity, demographics, attractiveness, credibility, etc.)
2. Message (appeal, inclusion/omission, organization, style, repetitiveness, etc.)
3. Channel (modality, directness, context, etc.)
4. Receiver (demographics, ability, personality, lifestyle, etc.)
5. Destination (immediacy/delay, prevention/cessation, direct/immunization, etc.)

Output persuasion steps
1. Tuning in (exposure to the communication)
2. Attending to the communication
3. Liking it, maintaining interest in it
4. Comprehending its contents (learning what)
5. Generating related cognitions
6. Acquiring relevant skills (learning how)
7. Agreeing with the communication's position (attitude change)
8. Storing this new position in memory
9. Retrieval of the new position from memory when relevant
10. Decision to act on the basis of the retrieved position
11. Acting on it
12. Postaction cognitive integration of this behavior
13. Proselytizing others to behave likewise

a. Persuasion steps typically occur sequentially.

difference variable) will tend to be more influenceable than those very high or very low in anxiety. A fourth, acute-chronic interaction, principle calls attention to how variations in the level of fear arousal in the message will interact with the audience's chronic level of anxiety in affecting persuasive impact. For example, in a campaign to get parents to bring their preschoolers in for immunizations, if the fear-arousing depiction of the dangers of noncompliance is raised in the persuasive message, this would tend to increase compliance in parents low in chronic anxiety and to decrease compliance in parents whose chronic anxiety level is high.

A fifth, situational weighting, principle asserts that the parameters of the nonmonotonic relation between a personality variable such as anxiety and influenceability will vary across situations, depending on the relative contributions to compliance made by each of the mediating steps in Table 2.1. For example, because anxiety decreases influenceability by reducing comprehension, but increases influenceability by increasing agreement with whatever part of the message is comprehended, anxiety will increase susceptibility to a health campaign whose message is simple and decrease susceptibility to campaigns involving complex instructions.

A sixth, confounded variable, principle states that the person's chronic level on a characteristic such as anxiety will tend to become embedded in a syndrome of compensatory coping characteristics. For example, a person high in anxiety will tend to develop threat-avoiding coping habits that protect him or her from experiencing anxiety. Therefore, the campaign must be designed to take into account not only the effects of the personality characteristic of initial interest but also the effects of the other characteristics with which it will have become clustered. A seventh, interaction, principle asserts that any personal characteristic is likely to interact with other communication variables in its effect on influenceability. Thus, personal characteristics such as anxiety will interact with whether frightening or reassuring appeals are used in the message and whether it is being transmitted by face-to-face or mass media channels.

Special Target Groups

Public policy and epidemiological considerations make certain age, sex, and ethnic groups of special interest in one or another health campaign. With regard to age, McGuire's (1985) mediational theory predicts a nonmonotonic inverted-U shaped relationship between age and influenceability; maximum suggestibility may occur at approximately age 9 (Eron, Huesmann, Brice, Fischer, & Mermelstein, 1983), with conformity maximizing at approximately age 12 (Costanzo & Shaw, 1966) and persuasibility peaking in adolescence, especially in the area of political susceptibility (Krosnick & Alwin, 1989; Tyler & Schuller, 1991). As people mature, their improving comprehension of persuasive messages makes them more susceptible to influence, but their decreasing tendency to agree with what they are told makes them less susceptible. It is also commonly assumed that because more educated people have characteristics such as being better informed, more critical, and more willing to maintain a deviant position, they will be less influenceable. However, education tends also to improve message comprehension, which tends to make better educated audiences more persuadable and explains why susceptibility to the U.S. Army's "Why We Fight" indoctrination films in World War II increased with the soldier's level of education (Hovland, Lumsdaine, & Sheffield, 1949).

With regard to sex differences in susceptibility to social influence (Eagly, 1983; McGuire, 1968, 1985), women are slightly more influenceable than men, but the difference is so slight as to be unimportant practically, although there are interactions with related variables such as eye contact or formality of dress (Cash et al., 1989; Orpen, 1989). It seems likely that audience ethnicity has even less intrinsic impact on influenceability than does sex. Because in most societies ethnic groups differ on other variables that do affect influenceability (e.g., education, self-esteem, and numerical predominance), however, differential susceptibility may be found in different ethnic groups, and there are likely to be interaction effects as well, such that the ethnicity of the source would tend to make more difference to minority group audiences than to the majority group in accord with distinctiveness theory (McGuire, 1984b).

Target Variables That Affect Persuasive Impact

Here, I consider how persuasive impact is affected by variables having to do with the kind of target attitudes or actions at which the campaign is aimed.

Beliefs Versus Attitudes Versus Behavior

Correlations between how a given communication affects knowledge about a topic, feelings regarding it, and behavior toward it tend to be modest (McGuire, 1989c; Pratkanis et al., 1989). There is some correlation among the three in that at any given time the person's information attitudes and behaviors tend to be positively correlated with regard to favorability to the topic at issue. Also, when a message produces a change in one, it tends to induce similar changes in the other two. Correlation between the three tends to be increased by variables such as familiarity and involvement with the topic, salience of the topic, personal traits such as need for cognition, similarity of the contexts in which the two effects are operating, and similar methods of measurement. More use should be made of causal models to test for theoretically derived multiple direct and indirect paths between these three components and other components in the total person (Bagozzi, 1982; Breckler, 1984).

Persistence of Persuasive Impact

Both practitioners and basic researchers tend to assume that the attitude change induced by a persuasive communication is at a maximum immediately after the audience receives the message and then decays progressively as time passes. However, the slope and even direction of time curves vary greatly with diverse variables such as source credibility, subtlety of argument, order of presentation, and channel (Cook & Flay, 1978; McGuire, 1985). The temporal decay of induced attitude change is further complicated because a delayed-action persuasion effect, such that in the early postcommunication period there is a progressive increase in persuasive impact, can be brought about by the discounting-cue sleeper effect, mutual postcommunication proselytizing, two-step flow, agenda-setting sensitization, the consistency reaction, reactance, and predispositional drift (McGuire, 1985; Pratkanis & Greenwald, 1985). Thus, evaluation studies should have delayed and immediate postcampaign measures of effectiveness (see Chapter 8, this volume).

Inducing Resistance to Persuasion

Public health campaigns are usually designed to produce a change but sometimes are designed to confer resistance to persuasion—for example, campaigns to prepare children to resist peer pressure to smoke or do drugs (McGuire, 1964, 1985).

One approach to producing resistance to persuasion is to use prior commitment, such as having the person express publicly (or even just think privately about) his or her initial position, as in Lewin's (1951) World War II group-decision research. A second approach is to induce resistant motivational states, such as preangering the person or increasing self-esteem or anxiety level. This approach is limited because such states tend to be nonmonotonically related to persuasibility so that increasing these motivational levels will make some people more persuadable and others less (Zellner, 1970). A third approach is to confer resistance by anchoring the person's initial stand on a given issue to the person's other beliefs or values or to esteemed reference groups (Holt, 1970; Nelson, 1968). A fourth immunizing approach is to educate people in critical thinking, recognizing persuasion attempts, detecting weaknesses in the attacking arguments, and summoning up counterarguments (Huesmann, Eron, Klein, Brice, & Fischer, 1983). However, increasing level of education can backfire by making the person more attentive to and comprehending of persuasive messages and therefore more persuadable, as described previously. A fifth means of conferring resistance to persuasion is to show the person unyielding models: People tend to succumb less to persuasive pressure after observing others resisting it (Evans, 1986; Milgram, 1974; Rushton, 1975). A sixth procedure for producing resistance to persuasion is the inoculation approach— that is, preexposing the believer to weakened belief-threatening material. Analogous to biological inoculation, exposure to the weak doses of attacking material is used to stimulate belief defenses without overcoming them, making the person more resistant to later strong attacks (McGuire, 1964).

PROMISING OUTPUT TOPICS
ON HOW PERSUASION WORKS

The output side of the communication-persuasion matrix can be usefully represented as a series of sequential mediating behavioral steps that persuasive communications tend to evoke and that culminate in the desired output behavior (e.g., the public's adopting the more healthful lifestyles being urged in a health campaign). Table 2.1, analyzing this process of being persuaded into 13 steps, deliberately errs on the side of being overly rational and thorough. The currently promising "multiple paths to persuasion" research proposes alternative short-cuts through this list. The "how persuasion works" topic involves three lines of work discussed in turn: research on how people use the media, processes that mediate persuasive impact, and where attitudes fit in the persuasion process.

Insights Into How People Use the Media

Who Selects Channels and Why?

Viewers engage in a high level of channel switching, particularly since the advent of remote channel selectors and since cable has made available dozens of channels. This brings into question viewer loyalty, not only to a given channel from program to program but also to a given episode from minute to minute (Barwise, Ehrenberg, & Goodhart, 1982). Because 30% of watchers switch channels at the beginning of a commercial break, PSAs, now shown in the commercial break, might more effectively be incorporated in the program (McGuire, 1984a; Piotrow et al., 1990).

Social Context of Media Exposure

There is evidence that people are more persuaded when exposed to a given message when they are alone (e.g., watching daytime soap operas and late-night movies) rather than with other people (e.g., with prime-time viewing) (Keating & Latané, 1976), which may favor impacts of PSAs that are typically shown at hours that attract the sole viewer. More work is needed on whether this high impact is due to cognitive or affective processes and on how the impact of others present depends on whether the others are passive or interacting with the audience member under study or talking to the actors on the screen (Singer & Singer, 1981; see also Chapters 29 and 30, this volume).

Mediators of the Persuasive Impact

Four currently active research areas illustrate the range of mediator issues (multiple paths and mediating substeps) currently receiving deserved attention.

Multiple Paths to Persuasion

Useful proposals of alternative routes to persuasion include Petty and Cacioppo's (1986a) proposed central versus peripheral paths and Chaiken's (1980) distinction between systematic versus heuristic processing. An audience uses the central route, involving a complex chain of behaviors such as that shown in Table 2.1, to the extent that the communication situation is important and deserving of careful scrutiny. Peripheral routes, involving much abbreviated paths, are used in the more typical low-involvement situations. Petty and Cacioppo (1986a) confirmed the implications that certain variables (such as argument strength) are important in central processing, whereas other variables (such as source credibility) are more important in peripherally processed persuasion. Identifying the paths likely to be used clarifies which communication variables will most enhance persuasive impact on the at-risk segment of the public.

Sequences of the Mediating Processes

The traditional, commonsensical output sequence shown in Table 2.1 is usually taken for granted by persuasion practitioners, such as those using the standard health belief model. However, several reversals of the commonsense relations among steps shown in Table 2.1 are likely. In perceptual distortion or selective exposure, Step 7 (attitude) precedes Step 4 (comprehension) or Step 2 (attending). Dissonance theorists note that Step 7 often follows Step 11, such as when people form their attitudes to justify their prior behavior rather than acting in accord with their prior attitudes, especially when the prior behavior is perceived as having serious consequences and as being volitional. The controversy regarding the primacy of affect versus cognition (Zajonc [1984] vs. Lazarus [1984]) suggests that the person may react affectively to the message content before he or she can report what that content is, reversing the order of Step 3 and Step 4. This poses a challenge to health campaigns (e.g., against drug abuse) in that high-risk members of the public would be able to tune out the unpleasant advice before they have processed the advice.

Communication Recall as a Mediator of Persuasion

The two mediating processes that researchers and practitioners in marketing and advertising most often use to evaluate communications and predict their ultimate persuasive impact on buying behavior are recall and liking for the communication (Steps 2-4 and 9) rather than the payoff (Step 11) of actually buying the advertised product (Beattie & Mitchell, 1985). A useful modification of the conventional Step 4 (comprehension) mediator deriving from the "cognitive responses" approach of the Ohio State University group (Greenwald, 1968; Petty, Ostrom, & Brock, 1981) has served as a corrective to the classical "information processing" model of persuasion popularized in the World War II army research by the Yale group (Hovland, Janis, & Kelley, 1953; Hovland et al., 1949). These researchers, who had a learning theory background, naturally stressed learning of the message arguments as the crucial mediator of the persuasive impact still popular in the health belief model. I criticized this passive recipient view of persuasion by theorizing that the person is persuaded not simply by the new information presented in the message from the external source but also by manipulating the salience of information already in the person's belief system (McGuire, 1960, 1964; McGuire & McGuire, 1991).

Communication Liking as a
Mediator of Persuasion

Ad liking (Step 3) is used almost as often as ad recall (Step 9) as an index of persuasive effectiveness in the advertising/marketing industry, but it is even more distal from the action payoff (Step 11). Any relation between enhanced liking and later action could be due to better attention to and learning of the message content, to increased source attractiveness that in turn leads to persuasive impact, or to a positive mood effect such that the humor or other inputs make the recipient more mellow and accepting.

The Decision Process Evoked
by Persuasive Communications

The following sections review four topics regarding how the decision to comply is evoked by the persuasive communication and how it is related to the prior and subsequent persuasion steps listed in Table 2.1.

Cognitive Algebra in Making Judgments

Since midcentury, most attitude theorists (Cartwright, 1949; Myrdal, 1944; Smith, 1949), as well as advertising and marketing practitioners (including those in the health area), have taken for granted the expectancy × value rational choice model (Feather, 1982) of how people integrate the information already in their cognitive arenas and in persuasive communications when making decisions. In its most common variant, the model assumes that a person, in choosing among health alternatives (e.g., a parent deciding what food to serve), generates (or abstracts from a persuasive message) a list of costs and benefits of each alternative food, attaches a scale value to each cost or benefit, and then multiplies this value by the probability that a given food will lead to that cost or benefit. The person then sums (or averages) these algebraic products for each food and serves the food with the highest score (Anderson, 1981).

One has only to observe one's own lazy cognition while doing the weekly shopping at the supermarket to realize that humans are unlikely to go through this tedious utility-maximizing calculus. Rather, the person may use some quick and dirty (but effective) approximation, such as using a sufficing rather than optimizing criterion, using only the most salient costs or benefits, or using only the benefits. For example, it may turn out that the cognitive space of child caregivers is such that they would be more persuaded to get their children immunized by a campaign that stresses nonhealth benefits and costs (e.g., the cost that failure to get immunizations might deprive the parents of the schools' babysitting function).

Shortcut Heuristics in Making Decisions

It seems likely that humans have developed phylogenetically and ontogenetically to have some appreciation for the structure of the environment and of their own needs, including heuristic biases that lead easily to behavioral choices similar to the choices that would have been yielded by an effortful consideration of the full information (Caverni, Fabre, & Gonzalez, 1990; Sherman & Corty, 1984; Tversky & Kahneman, 1974). There tends to be a positivity bias such that the public is more influenced by messages stressing health benefits gained than sickness dangers avoided (McGuire & McGuire, 1991). There is a representativeness heuristic such that the public is likely to misperceive the health danger of various behaviors unless considerations such as base rates, regression, and sample size are vigorously stressed in the message. The availability prototype and simulation heuristics indicate that persuasive communications should take into account the ease with which people can bring to mind instances of the various alternatives. There is also the anchoring-and-adjusting heuristic such that people tend to begin with some reference value (which the health communicator should be aware of) and adjust it until the final judgment is reached. The operation of such oversimplifying heuristics is likely to be particularly pronounced in high-risk and high-uncertainty situations (Covello et al., 1990) that often characterize decision making in matters of health.

Remote Ramifications of
Persuasive Communications

The impact of a communication campaign is usually measured by the extent to which it produces change on the explicit attitudes and behaviors. McGuire (1989c; McGuire & McGuire, 1991), however, has been investigating the remote ramifications of persuasive communications on topics and dimensions beyond those explicitly mentioned in the message. For example, a message that is successful in its explicit urging to get one's children immunized may generalize to other topics (e.g., to taking one's children for a dental checkup) and to other dimensions (e.g., proselytizing other parents to get their children immunized). Another asymmetry is that generalization tends to occur more vertically to antecedents and consequences of the explicit topic rather than to parallel topics.

Which informational source is most effective in changing health judgments depends on whether the communication is designed to induce a change on the likelihood or on the desirability dimension. For example, if we are trying to convince parents that they should have their children immunized, and if we are arguing for the likelihood of the children contracting the illness, it is more effective to communicate information from an outside source; if we are arguing for the undesirability of the threatening disease, it is more effective to elicit information from within the parent's own cognitive system, for example, by increasing the information's salience through Socratic questioning (McGuire & McGuire, 1991).

A related line of research deserving more study is people's implicit theory of biology (if devising a health campaign)—that is, their delusional systems regarding physiological topics such as how the body works and the nature of illness and recovery, perceptions that have major implications for how health messages are processed by the public (Leventhal, Meyer, & Nerenz, 1980; Pennebaker, 1982; see also Chapter 8, this volume).

The Decision Model and
Supplementary Processes

Users of the subjective expected utility (expectancy × value) and other decision models often go further by situating their decision model as a molecule within the context of a broader system. A widely used broader model is the theory of reasoned action (Fishbein & Ajzen, 1975), at whose core is the traditional additive expectancy × value model. With regard to further processes hypothesized to contribute to evoking the Step 11 behavior in Table 2.1, Fishbein's model adds a "subjective norm" term that behavior (or "behavioral intentions") depends not only on one's belief about the consequences of the behavior but also on one's perception of how one's valued reference groups feel about the behavior. A health message to induce parents to get their children immunized should mention not only favorable consequences of immunization but also that the parents' valued reference groups favor getting children immunized. Another addition that proves worthwhile is taking into consideration the recipient's initial "apperceptive mass" prior to receipt of the new information (Anderson, 1981). However, the addition of other plausible predictors has not been cost-effective in improving the model or enhancing impact (Bagozzi, 1982; Sheth, 1974; Triandis, 1980). A third type of elaboration is to use structural equation models to trace out alternative paths by which the attitudinal and decision processes relate to the other factors—for example, that beliefs can affect decisions via routes other than attitudes, and that attitudes may affect behavior via paths other than behavioral intention.

BASIC IMPLICATIONS

Uses of the Communication-Persuasion Matrix

The matrix is a user-friendly device for making the research findings conveniently available for those developing mass persuasion campaigns in areas ranging from promoting a more healthful lifestyle to commercial ads to sell products. Analyzing the output into successive mediational steps (exposure, attention, liking, etc.) provides the campaign designer with a diagnostic checklist that can be used to evaluate the capability of a proposed campaign to evoke each of the dependent variable mediational steps leading to persuasion and to identify which steps need bolstering. The input analysis into source, message, channel, audience, and target independent variables, each with subdivisions, provides a resource checklist that allows campaign designers to review a wide range of communication variables that can be added to bolster any of the campaign's weak spots and therefore increase its persuasive impact.

There are additional uses of this communication-persuasion matrix. It enables the campaign designer to keep current with the burgeoning literature on persuasion research. Specifically, new findings can be incorporated into what is already known by entering in one or more cells of the matrix the new empirically determined relations between a cell's column input variable and its row mediational output step. Also, by examining how many already determined relations can be found in each cell of the matrix, basic and applied researchers can judge what topics are relatively overstudied and which relations need more research.

Another benefit of the communication-persuasion matrix is that it suggests principles that help campaign designers avoid commonly made errors, and it suggests new insights. One such implication is the multistep principle, which reminds the campaign designer that any communication variable can affect persuasive impact via a dozen mediators. Another, compensatory, principle suggests that any communication variable typically affects impact in opposite ways via different mediating steps. A third, golden mean, corollary implication is that a moderate level of any communication variable usually has more persuasive impact than very high or very low levels.

Weaknesses of the Communication-Persuasion Matrix and Their Corrections

Many aspects of the communication-persuasion matrix need additional work. One problem is that many of the communication input variables interact in affecting persuasive impact, thus losing some of the convenience of being able to concentrate on one variable at a time. The information processing efficiency of the matrix is reduced because the importance and value of the research done are unequal among the various input categories. Another problem with the matrix is that in many situations, the persuasion process may be shortcut, with some mediators being eliminated (e.g., when the situation allows the use of cognitively undemanding peripheral paths to persuasion). Furthermore, the sequence of the mediators that remain is sometimes reversed in nonobvious ways (e.g., in selective exposure or rationalization). A fuller discussion of the many uses of the communication-persuasion matrix and of its shortcomings and alternatives for constructing persuasion campaigns can be found in McGuire (1984a, 1985).

NOTE

1. This chapter is adapted from McGuire (1994).

REFERENCES

Abrams, D., & Hogg, M. A. (1990). Social identification, self-categorization, and social influence. In W. Stroebe & M. Hewstone (Eds.), *European review of social psychology* (Vol. 1, pp. 195-228). London: Wiley.

Albion, M. S., & Farris, P. W. (1981). *The advertising controversy: Evidence on the economic effects of advertising.* Boston: Auburn House.

Anderson, N. H. (1981). *Foundations of information integration theory.* New York: Academic Press.

Bagozzi, R. P. (1982). A field investigation of causal relations among cognitions, affect, intentions, and behavior. *Journal of Marketing Research, 19,* 562-584.

Barwise, T. P., Ehrenberg, A. S. C., & Goodhardt, G. J. (1982). Glued to the box? Patterns of TV repeat-viewing. *Journal of Communication, 32*(4), 22-29.

Beattie, A. E., & Mitchell, A. A. (1985). The relationship between advertising recall and persuasion: An experimental investigation. In L. F. Alwitt & A. A. Mitchell (Eds.), *Psychological processes and advertising effects: Theory, research, and application* (pp. 129-155). Hillsdale, NJ: Lawrence Erlbaum.

Bless, H., Bohner, G., Schwarz, N., & Strack, F. (1990). Mood and persuasion: A cognitive response analysis. *Personality and Social Psychology Bulletin, 16,* 331-345.

Bowers, J. M., & Osborn, M. M. (1966). Attitudinal effects of selected types of concluding metaphors in persuasive speech. *Speech Monographs, 33,* 147-155.

Breckler, S. J. (1984). Empirical validation of affect, behavior, and cognition as distinct components of attitude. *Journal of Personality and Social Psychology, 47,* 1191-1205.

Calder, B. J., & Sternthal, B. (1980). Television commercial wear-out: An information-processing view. *Journal of Marketing Research, 17,* 173-186.

Campbell, D. T. (1965). Ethnocentrism and other altruistic motives. In D. Levine (Ed.), *Nebraska symposium on motivation, Vol. 13* (pp. 198-231). Lincoln: University of Nebraska Press.

Cartwright, D. (1949). Some principles of mass persuasion. *Human Relations, 2,* 253-267.

Cash, T. F., Dawson, K., Davis, P., Bowen, M., & Galumbeck, C. (1989). Effects of cosmetics use on the physical attractiveness and body images of American college women. *Journal of Social Psychology, 129,* 349-355.

Caverni, J. P., Fabre, J. M., & Gonzalez, M. (Eds.). (1990). *Cognitive biases.* Amsterdam: Elsevier.

Chaiken, S. (1979). Communicator's physical attractiveness and persuasion. *Journal of Personality and Social Psychology, 37,* 1387-1397.

Chaiken, S. (1980). Heuristic versus systematic information processing and the use of source versus message cues in persuasion. *Journal of Personality and Social Psychology, 39,* 752-766.

Comstock, G. (1982). Violence in television content: An overview. In D. Pearl, L. Bouthilet, & J. Lazar (Eds.), *Television and behavior: Ten years of scientific progress and implications for the eighties* (Vol. 2, pp. 108-125). Washington, DC: Government Printing Office.

Cook, T. D., & Flay, B. R. (1978). The persistence of experimentally induced attitude change. *Advances in Experimental Social Psychology, 11,* 1-57.

Costanzo, P. R., & Shaw, M. E. (1966). Conformity as a function of age level. *Child Development, 37,* 967-975.

Covello, V. T., von Winterfeldt, D., & Slovic, P. (1990). *Risk communication: Research and action.* Cambridge, UK: Cambridge University Press.

DeBono, K. G., & Telesca, C. (1990). The influence of source physical attractiveness on advertising effectiveness: A functional perspective. *Journal of Applied Social Psychology, 20,* 1383-1395.

Dion, K. K., & Stein, S. (1978). Physical attractiveness and interpersonal influence. *Journal of Experimental Social Psychology, 14,* 97-108.

Eagly, A. H. (1983). Gender and social influence: A social psychological analysis. *American Psychologist, 38,* 971-981.

Eagly, A. H., & Carli, L. L. (1981). Sex of researchers and sex-typed communications as determinants of sex differences in influenceability: A meta-analysis of social influence studies. *Psychological Bulletin, 90,* 1-20.

Eagly, A. H., & Chaiken, S. (1993). *The psychology of attitudes.* San Diego: Harcourt Brace Jovanovich.

Edwards, K. (1990). The interplay of affect and cognition in attitude formation and change. *Journal of Personality and Social Psychology, 59,* 202-216.

Eron, L. D., Huesmann, L. R., Brice, P., Fischer, P., & Mermelstein, R. (1983). Age trends in the development of aggression, sex-typing, and related television habits. *Developmental Psychology, 19,* 71-77.

Evans, R. I. (1986). How can health lifestyles in adolescents be modified? An analysis of a social psychological program in smoking prevention. In D. Routh (Ed.), *Handbook of pediatric psychology* (pp. 321-331). New York: Guilford.

Feather, N. T. (Ed.). (1982). *Expectations and actions: Expectancy-value models in psychology.* Hillsdale, NJ: Lawrence Erlbaum.

Fishbein, M., & Ajzen, I. (1975). *Belief, attitude, intention, and behavior.* Reading, MA: Addison-Wesley.

Geiselman, R. E., Haight, N. A., & Kimata, L. G. (1984). Context effects on the perceived physical attractiveness of faces. *Journal of Experimental Social Psychology, 20,* 409-424.

Gorn, G. J. (1982). The effects of music in advertising on choice behavior: A classical conditioning approach. *Journal of Marketing, 46,* 94-101.

Greenwald, A. G. (1968). Cognitive learning, cognitive response to persuasion, and attitude change. In A. G. Greenwald, T. S. Brock, & T. M. Ostrom (Eds.), *Psychological
foundations of attitudes* (pp. 147-170). New York: Academic Press.

Gunter, B., & Wober, M. (1983). Television viewing and public perceptions of hazards of
life. *Journal of Environmental Psychology, 3,* 325-335.

Hatfield, E., & Sprecher, S. (1986). *Mirror, mirror: The importance of looks in everyday
life.* Albany: State University of New York at Albany Press.

Hirsch, P. M. (1981). Distinguishing good speculation from bad theory: Rejoinder to
Gerbner et al. *Communication Research, 8,* 73-95.

Holt, L. E. (1970). Resistance to persuasion on explicit beliefs as a function of commitment to and desirability of logically related beliefs. *Journal of Personality and Social
Psychology, 16,* 583-591.

Hovland, C. I., Janis, I. L., & Kelley, H. J. (1953). *Communication and persuasion.* New
Haven, CT: Yale University Press.

Hovland, C. I., Lumsdaine, A. A., & Sheffield, F. D. (1949). *Studies in social psychology
in World War II: Vol. 3. Experiments on mass communication.* Princeton, NJ: Princeton University Press.

Huesmann, L. R., Eron, L. D., Klein, R., Brice, P., & Fischer, P. (1983). Mitigating the
imitation of aggressive behaviors by changing children's attitudes about media violence. *Journal of Personality and Social Psychology, 44,* 899-910.

Hughes, M. (1980). The fruits of cultivation analysis: A reexamination of some effects of
television watching. *Public Opinion Quarterly, 44,* 287-302.

Iyengar, S. (1991). *Is anyone responsible? How television frames political issues.* Chicago: University of Chicago Press.

Janis, I. L., Kaye, D., & Kirschner, P. (1965). Facilitating effects of "eating-while-read-
ing" on responsiveness to persuasive communications. *Journal of Personality and
Social Psychology, 1,* 181-186.

Keating, J. P., & Latané, B. (1976). Politicians on TV: The image is the message. *Journal
of Social Issues, 32*(4), 116-132.

Kellaris, J. J., & Cox, A. D. (1989). The effects of background music in advertising: A
reassessment. *Journal of Consumer Research, 16,* 113-118.

Kenrick, D. T., & Gutierres, S. E. (1980). Contrast effects and judgments of physical
attractiveness: When beauty becomes a problem. *Journal of Personality and Social
Psychology, 38,* 131-140.

Krosnick, J. A., & Alwin, D. F. (1989). Aging and susceptibility to attitude change. *Journal of Personality and Social Psychology, 57,* 416-425.

Krugman, H. E. (1965). The impact of television advertising: Learning without involvement. *Public Opinion Quarterly, 29,* 349-356.

Krugman, H. E. (1983). Television program interest and commercial interruption. *Journal of Advertising Research, 23*(1), 21-23.

Langlois, J. H., & Roggman, L. A. (1990). Attractive faces are only average. *Psychological Science, 1,* 115-121.

Langlois, J. H., Roggman, L. A., & Rieser-Danner, L. A. (1990). Infants' differential
social responses to attractive and unattractive faces. *Developmental Psychology, 26,*
153-159.

Lazarus, R. S. (1984). On the primacy of cognition. *American Psychologist, 39,* 124-129.

Leventhal, H., Meyer, D., & Nerenz, D. (1980). The common sense representation of illness danger. In S. Rachman (Ed.), *Medical psychology* (Vol. 2, pp. 7-30). New York: Pergamon.

Lewin, K. (1951). *Field theory in social change.* New York: Harper & Row.

Lincoln, A. J. (1977). Effects of the sex of the model and donor on donating to Amsterdam organ grinders. *Journal of Social Psychology, 103,* 33-37.

Malhotra, N. K. (1984). Reflections on the information overload paradigm in consumer decision making. *Journal of Consumer Research, 10,* 435-440.

McCullough, J. L., & Ostrom, T. M. (1974). Repetition of highly similar messages and attitude change. *Journal of Applied Psychology, 59,* 395-397.

McGuire, W. J. (1960). A syllogistic analysis of cognitive relationships. In M. J. Rosenberg & C. I. Hovland (Eds.), *Attitude organization and change* (pp. 65-111). New Haven, CT: Yale University Press.

McGuire, W. J. (1964). Inducing resistance to persuasion. *Advances in Experimental Social Psychology, 1,* 191-229.

McGuire, W. J. (1968). Personality and susceptibility to social influence. In E. F. Borgatta & W. W. Lambert (Eds.), *Handbook of personality theory and research* (pp. 1130-1187). Chicago: Rand McNally.

McGuire, W. J. (1983). A contextualist theory of knowledge: Its implications for innovation and reform in psychological research. *Advances in Experimental Social Psychology, 16,* 1-47.

McGuire, W. J. (1984a). Public communication as a strategy for inducing health-promoting behavioral change. *Preventive Medicine, 13,* 299-319.

McGuire, W. J. (1984b). Search for the self: Going beyond self-esteem and the reactive self. In R. A. Zucker, J. Aronoff, & A. I. Rabin (Eds.), *Personality and the prediction of behavior* (pp. 73-120). New York: Academic Press.

McGuire, W. J. (1985). Attitudes and attitude change. In G. Lindzey & E. Aronson (Eds.), *Handbook of social psychology* (3rd ed., Vol. 2, pp. 233-346). New York: Random House.

McGuire, W. J. (1986). The myth of massive media impact: Savaging and salvagings. In G. Comstock (Ed.), *Public communication and behavior* (Vol. 1, pp. 173-257). New York: Academic Press.

McGuire, W. J. (1989a). A mediational theory of susceptibility to social influence. In V. Gheorghiu, P. Netter, H. J. Eysenck, & R. Rosenthal (Eds.), *Suggestibility: Theory and research* (pp. 305-322). Heidelberg: Springer-Verlag.

McGuire, W. J. (1989b). A perspectivist approach to the strategic planning of programmatic scientific research. In B. Gholson, W. R. Shadish, Jr., R. A. Neimeyer, & A. C. Houts (Eds.), *The psychology of science: Contributions to metascience* (pp. 214-245). New York: Cambridge University Press.

McGuire, W. J. (1989c). The structure of individual attitudes and attitude systems. In A. R. Pratkanis, S. J. Breckler, & A. G. Greenwald (Eds.), *Attitude structure and function* (pp. 37-69). Hillsdale, NJ: Lawrence Erlbaum.

McGuire, W. J. (1989d). Theoretical foundations of campaigns. In R. E. Rice & C. K. Atkin (Eds.), *Public communication campaigns* (2nd ed., pp. 43-65). Newbury Park, CA: Sage.

McGuire, W. J. (1991). Guiding-idea theories of the person: Their use in developing educational campaigns against drug abuse and other health-threatening behavior. *Health Education Research: Theory and Practice, 6,* 173-184.

McGuire, W. J. (1994). Using mass media communication to enhance public health. In L. Sechrest, T. E. Backer, E. M. Rogers, T. F. Campbell, & M. L. Grady (Eds.), *Effective dissemination of clinical health information* (AHCPR Publication No. 95-0015, pp. 125-151). Rockville, MD: Agency for Health Care Policy and Research, Public Health Service.

McGuire, W. J. (1997). Creative hypothesis generating in psychology: Some useful heuristics. *Annual Review of Psychology, 48,* 1-30.

McGuire, W. J. (2000). Standing on the shoulders of ancients: Consumer research, persuasion, and figurative language. *Journal of Consumer Research, 27,* 1-23.

McGuire, W. J., & McGuire, C. V. (1991). The content, structure, and operation of thought systems. In R. S. Wyer, Jr. & T. K. Srull (Eds.), *Advances in social cognition* (Vol. 4). Hillsdale, NJ: Lawrence Erlbaum.

McGuire, W. J., & McGuire, C. V. (1992). Cognitive-versus-negative positivity asymmetries in thought systems. *European Journal of Social Psychology, 22,* 571-591.

Milavsky, J. R., Kessler, R. C., Stipp, H. H., & Rubens, W. S. (1982). *Television and aggression: Results of a panel study.* New York: Academic Press.

Milavsky, J. R., Pekowsky, B., & Stipp, H. (1975). TV drug advertising and proprietary and illicit drug use among teenage boys. *Public Opinion Quarterly, 39,* 457-481.

Milgram, S. (1974). *Obedience to authority: An experimental view.* New York: Harper & Row.

Millar, M. G., & Millar, K. U. (1990). Attitude change as a function of attitude type and argument type. *Journal of Personality and Social Psychology, 59,* 217-228.

Murphy, R. D. (1980). Consumer responses to cigarette health warnings. In L. A. Morris, M. B. Mazis, & I. Barofsky (Eds.), *Product labeling and health risks* (Banbury Report number 6, pp. 13-21). Cold Spring Harbor Laboratory, NY: Banbury.

Myrdal, G. (1944). *An American dilemma.* New York: Harper.

Nelson, C. E. (1968). Anchoring to accepted values as a technique for immunizing beliefs against persuasion. *Journal of Personality and Social Psychology, 9,* 329-334.

Orpen, C. (1989). The effect of gender on judgments of direct and indirect management influence methods. *Journal of Social Psychology, 129,* 119-120.

Patzer, G. L. (1985). *The physical attractiveness phenomena.* New York: Plenum.

Pearce, W. B., & Brommel, B. J. (1972). Vocalic communication in persuasion. *Quarterly Journal of Speech, 58,* 298-306.

Pennebaker, J. W. (1982). *The psychology of physical symptoms.* New York: Springer-Verlag.

Petty, R. E., & Cacioppo, J. T. (1986a). *Communication and persuasion: Central and peripheral routes to attitude change.* New York: Springer-Verlag.

Petty, R. E., & Cacioppo, J. T. (1986b). The elaboration likelihood model of persuasion. *Advances in Experimental Social Psychology, 19,* 123-205.

Petty, R. E., Ostrom, T. M., & Brock, T. C. (Eds.). (1981). *Cognitive responses in persuasion.* Hillsdale, NJ: Lawrence Erlbaum.

Piotrow, P. T., Rimon, J. G., II, Winnard, K., Kincaid, D. L., Huntington, D., & Convisser, J. (1990). Mass media family planning promotion in three Nigerian cities. *Studies in Family Planning, 21*(5), 265-274.

Pool, I. de S. (1983). Tracking the flow of information. *Science, 221,* 609-613.

Pratkanis, A. R., Breckler, S. J., & Greenwald, A. G. (Eds.). (1989). *Attitude structure and function* (pp. 37-69). Hillsdale, NJ: Lawrence Erlbaum.

Pratkanis, A. R., & Greenwald, A. G. (1985). A reliable sleeper effect in persuasion: Implications for opinion change theory and research. In L. F. Alwitt & A. A. Mitchell (Eds.), *Psychological processes and advertising effects: Theory, research, and application* (pp. 157-173). Hillsdale, NJ: Lawrence Erlbaum.

Ramirez, A. (1977). Social influence and ethnicity of the communicator. *Journal of Social Psychology, 102,* 209-213.

Reis, H. T., Wilson, I. M., Monestere, C., Bernstein, S., Clark, K., Seidl, E., Franco, M., Gioioso, E., Freeman, L., & Radoane, K. (1990). What is smiling is beautiful and good. *European Journal of Social Psychology, 20,* 259-267.

Reyes, R. M., Thompson, W. C., & Bower, G. H. (1980). Judgmental biases resulting from differing availabilities of arguments. *Journal of Personality and Social Psychology, 39,* 2-12.

Rossiter, J. R., & Robertson, T. S. (1980). Children's dispositions toward proprietary drugs and the role of television drug advertising. *Public Opinion Quarterly, 44,* 316-329.

Rothblum, E. D. (1990). Women and weight: Fad and fiction. *Journal of Psychology, 124,* 5-24.

Rushton, J. P. (1975). Generosity in children: Immediate and long-term effects of modeling, preaching, and moral judgment. *Journal of Personality and Social Psychology, 31,* 459-466.

Sherman, S. J., & Corty, E. (1984). Cognitive heuristics. In R. S. Wyer, Jr. & T. K. Srull (Eds.), *Handbook of social cognition* (Vol. 1, pp. 189-286). Hillsdale, NJ: Lawrence Erlbaum.

Sheth, J. N. (1974). A field study of attitude-structure and attitude-behavior relationship. In J. N. Sheth (Ed.), *Models for buyer behavior: Conceptual, quantitative, and empirical.* New York: Harper & Row.

Sidanius, J. (1993). The psychology of group conflict and the dynamics of oppression: A social dominance perspective. In S. Iyengar & W. J. McGuire (Eds.), *Explorations in political psychology* (pp. 183-224). Durham, NC: Duke University Press.

Singer, J. L., & Singer, D. (1981). *Television, imagination, and aggression: A study of preschoolers.* Hillsdale, NJ: Lawrence Erlbaum.

Smith, M. B. (1949). Personal values as determinants of a political attitude. *Journal of Psychology, 28,* 477-486.

Tajfel, H. (Ed.). (1982). *Social identity and intergroup relations.* Cambridge, UK: Cambridge University Press.

Taylor, S. E., & Thompson, S. C. (1982). Stalking the elusive "vividness" effect. *Psychological Review, 89,* 115-181.

Townsend, J. M., & Levy, G. D. (1990). Effects of potential partners' costume and physical attractiveness on sexuality and partner selection. *Journal of Psychology, 124,* 371-389.

Triandis, H. C. (1980). Values, attitudes and interpersonal behavior. In H. E. Howe, Jr. (Ed.), *Nebraska symposium on motivation, 1979* (Vol. 27, pp. 195-259). Lincoln: University of Nebraska Press.

Turner, J. C., & Oakes, P. J. (1989). Self-categorization theory and social influence. In P. B. Paulus (Ed.), *The psychology of group influence* (2nd ed.). Hillsdale, NJ: Lawrence Erlbaum.

Tversky, A., & Kahneman, D. (1974). Judgment under uncertainty: Heuristics and biases. *Science, 185,* 1124-1131.

Tyler, T. R., & Schuller, R. A. (1991). Aging and attitude change. *Journal of Personality and Social Psychology, 61,* 689-697.

Zajonc, R. B. (1984). On the primacy of affect. *American Psychologist, 39,* 117-123.

Zellner, M. (1970). Self-esteem, reception, and influenceability. *Journal of Personality and Social Psychology, 15,* 87-93.

3

Theory and Principles of Media Health Campaigns

Charles K. Atkin

This chapter applies key concepts from the mass communication and social science literature to the design of effective campaign strategies in the health domain. First, an overview of macrocampaign issues is presented: identification of target audiences and target responses, utilization of different types of messages, selection of communication channels, and optimization of quantitative dissemination factors such as volume of stimuli, repetition of presentations, length of campaign, and scheduling of messages. Then, the basic conceptualization underlying message design and suggestions for devising the content, form, and style of messages are discussed: strategic selection of substantive material, mechanical construction of message components, and creative execution of stylistic features. The chapter reviews conventional practices used in health campaigns and offers promising innovative strategies for future campaigns.

APPROACHING CAMPAIGN DESIGN

In designing and implementing successful health campaigns, the disciplined approach requires that the campaign team perform a thorough situational analysis, develop a pragmatic strategic plan, and execute the creation and placement of messages in accordance with principles of effective media campaign practices. It is usually advantageous to rely on research inputs at each phase in the process (see Chapters 2, 8, and 27, this volume).

The starting point in campaign design is a conceptual analysis of the situation comprising several forms of assessment. The initial step is to analyze the behavioral aspects of the health problem to determine which actions should be performed by which people to improve what aspects of health status. In particular, the design team needs to specify focal segments of the population whose health-related practices are to be changed and the bottom-line focal behaviors that the campaign ultimately seeks to influence. The next step is to trace backwards from the focal behaviors to identify the proximate and distal determinants and then create models of the pathways of influence via attitudes, beliefs, knowledge, social influences, and environmental forces. In most cases, the model will differ for each health topic, focal behavior, and population segment.

The next phase is to assess the model from a communication perspective, specifying target audiences and target behaviors that can be directly influenced by campaign messages. The communication campaign can then be designed to have an impact on the most promising pathways. This requires a comprehensive plan for combining the myriad strategic components subject to manipulation by the campaigner.

In formulating the plan, the campaign strategist is faced with basic decisions about allocating resources among the prospective pathways, focal behaviors, types of messages, channels, and dissemination options. Should the campaign seek to change fundamental behaviors or chip away at more readily altered peripheral actions? Should the most resistant or most receptive segments be the focus of campaign efforts? What proportion of the resources should be devoted to direct influence on the focal segment versus indirect pathways (e.g., by stimulating interpersonal influencers and by leveraging or combating environmental determinants)? Which influencers should be targeted? What is the optimum combination of awareness messages, instructional messages, and persuasive messages? How many messages should attack the competition (the unhealthy behavior) versus promote the healthy alternative? Is it more effective to disseminate the messages via expensive TV channels or to primarily use minimedia? Should the campaign messages be scheduled in concentrated bursts or spread out over a lengthy period of time?

During the past few decades, a relatively limited array of strategies has been typically used in media-based health campaigns. A basic theme of this chapter is that disciplined diversification can yield greater success in health campaigns by using a broader set of communication tactics that are coordinated in a more conceptually sophisticated manner and guided by formative research.

In media-based campaigns, strategy development entails sensitive application of mass communication theories and best practices campaign principles. The strategic guidelines presented in this chapter draw on models, processes, generalizations, and recommendations in the voluminous research literature on media health campaigns, particularly theoretical perspectives and reviews by Ajzen and Fishbein (1980), Atkin (1981, 1994), Atkin and Wallack (1990), Backer and Rogers (1993), Backer, Rogers, and Sopory (1992), Bandura (1986), Burgoon and Miller (1985), DeJong and Winston (1990), Donohew, Sypher, and Bukoski (1991), Hale and Dillard (1995), Janz and Becker (1984), Maibach and Parrott (1995), McGuire (1994), Petty, Baker, and Gleicher (1991), Prochaska and DiClemente (1983), Rogers (1983), Rosenstock (1990), Singhal and Rogers (1999), and Slater (1999).

The applicability of the general principles depends on the specific context (especially the types of audiences to be influenced and the type of product being promoted), so effective campaign design usually requires extensive formative evaluation inputs and message pretests. Surveys, focus groups, observation, interviewing, and lab testing provide useful information to guide campaign development and to provide feedback on effective and ineffective components (see Chapters 4 and 7, this volume).

LIMITED EFFECTS OF CONVENTIONAL CAMPAIGNS

Health campaigns that are directly targeted to the focal segment of the population tend to have a relatively modest degree of impact, but the effects vary substantially according to the palatability of the advocated behavior, receptivity of target audience, and the quality and quantity of messages (see Chapters 2 and 10, this volume).

There are many reasons why campaigns do not have a strong impact. Audience resistance barriers arise at each stage of response, from exposure to behavioral implementation. Perhaps the most elemental problem is reaching the audience and attaining attention to the messages. Other key barriers include misperception of susceptibility to negative outcomes, deflection of persuasive appeals, denial of applicability to self, rejection of unappealing recommendations, and inertia or lethargy.

Due to the wide variety of pitfalls, audience members are lost at each stage of message response. The messages may be regarded as offensive, disturbing, boring, stale, preachy, confusing, irritating, misleading, irrelevant, uninformative, useless, unbelievable, or unmotivating. Moreover, insufficient dissemination may render some of the campaign messages just plain invisible. The guidelines throughout this chapter should be helpful in avoiding or overcoming the problematic barriers to effectiveness, and formative evaluation data will help identify message weaknesses.

The motto "first do no harm" is applicable to media health campaigns because of imprecisely targeted messages and limited control over how receivers interpret the content. The problem is more acute for negative messages that depict problem behaviors and attempt to threaten individuals.

One significant problem is that campaigns may generate counterproductive boomerang effects in which significant portions of the audience are influenced in the opposite direction. Atkin (2000) presents an extensive discussion of boomerang effects, including the following types of unintended outcomes: Inadvertent social norming may occur when alarming prevalence statistics or portrayals of misbehavers may serve to normalize the unhealthy behavior. Depictions of the proscribed behavior may promote the competition as the audience becomes curious, learns it is fun, or regards it as challenging. The forbidden fruit appeal might sell the fruit; psychological reactance is particularly problematic with adolescents. Highly threatening fear appeals may backfire without a strong efficacy component, and frequent emphasis on a negative incentive may produce desensitization as the audience becomes accustomed to this harmful outcome. An underwhelming threat may also be counterproductive if the harmful outcome is less severe than expected, yielding a negative violation of expectations. Message pretesting is the best method to guard against counterproductive features that may produce undesired responses.

TARGET AUDIENCES

A typical health campaign might subdivide the population on a dozen dimensions (e.g., age, sex, ethnicity, stage of change, susceptibility, self-efficacy, values, personality characteristics, and social context), each with multiple levels. Combining these dimensions, there are thousands of potential subgroups that might be defined for targeting purposes.

Strategists must anticipate the array of likely audience reactions to campaign messages. In responding to media stimuli, individuals proceed through the basic stages of exposure and processing before effects can be achieved at the learning, yielding, and action levels (see Chapters 2 and 8, this volume). *Exposure* includes both the initial reception and the degree of attention to the campaign messages (it may be amplified by subsequent campaign-instigated seeking of further information or sensitization to other relevant media messages that are encountered). *Processing* encompasses mental comprehension, interpretive perceptions, pro- and counterarguing, and cognitive connections and emotional reactions produced by the campaign message (along with subsequent interpretation of other relevant stimuli, particularly developing resistance to countermessages). Audience predispositions play a crucial role in determining these responses.

There are two major strategic advantages of segmentation. First, message efficiency can be maximized if subsets of the audience are ordered according to importance (substantively: Who is most in need of change?) and receptivity (pragmatically: Who is most likely to be influenced?). Second, effectiveness can be increased if message content, form, and style are tailored to the predispositions and abilities of the distinct subgroups (see Chapters 4, 7, and 13, this volume). Three basic types of audiences can be targeted in media health campaigns: focal segments, influentials, and policymakers.

Focal Segments

The nature of the health problem dictates the broad parameters of the focal audience to be influenced (e.g., adolescents in a drug campaign and middle-aged females in a breast cancer campaign). Because audience receptivity is often a more central determinant of campaign effectiveness than the potency of the campaign stimuli, there will be differential success depending on which particular segment is targeted.

A fundamental factor is stage of readiness to perform the practice. Campaigns tend to achieve the strongest impact with reinforcing messages designed to maintain the healthy practices of those who are already favorably predisposed. A more important but somewhat less receptive target is composed of people who have not yet tried the unhealthy behavior but whose background characteristics suggest they are "at risk" in the near future. Those committed to unhealthy practices, however, are not readily influenced by directly targeted campaigns, so a heavy investment of resources to induce immediate discontinuation is likely to yield a marginal payoff.

Campaigners also need to consider other demographic, social, and psychological-based subgroups such as the high- versus low-income strata or high versus low sensation seekers (see Chapter 23, this volume). Influencing these varied population segments requires a complex mix of narrowly customized messages and broadly applicable multitargeted messages that use diverse appeals and optimally ambiguous recommended actions.

Interpersonal Influencers

It is often valuable for campaigners to supplement the direct approach (educating and persuading the focal segment) by influencing other target audiences that can exert interpersonal influence or help reform environmental conditions that shape behaviors of the segment to be changed. Mass media campaigns have considerable potential for producing effects on institutions and groups at the national and community level as well as motivating personal influencers in close contact with the focal individuals. These audiences are usually more receptive to media messages, and their indirectly stimulated activities are more likely to be effective than campaign messages directly targeted to the focal segment. These influencers can provide positive and negative reinforcement, exercise control (by making rules, monitoring behavior, and enforcing consequences), shape opportunities, facilitate behavior with reminders at opportune moments, and serve as role models. Furthermore, influencers can customize their messages to the unique needs and values of the local individuals.

For example, there are a variety of peer and authority figures in a position to personally educate, persuade, or control the focal segments of adolescents: parents, siblings, friends, coworkers, bosses, teachers, coaches, medical personnel, police officers, and store clerks (see Chapters 22 and 27, this volume).

An important role of the campaign is to stimulate interpersonal influence attempts by inspiring, prompting, and empowering influencers, especially those who are hesitant to wield their authority. The influencers are likely to be responsive to negative appeals that arouse concern about harmful consequences to those they are trying to help behave appropriately.

Societal Policymakers

Individuals' decisions about health practices are strongly shaped by the constraints and opportunities in their societal environment, such as monetary expenses, laws, entertainment role models, commercial messages, social forces, and community services. Through the interventions of government, business, educational, medical, media, religious, and community organizations, many of these influential factors can be altered to increase the likelihood of healthy choices or discourage unhealthy practices. These initiatives include direct service delivery, restrictions on advertising and marketing practices, and imposition of taxes. More fundamental long-range approaches might seek to restructure basic socioeconomic conditions by reducing poverty, improving schools, broadening access to the health care system, and enhancing employment opportunities.

Reformers have refined techniques that combine community organizing and media publicity to advance healthy public policies through media advocacy (see Chapter 31, this volume). Through agenda setting on health issues, news coverage can shape the public agenda and the policy agenda pertaining to new initiatives, rules, and laws. An important element is changing the public's beliefs about the effectiveness of policies and interventions that are advanced, which leads to supportive public opinion (and direct pressure) that can help convince institutional leaders to formulate and implement societal constraints and opportunities (see Chapter 1, this volume).

TARGET RESPONSES

In the health arena, the focal behavior is usually a specific behavioral practice or discrete action. The two fundamental approaches are to promote healthy behavior (e.g., enjoy a drug-free lifestyle) and to reduce or prevent unhealthy behavior (e.g., do not use drugs). The promotion of desirable practices works better for certain topic areas (e.g., it is easier to promote the designated driver arrangement for a safe ride home than to glamorize nonuse of drugs), and the negatively oriented prevention approach is more potent for topics for which harmful outcomes are genuinely threatening.

Prevention campaign messages focus primarily on the harmful consequences of the unhealthy practice rather than promoting a positive alternative to compete with it. This is especially the case for substances such as drugs and tobacco, where the positive behavior lacks explicit appealing features. Health campaigners typically attack the competition by threatening dire consequences for performing the proscribed behavior. Although threats can be effective if handled skillfully, the heavy reliance on negatively attacking the competition tends to restrict the strategic arsenal to a narrow array of options. A softer tactic is to discount the perceived benefits of the unhealthy practice, such as by asserting that smoking does not really impress peers.

In campaign messages that promote a positive product directly to a focal segment, there is a continuum of prospective target responses that can be explicitly recommended for adoption. These actions can vary in the acceptability to the audience, based primarily on effort and sacrifice required to perform the behavior and monetary expense. This barrier can be overcome with smaller or softer products that demand lower investment and generate fewer drawbacks. The campaign can create a "product line" of various behaviors featuring audience-appropriate forms of packaging. In creating this menu, the designer should take into account receptivity versus resistance of audience and the potency of the incentives associated with each product. With resistant audiences, it may be fruitless to advocate a sizable degree of change that is beyond the recipients' latitude of acceptability; for many health behaviors, the initial product representation should reflect the incremental "foot-in-the-door" strategy.

The array of products can be packaged in a manner that makes the recommended actions more appealing. Terminology and imagery such as "drug-free lifestyle" and "abstinence" have not been overwhelmingly effective in the alcohol, tobacco, and drug domains. Some messages might instead promote modestly demanding products such as prebehaviors (e.g., sign a pledge card or wear a red ribbon) or limited forms of abstaining (e.g., drug-free week and delay use until later).

In addition, there are numerous intermediate responses that might be targeted, such as awareness, knowledge, images, salience priorities, beliefs, expectancies, values, and attitudes; campaigns may seek to change key variables along the pathways leading to the focal behavior. Other types of target responses come into play when campaigns are aimed at influencers and societal policymakers.

TYPES OF CAMPAIGN MESSAGES

Depending on the most promising mechanisms of influence, campaigns use three basic communication processes by which messages move the target audience toward the desired response: awareness, instruction, and persuasion. The relative emphasis on the three types of messages will vary at different points of the campaign and for different target audiences because the pathways to impact depend on the existing pattern of knowledge and attitudes of the audience.

Awareness Messages

Most campaigns present messages that attempt to increase awareness: informing people what to do, specifying who should do it, and cuing them about when and where it should be done. These messages may be designed to create recognition of the topic or practice for a large portion of the public, to trigger activation among favorably predisposed audiences, to foster compliance with interpersonal influences or environmental forces in the focal segments, to encourage further information seeking about the topic, and to sensitize individuals to subsequently encountered messages. These last two processes will be discussed in detail.

Information Seeking

Campaign messages that have the broadest reach can deliver only a superficial amount of informational and persuasive content that is seldom customized to the individual recipient. To convey multiple appeals, elaborate evidence, and detailed instruction, media campaigns can stimulate the audience to seek out additional customized and especially salient material from specialized sources. A key role of awareness messages is to arouse interest or concern and to motivate further exploration of the subject. In particular, messages should include elements designed to prompt active seeking from elaborated information sources such as web sites, hotline operators, books, counselors, parents, and opinion leaders.

Sensitization

The everyday environment experienced by focal individuals has a rich array of existing influences that can complement the health campaign messages, but many of these stimuli are simply not salient enough to be recognized or processed. In the mass media, there are numerous news stories, advertisements, entertainment portrayals, and other public service campaigns that present content consistent with campaign goals. Similarly, individuals may not be conscious of certain social norms, interpersonal influences, behavioral models, or societal conditions that might contribute to performance of the focal behavior. Thus, some campaign messages can serve a priming function to cue the audience to available procampaign stimuli (see Chapter 12, this volume).

Instruction Messages

In many campaigns, there is a need to provide "how to do it" information that produces knowledge gain and skills acquisition. If the behavioral components are elaborate or complex, messages can educate the audience with a detailed blueprint. If certain individuals lack confidence to carry out the behavior, messages can provide encouragement or training to enhance personal efficacy. If the focal segment is subject to peer pressure or exposed to unhealthy media portrayals, instruction messages can teach peer resistance and media literacy skills. Given the potentially detrimental health effects of commercial advertising, entertainment media portrayals, and certain web sites, it may be wise to devote a modest proportion of campaign messages to inoculating viewers and listeners against these influences that might undermine the campaign.

Persuasion Messages

In addition to awareness and education, the campaign needs to present messages featuring reasons why the audience should adopt the advocated action or avoid the proscribed behavior. The classic case involves attitude creation or change, usually via knowledge gain and belief formation. For audiences that are favorably inclined, the campaign has the easier persuasive task of attaining reinforcement of predispositions: strengthening a positive attitude, promoting postbehavior consolidation, and motivating behavioral maintenance over time.

The promoting and attacking approaches used in persuasive campaign messages are generally accompanied by corresponding positive or negative incentive appeals. Messages for high-involvement health practices tend to emphasize substantive incentives, presenting persuasive arguments supported by credible messengers or evidence to move the audience through a lengthy hierarchy of output steps, such as attention, attitude change, and action (see Chapter 2, this volume). The most widely used frameworks (Theory of Reasoned Action, Protection Motivation Theory, and the Health Belief Model) draw on a basic expectancy value mechanism in which messages primarily influence an array of beliefs regarding the subjective likelihood of each outcome occurring; attitudinal and behavioral responses are contingent on each individual's valuation of these outcomes (see Chapter 12, this volume).

CHANNELS

In disseminating messages, designers most commonly rely on television, radio, newspapers, and printed materials, especially broadcast spots, press releases, and pamphlets. This narrow array of conventional choices has not consistently produced impressive results, and it may be worth exploring a more diverse variety of channels and vehicles, including secondary minimedia (e.g., billboards, posters, and theater slides), entertainment-education materials (e.g., songs, program inserts, and comics; see Chapter 28, this volume), and interactive media (e.g., web sites, CD-ROM disks, and computer games; see Chapters 29 and 30, this volume). The interactive capacity of these new technologies offers a promising advance over standard media channels because the messages can be customized to the individual's capabilities, readiness stage, stylistic tastes, knowledge levels, and current beliefs.

In assessing each option for channeling campaign messages, myriad advantages and disadvantages can be taken into consideration along many communicative dimensions. Atkin (1994) discusses channel differences in terms of *reach* (proportion of community exposed to the message), *specialization* (targetability for reaching specific subgroups), *intrusiveness* (capability for overcoming selectivity and commanding attention), *safeness* (avoidance of risk of boomerang or irritation), *participation* (active receiver involvement while processing stimulus), *meaning modalities* (array of senses employed in conveying meaning), *personalization* (human relational nature of source-receiver interaction), *decodability* (mental effort required for processing stimulus), *depth* (channel capacity for conveying detailed and complex content), *credibility* (believability of material conveyed), *agenda setting* (potency of channel for raising salience priority of issues), *accessibility* (ease of placing messages in channel), *economy* (low cost for producing and disseminating stimuli), and *efficiency* (simplicity of arranging for production and dissemination).

Health campaigners have traditionally underused public relations techniques for generating news and feature story coverage in the mass media. With recent trends making health topics increasingly central among journalistic priorities for newspapers, newsmagazines, and television newscasts (along with the long-standing interest on the part of specialty magazines, cable channels, and daytime TV talk shows), campaigns should take greater advantage of these opportunities for message dissemination (see Chapter 13, this volume).

Public relations in the health domain should move beyond the passive distribution of press releases to aggressively place guests on talk shows, regularly feed the feature writers with compelling story ideas, and creatively stage pseudoevents to attract journalist attention (including the dramatization of health-related statistics using "creative epidemiology" techniques). The source of public relations messages is especially important because these efforts tend to attain greater media acceptance when sponsored by high-profile and widely respected organizations that feature distinctive or compelling messengers (e.g., celebrity spokespersons, government officials, and charismatic experts who have gained prominence, along with victims and survivors who provide a human interest angle).

QUANTITATIVE DISSEMINATION FACTORS

Strategic dissemination considerations encompass the volume of messages, the amount of repetition, the prominence of placement, and the scheduling of message presentation.

A substantial volume of stimuli is needed to attain adequate reach and frequency of exposure, along with comprehension, recognition, and image formation. Moreover, maximum saturation conveys significance of the problem, which is an essential facilitator of agenda setting and heightened salience. Moderate repetition of specific executions may be needed to force low-involvement receivers to attend and process the message, but high repetition leads to wearout and diminishing returns. Prominent placement of messages in conspicuous positions within media vehicles (e.g., during prime-time and on the back page of newspapers) serves to enhance both exposure levels and perceived significance. To provide a common thread unifying the varied messages, the campaign should feature continuity devices (e.g., logo, slogan, jingle, and messenger), which increase memorability and enable the audience to cumulatively integrate material across multiple exposure impressions. Another quantitative consideration involves the scheduling of a fixed number of presentations; depending on the situation, campaign messages may be most effectively concentrated over a short duration, dispersed thinly over a lengthy period, or distributed in intermittent bursts of "flighting" or "pulsing."

Unlike commercial advertisers who can place numerous messages in the media and rely on high-repetition soft-sell strategies based on principles of mere exposure or other peripheral paths of influence, campaign designers relying on limited exposure through public service announcements need to achieve the greatest efficiency and effectiveness by making messages provocative, involving, and engaging to attract attention and facilitate processing.

To maximize quantity, campaigners need to diligently pursue monetary resources from government, industry, or association sources to fund paid placements and leveraged media slots, to aggressively lobby for free public service time or space, to skillfully employ public relations techniques for generating entertainment and journalistic coverage, and to use the low-cost Internet channel of communication. Moreover, pseudoquantity can be boosted by sensitizing audiences to appropriate content already available in the media and by stimulating information seeking from specialty sources (as noted previously).

The realities of health promotion and prevention often require exceptional persistence of effort over long periods of time. Perpetual campaigning is often necessary because focal segments of the population are in constant need of influence. There are always newcomers who are moving into the "at-risk" stage of vulnerability, backsliders who are reverting to prior misbehavior, evolvers who are gradually adopting the recommended practice at a slow pace, waverers who are needing regular doses of reinforcement to stay the course, and latecomers who are finally seeing the light after years of unhealthy habits.

MESSAGE DESIGN

In the rest of the chapter, the focus shifts to the content, form, and style of individual messages in the overall campaign. Sophisticated message design includes strategic selection of substantive material, mechanical construction of message components, and creative implementation of stylistic features.

The presentation begins with a discussion of incentives, which are central to persuasive messages, and then considers the messenger and stylistic concerns. For most of the pathways of influence, there are several other message qualities that increase effectiveness. *Credibility* is the extent to which the message content is believed to be accurate and valid; this is primarily conveyed by the trustworthiness and competence of the source and the provision of convincing evidence. The style and ideas should be engaging by using stylistic features that are superficially *attractive* and entertaining (and less pleasing components that are nevertheless arresting or refreshing) and substantive content that is interesting, mentally stimulating, or emotionally arousing. To influence behavior, the presentation must be personally involving and *relevant,* such that the receivers regard the recommendation as applicable to their situation and needs. Finally, the *understandability* of the message contributes to recipient processing and learning via presentation of material in a comprehensive and comprehensible manner that is simple, explicit, and sufficiently detailed.

Selection of Incentive Appeals

Rather than simply exhorting individuals to act in a specified way, it is preferable to present message content that links the desired health behavior to valued attributes or consequences that serve as positive incentives (or that links the unhealthy behavior to negative incentives). The classic incentive strategy in health messages is to offer a series of substantive arguments for or against a particular behavior, buttressed by credible evidence or source assertions.

The incentive appeals for complying with a recommendation should build on existing values of the target audience. The basic dimensions of incentives include physical health, time/effort, economic, psychological/aspirational, and social, each with possible positive and negative value predispositions. The most frequently used dimension in the health domain is physical health; negatively valued unhealthy outcomes (death, illness, and injury) tend to be featured more often than positive reinforcers, however. Clearly, there is a need to diversify the negative incentive strategies to include appeals not directly related to physical health per se (e.g., psychological regret and social rejection) and to give greater emphasis to reward-oriented incentives (e.g., valued states or consequences such as well-being, altruism, and attractiveness).

Appeals can emphasize either of the two basic components in the expectancy value formulation: the subjective probability of a consequence occurring or the degree of positive or negative valence of that outcome. For unhealthy behaviors, the operational formula is vulnerability × severity, positing that the audience is maximally motivated by a high likelihood of suffering a very painful consequence. The prime communication strategy is to change beliefs regarding the probability component. If there is a discrepancy between the audience's expectancy estimate and the actual likelihood, the message should stress the higher than expected probability (especially if the gap exists at the high end of the certainty scale). A second communication strategy is to intensify the valence by emphasizing the severity of negative consequences (or the positivity of benefits) or to raise the salience of those components of the expectancy value equation that the audience already regards as advantageous (e.g., positively valued and likely consequences of a recommended practice) so that each of these components is weighted more heavily in the audience's decision making.

Fear Appeals

A pervasive strategy in health campaigns is to motivate behavior change by threatening the audience with harmful outcomes from initiating or continuing an unhealthy practice. A strong fear-arousing message typically combines a severe negative physical consequence with an intense stylistic presentation (emotional, vivid, and involving). A mild fear appeal uses a toned-down style to threaten a more likely but less serious outcome. Fear appeals can be risky because there may be boomerang effects or null effects due to defensive responses by the audience members who attempt to control their fear rather than control the danger.

Despite these problems, the research indicates that well-designed fear appeals are quite effective in changing behavior (see Chapter 5, this volume). Threats are more successful if the message provides self-efficacy instructional material (demonstrating how to perform behaviors and boosting confidence that the individual can do so successfully) or response efficacy material (convincing the individual that the recommended behavior will reduce the danger).

Other Appeals

Strong negative incentives should play an important but limited role in campaigns. The design team should brainstorm less negative reasons why the audience should perform the healthy practice. This diversified approach encompasses messages featuring threats of a less severe nature, negative incentives beyond the physical health domain, and positive incentives.

When the designer is unable to offer any incentives that genuinely link strong valence with high probability, the next best approach seems to be to select a mildly valenced incentive that is highly probable rather than one that is strongly valenced but improbable. In the case of drug campaigns, minor negative physical incentives might be loss of stamina, weight gain, or physiological addiction.

Beyond the realm of physical health, there are dozens of potential motivational appeals along other dimensions. In the social incentive category, drug campaigns can present negative appeals about looking uncool, alienating friends, incurring peer disapproval, losing trust of parents, or deviating from social norms (see Chapter 22, this volume). The constellation of psychological incentives might include reduced ability to concentrate; low grades; feeling lazy and unmotivated; losing control; making bad decisions; and anxiety about getting caught or experiencing harm, guilt, and loss of self-respect. Among the economic incentives related to drugs are diminished job prospects, fines, cumulative cost of purchasing drugs, and inability to spend money on other needs and desires. Messages can also highlight penalties for violating laws and policies, such as incarceration, loss of driver's license, or suspension from school.

Positive Appeals

Campaigns should diversify by presenting a higher proportion of positive incentives. For each of the negative consequences of performing the proscribed practice, there is usually a mirror-image positive outcome that can be promised for performing the healthy alternative (e.g., avoiding drugs or enjoying a drug-free lifestyle). In the physical health dimension, messages can offer prospects ranging from a longer life span to enhanced athletic performance. Positive social incentives include being cool, gaining approval and respect, forming deeper friendships, building trust with parents, and being a good role model. On the psychological dimension, messages might promise such outcomes as gaining control over one's life, positive self-image, attaining one's goals, feeling secure, or acting intelligently. Positive appeals may effectively use the soft-sell approach to associate the desired behavior with positive images.

Multiple Appeals

There are dozens of persuasive appeals that are potentially effective, and the degree of potency is fairly equivalent in many cases. Rather than relying on a handful of incentives, it is advantageous to use multiple appeals across a series of messages in a campaign to influence different segments of the target audience (especially in media channels in which precise targeting is difficult) and to provide several reasons for the individual to comply. In selecting incentives, the key criteria are the salience of the promised or threatened consequences, the malleability of beliefs about the likelihood of experiencing these outcomes, and potential persuasiveness of the arguments that can be advanced. The designer should consider the absolute potency of each incentive and the relative contribution vis-à-vis other concurrent appeals and the influence that has already been achieved in the past. For messages about familiar health subjects, it is important to include some new appeals to complement the standard arguments. Preproduction research can test basic concepts to determine the absolute effectiveness of each one and to examine optimum combinations, and pretesting research can compare the relative influence of executions of various appeals.

Evidence

In conveying an incentive appeal, it is often necessary to provide evidence supporting claims made in the message. This is most important when belief formation is a central mechanism and when the source or sponsor is not highly credible. The type of evidence featured varies according to each audience. Sophisticated and highly involved individuals are more influenced by messages that cite statistics, provide documentation, and include quotations from experts, whereas dramatized case examples and testimonials by respected sources work better for those who are less involved. The message should demonstrate how the evidence is relevant to the situation experienced by the target audience to forestall denial of applicability.

In offering evidence, special care should be taken with the presentation of extreme claims (rare cases, implausible statistics, and overly dramatic depictions of consequences), highly biased marshalling of supportive facts, and misleading information. These elements may strain credulity and trigger counterarguing among audience members and may be challenged by critics in rebuttal messages.

One-Sided Versus Two-Sided Content

For most health-related target responses, behavioral compliance is impeded by a variety of disadvantages perceived by the audience, such as obstacles, drawbacks, and forsaken alternatives. The strategist is faced with the question of how to handle these drawbacks. A one-sided message strategy presents only the case favoring the desired behavior or against the competition and ignores the drawbacks. In a "two-sided" message, the elements of the opposing case are strategically raised and discounted to counteract current and future challenges.

The three basic techniques for addressing drawbacks are refutation, diminution, and tactical concession. First, supposed advantages of the unhealthy behavior or disadvantages of the promoted behavior can be directly refuted or diminished with contrary evidence or emotional attacks. Second, salient and substantive drawbacks of the focal behavior (and attractive features of alternative) can be mentioned and then downplayed by arguing that these factors are relatively unimportant compared with the beneficial features. Third, minor disadvantages can simply be conceded as a tactic for enhancing credibility and thus increasing the believability of other arguments in the message.

The research evidence indicates that the two-sided message is more persuasive if the audience is sophisticated and knowledgeable about the topic, predisposed against the position being advanced, wary of a manipulative intent, and already aware of the proarguments or likely to be exposed in the future. The main weakness of a two-sided presentation is that it may heighten the salience of certain drawbacks that audience members may not have been considering as they weighed their decisions. Formative research is useful in determining which of these factors are predominant in a particular health campaign situation.

Messengers

The *messenger* is the model appearing in messages who delivers information, demonstrates behavior, or provides a testimonial; this source presenter featured in the message is distinct from the institutional sponsor and the message creator. The health messenger is helpful in attracting attention, personalizing abstract concepts by modeling actions and consequences, bolstering belief formation due to source credibility, and facilitating retention due to memorability. Typically, eight categories of messengers are featured in health messages: a celebrity (e.g., a famous athlete or entertainer), a public official (a government leader or agency director), an expert specialist (e.g., a doctor or researcher), an organization leader (e.g., a hospital administrator or corporate executive), a professional performer (a standard spokesperson, attractive model, or character actor), an average person (e.g., a blue-collar man or a middle-class woman), a specially experienced person (e.g., a victim, survivor, or successful role model), or a unique character (e.g., animated, anthropomorphic, or costumed).

There are multiple dimensions of source credibility and attractiveness (see Chapter 2, this volume), and each type of messenger has variable potency in moving the audience through response stages. In selecting the appropriate messenger, the crucial factor is which component of the influence model needs a boost. For example, celebrities help draw attention to a dull topic, experts enhance response efficacy, ordinary people heighten self-efficacy, victims convey the severity of harmful outcomes, and victims who share similar characteristics of the audience should augment susceptibility claims. Atkin (1994) provides an elaborate discussion of strengths and weaknesses of various types of messengers.

Mechanical and Stylistic Factors

Many technical aspects of message production are used by the message designer in structuring and highlighting the substantive material, primarily to help attract attention and facilitate comprehension and retention. Atkin (1994) discusses guidelines for constructing key elements, such as the theme line (concise representation of a main idea with a headline, slogan, or provocative question), continuity devices (distinctive symbolic features providing a common thread across message executions), verbal copy (understandable vocabulary, sentence length, and copy density), arrangement of message elements (primacy vs. recency of key arguments), physical dimensions (size of print messages or length of broadcast messages), audio and visual factors (use of music or pictures), and technical production quality (sophisticated techniques and devices; see Chapter 14, this volume).

Stylistic features are primarily employed to convey substantive ideas in an engaging fashion (via artistic devices such as parody, suspense, sensuality, and wordplay) and can augment the other key message qualities of credibility, understandability, and relevance (via features such as serious tone, memorable slogans, and emotionally involving scenes). There are a variety of entertainment-oriented stylistic approaches for increasing the attractiveness of the message (see Chapter 28, this volume). Many message designers rely on humor, which has advantages in certain contexts (Atkin, 1994). Clever stylistic devices are a hallmark of health messages, especially the use of a play on words, ironic twist, or catchy slogan to attract interest and provoke thought. Vivid presentation styles, such as lively language, striking statements, fascinating facts, and vibrant visuals (and alluring alliteration), are helpful in communicating with low-involvement audiences. Content should be conveyed in a realistic and personalized manner by depicting situations and models that enable the audience to connect the material to their own experiences.

A serious tone is the safest strategy for delivering the substantive arguments, providing the messages are not overly preachy, boring, or bland. The rational style of presentation seems best suited for target responses in which the individual already perceives a need but seeks a solution, for target audiences who are more sophisticated and involved, for sources who are high in competence, and for print channels. Emotional appeals tend to work better for arousing drives and intensifying motivation by highlighting the severity of unhealthy outcomes or the rewards of healthy behavior.

Clarity Versus Strategic Ambiguity

The conventional rule of thumb in message construction is to be clear and straightforward, a proven technique for facilitating comprehension in educational and persuasive applications. In general, there is greater learning of material conveyed with simplified vocabulary, short sentences, sparse copy, graphic depictions, and a single major point per message.

In certain situations, however, it may be advantageous to communicate basic content components with ambiguous visual and verbal message executions that produce differential interpretations among audience segments. During message processing, ambiguity should reduce counterarguing and reactance and increase introspection and elaboration (thus minimizing the boomerang effect and maximizing audience involvement).

This approach is typically implemented by featuring vaguely worded behavioral recommendations or by presenting suggestive portrayals, arguments, and evidence. The ambiguity allows the individual receivers to draw their own implications based on predispositions; the strategic aspect involves manipulating the message content in a manner that plays off the perceptual tendencies of various subgroups. Strategically ambiguous executions are especially applicable to spot messages on TV, where targeting tends to be imprecise. If there are multiple segments that will attend the message, it can be both efficient and effective to influence several segments simultaneously with obliquely targeted or multitargeted messages.

The strategic ambiguity approach is adapted from the crafty communication practices of corporate executives and political candidates. It has been used quite shrewdly by the alcohol companies in their "private service" campaigns dealing with risky drinking, which use ambiguous slogans such as "know when to say when" or "think when you drink" to simultaneously attain multiple objectives: combat the drunk driving or alcohol poisoning problems among extreme drinkers (without significantly undermining consumption levels by regular heavy drinkers who perceive the drinking limitations in a liberal manner), favorably impress opinion leaders and the general public who perceive that the companies are exhibiting social responsibility by ostensibly targeting heavy drinkers with moderate-drinking messages, and promote product usage by portraying consumption in what viewers perceive to be a noncommercial context (Atkin, Wallack, & DeJong, 1992).

Even when the message is primarily aimed at a single audience segment, there are advantages of ambiguity and vagueness because the self-generated interpretation may be more persuasive than the concept that is concretely operationalized in a message. This simpler form of strategic ambiguity can be applied to the presentation of recommendations, consequences, and evidence in health messages. For example, an explicitly specified ideal behavior often falls outside the focal audience's latitude of acceptance, and explicit advocacy tends to be highly admonishing with words such as "don't" and "never." The alternative is to present vaguely worded, softened recommendations (e.g., indefinite time frames and limited situational applications) or to specify nothing and let recipients construct their own implication.

Messages can be vague in specifying exactly what is the harmful consequence by using subtle symbolic representations of harm or depicting someone experiencing distress of an uncertain nature; this allows the audience to mentally or emotionally imagine their own harmful outcome. For high-threat messages that seek to emphasize severity of harm, it may be advantageous to cite ambiguous consequences that are not readily observable (e.g., fried brain cells or silent disapproval by peers in a drug campaign) and thus are not readily refutable by those in a counterarguing mode. Messages might also cite concrete consequences of ambiguous origin (e.g., bad grades in school or loss of friends), for which the audience member can make the attribution that they are due to the risky behavior rather than other sources.

CONCLUSION

Most health campaigns have attained rather modest impact due to meager resources, poor conceptualization, and narrow strategic approaches. The limited potency of the media leads to several implications for campaign designers. First, set realistic expectations of success, especially in the short run. Be prepared for a long haul because many campaigns will take years to achieve and maintain significant impact. Second, employ some of the promising ideas presented throughout this chapter, and place more emphasis on relatively attainable impacts, by aiming at more receptive segments of the audience and by creating or promoting more palatable positive products. Augment the relatively small set of packaged campaign stimuli with message multipliers by stimulating information seeking and sensitization and by generating public relations publicity. Use a greater variety of persuasive incentives to motivate the audience, and include more educational material to help them perform the behaviors. Finally, the small direct effects may be augmented by shifting campaign resources to indirect pathways of facilitating and controlling the behavior of the focal segment via interpersonal, organizational, and societal influences.

This chapter has advocated greater diversification of pathways, products, incentives, and channels beyond the approaches conventionally used in health campaigns. This requires the disciplined development of strategies based on careful analysis of the situation, sensitive application of communication theory, and regular collection of formative evaluation information. In particular, the formulation of a comprehensive strategic plan is needed to effectively integrate the optimum combinations of campaign components that will directly and indirectly influence behaviors.

REFERENCES

Ajzen, I., & Fishbein, M. (1980). *Understanding attitudes and predicting social behavior.* Englewood Cliffs, NJ: Prentice Hall.

Atkin, C. (1981). Mass media information campaign effectiveness. In R. Rice & W. Paisley (Eds.), *Public communication campaigns* (2nd ed., pp. 265-280). Beverly Hills, CA: Sage.

Atkin, C. (1994). Designing persuasive health messages. In L. Sechrest, T. Backer, E. Rogers, T. Campbell, & M. Grady (Eds.), *Effective dissemination of clinical health information* (AHCPR Publication No. 95-0015, pp. 99-110). Rockville, MD: Public Health Service, Agency for Health Care Policy and Research.

Atkin, C. (2000). Promising strategies for media health campaigns. In W. Crano & S. Ostman (Eds.), *Mass media and drug prevention.* Mahwah, NJ: Lawrence Erlbaum.

Atkin, C., & Wallack, L. (1990). *Mass communication and public health: Complexities and conflicts.* Newbury Park, CA: Sage.

Atkin, C., Wallack, L., & DeJong, W. (1992). *The influence of responsible drinking TV spots and automobile commercials on young drivers.* Washington, DC: American Automobile Association Foundation for Traffic Safety.

Backer, T., & Rogers, E. (1993). *Organizational aspects of health communication campaigns: What works?* Newbury Park, CA: Sage.

Backer, T., Rogers, E., & Sopory, P. (1992). *Designing health communication campaigns: What works?* Newbury Park, CA: Sage.

Bandura, A. (1986). *Social foundations of thought and action: A social cognitive theory.* Englewood Cliffs, NJ: Prentice Hall.

Burgoon, M., & Miller, G. (1985). An expectancy interpretation of language and persuasion. In H. Giles & R. St. Clair (Eds.), *Recent advances in language, communication, and social psychology* (pp. 199-229). London: Lawrence Erlbaum.

DeJong, W., & Winston, J. (1990). The use of mass media in substance abuse prevention. *Health Affairs, 2,* 30-46.

Donohew, L., Sypher, H., & Bukoski, W. (1991). *Persuasive communication and drug abuse prevention.* Hillsdale, NJ: Lawrence Erlbaum.

Hale, J. L., & Dillard, J. P. (1995). Fear appeals in health promotion: Too much, too little or just right? In E. Maibach & R. Parrott (Eds.), *Designing health messages: Approaches from communication theory and public health practice* (pp. 65-80). Thousand Oaks, CA: Sage.

Janz, N. K., & Becker, M. H. (1984). The Health Belief Model: A decade later. *Health Education Quarterly, 11,* 1-47.

Maibach, E., & Parrott, R. (1995). *Designing health messages: Approaches from communication theory and public health practice.* Thousand Oaks, CA: Sage.

McGuire, W. (1994). Using mass media communication to enhance public health. In L. Sechrest, T. Backer, E. Rogers, T. Campbell, & M. Grady (Eds.), *Effective dissemination of clinical health information* (AHCPR Publication No. 95-0015, pp. 125-151). Rockville, MD: Public Health Service, Agency for Health Care Policy and Research.

Petty, R., Baker, S., & Gleicher, F. (1991). Attitudes and drug abuse prevention: Implications of the Elaboration Likelihood Model of persuasion. In L. Donohew, H. Sypher, & W. Bukoski (Eds.), *Persuasive communication and drug abuse prevention* (pp. 71-90). Hillsdale, NJ: Lawrence Erlbaum.

Prochaska, J., & DiClemente, C. (1983). Stages and processes of self change of smoking: Toward an integrative model. *Journal of Consulting and Clinical Psychology, 51,* 390-395.

Rogers, R. (1983). Cognitive and physiological processes in fear appeals and attitude change: A revised theory of protection motivation. In J. Cacioppo & R. E. Petty (Eds.), *Social psychophysiology* (pp. 153-176). New York: Guilford.

Rosenstock, I. (1990). The Health Belief Model: Explaining health behavior through expectancies. In K. Glanz, F. Lewis, & B. Rimer (Eds.), *Health behavior and health education: Theory research and practice* (pp. 39-62). San Francisco: Josey-Bass.

Singhal, A., & Rogers, E. M. (1999). *Entertainment-education: A communication strategy for social change.* Mahwah, NJ: Lawrence Erlbaum.

Slater, M. (1999). Integrating application of media effects, persuasion, and behavior change theories to communication campaigns: A stages-of-change framework. *Health Communication, 11*(4), 335-354.

4

Sense-Making Methodology: Communicating Communicatively with Campaign Audiences

Brenda Dervin
Micheline Frenette

The purpose of this chapter is to describe an approach to researching, designing, and implementing public communication campaigns based on a theoretically defined methodology called Sense-Making. We intentionally refer to members of our audiences as listeners and learners and as teachers and confidantes because the approach we describe rests on philosophic assumptions that mandate that communication (between researcher and researched, policy setter and citizen, and professional expert and intended recipient) be conceptualized, designed, and practiced dialogically. Treating communication as dialogue (i.e., communicatively) requires fundamental redefinitions of the terms *audiences* and *campaigns*. In one sense, both terms are no longer applicable— audiences become peers and collaborators—and if there are "campaigns" involved, they are two-way. We continue to use the familiar terms here with the assumption that audiences include both publics and institutions, and campaigns involve shared interaction and intentions (see Chapter 13, this volume).

To approach the communication campaign communicatively means facing ethical and procedural challenges. It means audiences will not only be heard but also that their perspectives will be acted on. It means approaching the campaign in a position of self-imposed reflection, being open to disagreement, even coming to understand that one's well-meaning intentions may be mistaken, may foster unintended deleterious consequences, or may simply be of no interest to another.

Calls for moving toward more dialogic campaigns have come from many quarters. We review these calls to provide context for our presentation of Sense-Making, which, as a methodology, is an example of one such call and also a systematic approach responding to it.

THE CALL FOR DIALOGIC CAMPAIGN DESIGN

There is widespread agreement that most communication campaigns directed at bettering audiences have either failed or have met only modest objectives, at extraordinarily high cost and with requisite high redundancy in message transmission. This negative analysis, however, applies to the traditional one-way public communication campaign assumed to infuse audiences with the will to change because of sheer transmission of "expert" information. In actuality, there have been calls to reconceptualize campaigns in more dialogic ways since the 1960s.[1]

Four Mandates to Approach Campaign Communication Dialogically

To summarize this literature, we have extracted four mandates, arrayed on a continuum from "soft" at one end to "hard" at the other because each successive mandate requires more changes in our conceptualizations.

Go Beyond Campaign-Designated Expert Information

The softest call for designing campaigns dialogically essentially retains the idea of the campaign as a one-way transmission of expert information. What differs is the idea that information transmission does not in itself produce change. A variety of strategies are proposed for adding "something more" than expert information to campaign messages. One strategy is to provide instructions on how to use information as a means of encouraging audience efficacy. Another is to incorporate message elements that are tailored to the information processing proclivities of the intended recipients or that in other ways trigger audience involvement. Given evidence of increasing distrust of experts among laypersons, other strategies call for engendering trust, using sources who are attractive and credible, emphasizing audience life interests and entertainment preferences, and highlighting human stories. Common to these strategies is that campaign messages still focus on information as prescribed by the campaign's designated experts, but something more is provided in hopes that messages will be more acceptable.

Appeal to Audiences in Their Social Contexts

The second mandate is still based on the top-down campaign. What differs is recognition that understandings of the world change markedly from culture to culture and community to community. The primary mandate here is to redirect major portions of campaign efforts from one-way mass-mediated designs to communication approaches anchored in specific audience social networks. Implementation takes one of two forms. The first involves target audiences in campaign design, such as by asking for their recommendations for achieving campaign goals. The second incorporates a variety of communicatively involving activities (e.g., call-in talk shows, hotlines, community forums, and family conferences) as relays for message transmission. Whereas the first form mandates attempts to make campaign messages more acceptable to audiences, the second goes further by using audience networks as vehicles for framing messages in ways suitable for the socially inscribed communication contexts in which audiences live.

Absorb and Reflect Audience Perspectives

The third mandate gives status to nonexpert views, even when these differ from those of experts. Campaigns typically focus on goals (e.g., quitting smoking, stopping drug use, and eating more vegetables) that are defined as remedial actions directed at problems (e.g., lung cancer, crack babies, and obesity). Campaigns rest on networks of causal and descriptive facts supported by scientific evidence, itself based on an assumed rightness in naming and explaining the world. Most campaigns measure success by compliance with goals. What is labeled noncompliance by institutions, however, may be strength and survival outside institutions, what institutions define as causal problem-solution chains may be debated outside institutions, and what experts consider facts today may be challenged by these same experts tomorrow. What differs in this mandate is the more radical idea that the assumptions and goals of experts must, at a minimum, be tested and tempered by audience input and, in a more genuine dialogic spirit, challenged, changed, or even replaced with alternatives.

Attend to Issues Relating Social Power and Ethics

Traditionally, campaign goals have been assumed to be universally applicable and benevolent. The fourth mandate—the most challenging, and which we identified as emerging in recent campaign literature—confronts this assumption and calls for attending to issues of ethics and social philosophy. This mandate involves two aspects: (a) problematizing truth claims about reality and (b) focusing on how issues of social class and structure, politics, and economics are implicated in expert knowledge statements and the uses of these statements in social policy. There are two primary arguments supporting the importance of this mandate. First, audiences are becoming weary of being judged wanting by experts and more savvy about contradictions in an increasingly uncontrolled information marketplace. Second, campaign environments that do not foster disagreement are likely to overlook unwittingly possible negative campaign outcomes (e.g., stigmatizing subgroups, depriving humans of pleasures, and exploiting community members).

SENSE-MAKING METHODOLOGY

Sense-Making as a methodology was developed to study and implement communication communicatively. It is based on a core assumption that dialogic communication intentions are not enough. Dialogue happens only if communication is designed to nurture its unfolding. Sense-Making assumes that all communication is designed but that most designs, even when well meaning, are habitual, unstated, and based on transmission assumptions. Sense-Making's intent is to provide general guidance for how to ensure as far as possible that dialogue is encouraged in every aspect of communication campaign research, design, and implementation.

Sense-Making has been under development by Dervin and colleagues since 1972. The approach is defined as a methodology for studying and facilitating the making and unmaking of sense in any communication situation, particularly when professionals are mandated to serve groups of people usually designated as audiences (e.g., patients, patrons, users, audiences, and customers). Many more formalized presentations are available (Dervin, 1992, 1999a, 1999b), so the following review focuses on major questions in campaign research and design.

Sense-Making's Basic Assumptions

Sense-Making rests on an elaborate set of theoretic assumptions and guidances for methods. The central idea is simple, however. Communication programs are doomed mostly to failure unless they focus on how audiences interpret their worlds and live and struggle in the complexes of social networks and everyday experiences that bind them. This focus on audiences, however, should not be merely a tool for constructing more persuasive messages. The communication campaign must place primary attention on creating procedural conditions that promote and invite two-way sharing and negotiating of meanings.

In Sense-Making, this is accomplished by refocusing attention away from nouns of interest to the campaign (e.g., its goals and its evidence) to verbs that permit a dialogic interface to be established. In simple terms, a nouning approach implies that we have come to a fixed understanding of a problem and its solution, whereas a verbing approach implies that we pay attention to how people are making and unmaking sense in the contexts of their lives. For example, in a nouning approach, obesity might be defined as a physical condition that must be alleviated to prevent ill health. In a verbing approach, we would learn how people make sense of obesity in their experiential contexts: One group may tell of its fat ancestors who lived long lives, another may tell of its anger at a society that promotes unhealthy eating habits but has made obesity one of its worst stigmas, and another may tell of lifelong struggles with physicians who have demanded that as patients they submit themselves to a succession of new diet regimes, each one presumably more efficacious than its predecessor.

In Sense-Making, understanding the sense that audiences have made and unmade as they move through their life experiences is achieved by applying the Sense-Making verbing analytic as the central organizing tool. Sense-Making's verbing analytic is based on two intersecting requisites. The first requisite is the assumption that the only way to hear another's world is to invite and assist the other in describing that world as much as possible entirely in the context of his or her own experiences, understandings, and meanings. The second requisite is that because of the power differentials inherent in the institution-audience or researcher-researched relationship, procedures must be found to bracket or tame the power of the institution or researcher.

It is assumed that there are both value constraints and time-space limitations to understandings created with the communication practices of science and expertise, just as there are constraints and limitations for understandings created with the communication practices of lived experience. Therefore, it is assumed that expert categorizations can be entirely wrong, irrelevant, or inappropriate impositions when applied in the contexts of other lived experiences. This does not mean that the voice of the institution or researcher should be silenced. Rather, it means putting that voice into dialogue along with other relevant voices—intended message recipients, their families, community, and so on. There is a yawning gap between institutional and researcher views and the world of the everyday. Sense-Making as an approach explicitly assumes that it is possible to bridge this gap by implementing alternative procedures.

The Sense-Making Verbing Analytic:
The Sense-Making Metaphor

Sense-Making incorporates a repertoire of potential procedures for accomplishing the goals discussed previously. All these are drawn from a central metaphor, shown in Figure 4.1. Here, one sees a human moving across time and space, facing a gap, building a bridge across the gap, and then constructing and evaluating the uses of the bridge. This metaphor rests on a discontinuity assumption—that gappiness is pervasive both in and between moments in time and space and in and between people. Gappiness is assumed to occur because of differences across time (e.g., self today versus self yesterday and scientific fact today versus scientific fact tomorrow) and across space (e.g., the experience of a particular condition in differing cultures, contexts, communities, material circumstances and the sense of an experience physically and the articulation of it verbally).[2]

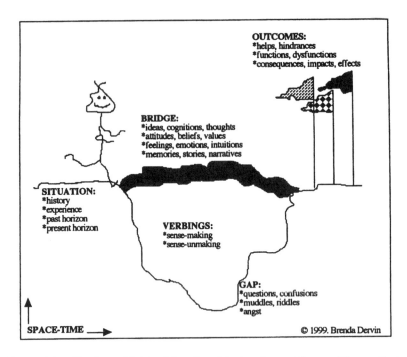

Figure 4.1. The Sense-Making Metaphor: Moving Across Time and Space, Facing a Gap, Building a Bridge Across the Gap, and Then Constructing and Evaluating the Uses of the Bridge. © Brenda Dervin, 1999.

The facing of gaps and building of bridges is Sense-Making's central metaphor. The metaphor is not intended to imply that life facing is only linear, logical, or problem-oriented. Sense-Making assumes there are many ways to bridge gaps. Sometimes we imitate a role model, repeat what was done in the past, do what we learned in our childhood, or follow a leader; sometimes we look to authority or expertise; sometimes we follow hunches, bumble along, and do what our feelings tell us; and sometimes we let circumstances toss us about. Across the range of conditions humans face, it is assumed that every potential mode of gap bridging is useful in some context. In Sense-Making, these myriad ways are conceptualized as verbings.

The implication of this in the campaign context is that a campaign objective is designed to bridge an institutionally perceived gap arising from an institutionally perceived worldview with its institutionally accepted categories. As an objective, it applies only to the time and place of its making and is constrained by the knowledge-making tools of its creation. Across time and across space, the objective may be seen as no bridge at all or as an entirely different kind of bridge. Every aspect of the campaign—every definition, goal, mandate, and argument—is open to potential challenge or reinterpretation when seen from another vantage point. Furthermore, because gappiness applies to both ontological conditions (i.e., the nature of reality) and epistemological conditions (i.e., the nature of knowing), there is no way to fix communicatively any particular campaign objective as absolutely correct. Hence, the only alternative is dialogue. The question becomes how to procedurally nurture dialogue between care-taking institutions with good intentions and mandated audiences. In working toward this goal, Sense-Making draws on the idea of pervasive gappiness, proposing that sense-making and sense-unmaking, whether institutionalized or individual, is usefully conceptualized as building bridges across gaps and then unmaking the bridges when they no longer serve. From this central metaphor is derived the core set of assumptions that Sense-Making mandates methodologically. Every Sense-Making application to campaign research and design requires the use of at least some, and ideally all, of the following assumptions:

1. Sense-making is gap bridging. Individual humans are conceptualized metaphorically as moving across time and space by bridging gaps inherent in the human condition—between times, spaces, people and events, self today and self yesterday, and so on. No amount of external information, prior instruction, or acculturation is sufficient to bridge a gap here and now. This is done by mind-body-heart-spirit step-takings of singular human entities, consciously or unconsciously, habitually or innovatively, and acting alone or in community.

2. There are many ways to make sense. Sense-making is accomplished by verbings that involve the making or using of ideas or both, cognitions, thoughts, and conclusions; attitudes, beliefs, and values; feelings, emotions, and intuitions; and memories, stories, and narratives. For example, sometimes sense-making involves borrowing an idea, sometimes it involves making one, and sometimes it involves rejecting one.

3. Sense-making is anchored in time and space. Each moment of sense-making is anchored in its own time and space, moving to another time and space. Sense-making is most usefully conceptualized as situated communicative practices, internal (e.g., thinking and remembering) and external (e.g., asking and objecting).

4. Sense-making occurs at the intersection of three horizons—past, present, and future. Every moment of sense-making is anchored at the intersection of horizons—past (histories, memories, and narratives), present (current conditions, material and experiential), and future (hopes, dreams, plans, and trajectories).

5. Sense-making can be either flexible or inflexible. It is assumed that there is potential for rigidity (habit, repetition, and stability) in human sense-making when compared across time and space but also potential for flexibility (innovation, responsiveness, and caprice). Attention must be paid to both possibilities.

6. Sense-making involves energy, both propelling and constraining. Every moment of sense-making involves energy—force, power, and constraint. These energies come from within (e.g., motivation and resistance) and without (e.g., barriers and help from society, others, and institutions) and from unique circumstances and enduring social conditions.

7. Every sense-maker is inherently a social theorist. Ordinary human beings are assumed to be capable of discussing the connections they see between past and present and between present and future, between self and one's own struggles, between self and others, and between self and society. These perspectives are assumed to be as essential to understanding campaign phenomena as are the perspectives of experts and researchers. The larger the power differential, the longer the time needed and the more difficult it will be to establish the necessary trust between researchers and researched.

8. Comparing sense-making across time, space, and people is more powerfully done with verbing analytics. If we focus only on the nouns of experience and phenomena, the understandings of the world of ordinary persons seem overbearingly unique and unamenable to systematic analysis. By focusing on the verbs of sense-making—how people see themselves as moving through life, the gaps they face, and the help they seek—we can compare sense-makings of one human to those of another, of one human to self across time and space, and so on without imposing nouns alien to sense-making experience.

9. Comparing sense-making across time, space, and people will yield patterns of both centrality and dispersion. Any comparison of sense-making activities will necessarily yield patterns of centrality (homogeneity and agreement) and patterns of dispersion (diversity and disagreement). Each is to be pursued by asking fundamental questions: Under what conditions would this occur? What implications result?

10. Campaign planners, researchers, and policymakers are sense-makers. The expertise of planners, researchers, and policymakers is sense-making and must be examined as such. This is a fundamental source of the self-reflexivity that is assumed to be essential for communicating communicatively.

How Sense-Making Is Applied in Campaign Research and Design

Each of the previous assumptions implies potential communicative procedures to be implemented in Sense-Making informed campaign research and design. There are three primary applications that will be discussed later: (a) interviewing, (b) analyzing data, and (c) planning campaign designs. It is important to first emphasize two points. First, Sense-Making is a methodology for communication practice in general; thus, Sense-Making applies to both research and campaign design. Second, Sense-Making has been developed to avoid traditional polarizations between so-called systematic quantitative and contextual qualitative approaches, aiming for qualitative sensitivity amid analytic systematization.

Applying Sense-Making to Interviewing

Sense-Making has been applied in both qualitative and quantitative interviews, in-depth and brief, phone and in-person, one-on-one and focus group, and interviewer-administered and self-administered. The use of Sense-Making rests on a foundational interviewing approach called the *Micro-Moment Time-Line*. In this approach, informants are asked to describe a situation relevant to the research focus—a situation important to them in some way (e.g., a time when they were concerned about AIDS or remembered hearing about it in the media and a time when they were concerned about their health or tried to take action to improve it). The situation is described in time line steps—what happened first, second, and so on. For each step, Sense-Making elements are extracted: What questions arose at this step? What thoughts? What feelings? What emotions? Each of these elements is then triangulated with the Sense-Making metaphor, with its emphasis on situation, gap, bridge, and outcome. For example, in triangulating a question, the informant is asked the following: What led to this question? How does it relate to your life? Society and power? Did you get an answer? How? Any barriers in the way? Did the answer help? Hinder? How?

From this basic approach, many variations have been derived. Some, for example, involve surveying an informant's entire lifeline of experiences vis-à-vis an issue (e.g., one's history with ill health) and then selecting one or more incidents for in-depth analysis. Others involve positioning informants directly as research collaborators. An example is an interview that asks informants to talk about how and why their views differ from those of others. A policy position established by an agency might be described in detail, with the informant asked for his or her thoughts, confusions, and conclusions. In another variation, the informant is asked to read an institutional policy statement and to indicate every place in the statement the person "stopped" to ask questions, raise objections, and so on. In both variations, each informant response is pursued with Sense-Making triangulations as described previously: What leads you to say this? How does this relate to your life? and so on.[3]

Applying Sense-Making to the
Analysis of Research Data

Each of the metatheoretical assumptions of Sense-Making mandates particular approaches to data analysis. The researcher is directed to look, for example, at how informant sense-making varies across time and space; for both stabilities and habits as well as flexibilities and changes; for connections between past, present, and future; and at how the informant sees self as constrained and struggling as well as moving and free. The aim of the Sense-Making informed analysis is to provide contextually unique detail and a means of ordering unique lived experience in terms of universal categories of movement.

From many Sense-Making studies, a set of universal verbing categories have been developed that allow researchers to interpret data without imposing institutional judgment on it. This is done by intersecting a deductive set of frameworks based on Sense-Making's verbing analytic with the inductive qualities of the data. For example, in one study (Dervin, Harpring, & Fore-man-Wernet, 1999), several informants described themselves as being concerned that their fetuses had been hurt by drug addiction, but each recollection of the lived experience was very different. This is a noun focus. The Sense-Making interview added a verbing focus by asking each informant how she saw this moment of concern—how it blocked her, how it related to her life, what would have helped, and what hindered. These kinds of data becomes the focus of a Sense-Making verbing analysis. By codifying how informants described themselves as stopped, struggling, and moving, what seems chaotic across different cases becomes more orderly.

The important idea here is that Sense-Making categories lay a verbing interface (how sense is made and unmade) over a noun interface (the goals of campaign designers). In this way, Sense-Making provides a set of universal descriptors that allow the researcher to compare audience members to campaign designers, audience members to themselves over time, and one group of audience members to another. Furthermore, quantitative Sense-Making studies have shown that in contrast to noun categories typically used in campaign research (e.g., demographic groups, personality factors, lifestyles, and interests), Sense-Making categories account for more variance in understanding audience sense-making with fewer categories. An explanation for this is that Sense-Making's verbing analytic attends to the essence of communicating—the making and unmaking of sense. In this way, Sense-Making provides a systematic means of addressing the interpretive world of target audience members without sinking into the overbearing contextual uniqueness that has for a long time seemed to be the outcome of interpretive analyses.

Figure 4.2 provides examples of two of Sense-Making's verbing-focused category schemes—situation movement states and utilities (helps). The former is a set of categories that focus on how the informant sees self as stopped or moving at a particular moment in time. The actual categories vary from study to study, but the nine category examples provided in Figure 4.2 are illustrative: decision (where one needs to choose between two or more roads ahead); problematic (being dragged down a road not of your own choosing); spinout, washout (not having a road, losing a road); barrier (knowing where you want to go but something blocks the way); being led (following someone down the road who has traveled it before); observing (watching without being concerned about movement); out to lunch (tuning out, escaping); waiting (waiting for something in particular); and passing time (spending time without waiting for something in particular).

Figure 4.2 also displays utilities (helps) used to evaluate outcomes in terms of how they facilitated movement through time and space. The 15 help catego-

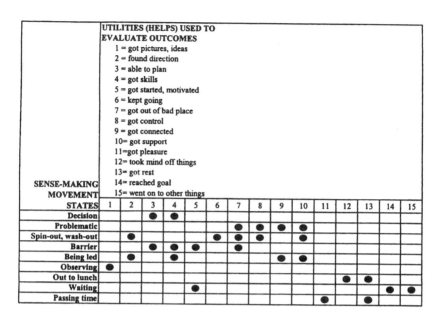

SENSE-MAKING MOVEMENT STATES	UTILITIES (HELPS) USED TO EVALUATE OUTCOMES 1 = got pictures, ideas 2 = found direction 3 = able to plan 4 = got skills 5 = got started, motivated 6 = kept going 7 = got out of bad place 8 = got control 9 = got connected 10= got support 11=got pleasure 12= took mind off things 13= got rest 14= reached goal 15= went on to other things														
	1	2	3	4	5	6	7	8	9	10	11	12	13	14	15
Decision			●	●											
Problematic							●	●	●	●					
Spin-out, wash-out		●				●	●	●		●					
Barrier			●	●	●		●								
Being led		●		●					●	●					
Observing	●														
Out to lunch											●	●			
Waiting				●										●	●
Passing time											●		●		

Figure 4.1. Application of Sense-Making Verbing Analytic to Data Analysis With a Portrait of Typically Strong Relationships Gleaned From Past Systematic Analyses.

ries displayed have been derived from many studies. Figure 4.2 also shows the typical patterns of significant relationships found between situation movement states and utilities in systematic analyses across Sense-Making studies. For example, it can be seen that informants in decision states have been more likely to evaluate outcomes in terms of whether they were able to plan or obtained skills. In contrast, informants in problematic situations were more likely to evaluate results in terms of whether they got out of a bad place, got control, got connected, or got support.

Applying Sense-Making to Campaign Design

There are two avenues for applying Sense-Making to campaign design: theoretically and empirically. Theoretically, the procedural mandates derived from Sense-Making must be implemented. For example, campaign interaction procedures would elicit the different situational conditions, paths of situation facing, and outcomes valued by different audience subsets. Major controversies would be acknowledged and made a topic of focus. Campaign messages would attend to both centralities and agreements across informants and to dispersion and contests, and they would also elicit a variety of explanations for these differences.

Empirical applications of Sense-Making to campaign design involve using results of Sense-Making informed research. For example, each of the intersections of movement states and helps shown in Figure 4.2 implies a different set of sense-making needs that could guide message development. Alternatively, systematic analyses informed by the Sense-Making metaphor focusing on where informants are coming from, what they are struggling with, and where they are going could be used as a basis for evaluating proposed campaign messages and designing new ones. This alternative is shown in Table 4.1, resulting from Frenette's (1998, 1999) explorations of the potentials of Sense-Making specifically for media campaigns. Table 4.1 is intended to be suggestive rather than exhaustive. The specific ways in which Sense-Making might apply to campaign message evaluation and design would vary across subject areas, population, and media. The important point is that Table 4.1 illustrates the use of Sense-Making in designing the campaign as dialogue.

SENSE-MAKING APPLICATIONS TO CAMPAIGN FOCI

In this section, we describe four actual applications of Sense-Making and then draw the strands together by focusing on how these examples implement the mandate to communicate communicatively in the campaign context.

Sense-Making has been applied in a wide variety of public education and communication contexts (e.g., utility restructuring, interracial dialogue, and everyday problem solving). It has been used to evaluate existing or proposed campaigns and to conduct formative research as a basis for campaign design. In all cases, research has culminated in recommendations for campaign practice, some of which have been implemented. The following four examples from the health communication context span approximately 20 years of applications, representing some of the earliest efforts and some of the most recent, and they exemplify different ways in which Sense-Making has been used as a tool to address communication communicatively.[4]

Goal: Seeing Antismoking
Messages Through Adolescent Eyes

In a series of qualitative studies, Frenette (1998, 1999) analyzed focus group interviews conducted with approximately 100 French-speaking adolescents in Quebec, Canada, about their experiences with cigarettes and their perceptions of different antismoking campaign messages. Although there was a wide range of individual circumstances that guided the sense-makings of her informants, Frenette extracted three categories of patterns revealing the conditions under which adolescents found antismoking messages to be supportive of their sense-making, neutral, or hindering. On the positive side, her results showed that antismoking messages were sometimes used by adolescents as

Table 4.1 A Model Applying Sense-Making's Metatheory to the Potential
Construction of Campaign Messages

Sense-Making Metaphor	*Aspects of Life-Facing Situations*	*Potential Audience Member Goal*	*How a Campaign Message Might Help*
Where one is coming from	Experiences preceding the current situation	To acknowledge	To reflect
	Situation currently experienced	To identify	To reflect To clarify
	Needs served by the situation	To recognize	To reflect To identify
What one is struggling with	Problems seen as requiring solution	To clarify	To reflect To identify
	Questions and confusions faced	To express	To reflect To raise
	Obstacles, constraints standing in way	To overcome	To reflect To identify
	Gaps preventing movement forward	To bridge	To reflect To bridge
Where one is going	Resources (helps, answers, information)	To identify To obtain	To suggest
	Solutions (ways to move forward)	To apply	To suggest To demonstrate
	Uses (helps, hindrances from solutions)	To evaluate	To confirm

stepping-stones. This happened, for example, when adolescents saw messages relating to personal experiences and current life situations and had no restraining conditions that led them to be defensive about themselves or their peers. Likewise, when adolescent smokers viewed messages as acknowledging needs satisfied by smoking, they felt respected and were more inclined to listen to suggestions of alternative ways to meet these needs.

On the negative side, Frenette's (1998, 1999) results showed numerous instances in which antismoking messages were neutral with regard to teenager sense-makings. This happened when the lived context of smoking was ignored and when obstacles encountered by those attempting to quit were not acknowledged nor gaps attended to. Finally, there were circumstances in which teenager sense-makings about smoking seemed to actually be hindered by antismoking messages. Examples include the following: (a) when young smokers were unfairly portrayed as dependent or uncaring of others, (b) when messages seemed oblivious to the social dynamics surrounding smoking, and (c) when message ambiguity was such that it drew teenager attention away from thinking about their lives and absorbed them instead in trying to figure out what the message meant. Frenette's primary conclusion was that media messages (i.e., public service announcements, which often provide the foundation of a communication campaign) can play a more vital role in campaigns if we understand more fully how potential audience members use them in their sensemakings.

Goal: Understanding How
General Population Adults Theorize AIDS

Brendlinger, Dervin, and Foreman-Wernet (1999) compared general population responses to a traditional health department survey of knowledge, attitudes, and behaviors to an exploratory Sense-Making survey. The traditional survey consisted of a series of close-ended knowledge, attitude, and behavioral report items; the Sense-Making survey consisted of a series of open-ended items appropriate to Sense-Making's verbing analytic. Each informant was asked to describe three situations—a time when he or she had heard or learned something about AIDS; when he or she or someone he or she knew was exposed to AIDS; and when he or she read, heard, or saw something about AIDS in the mass media. For each situation, informants were asked to (a) describe the situation; (b) indicate any new ideas they derived during the situation and what effect these ideas had on them; (c) indicate any questions they had during the situation; and (d) for their most important question, report how important the question was, how easy or difficult it was to answer, if they tried to get an answer and if not, why not, whether they ever got an answer, how they tried, what barriers they encountered, and how the answer impacted them.

Results showed that the map of categories regarding AIDS imposed by the traditional survey was a weak fit when applied deductively to narratives provided by Sense-Making informants. Only 31.7% of 63 Sense-Making informants mentioned one or more of the specific issues implied by the traditional survey's 10 knowledge items, only 17.5% mentioned any of the specific attitudinal items, and only 25.4% mentioned one or more of the risky or protective behaviors named by the health department. The authors concluded that their informants were neither apathetic nor passive in their relationship to AIDS. On average, their informants named five cognitions (new ideas or questions) each, but their cognitions rarely coincided with health department framings. The difference was that Sense-Making informants did not focus on technical details that interested a health department intent on transmitting expert information but rather on issues pertaining directly to their lives.

Goal: A Blood Center Wants Donors to Donate Again

A city blood center commissioned two studies because staff were convinced, based on prior evidence, that the center was losing some potential donors because of ignorance regarding eligibility requirements. Two Sense-Making studies were conducted (Dervin, Jacobson, & Nilan, 1982; Dervin, Nilan, & Jacobson, 1981). One did in-depth time line interviews asking the 80 randomly selected frequent and new donors, "What happened during your most recent donating experience?" For each time line step, informants were asked what gaps they faced, what questions they had, whether they got answers to their questions, and how they were helped or hindered in each step of the way. Results showed that although demography did not predict donor information needs and seeking, where informants were in the process did predict information needs. Each step in the donating time line was associated with its own complex of questions. For example, eligibility questions were more likely to be in donor minds when they checked in to donate. Instead, blood center personnel had been trying to convey eligibility information when donors were recovering and leaving.

The second study compared 105 new, drop-out, and frequent female blood donors in terms of their recollections of their donating experience—what facilitated and what stood in the way. Results showed that the primary difference between drop-out and frequent female donors was access to donation sites. The frequent donors were more likely to report that signing up and participating in donating was available to them through their workplace or near their homes or because of their association with someone who donated and provided transportation.

The two studies provided directions for communication planning. They showed that a campaign to convince women to repeatedly donate would be ineffective and that attention should be redirected to improving access. Second, a plan was established to provide a user-friendly question-answering system at five different times during the donating process. Typical questions at each time were to be displayed on a computer screen that donors could activate to obtain answers. Answers were to be provided on screen from a variety of sources implementing the Sense-Making assumption that a given question rarely leads to only one answer.

Goal: A Cancer Clinic Staff Wants to
Reduce Stress From Anxious Patients

A cancer clinic staff believed that patient confusion and resentment were contributing as much to the daily stress of their jobs as the seriousness of cancer.[5] A Sense-Making study of 30 randomly selected patients asked them to detail the events of their contacts with the clinic, the ways in which they felt impeded, the confusions they had, and the ways in which they wanted to be helped or were actually helped or both. Results showed that patients wanted more chances to explore and discuss their confusion and concern with others who were sympathetic; acknowledgment of the contested nature of the information circulating about cancer and its treatment; help getting more information, particularly from other cancer patients; social support; and staff to view them as human beings and not walking tumors. Clinic staff responded by designing group support sessions for patients in which questions and concerns would be openly discussed and disagreements openly admitted. They also instituted a wall of "info sheets," each of which addressed a common patient question (e.g., Can you get well without any treatment at all?).

"Answers" to the questions were provided by different doctors and nurses as well as by patients, thus implementing the Sense-Making mandate to attend both to centrality and to dispersion. Each answerer was asked to provide his or her own explanations for why answers differed across sources. In addition, clinic intake personnel were trained to use Sense-Making questioning when they talked with patients as they approached the desk: "What brings you here today?" "What confusions or problems are you facing?" and "How do you hope we can help you today?" Sense-Making interviews were also conducted with clinic staff—nurses, technicians, and doctors. Results indicated that staff needed their own support groups to handle the daily sadness of their jobs, and they needed to connect with their patients outside the reality of their "cancerness." They also indicated that they needed a more rational way of handling the inherently contestable nature of the medical services they were providing. These results led to regular required attendance at staff support groups and to staff volunteering to rotate attendance at patient support groups to keep in touch with the dialogic spirit they represented. In addition, staff decided to do whatever was needed to make it possible for each patient or patient's family to make their own decisions.

COMMUNICATING COMMUNICATIVELY

Our primary intent in this chapter was to use Sense-Making as a exemplar of what it means to address communication communicatively. In each of the previous examples, the audience was no longer conceptualized as an amorphous mass. Rather, informants became situated in real circumstances for which the logic of what was said was validated and anchored in that experience. In each case, institutions learned something they did not know and even had their expectations changed. Teenage smokers, for example, listened to campaign messages if the realities of their lives and conditions were respected. General population adults paid much attention to AIDS, even if close-ended surveys judged them otherwise. The problem for women donors was not ignorance about eligibility requirements but ease of access. Many cancer clinic patients wanted exposure to the very contradictory kinds of information from which cancer clinic staff were trying to protect them. They too, however, became willing to listen when their questions and points of view were acknowledged.

It could be said that the potential directions for campaign design derived from what informants said. They became our teachers and our confidantes and trusted that we had listened; they also became our listeners and our learners. This is the essence of what it means to design communication communicatively to be dialogic. Being dialogic is not simply a matter of packaging messages to match audience information processing styles or finding ways to transmit messages via trusted, credible, or intimate others. It is a matter of acknowledging in the core of the campaign the everyday sense-makings of audiences. All communication is ultimately dialogic. The dialogue will either be driven underground by institutions that cannot hear and therefore will not be heard, or be nurtured into the open.

Traditionally, communication efficiency and effectiveness have been conceptualized as opposing trade-offs (see Chapter 9, this volume). In contrast, Sense-Making addresses both simultaneously by reconceptualizing what attention to individuality means. Sense-Making does not focus on static characterizations of individual people who are assumed to behave the same in varying circumstances. Rather, it focuses on the idea that communicating is responsive to situational conditions—a moment of sense-making replaces the person as primary focus. These situational moments are addressed in interviewing, analysis, and design with Sense-Making's verbing analytic, which focuses on aspects of audience needs that were formerly construed as chaotic and elusive. It is this reconceptualization that is the foundation of Sense-Making's claim that it is possible for institutions to implement dialogic communication systematically—in essence, to communicate communicatively with audiences.

NOTES

1. This section is based on an extensive review of the public communication campaign and audience survey research literature. Because of space limitations, we list only a few especially helpful recent works: Baer (1996), Cheek (1999), Clatts (1994), Guttman (1997), Krosnick (1999), Proctor (1999), Tardy and Hayle (1998), and Yankelovich (1996). For a copy of our full bibliography, contact *dervin.1@osu.edu* or *frenettm@ com.umontreal.ca*. Our bibliography for this chapter also builds on that used in the chapter on Sense-Making in the second edition of this book (Dervin, 1989).

2. Sense-Making owes a debt to many philosopher-theorists. See Dervin (1999b) for a recent list, and see Carter (1990, 1991) for his work focusing on the development of theory for the study of communicating. For bibliographies and exemplars relating to the uses of Sense-Making in research and practice, see *http://communication.sbs.ohio-state.edu/ sense-making/*.

3. The use of Sense-Making triangulations in conjunction with message stops builds on Carter's "signaled stopping technique" (Carter, Ruggels, Jackson, & Heffner, 1973).

4. See *http://communication.sbs.ohio-state/sense-making* for up-to-date listings of Sense-Making studies. Volume 9 (issues 2-4) of the *Electronic Journal of Communica-*

tion (1999; *http://www.cios.org/www/ejcrec2.htm*) reports 18 empirical Sense-Making studies, including 5 focusing directly on public communication campaigns. Two are described briefly in this section. The other three are Dervin et al. (1999), Madden (1999), and Murphy (1999).

5. The cancer clinic permitted access on the proviso that the data would not be published except in brief abstract.

REFERENCES

Baer, R. D. (1996). Health and mental illness among Mexican American migrants: Implications for survey research. *Human Organization, 55*(1), 58-66.

Brendlinger, N., Dervin, B., & Foreman-Wernet, L. (1999). When informants are theorists: An exemplar study in the HIV/AIDS context of the use of sense-making as an approach to public communication campaign research. *Electronic Journal of Communication* [On-line serial], *9*(2-4). Available: *http://www.cios.org/www/ejcrec2. htm*.

Carter, R. F. (1990). Our future research agenda—confronting challenges—or our dying grasp. *Journalism Quarterly, 67*(2), 282-285.

Carter, R. F. (1991, May). Comparative analysis, theory, and cross-cultural communication. *Communication Theory, 1*, 151-158.

Carter, R. F., Ruggels, W. L., Jackson, K. M., & Heffner, M. B. (1973). Application of signaled stopping technique to communication research. In P. Clarke (Ed.), *New models for communication research* (pp. 15-43). Beverly Hills, CA: Sage.

Cheek, J. (1999). Influencing practice or simply esoteric? Researching health care using postmodern approaches. *Qualitative Health Research, 9*(3), 383-392.

Clatts, M. C. (1994). All the king's horses and all the king's men: Some personal reflections on ten years of AIDS ethnography. *Human Organization, 53*(1), 93-95.

Dervin, B. (1989). Audience as listener and learner, teacher and confidante: The sense-making approach. In R. E. Rice & C. K. Atkin (Eds.), *Public communication campaigns* (2nd ed., pp. 67-86). Newbury Park, CA: Sage.

Dervin, B. (1992). From the mind's eye of the user: The sense-making qualitative-quantitative methodology. In J. D. Glazier & R. R. Powell (Eds.), *Qualitative research in information management* (pp. 61-84). New York: Libraries Unlimited.

Dervin, B. (1999a). Chaos, order, and sense-making: A proposed theory for information design. In R. Jacobson (Ed.), *Information design* (pp. 35-57). Cambridge: MIT Press.

Dervin, B. (1999b). On studying information seeking methodologically: The implications of connecting metatheory to method. *Information Processing and Management, 35*, 727-750.

Dervin, B., Harpring, J., & Foreman-Wernet, L. (1999). In moments of concern: A sense-making study of pregnant drug-addicted women and their information needs. *Electronic Journal of Communication* [On-line serial], *9*(2-4). Available: *http:// www.cios. org/www/ejcrec2.htm*.

Dervin, B., Jacobson, T., & Nilan, M. (1982). Measuring information seeking: A test of a quantitative-qualitative methodology. *Communication Yearbook, 6*, 419-444.

Dervin, B., Nilan, M., & Jacobson, T. (1981). Improving predictions of information use: A comparison of predictor types in a health communication setting. *Communication Yearbook, 5*, 807-830.

Frenette, M. (1998). Une perspective constructiviste sur les messages antitabagiques destinés aux jeunes [A constructivistic perspective on anti-smoking messages aimed at youth]. *Revue Québécoise de Psychologie, 19*(1), 109-134.

Frenette, M. (1999). Explorations in adolescents' sense-making of anti-smoking messages. *Electronic Journal of Communication* [On-line serial], *9*(2-4). Available: *http://www.cios.org/www/ejcrec2.htm.*

Guttman, N. (1997). Ethical dilemmas in health campaigns. *Health Communication, 9*(2), 155-190.

Krosnick, J. A. (1999). Survey research. *Annual Review of Psychology, 50,* 337-367.

Madden, K. M. (1999). Making sense of environmental messages: An exploration of households' information needs and uses. *Electronic Journal of Communication* [On-line serial], *9*(2-4). Available: *http://www.cios.org/www/ejcrec2.htm.*

Murphy, T. (1999). The human experience of wilderness. *Electronic Journal of Communication* [On-line serial], *9*(2-4). Available: *http://www.cios.org/www/ejcrec2.htm.*

Proctor, R. N. (1999). *The Nazi war on cancer.* Princeton, NJ: Princeton University Press.

Tardy, R. W., & Hayle, C. L. (1998). Bonding and cracking: The role of informal interpersonal networks in health care decision making. *Health Communication, 10*(2), 151-173.

Yankelovich, D. (1996). A new direction for survey research. *International Journal of Public Opinion Research, 8*(1), 1-9.

5

Creating Fear in a Risky World

Generating Effective Health Risk Messages

Michael T. Stephenson
Kim Witte

It is often considered a quirk of human nature that we are unrealistically optimistic about our likelihood of experiencing negative events (Weinstein, 1980). Most people—in one way or another—engage in behaviors that are considered health risks. There is almost always an excuse, however: We have one more drink because our friends insist, or we fail to get a flu shot because we were just really busy this year. We believe that others might experience harmful effects of their behaviors, but not us (Weinstein, 1984).

In response, some health educators and practitioners have adopted the use of scare tactics, or fear appeal messages, to enhance perceptions of risk. The logic is that fear will get our attention and drive home the social or physical consequences associated with risky behaviors, thereby increasing our perceived vulnerability to such actions and decreasing risky behaviors. Consequently, fear appeals have become a viable alternative to diminishing risky behavior and increasing adaptive behaviors (Witte, 1994). Research on the effectiveness of fear appeals actually began in the early 1950s and continued for many years with mixed results (Dillard, 1994; Witte, 1992a, 1998). Recent theoretical advances, however, have substantiated the effectiveness of fear appeals in enhancing perceived risk and motivating adaptive behavior change in many health domains (Hale & Dillard, 1995; Witte & Allen, 2000). Despite this recent supportive evidence, using fear to motivate behavior change has not gained universal acceptance in many applied communities (Backer, Rogers, & Sopory, 1992; Covello, von Winterfeldt, & Slovic, 1986).

This chapter discusses how to position fear within risk messages to effectively promote health-related behaviors. To begin, we review the research on how individuals estimate health risks. Then we elaborate on the relationship between risk, perceived vulnerability, and behavior. Finally, we outline a way to effectively influence perceptions of vulnerability to promote health-related behaviors and prevent maladaptive responses through the use of an empirically supported fear appeal theory, the Extended Parallel Process Model (EPPM) (Witte, 1992a).

EVALUATING AND COMPARATIVELY ESTIMATING RISK

Risk is defined as the likelihood of a specific event occurring multiplied by the magnitude of consequences associated with that event (Douglas, 1985). Usually, these events and consequences are considered negative, such as the onset of disease (the event) and associated symptoms (the consequences). Consistent with Slovic (1987), Rothman, Klein, and Weinstein (1996) found that study participants overestimated their vulnerability to hazards that have lower probabilities of occurring, such as dying from chronic liver disease, dying from colon cancer, or dying by committing suicide. In contrast, participants underestimated their risk to hazards that occur more frequently, including contracting a sexually transmitted disease, becoming pregnant, or getting a divorce.

Furthermore, we "consistently and substantially" overestimate risks to others, particularly when making comparisons to our own vulnerability (Rothman et al., 1996, p. 1231). This relative optimistic bias (Weinstein, 1984, p. 432) is maintained by distorting our beliefs about risk factors that are controllable. For example, skin cancer, HIV, and pneumonia are all partly preventable by controllable behaviors: regularly wearing sun screen, using condoms, and seeking medical attention, respectively.

Denial helps to maintain this relative optimistic bias: "People are unrealistic about their vulnerability to hazards perceived to be controllable at least in part because they are biased about the actions and psychological attributes that determine their susceptibility to such hazards" (Weinstein, 1984, p. 439). In addition, Rothman and colleagues (1996) determined that we alter or generate self-serving beliefs regarding our superiority over others. Perhaps most striking, Klein and Kunda (1993) found that individuals modified reports of their own behavior, such as drinking alcohol, to distinguish their own behavior as more acceptable than that of others.

A different line of research explains that some people, by nature, are genetically driven to take risks. Those high in a psychobiological trait called sensation seeking (Zuckerman, 1979, 1994; see Chapter 23, this volume) are inherently more likely to seek out physical, emotional, or legal risks, such as earlier and greater use of tobacco, alcohol, and drugs (Teichman, Barnea, & Rahav, 1989) or risky, unprotected sex (Donohew et al., 2000). Thrill-seeking behaviors release the brain-reward chemical dopamine, leaving sensation seekers with a "rush" after engaging in thrill-seeking activities (e.g., bungee jumping, fast and dangerous driving, and smoking marijuana).

WHY USE FEAR TO INCREASE RISK SUSCEPTIBILITY?

Why would health planners use fear appeals to enhance our perceptions of vulnerability to certain risks? Because increased fear arousal and perceived threat are positively associated with recommended attitude and behavior changes (Boster & Mongeau, 1984; Mongeau, 1996; Sutton, 1982; Witte & Allen, 2000). Fear arousal appears to be the emotional reaction to a fear appeal, and perceived threat appears to be the cognitive reaction to a fear appeal. Campaigners have often relied on fear appeals to convey risks and increase vulnerabilities to certain behaviors. For example, Freimuth, Hammond, Edgar, and Monohan (1990) found that one of every four HIV/AIDS-related public service announcements was a fear appeal. Perhaps the most common fear appeal ever used was the egg-in-frying-pan message produced by the Partnership for a Drug Free America designed to convince viewers that using drugs literally fries your brain. The frying pan concept, apparently still appealing to viewers and antidrug campaigners, was modernized and re-created in 1998 to introduce the Office of National Drug Control Policy's $2-billion, 5-year attack on adolescent drug use.

HOW FEAR HAS BEEN USED TO CONVEY RISK

Although not fear appeal theories, per se, the following approaches clearly highlight those variables most central to the fear appeal domain.

Health Belief Model

Some of the earliest assessments of risk in relation to health behaviors were conducted by Hochbaum and a team of social psychologists working for the United States Public Health Service in the early 1950s (Rosenstock, 1990). Their investigations led health education specialists to focus on four major components that eventually evolved into the Health Belief Model (HBM) (Rosenstock, 1974): severity, susceptibility, benefits, and barriers (Janz & Becker, 1984). A fifth but less addressed component of the HBM, cues-to-action, represents the internal or external stimulus that prompts one to make decisions or engage in health-related behaviors (Bruce, Shrum, Trefethen, & Slovik, 1990; Mattson, 1999; Witte, Stokols, & Ituarte, 1993). Self-efficacy was later incorporated as a sixth component into the HBM (Rosenstock, Strecher, & Becker, 1988). Two meta-analyses (Janz & Becker, 1984;

Zimmerman & Vernberg, 1994) reveal that perceived barriers exhibit the strongest relationship with behaviors in a variety of domains. Perceived susceptibility, or one's vulnerability to an illness or injury, was also a strong predictor of various health behaviors and understanding.

Precaution Adoption Process

While conducting his program of research on risk perception, Weinstein (1980, 1982, 1983, 1984) became dissatisfied with existing preventive behavior theories. His answer was the multistage theory called the Precaution Adoption Process (PAP), which models the "processes that lead individuals to adopt new preventive health behaviors and other precautions" (Weinstein, 1988, p. 357) and reflects perceptions of costs and benefits associated with preventive behaviors.

Stage theories, such as the PAP, suggest that individuals in different stages exhibit distinct beliefs about susceptibility and distinct behavioral characteristics. The first two stages of the PAP ("Has heard of hazard" and "Believes in significant likelihood for others") reflect our awareness that a specific hazard is a significant problem. The third stage ("Acknowledges personal susceptibility") occurs when individuals acknowledge their personal susceptibility to a specific threat. A fourth stage ("Decides to take precaution") occurs for those who have decided to take a precaution against the threat, whereas the fifth and final stage ("Takes precaution") occurs when individuals act to take a precaution. Weinstein (1988) noted, "The decision to act . . . will not occur until people have reached the final stages of all three relevant beliefs: susceptibility, severity, and precaution effectiveness" (p. 365).

Weinstein specifies the identifying characteristics for each stage in combination with what he believes are the important components to emphasize in risk messages. The framework is practical and potentially valuable, although there is little research in health communication adopting this method. We would be more inclined to use the approach advocated by Slater (1999), which links specific communication message theories such as the EPPM (described later) with classification schemes such as PAP. Slater (1999) and others (Maibach & Cotton, 1995) have incorporated theory-based message design into a more frequently used stage theory, the Transtheoretical Model (which is also known as Stages of Change Model) (Prochaska & DiClemente, 1982, 1983; see also Chaper 29, this volume).

Message Framing

A third approach to enhancing perceptions of risk advocates "framing" messages by emphasizing potential gains or potential losses associated with specific health behaviors. *Gain-framed* messages emphasize the advantages or benefits of certain behaviors or the likelihood that one would gain by adopting them. In contrast, *loss-framed* messages highlight the disadvantages or costs of certain behaviors or the odds that individuals will lose or not be successful in taking certain actions. Framing is generally based on the invariance postulate of Kahneman and Tversky's (1979; Tversky & Kahneman, 1981) prospect theory, which suggests that people are *risk averse* when presented choices involving gains and *risk seeking* when presented choices involving losses, even though the gain and loss options are different representations of the same choice (Rothman & Salovey, 1997, p. 7).

To date, there are no theoretical guidelines with which one could consistently generate gain- or loss-framed messages. To account for a hodgepodge of contradictory results in such research, Rothman and Salovey (1997) determined that the effectiveness of either gain- or loss-framed messages is dependent on multiple factors, including the perceived (un)desirability of the specified outcomes, the salience of the outcomes, the context from which a decision is made, and the type of behavior addressed by the message.

Thus, because a preventive behavior, such as using condoms, generally involves little risk and provides more certainty, a gain-framed message should bemost effective in facilitating this behavior (Christopherson & Gyulay, 1981; Rothman, Salovey, Antone, Keough, & Martin, 1993; Treiber, 1986). In contrast, loss-framed messages should be more effective in promoting detection-oriented behaviors that have perceived risks associated with detecting a potentially unpleasant health outcome, such as breast exam screenings or skin cancer examinations (Rothman & Salovey, 1997). Research by Meyerowitz and Chaiken (1987; see also Meyerowitz, Wilson, & Chaiken, 1991) supports this assertion, as they determined that loss-framed messages were more successful in generating positive breast self-exam intentions and behaviors compared to the messages framed in gain language and a control condition (Kalichman & Coley, 1995). In general, this line of research remains troubled by its atheoretical nature and the inherent subjective variation in the interpretation of multiple contexts and health behaviors (Rothman & Salovey, 1997, p. 16).

FEAR APPEAL THEORIES

Fear appeal messages can be distinguished from the previous theories and strategies in that they "attempt to change our attitudes by appealing to [the] unpleasant emotion of fear" (Rogers, 1983, p. 153). They more narrowly focus on eliciting fear by describing the "terrible things" that will happen to people if they do not adhere to recommended behaviors (Witte, 1992a). Fear messages may accentuate potential risk from either physical threats (e.g., unprotected sex and HIV) or social threats (e.g., harmed relationships with family and friends from marijuana use).

Fear has not always been considered a viable and effective means to promote behavior change. In fact, fear was first viewed as an inhibitor to message acceptance by Janis and Feshbach (1953) because they detected a negative relationship between the strength of fear appeals and conformity with recommendations to carefully brush one's teeth. Interestingly, even some current experts and health entertainment industry chiefs remain skeptical about the effectiveness of fear appeals (Backer et al., 1992, p. 113), although the empirical research of the past 25 years shows that they often work. Three theoretical perspectives have historically dominated fear appeal research; Fear-as-Acquired Drive Model, the Parallel Process Model, and the protection motivation theory are reviewed in considerable detail by Dillard (1994), Hale and Dillard (1995), and Witte (1992a).

Drive Models

Hovland, Janis, and Kelly (1953) claimed that anything that reduced the negative drive that motivates people to take action would become the preferred, habitual response to a threat because it was rewarding to eliminate the negative drive. Their answer was to provide assuring recommendations in a fear appeal to reduce a negative drive state. If these recommendations did not work to reduce the drive state, however, other more maladaptive strategies, such as defensive avoidance (i.e., not thinking about the threat) or perceived manipulation (i.e., feeling angry because of a perception of manipulation) might be tried by recipients. Whichever method worked best to reduce fear, the recommendation or the maladaptive behavior, would become the preferred and habitual response to the threat. Within this same paradigm, Janis (1967) argued that moderate fear appeals were most effective in motivating action, maintaining a curvilinear (or inverted-U shaped) relationship between fear and message acceptance.

Parallel Response Model

In introducing his Parallel Response Model (later Parallel Process Model), Leventhal (1970) challenged the assumptions of the drive models that "fear arousal instigates the cognitive processes that mediate acceptance of fear appeals' recommendations" (Eagly & Chaiken, 1993, p. 440). Instead, he denounced the curvilinear relationship with his research, which revealed that strong fear appeals worked best (Leventhal & Singer, 1966). Leventhal, however, maintained that there were two distinct reactions to fear appeals. The first was a primarily cognitive process, called danger control, that occurred when people thought about the threat and ways to avert it (e.g., they tried to control the danger). The second was a primarily emotional process, called the fear control process, during which people reacted to their fear and engaged in coping strategies to control their fear.

Protection Motivation Theory

Rogers's (1975, 1983) protection motivation theory focused on the danger control side of Leventhal's model. It claimed that four components were needed in a fear appeal: the probability of occurrence of a threat, the magnitude of noxiousness of a threat, the effectiveness of the recommended response, and information about one's ability to perform a recommended response. These four components produced corresponding cognitive mediating processes resulting in perceptions of one's vulnerability, severity, response efficacy, and self-efficacy. If all these cognitive mediators were at high levels, then the maximum amount of protection motivation and thus attitude or behavior change would be elicited.

THE EXTENDED PARALLEL PROCESS MODEL

The EPPM (Witte, 1992a), summarized in Figure 5.1, expands and integrates the previously discussed fear appeal theories, although it is largely based on Leventhal's (1970) parallel danger and fear control framework.

Threat and Efficacy in the EPPM

According to the EPPM, the evaluation of a fear appeal initiates two appraisals of the message. First, individuals appraise the threat of the hazard based on perceptions about the severity of the threat and on how susceptible individuals believe themselves to be to the threat. Consider, for example, a portion of the threat message designed to convey the severity of skin cancer to college students from overexposing themselves to the intense summer sun (for study results, see Stephenson & Witte, 1998). A portion of the threat component stated,

> The sun's rays can be intense and deadly; in fact, unprotected skin in the hot Texas sun can result in deep red, heat-filled, painful sunburns, some of which turn into blisters that form, ooze, crust over, and break again letting the sappy liquid drain from the open wound.

To convey individuals' susceptibility to skin cancer, the message was personalized by noting that "everyone is at risk, especially those of us in Texas who live in an extremely sunny region of the United States." The more individuals believe the threat is severe and that they are susceptible to serious danger, the more motivated they are to begin the second appraisal, which is an evaluation of the efficacy of the recommended response. Specifically, individuals gauge the *response efficacy*, or the perceived effectiveness of the response to avert the threat. In addition, individuals assess *self-efficacy*, beliefs about their own ability to effectively avoid the hazard. Continuing the skin cancer example, one response effi-

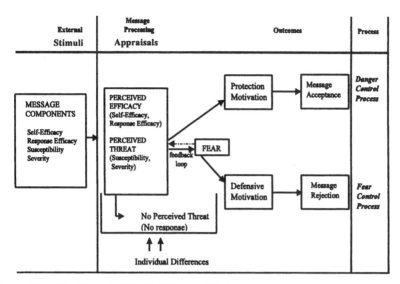

Figure 5.1. The Extended Parallel Process Model

cacy component revealed how "studies have shown that using sunscreen with a Sun Protective Factor (SPF) rating of 15 or higher greatly decreases your chances of sunburn and skin cancer." Self-efficacy was bolstered in one instance by stating that "each and every one of us is capable of protecting ourselves against sunburn and skin cancer. . . . Having fun in the sun is as easy as using some common sense."

Perceived threat determines the *extent* of a response (i.e., the strength of the danger or fear control responses), whereas perceived efficacy determines the *nature* of the response (i.e., whether danger or fear control responses are elicited). If no information regarding the efficacy of the recommended response is given, individuals will rely on past experiences and prior beliefs to determine perceived efficacy.

Processing Fear Appeal Messages

The EPPM maintains that individuals do one of three things following the appraisals of a fear appeal. Individuals may engage in danger control, in which they cognitively process the message and take action to avoid the threat. An alternative response is fear control, in which individuals emotionally repress the message and ignore the threat. A third alternative is to ignore the message, which typically occurs if the threat is perceived as irrelevant or insignificant, leaving no motivation to process the message.

Danger control processes dominate when people realize they are susceptible to a serious threat and believe they can successfully avert it. These realizations are created by a high threat-high efficacy message (e.g., "Skin cancer is a deadly disease to which I am susceptible, but I am easily and successfully able to prevent it by using sun screen"). These cognitive efforts generate protection motivation, which stimulates actions such as attitude, intention, or behavior changes that reduce or diminish the threat (e.g., "I am going to wear sun screen the next time I go to the beach to prevent getting skin cancer").

Fear control processes are also elicited on exposure to a serious threat to which individuals believe themselves to be susceptible. With fear control, however, individuals do not believe they can successfully avoid the threat. Such beliefs emerge from exposure to a high threat-low efficacy message (e.g., "Skin cancer is a deadly disease to which I am susceptible, but there is nothing I can really do to effectively prevent it, so it may be too late for me"). Low efficacy may occur for several reasons: Individuals realize they cannot prevent the serious threat from occurring, they believe the response to be futile, individuals had no prior efficacy-related thoughts or beliefs, or people believe they are incapable of carrying out the recommended response. In contrast to the cognitive danger control processes, fear control processes are primarily emotional, in which people respond to and cope with their fear and not the danger. This heightened fear arousal typically leads people to defensive avoidance (e.g., "I'm just not going to think about skin cancer, it scares me too much"), denial (e.g., "I'm not going to get skin cancer, no one else I know has it"), or message manipulation (e.g., "They are just trying to scare me, but it won't work on me"). Witte (1992b) showed that fear control processes interfere with danger control processes, producing an inverse relation between fear control and danger control responses. For example, when a person is denying the threat of AIDS (controlling one's fear), he or she is not asking a partner to use condoms (controlling the danger).

In summary, the EPPM states that a fear appeal message's recommendations are accepted when danger control processes dominate, but the message's recommendations are rejected when fear control dominates. Message acceptance is defined as attitude, intention, and behavior change, and message rejection is defined as defensive avoidance, denial, and perceived manipulation.

Application of the EPPM

The theoretical tenets of the EPPM have been empirically tested and validated in several health contexts. The initial test of the model was employed in the context of AIDS. The high threat component, describing and depicting the severity of disease, in combination with a high condom efficacy message, increased condom usage and decreased unprotected sex among heterosexual partners. The high threat component in combination with the low condom efficacy message produced strong fear control responses and generated no significant increase in condom use (Witte, 1992b, 1994). In addition, the EPPM has been employed concerning the spread of sexually transmitted diseases (Witte, Berkowitz, Cameron, & Lillie, 1998), radon awareness (Witte et al., 1998), and skin cancer (Stephenson & Witte, 1998). The EPPM has also been used to analyze breast cancer messages (Kline & Mattson, 2000), to conduct formative research for a tractor safety campaign (Witte, Peterson, et al., 1993), to design messages (Witte, 1995), and to reduce the occupational hazards associated with overexposure to beryllium (Tan-Wilhelm et al., 1999).

Witte, Cameron, Lapinski, and Nzyuko (1998) analyzed a sample of African HIV/AIDS campaign materials, most of which have been criticized for being atheoretical and failing to address audience beliefs (Nzyuko, 1996). For example, the posters designed to encourage preventive behaviors instead elicited denial or reactance processes because they made people feel susceptible to a very serious threat but gave them no mechanisms or hope of successfully averting the threat. In contrast, pamphlets were more likely to emphasize self and response efficacy at the expense of downplaying threat. Although the EPPM clearly would encourage greater levels of threat, most participants already had extremely high levels of existing perceived threat. In fact, most thought they definitely or maybe were infected with the virus (Witte, Cameron, & Nzyuko, 1996). Consequently, the researchers concluded that the emphasis on efficacy was desirable.

SPECIFIC RECOMMENDATIONS

Theoretical Recommendations

Future research should examine message design features in greater detail, using both physiological and self-report measures. More precisely, what specific message features differentiate a strong fear appeal from a weak fear appeal? For example, Witte (1993) initially advocated the use of vivid pictures to elicit fear arousal, but Stephenson and Witte (1998) found that vivid and grotesque pictures of individuals in the advanced stages of skin cancer did not contribute to the overall effectiveness of fear appeal messages. Is it possible that pictures do not enhance perceptions of severity, or is the issue more deeply methodological? A related issue is how vivid language must be to elicit an appropriate high fear arousal, especially in light of Boster and Mongeau's (1984) contention that many of the studies in their meta-analysis did not adequately elicit fear. What is it about fear appeals that promotes fear, threat, or efficacy?

Our understanding of fear appeals could be substantially improved by evaluating the appraisal process. The EPPM and other fear appeal reviews (Hale & Dillard, 1995) suggest that the threat component and appraisal occur before the efficacy component and appraisal. If efficacy preceded threat, however, what type of processing occurs and what claims would this allow in terms of a primacy or recency effect for threat or efficacy? Witte has also advocated the need for more naturalistic fear appeal research. Witte and Allen (2000) noted, "We have no idea, for example, if the average television viewer actually watches a fear appeal if exposed, or if s/he immediately changes the channel."

Recommendations for Practice

Fear appeals remain an effective and viable alternative for changing risky behaviors, providing the appeals are appropriately developed (Witte, 1993, 1995, 1998). Enhanced perceptions of threat alone may not adequately motivate behavior, however (Weinstein, 1984, p. 453). In addition to severity, fear appeal messages should also accentuate one's susceptibility to the threat, with particular attention given to the relationship between performing the risky behavior and the susceptibility to risks associated with that behavior. For example, Witte, Peterson, et al. (1993) found that farmers clearly understood the threats posed to them from operating farm equipment; consistent with the risk literature, however, the same farmers did not believe they were vulnerable to the risks.

Susceptibility can be conveyed with personalized references to an audience's vulnerability, emphasizing the word "you" and addressing salient behaviors by members of the target audience. Rothman et al. (1996) specifically suggest providing information about a "specific similar other" rather than the average person within the target audience's demographic. Weinstein's (1988) Precaution Adoption Process stage model would further enhance the targeting effort by framing the message for the varying cognitive stages of the target audience.

Perhaps the most important practical recommendation, however, is that a highly threatening fear appeal will backfire without an equally strong efficacy component. Kline and Mattson (2000) demonstrated that this critical component is often overlooked, particularly in their analysis of breast cancer prevention messages. One-liners, common in health prevention materials (e.g., the "Fry Now, Pay Later" brochure from the American Cancer Society), may actually do more harm than good by eliciting defensive responses (Stephenson & Witte, 1998).

CONCLUSION

Our goal in this work was to discuss how to effectively employ fear in health risk messages. A review of the risk literature revealed that most people are incapable of accurately assessing their own vulnerabilities to risky health behaviors. Likewise, people engage in relative optimistic bias, cultivating the inaccurate belief that others are more likely to be adversely affected by the consequences of risky behavior than themselves. This denial of personal vulnerability substantially decreases the chances of engaging in risk-reduction behaviors. Research has documented, however, that increased perceived vulnerability is positively associated with preventive behaviors. Fear appeals offer a common, viable, and effective means by which to increase the awareness of vulnerabilities to specific health threats. The EPPM (Witte, 1992a) offers an empirically verified message framework with which to generate effective risk-reducing messages. Highly threatening messages emphasizing the severity of a risky behavior and the vulnerability of a specific target group that routinely engages in such behaviors are successful provided a strong efficacy component is also part of the message. Such messages position fear in such a way so as to enhance an individual's perceived personal susceptibility to a risk and still foster positive attitudes and behaviors of the recommended risk-reducing alternative.

REFERENCES

Backer, T. E., Rogers, E. M., & Sopory, P. (1992). *Designing health communication campaigns: What works?* Newbury Park, CA: Sage.

Boster, F. J., & Mongeau, P. A. (1984). Fear-arousing persuasive messages. In R. Bostrom (Ed.), *Communication yearbook, Vol. 8* (pp. 330-375). Beverly Hills, CA: Sage.

Bruce, K. E., Shrum, J. C., Trefethen, C., & Slovik, L. F. (1990). Students' attitudes about AIDS, homosexuality, and condoms. *AIDS Education and Prevention, 2,* 220-234.

Christopherson, E. R., & Gyulay, J. E. (1981). Parental compliance with car seat usage: A positive approach with long-term follow-up. *Journal of Pediatric Psychology, 6,* 301-312.

Covello, V., von Winterfeldt, D., & Slovic, P. (1986). Risk communication: A review of the literature. *Risk Abstracts, 3,* 171-182.

Dillard, J. P. (1994). Rethinking the study of fear appeals. *Communication Theory, 4,* 295-323.

Donohew, L., Zimmerman, R., Cupp, P. S., Novak, S., Colon, S., & Abell, R. (2000). Sensation seeking, impulsive decision-making, and risky sex: Implications for risk-taking and design of interventions. *Journal of Personality and Individual Differences, 28,* 1079-1091.

Douglas, M. (1985). *Risk acceptability according to the social sciences.* New York: Russell Sage Foundation.

Eagly, A. H., & Chaiken, S. (1993). *The psychology of attitudes.* Orlando, FL: Harcourt Brace.

Freimuth, V. S., Hammond, S. L., Edgar, T., & Monohan, J. L. (1990). Reaching those at risk: A content analytic study of AIDS PSAs. *Communication Research, 17,* 775-791.

Hale, J. L., & Dillard, J. P. (1995). Fear appeals in health promotion: Too much, too little or just right? In E. Maibach & R. Parrott (Eds.), *Designing health messages: Approaches from communication theory and public health practice* (pp. 65-80). Thousand Oaks, CA: Sage.

Hovland, C., Janis, I., & Kelly, H. (1953). *Communication and persuasion.* New Haven, CT: Yale University Press.

Janis, I. L. (1967). Effects of fear arousal on attitude change: Recent developments in theory and experimental research. In L. Berkowitz (Ed.), *Advances in experimental social psychology* (Vol. 3, pp. 166-225). New York: Academic Press.

Janis, I. L., & Feshbach, S. (1953). Effects of fear-arousing communications. *Journal of Abnormal and Social Psychology, 48*, 78-92.

Janz, N. K., & Becker, M. H. (1984). The Health Belief Model: A decade later. *Health Education Quarterly, 11*, 1-47.

Kahneman, D., & Tversky, A. (1979). Prospect theory: An analysis of decision under risk. *Econometrica, 47*, 263-291.

Kalichman, S. C., & Coley, B. (1995). Context framing to enhance HIV-antibody-testing messages targeted to African American women. *Health Psychology, 14*, 247-254.

Klein, W. M., & Kunda, Z. (1993). Maintaining self-serving social comparisons: Biased reconstruction of one's past behaviors. *Personality and Social Psychology Bulletin, 19*, 732-739.

Kline, K. N., & Mattson, M. (2000). Breast self-examination pamphlets: A content analysis grounded in fear appeal research. *Health Communication, 12*(1), 1-22.

Leventhal, H. (1970). Findings and theory in the study of fear communications. In L. Berkowitz (Ed.), *Advances in experimental social psychology* (Vol. 5, pp. 119-186). New York: Academic Press.

Leventhal, H., & Singer, R. P. (1966). Affect arousal and positioning of recommendations in persuasive communications. *Journal of Personality and Social Psychology, 4*, 137-146.

Maibach, E. W., & Cotton, D. (1995). Moving people to behavior change: A staged social cognitive approach to message design. In E. Maibach & R. L. Parrott (Eds.), *Designing health messages* (pp. 41-64). Thousand Oaks, CA: Sage.

Mattson, M. (1999). Toward a reconceptualization of communication cues to action in the Health Belief Model: HIV test counseling. *Communication Monographs, 66*(3), 240-265.

Meyerowitz, B. E., & Chaiken, S. E. (1987). The effect of message framing on breast self-examination attitudes, intentions, and behaviors. *Journal of Personality and Social Psychology, 52*, 500-510.

Meyerowitz, B. E., Wilson, D. K., & Chaiken, S. (1991, June). *Loss-framed messages increase breast self-examination for women who perceive risk.* Paper presented at the annual convention of the American Psychological Society, Washington, DC.

Mongeau, P. (1996). Another look at fear arousing persuasive appeals. In M. Allen & R. Preiss (Eds.), *Prospects and precautions in the use of meta-analyses* (pp. 75-100). Dubuque, IA: William C. Brown.

Nzyuko, S. (1996). Does research have any role in information/education/communication programs in Africa? An insider's view. *Journal of Health Communication, 1*, 227-229.

Prochaska, J. O., & DiClemente, C. C. (1982). Transtheoretical therapy: Toward a more integrative model of change. *Psychotherapy: Theory, Research, and Practice, 20*, 161-173.

Prochaska, J. O., & DiClemente, C. C. (1983). Stages and processes of self change of smoking: Toward an integrative model. *Journal of Consulting and Clinical Psychology, 51*, 390-395.

Rogers, R. W. (1975). A protection motivation theory of fear appeals and attitude change. *Journal of Psychology, 91*, 93-114.

Rogers, R. W. (1983). Cognitive and physiological processes in fear appeals and attitude change: A revised theory of protection motivation. In J. Cacioppo & R. E. Petty (Eds.), *Social psychophysiology* (pp. 153-176). New York: Guilford.

Rosenstock, I. M. (1974). Historical origins of the Health Belief Model. *Health Education Monographs, 2,* 328-335.

Rosenstock, I. M. (1990). The Health Belief Model: Explaining health behavior through expectancies. In K. Glanz, F. M. Lewis, & B. K. Rimer (Eds.), *Health behavior and health education: Theory research and practice* (pp. 39-62). San Francisco: Jossey-Bass.

Rosenstock, I. M., Strecher, V. J., & Becker, M. (1988). Social learning theory and the Health Belief Model. *Health Education Quarterly, 15,* 175-183.

Rothman, A. J., & Salovey, P. (1997). Shaping perceptions to motivate healthy behavior: The role of message framing. *Psychological Bulletin, 121*(1), 3-19.

Rothman, A. J., Klein, W. M., & Weinstein, N. D. (1996). Absolute and relative biases in estimations of personal risk. *Journal of Applied Social Psychology, 26,* 1213-1236.

Rothman, A. J., Salovey, P., Antone, C., Keough, K., & Martin, C. D. (1993). The influence of message framing on intentions to perform health behaviors. *Journal of Experimental Social Psychology, 29,* 408-433.

Slater, M. D. (1999). Integrating application of media effects, persuasion, and behavior change theories to communication campaigns: A stages-of-change framework. *Health Communication, 11*(4), 335-354.

Slovic, P. (1987). Perceptions of risk. *Science, 236,* 280-285.

Stephenson, M. T., & Witte, K. (1998). Fear, threat, and perceptions of efficacy from frightening skin cancer messages. *Public Health Reviews, 26,* 147-174.

Sutton, S. R. (1982). Fear-arousing communications: A critical examination of theory and research. In J. R. Eiser (Ed.), *Social psychology and behavioral medicine* (pp. 303-337). London: Wiley.

Tan-Wilhelm, D., Witte, K., Liu, W. Y., Newman, L. S., Janssen, A., Ellison, C., Yancey, A., Sanderson, W., & Henneberger, P. (1999). Impact of a worker notification program: Assessment of attitudinal and behavioral outcomes. *American Journal of Industrial Medicine, 36,* 1-9.

Teichman, M., Barnea, Z., & Rahav, G. (1989). Sensation seeking, state and trait anxiety and depressive mood in adolescent substance users. *International Journal of Addictions, 24,* 87-99.

Treiber, F. A. (1986). A comparison of positive and negative consequences approaches upon car restraint usage. *Journal of Pediatric Psychology, 11,* 15-24.

Tversky, A., & Kahneman, D. (1981). The framing of decisions and the psychology of choice. *Science, 211,* 453-458.

Weinstein, N. D. (1980). Unrealistic optimism about future life events. *Journal of Personality and Social Psychology, 39,* 806-820.

Weinstein, N. D. (1982). Unrealistic optimism about susceptibility to health problems. *Journal of Behavioral Medicine, 5,* 441-460.

Weinstein, N. D. (1983). Reducing unrealistic optimism about illness susceptibility. *Health Psychology, 2,* 11-20.

Weinstein, N. D. (1984). Why it won't happen to me: Perceptions of risk factors and susceptibility. *Health Psychology, 3*(5), 431-457.

Weinstein, N. D. (1988). The precaution adoption process. *Health Psychology, 7*(4), 355-386.

Witte, K. (1992a). Putting the fear back into fear appeals: The extended parallel process model. *Communication Monographs, 59,* 329-349.

Witte, K. (1992b). The role of threat and efficacy in AIDS prevention. *International Quarterly of Community Health Education, 12,* 225-249.

Witte, K. (1993). Message and conceptual confounds in fear appeals: The role of judgment methods. *Southern Communication Journal, 58,* 147-155.

Witte, K. (1994). Fear control and danger control: An empirical test of the Extended Parallel Process Model. *Communication Monographs, 61,* 113-134.

Witte, K. (1995). Fishing for success: Using the persuasive health message framework to generate effective campaign messages. In E. Maibach & R. Parrott (Eds.), *Designing health messages: Approaches from communication theory and public health practice* (pp. 145-166). Thousand Oaks, CA: Sage.

Witte, K. (1998). Fear as motivator, fear as inhibitor: Using the Extended Parallel Process Model to explain fear appeal successes and failures. In P. A. Andersen & L. K. Guerrero (Eds.), *The handbook of communication and emotion: Research, theory, applications, and contexts* (pp. 423-450). San Diego: Academic Press.

Witte, K., & Allen, M. (2000). When do scare tactics work? A meta-analysis of fear appeals. *Health Education and Behavior, 27,* 608-632.

Witte, K., Berkowitz, J., Cameron, K., & Lillie, J. (1998). Preventing the spread of genital warts: Using fear appeals to promote self-protective behaviors. *Health Education & Behavior, 25,* 571-585.

Witte, K., Berkowitz, J., Lillie, J., Cameron, K., Lapinski, M. K., & Liu, W. Y. (1998). Radon awareness and reduction campaigns for African-Americans: A theoretically-based formative and summative evaluation. *Health Education & Behavior, 25,* 284-303.

Witte, K., Cameron, K. A., Lapinski, M. K., & Nzyuko, S. (1998). Evaluating HIV/AIDS prevention programs according to theory: A field project along the Trans-Africa Highway in Kenya. *Journal of Health Communication, 4,* 345-363.

Witte, K., Cameron, K., & Nzyuko, S. (1996). *HIV/AIDS along the Trans-Africa Highway in Kenya: Examining risk perceptions, recommended responses, and campaign materials.* Report submitted to the All-University Research Initiative Grant program, Michigan State University, East Lansing.

Witte, K., Peterson, T. R., Vallabhan, S., Stephenson, M. T., Plugge, C. D., Givens, V. K., Todd, J. D., Becktold, M. G., Hyde, M. K., & Jarrett, R. (1993). Preventing tractor-related injuries and deaths in rural populations: Using a Persuasive Health Message (PHM) framework in formative evaluation research. *International Quarterly of Community Health Education, 13,* 219-251.

Witte, K., Stokols, D., & Ituarte, P. (1993). Testing the Health Belief Model in a field study to promote bicycle safety helmets. *Communication Research, 20,* 564-586.

Zimmerman, R. S., & Vernberg, D. (1994). Models of preventive health behavior: Comparison, critique, and meta-analysis. *Advances in Medical Sociology, 4,* 45-67.

Zuckerman, M. (1979). *Sensation seeking: Beyond the optimal level of arousal.* Hillsdale, NJ: Lawrence Erlbaum.

Zuckerman, M. (1994). *Behavioral expressions and biosocial bases of sensation seeking.* New York: Cambridge University Press.

PART II

Campaign Design and Evaluation

6

Evaluating
Communication Campaigns

Thomas W. Valente

Communication campaign evaluation represents an exciting and challenging field of research that provides the opportunity to improve programs and conduct theoretically interesting research. Although public communication campaigns are exciting to create and conceptualize, their true worth is not measured by the degree people like them or whether implementers "feel" a campaign has succeeded but, rather, in the program's influence on the communities and stakeholders it is created to benefit.

This chapter provides an introduction to communication campaign evaluation. It presents an evaluation framework that delineates the steps in the evaluation process and presents study designs used to conduct evaluation research. The importance of specifying a theoretical basis for an evaluation is stressed. The chapter distinguishes evaluation procedures based on sample types (cross-sectional versus panel) and levels of assignment (group, individual, and self-selected). Data from an evaluation of a mass media campaign broadcast in Bolivia are used to illustrate many of the concepts. The chapter concludes with a discussion of impact assessment and dissemination procedures.

AUTHOR'S NOTE: I thank Rebecca Davis, Phyllis Piotrow, and Ronald E. Rice for comments on earlier drafts of the manuscript. Support for this research was provided by the U.S. Agency for International Development cooperative agreement No. DPE-3052-A-00-0014, The Johns Hopkins University, Population Communication Services, and National Institute on Drug Abuse Grant DA10172.

EVALUATION MODELS

Evaluation is the systematic application of research procedures to understand the conceptualization, design, implementation, and utility of interventions. Evaluation research determines whether a program was effective, how it did or did not achieve its goals, and the efficiency with which it achieved them (Boruch, 1996; Mohr, 1992; Rossi, Freeman, & Lipsey, 1999; Shadish, Cook, & Leviton, 1991). Evaluation contributes to the knowledge base of how programs reach and influence their intended audiences so that researchers can learn lessons from these experiences and implement more effective programs in the future. Although the term evaluation can evoke negative reactions among those whose programs are being evaluated, because the evaluation process does inevitably determine the "value" of some activities, evaluators can alleviate these concerns by being sensitive to the fears and concerns of program staff and personnel.

Empirical work on evaluation as a specialty field has blossomed in the past few decades, and many scholars have made notable contributions with the result that today, evaluation is seen as a distinct research enterprise (Shadish et al., 1991). Three major debates often frame an evaluation enterprise. One debate concerns the use of quantitative versus qualitative methodologies (Guba & Lincoln, 1981). Both methods are valid and serve their purposes, which should complement one another. The choice of research methods should be driven by their ability to answer the research questions being posed and the availability of data. A second debate concerns whether nonexperimental designs can adequately control for selectivity and other biases inherent in the public communication evaluation process. With proper theoretical and methodological specification, researchers can use quasi-experimental designs to evaluate campaigns. A third debate concerns the advantages and disadvantages of internal versus external evaluators. External evaluators often have more credibility, but they are usually less informed than internal evaluators about aspects of the campaign's implementation that may influence its effectiveness. The reader can consult Valente (in press) for more details on these issues.

Evaluation is an essential component of any communication campaign because it improves the probability of achieving program success by forcing campaign programmers to specify explicitly the goals and objectives of the campaign. Once the campaign objectives are specified, it becomes possible to create programs to meet these objectives and develop instruments to measure them. The first function of an evaluation, then, is to determine the degree to which the campaign reached its objectives. For example, if a campaign was designed to increase the awareness of the dangers of substance abuse, the evaluation proposal should state the percentage increase expected in this awareness. The second function of a campaign evaluation is to help planners and scholars understand how or why a particular campaign worked. Knowing how or why a program worked increases the likelihood that successes can be repeated and failures avoided in future behavioral promotion programs. Finally, a third function of evaluation is to provide information relevant for planning future activities. Evaluation results can indicate what behaviors or which audiences should be addressed in the next round of activities. In summary, we conduct evaluation to know whether the program worked, how and why it worked, and how to make future programs better.

There are many barriers to rigorous evaluation. One major barrier is the perceived cost of evaluation. Many programmers argue that money spent on evaluation research should not be diverted from program activities. This argument neglects the fact that evaluation should be an integral part of any program. Research costs should normally be limited to approximately 10% to 15% of the total project budget (Piotrow, Kincaid, Rimon, & Rinehart, 1997). These costs, however, provide a high rate of return to the program by improving its implementation. A second barrier to rigorous evaluation is the perception that research takes too much time. As a rule, evaluation results should be available before, during, immediately after, and some later time after the program is completed. Finally, many people object to evaluation on the grounds that it detracts from program implementation. Evaluations should not interfere with programs but, rather, should be considered an integral part of, and a complement to, the program. Indeed, planning and implementing a rigorous evaluation clarifies the timing and objectives of various program components, such as when to conduct the program launch, when to start broadcasts, and how to space supplementary activities to maximize reach and effectiveness (see Chapter 8, this volume).

Figure 6.1 provides a conceptual framework of the campaign evaluation process. Evaluation research is often conducted in three distinct phases: formative, process, and summative. The first step in the evaluation process is to identify and assess the needs that drive the desire for a communication campaign. Once needs are identified, formative research is conducted to more clearly understand the subject of the program. *Formative research* consists of those activities that define the scope of the problem, gather data on possible intervention strategies, learn about the intended audience, and investigate possible factors that might limit program implementation. Formative research is also used to test message strategy, test the effectiveness of possible communication channels, and learn about audience beliefs, motivations, perceptions, and so on (see Chapter 7, this volume). Typically, formative research is conducted using qualitative research methods, such as focus group discussions (FGDs), in-depth interviews, and ethnographic observations, although initial surveys are useful as well. In the Bolivia National Reproductive Health Program (NRHP) campaign, we conducted FGDs among married and unmarried men and women to determine their perceptions regarding contraceptives and family planning. We were surprised to find that many Bolivians were eager to adopt contraceptive methods, but they did not know where to get such services.

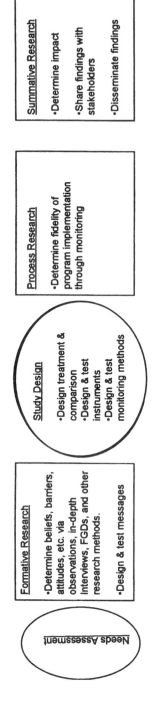

Figure 6.1. Communication Campaign Evaluation Framework

The evaluator then develops a study design. The study design (discussed in detail later; see Table 6.1) should be the most rigorous design feasible that meets the need of program implementers. Evaluators seek to find a balance between research rigor, the needs of stakeholders, and the practical limitations of conducting applied research. For example, in the Bolivia NRHP project, the evaluation would have been stronger if we had been able to restrict the campaign broadcast to certain areas, thus providing a comparison region that did not receive the campaign. Bolivian government officials were opposed to this idea because it would have denied some Bolivians access to information that they deserved; therefore, a one-group pre-/posttest design was used.

Process research (also known as monitoring) consists of those activities conducted to measure the degree of program implementation to determine whether the program was delivered as it was intended. Process research is usually conducted by collecting data on when, where, and for how long the campaign is broadcast. The evaluator might want to hire individuals to watch TV or listen to the radio at prespecified times to record the program. In the Bolivia NRHP project, we requested advertising log books from the advertising agency contracted to produce and broadcast the campaign. We discovered that the campaign was not implemented as intended in the smaller cities of Bolivia, and this warranted a rebroadcast of the campaign (Valente & Saba, 1998).

Summative research consists of those activities conducted to measure the program's impact, to determine the lessons learned from the study, and to disseminate research findings. Summative research is usually conducted by analyzing quantitative data collected before, during, and after (both short term and long term) the campaign. Summative research is an interactive and iterative process in which preliminary findings are shared with program planners and other stakeholders prior to widespread dissemination. The stakeholders provide insight into the interpretation of data and can help set the agenda for specific data analyses. Once the summative research is completed, findings can be disseminated through a variety of channels, including debriefing meetings, conferences, preliminary findings reports, web sites, working papers, and peer-reviewed journal articles. The evaluation framework in Figure 6.1 delineates the steps in the evaluation process, but it is theory concerning human behavior that informs it.

THEORETICAL CONSIDERATIONS

Program goals and objectives should not emerge spontaneously but, rather, stem from theoretical explanations for behavior. The choice of a theoretical orientation to develop a model for and explain the behavior under study can drive both the design of the program and the design of the evaluation, particularly the design of the study instruments. For example, if self-efficacy is theorized to be an important influence on whether individuals use condoms during sex, then the program may try to increase self-efficacy among the intended audience; the evaluation therefore needs to measure self-efficacy before, during, and after the campaign to determine whether the program did indeed deliver self-efficacy messages or training and change self-efficacy levels in the appropriate communities.

Weiss (1972, 1997) made a useful distinction between successful theoretical specification and successful program implementation via three different scenarios in which the program or the theory or both might succeed or fail. In the first scenario, a successful program sets in motion a causal process specified by a theory that results in the desired outcome. In the second scenario, there is a failure of theory in which there is a successfully implemented program (as measured by process evaluation) that sets in motion a causal process that did not result in the desired outcome. In the third scenario, because of a program failure, the intervention did not start an expected causal sequence, so the theory could not be tested.

Thus, the congruence between theory and program implementation can be very important, and a tight linkage between the two increases the likelihood that the program will be judged a success by avoiding cases in which there is a theory failure (Chen & Rossi, 1983). If the program fails, one may not be able to test theory, but if the theory fails, one may incorrectly conclude that the program failed (or succeeded). Having set goals and objectives and determined the theoretical underpinnings for the program and the evaluation, the researcher must then specify a study design.

STUDY DESIGNS

Study design is the specification and assignment of intervention and control conditions, the sampling methodology and sample selection procedures, and the statistical tests to be used to make decisions about the effectiveness of a campaign. A thorough understanding of study designs and terminology enables the evaluator to choose the most appropriate methods for his or her research. An appropriate research design is one that minimizes threats to internal and external validity given the constraints of program implementation and resources. *Threats to validity* are factors that conspire to provide alternative explanations for intervention effects. Examples of threats to validity include history, maturation, testing, selectivity, and sensitization. Study design terminology also permits researchers to communicate efficiently with one another concerning their research procedures. This section addresses levels of assignment and sampling procedures and then presents six study designs.

Specification of intervention and control conditions can occur at the individual, group or community, or self-selection level. *Individual assignment* occurs when the researcher can specify which individuals will be exposed to the intervention and which ones will not. Ideally, researchers can identify a population, select a random sample, and then randomly assign individuals to groups that receive the intervention and groups that do not (a control group). *Group assignment* occurs when the researcher specifies that certain groups, such as schools, organizations, or communities, will be the focus of the intervention and that the intervention can be restricted to these groups. In such cases, the intervention is applied to one or some groups, whereas other groups that do not receive the intervention act as comparison groups (most scholars prefer the term "comparison" rather than "control" for group assignment). It is important to match the comparison and intervention groups or communities on as many characteristics as possible to maximize comparability so as to minimize the alternative explanation that group differences, rather than the intervention, caused the effect. *Self-selection assignment* occurs when the study subjects determine who is exposed to the intervention. Self-selection assignment occurs most commonly in mass media campaign studies because a majority of the population has the ability to selectively hear or see the program (including across treatment and comparison regions, discussed later), and many people may selectively recall it.

Once the level of assignment is specified, researchers then determine whether it is feasible to collect panel or cross-sectional (independent) samples. A *panel sample* consists of interviews with the same respondents at multiple points in time. A *cross-sectional* or *independent sample* consists of interviews with different respondents at one or multiple points in time. The data management, statistical procedures, and statistical inferences for panel and cross-sectional samples are quite different (Valente, in press). The advantages of panel data compared to cross-sectional data are that panel data (a) can measure change with lagged analysis or difference scores; (b) can pinpoint exactly which individuals, with what characteristics, changed their scores or behaviors; (c) require smaller sample sizes because they are collected on the same individuals and hence variance estimates are smaller; and (d) may be easier to analyze because fewer control variables are required. The disadvantages of panel data are that (a) it may be difficult to follow-up with respondents, (b) attrition can bias the study results, and (c) there may be some loss of validity due to repeated testing or interviewing. Ideally, evaluators collect both panel and cross-sectional data to strengthen their inferences, as was done in the cardiovascular disease community trials (Shea & Basch, 1990).

A standard way to depict study designs is to use X's to refer to an intervention condition (the group exposed to the campaign) and O's to refer to a data collection observation (e.g., administration of a survey questionnaire). Subscripts distinguish different X's and O's. For example, X_1 and X_2 may refer to different interventions, such as a media campaign and a media campaign and accompanying interpersonal counseling. For observations, subscripts are often used to refer to observations in different conditions (e.g., intervention and control groups) and at different time periods (e.g., before and after a campaign) (Campbell & Stanley, 1963; Cook & Campbell, 1979).

Table 6.1 arrays the six study designs in increasing order in terms of the number of observation groups for each. Design 1, postcampaign only, collects

Table 6.1 Study Designs

Design	Baseline	Intervention	Follow-up	Validity Threats Reduced
1. Postcampaign only	—	X	O	None
2. Pre-/postcomparison	O	X	O	Selectivity
3. Pre-/postcomparison and post-only control group	O —	X —	O O	Testing
4. Pre-/postcomparison and predetermined control group	O O	X —	O O	History and maturation
5. Pre-/postcomparison and predetermined control group and post-only intervention group	O O —	X — X	O O O	Sensitization
6. Solomon Four Group	O O — —	X — X —	O O O O	All of the above

NOTE: — = No observation or intervention; X = intervention/campaign; O = observation such as survey.

data on the degree of exposure to the campaign, any self-reports of whether respondents believe that the campaign influenced them, and possibly behavioral data. Design 1 is the weakest evaluation design because it provides data only on posttreatment conditions and does not control for any threats to validity.

Design 2, pre-/postcomparison, reduces some threats to validity because it provides a baseline against which to compare the postcampaign scores. Design 2 is often used when it is not feasible to identify or create a control group. A cross-sectional pre-/postcomparison consists of selecting two comparable independent samples before and after the campaign and making population-level comparisons. For example, Valente, Kim, Lettenmaier, Glass, and Dibba (1994) interviewed 400 randomly selected respondents in one region of The Gambia before and after a 9-month radio soap opera and showed that family planning knowledge, attitudes, and practices increased significantly between the two surveys. The shortcoming of this methodology is that there may be fluctuations in sample characteristics that account for differences in outcomes between the two surveys. Moreover, secular trends, historical events, or other factors may have created the behavior change.

A panel pre-/postdesign can help eliminate some of the rival explanations because the same persons are interviewed and changes can be measured on individuals (i.e., not solely at the population level). For example, in an evaluation of a street theater's effectiveness at reducing family planning misinformation,

Valente, Poppe, Alva, de Briceno, and Cases (1994) interviewed passersby about their family planning knowledge before and after the drama. The study found that the drama reduced misinformation by 9.4%. The shortcoming of the pre-/postdesign, however, is that because there is no control group, it is difficult to say what would have happened in the absence of the campaign and difficult to determine the influence that taking the survey had on respondents' misinformation scores (validity threats of history, testing, sensitization, etc.).

Designs 3 and 4 include a post-only control group and a pre-/postcontrol group, respectively. Both of these designs are strong and provide relatively good measures of program impact because the intervention group's scores can be compared to the control group's scores. Design 3 includes a post-only control group in which respondents are not interviewed before the intervention, and therefore the researcher can determine the degree that taking a pretest influences the impact of the intervention. For example, Valente and Bharath (1999) interviewed 100 randomly selected people who attended a 3-hour drama designed to improve knowledge about HIV/AIDS transmission. The same 100 persons were interviewed immediately after the drama, and an additional 100 persons were interviewed after the drama only. Results indicated that the drama increased knowledge by 26%. Comparison of the postdrama scores between those interviewed before and those not interviewed before provided an estimate of the effect of the intervention attributable to taking the pretest (3% in this case). Note that this design cannot distinguish how much of this difference was due to the pretest alone or due to a pretest/intervention interaction known as sensitization. The main limitations of Designs 1 through 3 are that they cannot measure the degree of change due to history or maturation or both, which are threats to validity that happen over time.

Design 4 enables the comparison of difference scores for both the treatment and the control groups and a computation of the difference of differences. Because Design 4 measures a group before and after the intervention that did not receive the intervention, the scores for the control group can be used to estimate the amount of change attributable to history and maturation. A classic example of Design 4 was conducted by Douglas, Westley, and Chaffee (1970) in a study that demonstrated the effectiveness of a campaign designed to change community attitudes toward community programs to help the disabled. They interviewed randomly selected respondents from two communities—one that was exposed to an informational campaign and one that was not. Results showed that the experimental community increased its positive attitude significantly more than did the comparison community. Design 4 enables researchers to subtract pretest scores from the posttest ones for both experimental and control groups and then subtract these differences from one another (the difference of differences). This value provides a measure of program effectiveness; it does not, however, control for testing and sensitization effects. That is, changes in scores for the intervention group may not be solely due to the intervention but, rather, due to the fact that the persons exposed to the intervention also took a pretest that may have sensitized them to the content of the intervention, making them more likely to change their behavior. It would be unclear, then, whether the intervention would have the same effect among people who did not take a pretest.

Design 5 adds a second intervention group that does not get pretested so as to control for the effects of the pretest sensitization. Design 5 is quite rigorous because it controls for most threats to validity. The only limitation to Design 5 is that it is restrictive in its ability to determine how much of the effects due to validity threats can be attributed to specific validity threats. For example, the post-only intervention groups may have scores comparable to those of the control group due to historical factors that the researcher wants to separate from those effects due to the pretest sensitization. As a hypothetical example, suppose a campaign was launched to improve knowledge on the harmful effects of substance abuse. Also suppose that a historical event such as the death of a famous person due to a drug overdose occurs during the study period. Comparisons of group scores will not be able to differentiate whether posttest scores changed due to the interaction between the program and the historical event or to interactions between the pretest and the historical event.

Design 6, the Solomon (1949) Four Group Design, adds a final control group that receives no intervention and no pretest survey. The Solomon Four Group design is the most rigorous because it controls for all threats to validity. These six study designs are usually implemented with panel samples because Designs 4 through 6 cannot be implemented with cross-sectional samples unless groups are used as the level of assignment, which requires large numbers of groups.

POWER

Once the study design is specified, researchers must determine the needed sample size to conduct the study. Available resources often determine the sample size used for a study because many studies have a fixed budget, and researchers often decide that they will spend a fixed amount for data collection and entry. Regardless of the available resources, it is prudent to conduct power analysis to determine (a) the appropriate sample size needed before the study is conducted and (b) the degree of reliability in the study results. *Power* is the ability of a statistical test to detect a significant association when such an association actually exists (i.e., avoiding Type II error) (Borenstein, Rothstein, & Cohen, 1997; Cohen, 1977; Kraemer & Thiemann, 1987).

For example, suppose a study finds that participants improved their knowledge 10% but reports that this increase was not statistically significant. Power analysis may show that the power is only 40%, meaning that of 100 tests conducted among this population and with this effect size, 40 of the tests would be considered significant, and that a larger population or greater control of other variables would reveal this effect size as significant. Thus, power was insufficient to reject the threat of Type II error and to enable the analysis to "find" the actual effect as statistically significant.

Power analysis consists of the interrelationship between four components of study design: (a) effect size (magnitude of difference, correlation coefficient, etc., also known as Δ); (b) significance level (Type I error or alpha level—usually .05 or .01); (c) sample size; and (d) power (Type II error or beta level—usually .80 or .90). These components are related to one another by power formulas (equations) so that if any three components are known, the fourth can be computed (Snedecor & Cochran, 1989). Thus, a researcher can determine minimum sample size needed for a study by specifying the expected or presumed effect size, the desired significance level, and the desired power.

The most common way to determine sample size is to first determine the magnitude of effect the campaign is expected to achieve, which is often calculated using theoretical assumptions or meta-analysis techniques (Durlak & Lipsey, 1991; Freimuth & Taylor, 1998; Hunter & Schmidt, 1990). In a meta-analysis of communication campaign effects, Snyder et al. (in press; see Chapter 10, this volume) found that the association between a campaign and the behavior being promoted was $r = .09$, which translated into an effect size of 8.6%. Given this estimated effect size and a decision regarding which test statistic will be used, the researcher can calculate the desired sample size needed for this effect size to be considered statistically significant before the study is conducted.

Other factors affect the final and thus optimal initial sample size: (a) survey response rates, (b) data collection type, (c) mortality in panel studies, (d) weighting schemes, and (e) adequate representation for subgroups. Once a researcher determines a minimum sample size needed based on power analysis, this number has to be increased to account for these other factors.

LEVELS OF ASSIGNMENT AND ANALYSIS

Many interventions are developed for specific communities or are tested in multiple communities before being scaled up to regional or national audiences. In many studies, certain communities (schools, organizations, towns, etc.) act as intervention sites, whereas other communities act as controls (Bertrand, Santiso, Linder, & Pineda, 1987; Rogers et al., 1999). Study designs in which the group is the unit of randomization are referred to as group-randomized trials (Murray, 1998). In group-randomized trials, data are collected on individual and sometimes appropriate group-level behavior, but because individuals are clustered into groups, researchers need to conduct their analysis in a manner that accounts for differences in variation between groups versus variation within groups. Generally, individuals in the same group will be more like one another (have less variation) than like individuals from different groups (have more variation). Given the group difference in variances, statistical clustering correction techniques such as the intraclass correlation should be used (Murray, 1998).

When impact studies are conducted using groups as the unit of assignment such that some groups or communities are exposed to the campaign and others serve as comparisons, the researcher can compute group-level values for the variables and conduct statistical analysis using the group as the unit of analysis (Kirkwood, Cousens, Victora, & de Zoysa, 1997). This analytic technique provides a test of program impact at the community level. This technique is not often used, however, because the number of communities used in any study is usually not very large and so the statistical tests will have few degrees of freedom (and low power). The advantage, however, is that most variable estimates will be accurate (have narrow variance estimates), and thus the likelihood of finding statistically significant differences increases (i.e., Type II error declines).

The more common analytic approach for community-based data is to create dummy variables indicating whether the respondent was in the intervention or control group. For example, when the campaign is broadcast in multiple communities, a variable is created that indicates which respondents were in intervention groups and which were in comparison groups. A statistical test such as analysis of variance (ANOVA) is conducted to determine whether outcomes were significantly different between conditions. If there are multiple conditions—for example, mass media supplemented with interpersonal persuasion—then a dummy variable is created with values for each condition, and differences across each condition are tested. Murray (1998) presented techniques that control for the within-group variations inherent in this analysis.

Many mass media campaigns cannot be restricted to intervention and control conditions because they are broadcast to an entire region or even to an entire country. In such cases, comparison between conditions is not possible, and the researcher has to rely on before-after surveys with independent or panel surveys. Although such designs, referred to as quasi-experimental, are usually considered less rigorous, evidence suggests (Freimuth & Taylor, 1998; Snyder et al., in press) that they still provide valid evaluations of campaign effects. The chief threat to validity for quasi-experimental campaign evaluations is that researchers have difficulty determining whether associations between program exposure and outcomes are genuine or spurious. In other words, respondents may report an increase in campaign exposure and state that they started a new behavior, but the researcher cannot determine whether campaign exposure preceded behavior change or vice versa.

To address the problem of spuriousness and other validity threats with cross-sectional data, researchers can (a) include a time variable to control for any secular trends and sample variations, (b) control for sociodemographic and other characteristics with multivariate statistical techniques, (c) create valid and reliable measures of campaign exposure (verified by process evaluation) that can be linked in a dose-response relationship (Jato et al., 1999), and (d) attempt to eliminate rival or alternative explanations. In panel studies, researchers can also do the previously mentioned activities, but they have the additional advantage of controlling for and measuring the influence of past behavior. A further recommendation in both panel and cross-sectional studies is to collect data from respondents on their recollections of exactly when or for how long they had been engaging in the behavior. Such data provide a link between self-reports and the timing of programmatic interventions. For example, in the Bolivia NRHP campaign (Valente & Saba, in press), we knew when the specific advertisements promoting contraceptive methods were broadcast, and we asked respondents how long they had been using their current contraceptive method. We linked the two pieces of information and found that the modal month that new adopters of contraceptives starting using their method was the same month that the TV and radio spots were broadcast.

No single methodological technique completely solves the spuriousness problem. The best approach is to start with a plausible theoretical model and use multiple sources of data at multiple points in time to construct a coherent explanation for a campaign's impact (or lack thereof).

CAMPAIGN EXPOSURE

A critical variable used to evaluate public communication campaigns is campaign exposure. *Campaign exposure* is the degree to which audience members have access to, recall, or recognize the intervention. High levels of campaign exposure can indicate that the message reached the audience. Campaign exposure measures are valued by programmers because they indicate whether the program was implemented as intended. Campaign exposure often provides the first step in a behavior change sequence and provides a necessary indicator to distinguish between program and theory failure. Note that process evaluation can help identify how much of the planned exposure or treatment is actually engaged by particular audiences (see Chapter 8, this volume).

As mentioned previously, analysis can determine whether there is an association between campaign exposure and outcomes. An association between exposure and outcomes, however, is a necessary but not a sufficient condition to show that the campaign caused the outcomes; rather, it is one piece of a causal linkage between campaign implementation and intended effect. Even within an appropriate research design, the main reason that an association between exposure and outcomes does not guarantee a causal linkage is that the audience members may selectively expose themselves to the campaign for a variety of reasons not related to the theorized impact process.

Selective exposure occurs when nonrandom and nonintervention factors influence who was exposed to the intervention (Zillman & Bryant, 1985). Many factors create selective exposure, including the fact that (a) some audience members already practice the behavior, (b) some people already intend to practice the behavior, and (c) some people may have differential media access and preferences. The researcher has to eliminate or reduce these competing factors (by study design or statistical analysis) before he or she can argue that the campaign caused the outcome. Random-controlled trials attempt to minimize selectivity and other validity threats through random assignment. In panel studies, many of these factors can be controlled because data are collected on the same individuals and prior behavioral states can be controlled.

INTERPERSONAL COMMUNICATION

Public communication campaigns can be very effective at stimulating interpersonal communication (Valente, Poppe, & Merritt, 1996). This interpersonal communication can be a nuisance to some evaluators because it often results in persons in the intervention group talking to people in the comparison groups and thus contaminating the research design. In fact, many campaign evaluations collect data immediately after the campaign is broadcast to maximize the degree that the respondents recall the campaign before it fades in their memory and to capture its impact before people can talk about and spread the effect beyond the boundaries of the intervention region.

Understanding how interpersonal influence and public campaigns complement one another, however, should be a major goal for campaign evaluators and incorporated explicitly in the design. Campaigns often stimulate interpersonal communication, but the impact of this media-generated communication will not be apparent until the information percolates through interpersonal networks and individuals have time to share their attitudes, experiences, and opinions with one another (Boulay, 2000; Valente, 1995).

Valente extended the two-step flow hypothesis (whereby media influence opinion leaders, who in turn influence others; Katz, 1957; Katz & Lazersfeld, 1955; Valente & Saba, 1998) by developing a threshold model in which the media influence those with low thresholds, who in turn influence others in their personal networks with higher thresholds (Valente, 1995, 1996; Valente & Saba, 1998). More generally, the characteristics of who talks to or influences whom within the context of communication campaigns warrant further investigation.

MEASURING IMPACT

A primary goal of evaluation research is to measure the effects, both anticipated and unanticipated, short and long term, individual and system level, of an intervention (see Chapter 8, this volume). If evaluators constructed an evaluation design before the program was launched, then baseline and comparison data exist to enable computation of indicators to measure impact. Often, the immediate impacts of a program are determined by assessing whether there has been a change in relevant variables that can be attributed to the campaign (i.e., theory success given program success). Typically, evaluators are testing a conceptual model similar to that depicted in Figure 6.2 in which the campaign is designed to change individual knowledge, attitudes, and practices.

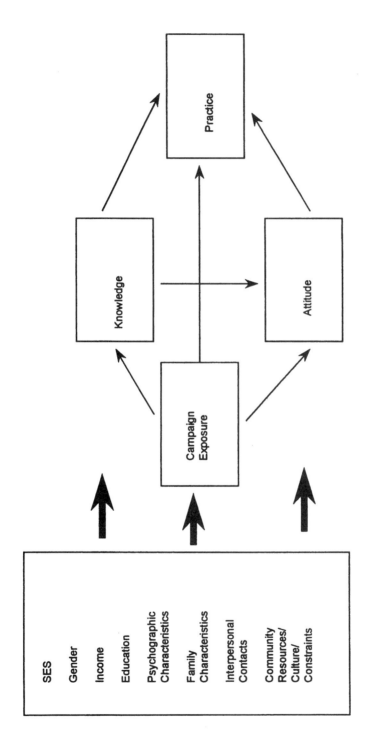

Figure 6.1. Conceptual Model of Campaign Impact

Table 6.2 Regression for Contraceptive Awareness (β) and Use (Adjusted Odds
Ratios [AORs]) on Demographic Characteristics, Campaign Exposure,
and Personal Network Exposure for Randomly Selected Urban Bolivians

| | Cross-Sectional Surveys (N = 4,620) | | Panel Surveys (N = 545) | |
| | Awareness (β) | Current-Use AOR | Awareness (β) | Current-Use AOR |
Measure				
Baseline	—	—	.18***	4.92***
Education	.34***	1.27***	.23***	1.16
Income	.13***	1.22***	.09*	0.86
Female	.08***	0.59***	.17***	0.65
Married	.03**	1.72***	−.02	0.67
Age	.01	−0.99*	.17***	0.99
Number of children	.02	1.03	−.12*	1.01
City prevalence	.02	1.17***	—	—
Time	−.06**	1.05	—	—
Network exposure	.16***	1.32***	.20***	1.50***
Campaign exposure	.15***	1.43	.13***	1.06
Adjusted R²	.22***	0.10***	.29***	0.15***

*p < .05; **p < .01; ***p < .001.

The researcher first determines whether outcomes have changed between
baseline and follow-up (e.g., with a *t* test). Change scores can then be computed and ANOVA tests conducted to determine whether change was different
for different demographic and socioeconomic groups, such as between males
and females. Typically, the researcher will then compute a regression equation
with the follow-up score as the dependent variable and the baseline and intermediate time period scores as independent variables (this is known as lagged
analysis) and include sociodemographic and system constraint variables as
controls. Importantly, campaign researchers should also include variables that
measure access to (or literacy of) the media channels over which the campaign
is disseminated (perhaps obtained through the process evaluation) and include
variables for campaign exposure (Valente, in press).

Table 6.2 reports the results from the Bolivia NRHP campaign evaluation
based on cross-sectional and panel samples of respondents interviewed before
and after the 9-month campaign. Two of the outcomes were an index of awareness of contraceptive methods and self-reported use of a modern method of
contraception (Valente & Saba, 1998). We hierarchically regressed method
awareness using ordinary least squares on (a) the sociodemographic variables
education, income, gender, marital status, age, and number of children; (b) city
method prevalence rate; (c) time (baseline or follow-up); (d) network exposure
(number of the respondent's network whom he or she thinks uses a contraceptive method); and (e) campaign exposure. We regressed contraceptive method

use using logistic regression (Hosmer & Lemeshow, 1989), because it is a dichotomous variable, on the same variables. Note that the panel data include the baseline variables, whereas the cross-sectional data include a variable for the time of the measure (i.e., baseline and follow-up).

For awareness, we report standardized beta coefficients so that we can compare the magnitude of the different independent variables' associations with method awareness. Education, income, being female, network, and campaign exposure were all significantly positively associated with method awareness in the cross-sectional data. Time had a slight negative association, which indicates that the follow-up sample had lower method awareness. For method use, we report adjusted odds ratios (AORs), which indicate the percentage change in the outcome for each unit change in the independent variable. All variables except number of children, time, and campaign exposure were associated with method use.

The panel data analysis showed similar results for method awareness, with the exception that age and number of children were also significantly associated with method awareness. Also, note that method awareness at baseline was significantly associated ($\beta = .18$, $p < .001$) with method awareness at follow-up. For contraceptive method use, the main variable associated with method use was method use at baseline (AOR $= 4.9$, $p < .001$). The AOR indicates that persons who used a method at baseline were 4.9 times more likely to use a method at follow-up than those who did not use a method at baseline. Notice that network exposure (the proportion of friends and family that the respondent thinks use contraceptive methods) was significantly associated with both knowledge and method use. Campaign exposure was significantly associated with method awareness but not with method use, indicating that the campaign influenced knowledge but did not directly influence use. This analysis lends support to an interpretation of the campaign's effect as indirectly influencing behavior through method awareness (but see Valente & Saba, 1998).

DISSEMINATION

Once the study has been completed, it is strongly recommended that the researcher disseminate the results. Dissemination (sometimes referred to as feedback or feed-forwarding) is often neglected in evaluation plans because researchers are preoccupied with planning and conducting the study and often believe that the results will speak for themselves. Moreover, it is difficult to anticipate the appropriate audiences and channels for dissemination before the findings are known.

Dissemination plans are needed because dissemination can be controversial. Controversy and conflict may emerge during dissemination of research results for several reasons. First, programmers and evaluators may disagree on the appropriate audience or the vehicle to disseminate the findings. For example, many researchers are interested in publishing the research results in prestigious, peer-reviewed journals, which can be time-consuming and may result in emphasis on the methodology, subtleties of the underlying theory, or particular results. In contrast, programmers are usually interested in immediately producing a report that looks good, is comprehensive, is understandable to a professional audience of other programmers and planners, and can lead to specific practice improvements.

Second, there is usually pressure for the evaluation findings to report something (if not many things) positive about the program. Programmers obviously want the evaluation to stress the successes of the project because it is, after all, partly an evaluation of their performance. The evaluator, of course, is interested in accurately reporting on the study results, regardless of the positive or negative effects that were detected. Finally, proper dissemination of findings requires resources usually earmarked for other activities.

Despite these potential controversies, the researcher is not only obligated but also well served by expending considerable effort in disseminating evaluation results. Evaluation findings can be disseminated in at least five ways: (a) via scheduled meetings with the programmers, (b) at scientific conferences relevant to the topic, (c) through key findings or technical reports, (d) via the Internet and World Wide Web, and (e) through academic papers published in refereed journals. Most campaigns not documented in evaluation reports are forgotten within a year or two.

SUMMARY

Public communication campaign evaluation represents an exciting intellectual opportunity to bridge behavioral theory with important practice. The value of these behavior change programs, however, is fundamentally dependent on determining who was reached, how the program influenced them, and how programs can be improved in the future. Without evaluation, the utility of implementing public communication campaigns is subject to debate, criticism, and even ridicule. Disseminating information to foster a more informed and hence more empowered populace represents a significant means to improve the quality of life for all. The challenge for communication campaign evaluators is to implement rigorous evaluations that advance the science of communication and simultaneously provide relevant information to the practice of communication.

REFERENCES

Bertrand, J. T., Santiso, R., Linder, S. H., & Pineda, M. A. (1987). Evaluation of a communications program to increase adoption of vasectomy in Guatemala. *Studies in Family Planning, 18,* 361-370.

Borenstein, M., Rothstein, H., & Cohen, J. (1997). *Power and precision: A computer program for statistical power analysis and confidence intervals.* Teaneck, NJ: Biostat.

Boruch, R. (1996). *Randomized experiments for planning and change.* Thousand Oaks, CA: Sage.

Boulay, M. (2000). *Indirect exposure to a mass media campaign.* Manuscript submitted for publication.

Campbell, D. T., & Stanley, J. C. (1963). *Experimental and quasi-experimental designs for research.* Boston: Houghton Mifflin.

Chen, H. T., & Rossi, P. H. (1983). Evaluating with sense: The theory-driven approach. *Evaluation Review, 7*(3), 283-302.

Cohen, J. (1977). *Statistical power analysis for the behavioral sciences* (rev. ed.). New York: Academic Press.

Cook, T. D., & Campbell, D. T. (1979). *Quasi-experimentation: Design and analysis issues for field settings.* Boston: Houghton Mifflin.

Douglas, D., Westley, B., & Chaffee, S. H. (1970). An information campaign that changed community attitudes. *Journalism Quarterly, 47,* 479-487.

Durlak, J. A., & Lipsey, M. W. (1991). A practitioner's guide to meta-analysis. *American Journal of Community Psychology, 19,* 291-332.

Freimuth, V. S., & Taylor, M. (1998). *Are mass mediated health campaigns effective? A review of the empirical evidence.* Paper prepared for the National Heart, Lung, and Blood Institute, National Institutes of Health, Bethesda, MD.

Guba, E. G., & Lincoln, Y. S. (1981). *Effective evaluation: Improving the usefulness of evaluation results through responsive and naturalistic approaches.* San Francisco: Jossey-Bass.

Hosmer, D. W., & Lemeshow, S. (1989). *Applied logistic regression.* New York: Wiley.

Hunter, J. E., & Schmidt, F. L. (1990). *Methods of meta-analysis.* Newbury Park, CA: Sage.

Jato, M., Simbakalia, C., Tarasevich, J., Awasum, D., Kihinga, C., & Ngirwamungu, E. (1999). The impact of multimedia family planning. *International Family Planning Perspectives, 25*(2), 60-67.

Katz, E. (1957). The two-step flow of communication: An up-to-date report on a hypothesis. *Public Opinion Quarterly, 21,* 61-78.

Katz, E., & Lazersfeld, P. (1955). *Personal influence.* New York: Free Press.

Kirkwood, B. R., Cousens, S. N., Victora, C. G., & de Zoysa, I. (1997). Issues in the design and interpretation of studies to evaluate the impact of community-based interventions. *Tropical Medicine and International Health, 2,* 1022-1029.

Kraemer, H. C., & Thiemann, S. (1987). *How many subjects? Statistical power analysis in research.* Newbury Park, CA: Sage.

Mohr, L. B. (1992). *Impact analysis for program evaluation.* Newbury Park, CA: Sage.

Murray, D. M. (1998). *Design and analysis of group-randomized trials.* New York: Oxford University Press.

Piotrow, P. T., Kincaid, D. L., Rimon, J., & Rinehart, W. (1997). *Health communication: Lessons for public health.* New York: Praeger.

Rogers, E. M., Vaughan, P. W., Swalehe, R. A., Rao, N., Svenkerud, P., Sood, S., & Alfred, K. (1999). Effects of an entertainment-education radio soap opera on family planning behavior in Tanzania. *Studies in Family Planning, 30,* 193-211.

Rossi, P. H., Freeman, H. E., & Lipsey, M. (1999). *Evaluation: A systematic approach.* Thousand Oaks, CA: Sage.

Shadish, W. R., Cook, T. D., & Leviton, L. C. (1991). *Foundations of program evaluation: Theories of practice.* Newbury Park, CA: Sage.

Shea, S., & Basch, C. E. (1990). A review of five major community-based cardiovascular disease prevention programs. Part II: Intervention strategies, evaluation methods, and results. *American Journal of Health Promotion, 4*(4), 279-287.

Snedecor, G. W., & Cochran, W. M. (1989). *Statistical methods* (8th ed.). Ames: Iowa State University Press.

Snyder, L. B., Hamilton, M. A., Mitchell, E. W., Kiwanuka-Tondo, J., Flemin-Milici, F., & Proctor, D. (in press). The effectiveness of mediated health communication campaigns: Meta-analysis of differences in adoption, prevention, and cessation behavior campaigns. In R. Carveth & J. Bryant (Eds.), *Meta-analysis of media effects.* Mahwah, NJ: Lawrence Erlbaum.

Solomon, R. L. (1949). An extension of control group design. *Psychological Bulletin, 46,* 137-150.

Valente, T. W. (1995). *Network models of the diffusion of innovations.* Cresskill, NJ: Hampton Press.

Valente, T. W. (1996). Social network thresholds in the diffusion of innovations. *Social Networks, 18,* 69-79.

Valente, T. W., & Bharath, U. (1999). An evaluation of the use of drama to communicate HIV/AIDS information. *AIDS Education and Prevention, 11,* 203-211.

Valente, T. W., Kim, Y. M., Lettenmaier, C., Glass, W., & Dibba, Y. (1994). Radio and the promotion of family planning in The Gambia. *International Family Perspectives Planning, 20*(3), 96-100.

Valente, T. W., Paredes, P., & Poppe, P. R. (1998). Matching the message to the process: Behavior change models and the KAP gap. *Human Communication Research, 24,* 366-385.

Valente, T. W., Poppe, P. R., Alva, M. E., de Briceno, V., & Cases, D. (1994). Street theater as a tool to reduce family planning misinformation. *International Quarterly of Community Health Education, 15*(3), 279-289.

Valente, T. W., Poppe, P. R., & Merritt, A. P. (1996). Mass media generated interpersonal communication as sources of information about family planning. *Journal of Health Communication, 1,* 259-273.

Valente, T. W., & Saba, W. P. (1998). Mass media and interpersonal influence in the Bolivia National Reproductive Health Campaign. *Communication Research, 25,* 96-124.

Valente, T. W., & Saba, W. P. (in press). Campaign recognition and interpersonal communication as factors in contraceptive use in Bolivia. *Communication Research.*

Weiss, C. (1972). *Evaluation research: Methods for assessing program effectiveness.* Englewood Cliffs, NJ: Prentice Hall.

Weiss, C. (1997). How can theory-based evaluation make greater headway? *Evaluation Review, 21,* 501-524.

Zillman, D., & Bryant, J. (Eds.). (1985). *Selective exposure to communication.* Hillsdale, NJ: Lawrence Erlbaum.

7

Formative Evaluation Research in Campaign Design

Charles K. Atkin
Vicki S. Freimuth

Public communication campaigns have achieved a mixed record of effectiveness in influencing health and prosocial behavior, as reflected by the array of cases cited in this book. A key determinant of success is the development of sophisticated strategies based on formative evaluation research.

Evaluation research seeks to answer questions about target audiences for a program or campaign, encompassing the collection of background information about audience orientations before initiating a campaign and assessment of the implementation and effectiveness during and after a campaign (Flay & Cook, 1989; see Chapter 6, this volume). According to Palmer (1981), *formative research* provides data and perspectives to improve messages during the course of creation. He divides this type of evaluation into two phases. The first involves *preproduction research,* "in which data are accumulated on audience characteristics that relate importantly to the medium, the message, and the situation within which the desired behavior will occur" (p. 227). The second type of formative research is *production testing,* also known as pretesting, in which prototype or pilot messages are tested to obtain audience reactions prior to final production.

Health campaigners do not regularly use systematic approaches at the preproduction stage, and many mass media campaign efforts proceed in the absence of a research foundation. Instead, messages tend to be produced in a haphazard fashion based on creative inspiration of copywriters and artists, patterned after the normative standards of the health campaign and advertising genres. Only minimal background information about the audience is used in devising message appeals and presentation styles, in selecting source spokespersons and channels, and in identifying specialized subgroups to be reached. Furthermore, the formulation of basic campaign goals and specific objectives is seldom based on research identifying priority areas of concentration and critical stages of the communication process that must be addressed.

In designing and implementing successful health campaigns, a disciplined approach requires that the campaign team perform a thorough situational analysis, develop a pragmatic strategic plan, and execute the creation and placement of messages in accordance with principles of effective media campaign practices, each based on appropriate research results.

Moreover, more diligent efforts are needed to improve the working relationship between campaign designers and evaluation researchers versus the media professionals who implement message creation and dissemination. A major role of the strategist in the collaborative process is to develop a framework for setting specifications and providing feedback as messages are prepared, channels are selected, and campaign interventions and messages are implemented.

This approach is seldom fully practiced because many organizations that sponsor health campaigns (and campaign designers) succumb to various irresistible temptations: They are occasionally contemptuous (regarding the focal segment as misbehavers who are ignorant and misguided), righteous (admonishing unhealthy people about their incorrect behavior), extremist (rigidly advocating unpalatable ideals of healthy behavior), politically correct (staying within tightly prescribed boundaries of propriety to avoid offending overly sensitive authorities and interest groups), colleague oriented (seeking to impress professional peers and overly reliant on normative practices for the genre), or self-indulgent (attempting sophisticated executions in which creativity and style overwhelm substantive content considerations).

Thus, campaigns tend to overemphasize creative self-expression, clever sloganeering, artistic production values, celebrity spokespersons, exciting visual channels, and powerful fear appeals threatening severe harm. This approach can occasionally produce creatively brilliant messages that win awards and generate positive reactions from the audience, but the overall campaign does not necessarily contribute to changes in health behavior.

It should be kept in mind that public service campaigns differ from other media forms, such as news and entertainment, because the messages are purposively focused on achieving changes in knowledge, attitudes, and behavior. In many respects, campaigns in the health and prosocial domains are similar to commercial advertising campaigns. It is useful to adapt concepts from the social marketing perspective, which emphasizes an audience-centered consumer orientation and calculated attempts to package the social product and use the optimum combination of components to attain pragmatic goals (see Chapter 27, this volume). Because it is more difficult to sell healthy practices than commercial goods, there is even a greater need for health campaigners to exercise pragmatic self-discipline.

Health specialists are not always conscious of the fact that they differ substantially from their audiences in knowledge, values, priorities, and level of involvement; therefore, they lack the perspective of the "average" person. Research data from samples of the target audiences can help overcome the gulf between sender and receiver.

The campaign designer must adeptly consider and respond to audience resistance barriers at each stage of response, from exposure to processing, learning, yielding, and behavioral implementation. Perhaps the most elemental problem is reaching the audience and attaining attention to the messages. Other key barriers include misperception of susceptibility to negative outcomes, deflection of persuasive appeals, denial of applicability to self, rejection of unpalatable recommendations, and inertia.

In particular, campaign designers need to be vigilant of unintended side effects that run counter to the campaign objectives or that undermine other health practices. Avoiding undesired responses and unintended negative outcomes, including the boomerang effect (see Chapters 2 and 9, this volume), requires careful formative evaluation inputs, both preproduction information gathering and rough message pretesting.

There are more important issues involving counterproductive problem shifting across the health problems. For example, if adolescents are successfully scared away from marijuana, they may drink more alcohol because it is viewed as relatively less harmful. If teenage drinkers adopt the heavily promoted designated driver practice (see Chapter 21, this volume), it may disinhibit drunkenness among their nondriving companions. If teenage drivers are convinced that safety belts will protect them, they may drive faster and suffer high-speed crashes. More fundamentally, the conventional campaign focus on individual behavior change puts the onus of responsibility on the "victim" while deflecting attention from social and structural determinants of the health problem (see Chapters 4, 9, and 31, this volume).

This chapter provides a conceptual framework explaining why formative evaluation research is a valuable resource in developing more effective health campaigns, describes the two phases of formative research (preproduction and pilot testing), and illustrates the preproduction process in the case of drunk driving prevention.

CONCEPTUAL FRAMEWORK
FOR CAMPAIGN PERSUASION

The conventional approach to designing persuasion strategies involves separating the communication process into source, message, channel, and receiver variables as inputs and a series of information processing and response variables as outcomes. One widely used model is McGuire's input-output matrix, which includes the four variables mentioned previously along with destination factors on the input side of the matrix (see Chapter 2, this volume).

The source, message, and channel components are manipulable by the campaign designer. The source concept includes both the messenger who delivers the message and the organization that sponsors the message, which can be characterized in terms of demographics (age, sex, and socioeconomic status), credibility (expertise and trustworthiness), and attractiveness. Each message can feature a variety of content dimensions (themes, appeals, claims, evidence, and recommendations) using various formats of organization and styles of packaging; the overall series of messages in a campaign can vary in volume, repetition, prominence of placement, and scheduling. The channel variables comprise both the medium of transmission (television, radio, newspapers, magazines, booklets, and web sites) and the particular media vehicle (e.g., specific radio station or magazine title).

Although receiver factors are not subject to manipulation, sensitivity to the background attributes, abilities, and predispositions of individuals enhances the effectiveness of campaign stimuli. Finally, the destination encompasses the array of impacts that the campaign aims to produce, such as immediate versus long-term change, prevention versus cessation, direct versus two-step flow of influence, and intermediate responses versus ultimate behavioral outcomes (see Chapter 8, this volume).

The output variables have been conceptualized in many ways, typically beginning with exposure and processing, followed by the hierarchy of cognitive, affective, and behavioral consequences of the campaign inputs. Combining elements from various models, this chapter proposes that receivers move through five basic stages, each with several substeps. The first is *exposure,* which includes encountering the stimulus and paying attention to it. The next stage is *information processing,* including comprehension of the content, selective perception of source and appeals, and evaluative reactions such as liking, agreeing, and counterarguing. The third stage is *cognitive learning,* which involves knowledge gain and skills acquisition. Fourth, the *yielding* stage encompasses the formation or change of affective orientations, such as beliefs, saliences, values, attitudes, and behavioral intentions. Finally, a *utilization* stage includes retrieval and proximate motivation, the action itself, postbehavioral consolidation, and long-run continuation and maintenance of the practice.

Considering the dynamic forces that explain how campaign inputs and individual predispositions move the audience through the output stages, several social psychological theories are relevant to mediated campaigns on topics such as health. The instrumental learning perspective of Hovland, Janis, and Kelley (1953) focuses attention on factors such as source credibility, the incentives in the message appeal, and repetition. The social cognitive approach articulated by Bandura (1986) emphasizes the importance of the characteristics of source role models, the explicit demonstration of target behaviors, and the depiction of vicarious positive and negative reinforcements. The cognitive response perspective focuses on the thoughts that the receiver generates while processing messages (Petty & Cacioppo, 1986); the individual actively relates content to prior knowledge and experience and forms new connections or arguments (see Chapters 5 and 12, this volume).

Most pertinent are expectancy-value formulations, particularly the Ajzen and Fishbein (1980) theory of reasoned action. Their model stresses the role of beliefs concerning the likelihood that performance of a behavior leads to certain consequences that, when combined with evaluations of the outcomes, determine the attitude. Another feature of their model is the influence of subjective norms, based on beliefs about the orientations of particular referent groups or persons toward the behavior. Also relevant to microlevel processes in health persuasion are concepts from the Health Belief Model (Janz & Becker, 1984; Rosenstock, 1990), protection motivation theory (Rogers, 1983), the Stages of Change Model (Prochaska & DiClemente, 1983), and self-efficacy theory (Bandura, 1977). This brief overview of the campaign influence variables suggests some types of information that should be obtained to facilitate campaign planning.

PREPRODUCTION RESEARCH

In preproduction formative evaluation research, the strategist attempts to learn as much as possible about the intended audience and community before specifying goals and devising strategies (see Chapters 8 and 27, this volume). The campaign designer needs to identify target audiences and target behaviors, specify critical intermediate response variables, ascertain channel exposure patterns, and determine receptivity to potential message components. Atkin (see Chapter 3, this volume) and McGuire (see Chapter 2, this volume) identify the key factors in campaign and message design.

To collect these kinds of information, two research techniques are most commonly employed at the preproduction stage (see Chapter 4, this volume). Focus group sessions are conducted by a moderator who stimulates extensive open-ended discussions of selected issues in a small group setting. More quantitative data are provided by formal sample surveys of audience members using standardized questionnaires or interview schedules to measure a broad array of variables systematically.

The preproduction stage of the formative research process will be illustrated in the following sections with selected findings from a series of surveys and supplemental focus group interviews of teenagers, parents, college students, party hosts, and the general adult public on the subject of drunk driving prevention (Atkin, Garramone, & Anderson, 1986).

Identifying the Target Audiences

Effective campaigns seldom aim at a broad cross section of the public; instead, they focus on specialized segments of the overall audience. Formative research is useful in identifying the high-priority target subgroups by providing data regarding which categories of individuals are at risk, which are most receptive to media persuasion on the topic, and which are in a position to influence high-risk persons interpersonally.

Survey measures with representative samples (as well as preexisting media, demographic, psychographic, census, and consumer data) are typically used to segment the audience along many dimensions defined in terms of demographic and psychographic characteristics, social role position, behavioral risk profile predispositions, future behavioral intentions, and media exposure patterns.

In the case of drunk driving, the surveys show that 16- to 24-year-old males who drink heavily at weekend parties are far more likely than other groups to drive while intoxicated or ride with a drunk driver; this high-risk segment constitutes less than 5% of the population. The research also indicates that several other target audiences display promising potential for attempting interpersonal intervention to prevent drunk driving: parents of high school students (who can prohibit their teenagers from attending unsupervised drinking parties), adult party hosts (who can discourage excessive drinking by guests or arrange alternative transportation for intoxicated drivers), and female passengers riding with heavy-drinking dates or mates (who can warn their drivers not to overconsume or take over the driving role on the ride home). In terms of receptivity, parents are an example of a favorably predisposed segment; the data show that most disapprove of teenage drinking, believe that teenage drunk driving is a serious problem, and desire to know techniques to prevent their sons or daughters from becoming involved in drunk driving incidents.

Specifying the Target Behavior

The ultimate goal of a campaign is typically behavioral change, such as reduction in the incidence of drunk driving. Most practices, however, are a product of various component behaviors (e.g., drunk driving may be reduced if the driver abstains from alcohol, drinks limited quantities, or allows a sober person to drive home), which in turn are determined by social and environmental factors (e.g., availability of attractive nonalcoholic drinks, suggestions by companions to limit consumption, or inaccurate perceptions of social norms concerning drinking). Formative research is helpful in specifying which particular behaviors and external factors are most influential in altering the focal practices and which are most amenable to change via campaign messages; these variables are then incorporated as concrete objectives in the campaign plan.

In the case of social intervention to prevent drunk driving, survey research reveals two examples of priority target behaviors. One potentially effective tactic is to encourage the female passenger to drive the car back from a drinking occasion because data show that women tend to become less intoxicated than their male drivers, and yet most allow the male to drive. Findings also indicate that half of young adults planning to ride home from a party with the person who drove them to the party hesitate to put pressure on that person to remain sober enough to drive safely, whereas most drivers say they would respond cooperatively to such dissuasion by cutting back on consumption; thus, an important target behavior is more frequent influence attempts by companions to prevent their driver from exceeding the safe drinking limit.

Regarding target audience receptiveness to behavioral recommendations, the survey of party hosts asked the sample to rate 22 potential hosting techniques in terms of acceptability (how comfortable they would feel in using each strategy and how offensive they believed each strategy would be regarded by guests). Results indicated that many effective techniques are rated as highly acceptable (e.g., actively offering food to drinkers, arranging for another guest to drive an intoxicated person home, and expressing concern that a driver is drinking too much), whereas other actions are disdained (e.g., having guests check-in their car keys on arrival, warning drinking drivers about accident risks, and stopping service of alcohol 2 hours before the party's end). Such formative evaluation data enable designers to narrow the list to the most promising techniques and to isolate which less acceptable but critically important behaviors would require extra persuasive emphasis to be changed.

Elaborating Intermediate Responses

As a means to attaining the behavioral objectives, campaign messages must first have an impact on preliminary or intermediate target variables along the response chain, ranging from exposure and processing to learning and yielding and actual utilization. In particular, campaign designers must overcome individual resistance characteristics such as misconceptions, dysfunctional attitudes, and behavioral inhibitions. Isolation of the most crucial response stages is facilitated by an understanding of the characteristics and predispositions of the target audience. Focus groups and sample surveys are both valuable tools providing topic-specific background information for mapping the domains discussed here.

Knowledge and Lexicon

Research illuminates the target audience's entry-level awareness and information holding about the subject of the campaign, identifying what is already known, what gaps exist, what confusions must be clarified, and what misinformation must be corrected (see Chapter 4, this volume); the level of familiarity with and comprehension of topic-related vocabulary and terminology can also be ascertained. For example, only one fourth of the surveyed drinkers knew the legal blood alcohol level (0.10%) that would result in arrest for driving under the influence, just half realized that eating food before drinking substantially reduces intoxication, and one fifth incorrectly thought that drinking coffee helps to sober up a driver. The surveys show that people have diverse meanings for key terms such as "social drinker" and "moderation," diverse labels for the state of intoxication, and limited understanding of concepts such as intervention and designated driver.

Beliefs and Images

Because many campaign message strategies seek to alter subjective conceptions such as perceived social norms or estimated probability of outcomes associated with the behavioral practice, it is important to measure precisely the preexisting cognitive orientations held by individuals. For example, data show that drinkers underestimate the degree of social disapproval of drunk driving (two fifths believe that others excuse drunk driving, whereas just 5% of the public is actually tolerant; see Chapter 22, this volume) and overestimate the statistical risks of both crashes and police apprehension (the typical driver perceives that the odds of arrest while driving drunk on a given evening are 1 in 100, whereas police data indicate the chances are 1 in 2,000). This tells a strategist that messages should feature information about social norms but should not emphasize facts about arrest probability.

Attitudes and Values

Affective predispositions are also a significant consideration in message design, particularly evaluations of outcomes associated with practices. Depending on the direction, intensity, and structure of relevant values and attitudes, the campaign may concentrate on creation, conversion, reinforcement, or activation. Reinforcement and activation are appropriate for most drivers, who already hold a negative attitudinal set toward the act of drunk driving and regard the crash and apprehension consequences as undesirable. Thus, messages that intensify the negativity of outcomes (e.g., monetary costs of conviction or difficulty of coping without a license) appear to be promising. The research shows, however, that most men dismiss the embarrassment or threat to masculinity resulting from a wife or girlfriend driving them home, indicating that this presumed obstacle need not be addressed in campaign appeals.

Salience Priorities

Research also provides guidance concerning which cognitive and affective orientations need to be made more or less salient. Because most drivers already believe that there is a substantial risk of crash involvement, but only one fourth consciously contemplate this possibility, increasing the salience of this outcome would lead drivers to give it greater weight relative to other factors when setting a limit or deciding whether or not to consume additional drinks. In contrast, the vast majority regard drunk driving as a serious problem in society, indicating little need for campaigning designed to raise this issue on the public's agenda (on issue agendas, see Chapters 2 and 31, this volume).

Efficacy and Skills

For certain practices, many well-intentioned and highly motivated individuals fail to carry out appropriate acts because they lack confidence in their ability to perform the behaviors competently. For example, some people might be inhibited about taking the car keys from an impaired friend. Survey findings demonstrate that although most companions agree that it is important to help drivers limit consumption and to prevent intoxicated friends from driving, many of them wish they knew better techniques for discouraging excessive drinking or handling a drunk friend who insists on driving. If research shows that this is a barrier, messages can seek to enhance personal efficacy or provide training for specific skills.

Ascertaining Channel Use

In deciding which channels are most efficient and effective for disseminating campaign messages, strategists need to determine the mass media preferences and interpersonal communication patterns of target audiences. Although many basic exposure data are available from commercial audience measurement services such as Nielsen, customized surveys provide a much more elaborate and relevant array of data.

At a general level, it is useful to know the following information about the intended receivers: amount of time spent watching television, listening to radio, reading magazines and newspapers, and surfing the Internet; usage of specific media vehicles (local radio stations and magazine titles); attention to various types of media content (news and public service messages); exposure to secondary channels (movie theater slides, pamphlets, direct mail, billboards, bumper stickers, posters, and matchbooks); and interpersonal contact networks.

Topic-specific data are more pertinent to campaign planning: consumption of media content presenting subject matter that complements or competes with campaign messages (product ads, news items, feature stories, entertainment portrayals, and web sites), interpersonal communication about topic (interactions with opinion leaders, informal conversations, and peer pressures), and exposure to prior campaign messages (attention to topical public service announcements [PSAs] and posters).

In addition to sheer exposure, formative researchers can obtain credibility ratings for media channels, vehicles, and content categories, measure audience recall, and evaluate reactions to messages disseminated in previous campaigns. For example, the drunk driving surveys found that teenage male drinkers tend to listen to rock music stations, whereas adult party hosts are heavy readers of local newspapers; the typical person is exposed each day to a dozen prodrinking portrayals in beer commercials and prime-time television shows and to several depictions of risky driving behavior in crime dramas; one fourth of adults have tried to discourage a drunk person verbally from driving; teenage drivers perceive moderately strong peer pressure to avoid getting drunk if driving; young adults pay attention to an average of two antidrunk driving TV PSAs per week but see almost no promoderation spots; more than half the public has noticed news stories about local police efforts to catch drunk drivers, and most of these people report being more likely to drink safely or warn companions as a result of the publicity; and many teenage drinkers discredit safety threats featured in PSAs.

Preliminary Evaluation of Message Components

Before campaign stimuli are drafted, strategic and creative approaches are facilitated by both informal feedback and formal ratings for prospective source presenters, message themes, persuasive arguments, and stylistic devices. In the drunk driving project, focus group discussions explored reactions to altruistic versus fear appeals for motivating intervention attempts and examined the appropriateness of humorous versus serious treatment of the subject. Survey questionnaires presented a listing of several dozen spokespersons, arguments, and claims under consideration for campaign messages; believability and effectiveness scores for each component were measured on a scale from 0 to 10.

Armed with the background information collected in the preproduction phase of campaign design, the strategy and research specialists are in a position to work with creative personnel in formulating potential message ideas (and specific headlines, slogans, copy points, layouts, formats, artwork, music, and special effects), selecting visible source presenter talent to appear in the messages, and determining the most appropriate media for communicating the material (such as the telenovelas or rock music videos discussed in Chapter 28, this volume).

Database Resources for Preproduction

There are a wide variety of governmental and commercial data resources available for audience segmentation research, including those discussed in the following sections.

Prizm Lifestyle Segmentation Data

This is a system of integrated data sets and software for statistical analysis, reporting, charting, and mapping available from Claritas, Inc., including

1. U.S. census data on sociodemographic variables for all block groups and higher levels of census geography (tracts, counties, metropolitan statistical areas, states, and nation). The data are also available by ZIP code geography and A. C. Nielsen Designated Market Area geography, which encompasses television markets. An annual proprietary update of all items is conducted by Claritas.
2. Cartographic data on features for geographic information system analysis.
3. Market research data on 20,000 respondents annually from Simmons Market Research Bureau Study of Media and Markets (SMM) on consumer behavior and lifestyle, including Magazines, Lifestyle, Television, Media Usage, General Product Usage, and Financial Product Usage.
4. User-supplied data on variables relevant to particular (health-related) problems, such as AIDS incidence by ZIP code.

Data integration is achieved through a link between geographic areas and Prizm lifestyle clusters. Every block group, census tract, and ZIP code in the United States can be classified into 1 of 62 neighborhood types or lifestyle segments (clusters) in the Prizm segmentation framework. Any item in these integrated data sets associated with a public health issue, a demographic characteristic, a geographic area, a consumer behavior, or a user-supplied health variable can be linked to information in the other data sets to address questions such as the following: Who are the target audiences? What are they like? Where are they? and How can they be reached? COMPASS software and Claritas Mapping are used to conduct the analyses.

American Healthstyles Data

This survey-based data set combines health behavior and communication-relevant questions with general lifestyle, sociopolitical, and media usage questions to provide a comprehensive understanding of potential audiences. The mail questionnaire contains five core health areas: smoking, alcohol use, exercise, diet and nutrition, and weight control. The items are based on theories of health behavior and are designed to measure outcome expectations, self-efficacy, motivation, personal goals and behavioral intentions, perceptions of social norms, and social support. In addition, an advisory panel with representatives from a variety of health organizations makes recommendations on topical areas to be included in the survey. The survey is conducted for Porter Novelli by Market Facts, Inc., in conjunction with the annual DDB Needham Lifestyles Survey. The lifestyles survey employs quota sampling from a consumer mail panel of 500,000 persons to generate a list of 5,000 adults who are representative of all U.S. adults, stratified by age, sex, marital status, race and ethnicity, income, region, household size, and population density. The Healthstyles survey is administered annually to between 2,500 and 3,000 respondents to the Lifestyle Survey.

American Youthstyles Data

This survey-based data set, collected via questionnaire, provides information on health behavior and communication-relevant items for middle school and high school students. The questionnaire includes items on health behaviors and attitudes as well as general interests, social relationships, and psychographic self-concept ratings. The planned sample size is 3,000 middle school and 3,000 high school respondents. The survey is conducted for Porter Novelli by Audit Systems Worldwide.

Simmons Teenage Research Study Data

This data set contains information on a wide range of consumer behaviors and lifestyle characteristics for persons 18 years old and younger. It includes information on print and broadcast media usage, product usage, lifestyle, and psychographics. Simmons Teenage Research Study data are obtained through a national probability sample of teenagers in households that participated in the Simmons SMM data collection described previously. The data are collected through interviews and questionnaires. The current data set contains information from 2,373 respondents.

PRETESTING RESEARCH

The second basic phase of formative evaluation is pretesting, the process of systematically gathering target audience reactions to preliminary versions of messages before they are produced in final form (U.S. Department of Health and Human Services [DHHS], 1992). Pretesting can help determine which of several alternative ideas or draft messages are most effective, or it can identify strengths and weaknesses in single messages. Pretesting research is used at two stages in message creation: concept development and message execution.

Developing the Concept

Concepts are partially formulated message ideas consisting of visual sketches and key phrases that convey the main elements to be represented in the finished product. Pretesting at this stage provides direction for eliminating weaker approaches and identifying the most promising concepts, saving considerable time and money during production. Sometimes, entirely new concepts emerge from audience responses, whereas original ideas are revised and refined. Another advantage to pretesting rough concepts is the generation of words, phrases, and vernacular used by the target audience so that appropriate language can be used in formulating complete messages. For example, pathologists believed that a lay description of the symptoms of melanoma (a form of skin cancer) should be "notched, blue-black, irregular spots." Interviews with members of the target population, however, suggested different adjectives. When shown pictures of the symptoms, respondents' descriptions included "looks like a bad sunburn," "a small rash," "blotchy," or "a bad scrape" (DHHS, 1984; see also Chapter 4, this volume).

Creating the Test Message

Complete messages can then be created in rough form for the next stage of pretesting: message execution. Rough executions of televised PSAs may include *animatics* (motion is simulated by sequentially videotaping or filming artwork, storyboards, or cartoon frames that realistically represent the planned final product), *photomatic spots* (simulate motion through the sequential videotaping or filming of a minimum of eight still-frame photographs), or a *rough live-action spot* (an actual "run-through" of the spot filmed or videotaped using simplified sets, nonprofessional talent, and preliminary audio tracks). Radio PSAs and print materials can also be prepared for testing in rough form. If music or sound effects will be used in the final audio product, they should also be included in the rough message.

At this stage, pretesting can be used to predict how effectively a message will move the target audience through the five basic stages of reaction to campaign stimuli discussed earlier by (a) assessing the attention value of a message, (b) measuring its comprehensibility, (c) determining its relevance to the target audience, (d) identifying strengths and weaknesses, and (e) gauging any sensitive or controversial elements.

Assessing Attention

An essential ingredient of messages is their ability to attract the target audience's attention in the context of competing media and messages. Typically, after exposure to a clutter format of five to seven spot messages placed within an entertainment program, the audience is asked to list all the ads or public service messages they remember seeing. More direct observational methods have also been used to assess attention, especially with very young children. Children's Television Workshop has used the distracter method, which measures attention by observing whether children are focused on the program or on a competing stimulus—one measure of program appeal. In the most recent version of this method, if children watch at least half of a segment of a complete show, then that segment receives an "eyes-on-screen" score. Observational data are also gathered about the children's verbal comments, their singing and dancing in response to the show, and off-task activities such as talking or playing with their friends. Finally, these observations are followed with one-on-one interviews to test for comprehension and appeal.

Measuring Comprehension

Messages must be understood before they can be processed and accepted. Procedures for measuring comprehension range from highly structured, closed-ended questions to open-ended requests for recall of main ideas. For example, the rough form of a PSA on teenage smoking used "balloons" similar to those found in cartoon strips to represent the characters' thoughts. During pretesting, it was discovered that this approach confused the audience, so the balloons were dropped from the finished spot.

Identifying Strong and Weak Points

Pretesting prior to final production and distribution can help ensure that each element of a message is likely to meet the information needs of the audience. For example, messages promoting long-term compliance with high blood pressure medication regimens have been pretested and found to have some weaknesses. First, there was a question as to whether the most important point in the messages—the need for daily medication—was understood to be about medication for hypertension or simply to be about the need for medication in general, as prescribed for any illness. Second, respondents had trouble understanding the jingle lyrics even after two exposures. As a result, these PSAs were changed by clarifying the specific need for daily antihypertension medication and by rearranging the musical delivery (DHHS, 1984).

Determining Personal Relevance

Target audiences must perceive that a message personally applies to them for the message to be effective. Pretest results for a booklet on high blood pressure revealed that hypertensives recalled and understood more specific points related to high blood pressure control than did the general audience group. Furthermore, when asked for whom the booklet was intended, a higher proportion of hypertensives believed the booklet was "talking to someone like me" (DHHS, 1984).

Gauging Sensitive or Controversial Elements

Pretesting can help in determining whether messages may alienate or offend target audiences, often rejecting sponsors' or interest groups' assumptions about the general public's responses.

TYPES OF PRETESTING

The following sections summarize a variety of pretesting techniques in developing public service messages: (a) focus group interviews, (b) individual in-depth interviews, (c) central-location intercept interviews, (d) brief surveys, (e) self-administered questionnaires, (f) theater testing, (g) day-after recall, and (h) other approaches.

Focus Group Interviews

Focus group interviews are a form of qualitative research adapted by marketing researchers from group therapy (Krueger, 1994; Stewart & Shamdasani, 1990). They are conducted with a group of approximately 8 to 10 respondents simultaneously. Using a discussion outline, a moderator keeps the session on track while allowing respondents to talk freely and spontaneously. As new topics related to the outline emerge, the moderator probes further to gain useful insights. Focus groups are a very flexible formative research method. We have conducted groups in animal sheds, sitting on straw in Africa, via telephone, over the Internet, and in sophisticated facilities with one-way mirrors and video cameras in large cities. On-line focus groups can be held in a modified "chat room." Respondents may be recruited by phone or e-mail and log on to a designated web site at a certain prearranged time. Once in the "room," the participant's screen is usually divided into two sides: One side has the text of the discussion and the other shows messages and materials. In addition to obvious lower costs due to eliminating expenses for travel, food, and renting facilities, chat discussion "threads" create an instant transcription, although they lack the in-depth emotional information obtained by personally observing the participants (Heckman, 2000).

Focus group interviews provide insights into target audience beliefs on an issue, allow program planners to obtain perceptions of message concepts, and help trigger the creative thinking of communication professionals. The group discussion stimulates respondents to talk freely, providing valuable clues for developing materials in the consumers' language.

As with any qualitative research approach, however, care must be taken not to interpret focus group interview results quantitatively; focus group testing is indicative, not definitive. As with all pretesting research, focus group respondents should be typical of the intended target audience. Subgroups within the target audience representing relevant positions on the issues should be included, usually in separate focus groups. For example, in testing message concepts on smoking aimed at a general audience of smokers, a cross section of individuals—males and females, heavy and light smokers, and older and younger—might be recruited for the groups.

An experienced, capable moderator should lead the groups. The moderator must be well informed about the subject and the purpose of the group sessions.

A good moderator builds rapport and trust and should probe respondents without reacting to and thereby influencing their opinions. A good moderator keeps the discussion on track while talking as little as possible and makes it clear that he or she is not an expert on the subject under discussion (Krueger, 1994; Stewart & Shamdasani, 1990).

Individual In-Depth Interviews

Individual in-depth interviews are used for pretesting issues that are very sensitive or must be probed very deeply and for respondents who are difficult to recruit for focus group interviews, such as physicians, dentists, and chief executive officers. Such interviews can be quite long, lasting from 30 minutes to 1 hour, and are used to assess comprehension as well as feelings, emotions, attitudes, and prejudices. Although in-depth interviews are very costly and time-consuming, they may be the most appropriate form of pretesting for sensitive subjects (e.g., breast reconstruction) (see Chapter 4, this volume).

Central-Location Intercept Interviews

Central-location intercept interviews involve stationing interviewers at a location frequented by individuals from desired target audiences and, after asking a few screening questions, asking qualified respondents to participate in the pretest. If they are willing to participate, respondents are taken to the interviewing station, shown the pretest messages, and asked a series of questions to assess their reactions to the message concepts or executions. One advantage to this type of pretesting is that a high traffic area can yield many interviews in a reasonably short time. For instance, low-income women who were enrolled in the Special Supplemental Nutrition Program for Women and Children were recruited during food voucher distribution so that large numbers of participants were available for interviewing. The interviews took only 10 minutes, and very few women refused to participate (Treiman et al., 1996). The second advantage is that using a central location for hard-to-reach target audiences can be a cost-effective means of gathering data. For example, in Africa, an official check-in station was used to pretest HIV messages designed for long-distance truck drivers. As with focus groups, sampling is not random, and the results cannot be generalized to a larger population. A significant disadvantage of this pretesting method is the lack of camouflage; because respondents know they are participating in a test, their responses may be less valid.

New technology has enhanced the way this method can be used for pretesting. The National Youth Anti-Drug Media Campaign uses touch-screen multimedia methodology to pretest its antidrug messages. Questions are administered on screen (with voice-over support), and responses are recorded via a 21-inch touch-screen monitor, with all verbal responses digitally recorded for playback and transcription purposes. Respondents can proceed through the interview at their own pace, free of any risk of interviewer bias; confidentiality and anonymity are enhanced because no interviewer is present; and visual cues can be added to questions (showing pictures of beer, tobacco, and drugs to illustrate "gateway drugs") (Office of National Drug Control Policy, 1998).

Self-Administered Questionnaires

Self-administered questionnaires can also be used to pretest concepts and rough messages. These questionnaires can be mailed to respondents along with pretest materials or distributed at a central location. Each respondent is asked to review the materials, complete the questionnaire, and return it by a certain date. The Internet has enhanced the use of this method. It is now possible to conduct these tests on a web site, which speeds up the data collection process and encourages more participation because it is easier for respondents to answer. For example, a large organization used this approach to pretest new logo designs and taglines. Although the use of self-administered questionnaires is relatively inexpensive, they do have several disadvantages. First, response rate may be very low, even with several follow-up contacts. Second, only individuals who love or hate the pretest materials may respond, resulting in a systematic bias in the pretest results and possibly in the completed message.

Brief Surveys

An efficient approach for assessing audience responses to messages is a two-page questionnaire that can be administered following exposure to a specimen message (e.g., TV spot, pamphlet, or web page). The instrument measures the perceived effectiveness of the message for producing an impact on a target audience (e.g., "How effective is this message in influencing college students to avoid driving drunk?" with response categories such as Very Effective, Fairly Effective, Slightly Effective, and Not Effective) and overall rating of the message (Excellent, Good, Fair, and Poor).

Then, respondents are asked to evaluate the message along perhaps a dozen qualitative dimensions on a numerical scale ("What is your personal reaction to the message? Give ratings using a scale from 0 to 10 [with 10 being the highest score] on each of these factors"). Typical factors and accompanying definitions include *informative* (tells you something new and increases your knowledge), *sensible* (presents wise advice that seems reasonable), *memorable* (vivid image, fascinating fact, and catchy slogan), *enjoyable* (interesting, entertaining, and stimulating message), *useful* (valuable information and helpful advice worth remembering), *imaginative* (style is refreshing, novel, unique, and clever), *believable* (accurate information and sincere/trustworthy characters are used who know what they are talking about), *convincing* (presents ideas with which you agree), *professional* (production quality is high), *moti-*

vating (presents influential reasons to prompt change in behavior), and *on-target* (content is personally meaningful and people and situations are used with which you can identify).

Next, respondents provide assessments of "whether or not the message has any of these negative features" using a simple yes/no response to a series of question on factors such as the following: *preachy* ("Was the tone of message too moralistic or righteous?"), *disturbing* ("Were you turned off because it is too emotional or threatening?"), *confusing* ("Is anything unclear, vague, or difficult to understand?"), *irritating* ("Did you find anything offensive or annoying?"), *dull* ("Was the style boring, stale, or trite?"), *misleading* ("Were there any biased arguments or exaggerated claims?"), and *irrelevant* ("Was the content unrealistic, distant from your experience, or not related to your needs?"). These standardized evaluations can be supplemented with a set of open-ended questions for which respondents are asked to give positive or critical comments about the themes, appeals, styles, or other components of the message. Their suggestions for improving the message can also be solicited. The comments are written in large group administration or given orally in the focus group setting.

Theater Testing

Theater testing uses forced exposure to test rough television message executions in controlled settings. Although this technique is generally used with commercial messages, it has been modified to test PSAs for television. Testing takes place with several hundred respondents representative of the message's target audience. Respondents are recruited by random-digit telephone calls that invite them to preview and evaluate new television or radio program materials. The television or radio program material is used to camouflage the intent of the testing situation. At each test location, respondents are seated in groups of approximately 25 around large TV monitors. To avoid interviewer bias, all questions are prerecorded and administered over TV monitors.

Test commercials and the PSA are embedded in two 30-minute TV programs. Respondents are exposed to each message twice. The first exposure occurs in a program consisting of four variety acts that are interrupted by a station break in which seven commercials are played consecutively. This "clutter" sequence is meant to stimulate an on-air viewing situation, with four test spots separated by three constant control commercials. After respondents answer a series of questions on their opinion of the variety acts, two open-ended response items are administered, approximately 30 minutes following exposure to the test messages. Respondents are asked to recall, on an unaided basis, all the messages they remember by brand name, product type, or public service (the attention measure). They are then asked to write down the central point each message was trying to convey (the main idea communication measure). Another exposure to the test messages occurs in the context of a pilot situation comedy. In this case, each message is shown individually, separated by approximately 6 minutes of program content. After the second exposure, diagnostic questions are administered that probe respondent reactions, including personal relevance and a believability measure (i.e., is the message convincing?). Theater testing also provides an opportunity to use electronic devices to record and display moment-to-moment evaluations of messages, which can later be overlaid on the actual PSA to identify particularly positive or negative components (Baggaley, 1988).

Day-After Recall

A more naturalistic pretesting technique that is used primarily to test televised commercials, or pretest PSAs, is day-after recall. Potential respondents are contacted by telephone and invited to view a program on cable TV in their own homes that evening and then participate in a follow-up telephone interview the next day. Test commercials and PSAs are embedded in the program. The interviewer calls back the next day to determine if the viewers remember seeing the commercials or PSAs and if they recall any details about the test messages. One variation intended as an alternative to theater testing presents the questions on screen for immediate telephone interviews.

Other Formative Evaluation Techniques

Readability testing is critical when producing print materials. It estimates the educational level required for target populations to adequately comprehend written materials. Readability tests are available on many standard word processing packages, or a test can easily be computed by hand (DHHS, 1992).

Public communication campaigns often rely on various gatekeepers to disseminate materials. In the broadcast media, for example, the PSA director or station manager decides if the PSA is aired, when, and for how long. Frequently, the flow of print messages is controlled by "intermediaries" such as health professionals and organizations. If these gatekeepers do not like the messages, it is unlikely that the target audiences will ever be reached. Thus, a gatekeeper review includes them in reviewing materials in a rough stage of production concurrent with audience pretesting.

The traditional formative research methods described in the previous sections have been criticized because the audiences are seldom involved in problem identification. In contrast, participatory rapid appraisal, usually applied in work in developing countries, is a semistructured process of learning from, with, and by rural people about rural conditions (Clift & Freimuth, 1997; see Chapters 4 and 13, this volume). A variety of methods can be used: direct observation and participation, group walks through the village, mapping, wealth ranking, diagramming, and the creation of time lines. For example, in India, maps have been drawn on the ground in a matter of minutes to show all the huts in a small village. These maps can be followed with social information, such as markers of households and number of children. Even more sophisticated information, such as immunization status of children, can be indicated by seeds or stones. This mapping process is participatory, with villagers working together, challenging and correcting each other. These maps often become permanent models, providing a visible record of goals and achievements. These participatory rapid appraisal methods might be very appropriate ways for underserved groups to create content that meets their own information needs.

Finally, multiple formative evaluation methods are frequently combined as the campaign is developed (Freimuth, Plotnick, Ryan, & Schiller, 1997).

CONCLUSION

By collecting preproduction information and feedback reactions to pretest versions of the message concepts and executions, the campaign designers are in a much better position to devise more effective campaign plans and messages before final production and full-scale dissemination. Formative evaluation facilitates the development of more sophisticated campaign strategies, helps avoid pitfalls, and improves the quality of the created messages.

REFERENCES

Ajzen, I., & Fishbein, M. (1980). *Understanding attitudes and predicting social behavior.* Englewood Cliffs, NJ: Prentice Hall.

Atkin, C., Garramone, G., & Anderson, R. (1986, May). *Formative evaluation research in health campaign planning: The case of drunk driving prevention.* Paper presented at the annual meeting of the International Communication Association.

Baggaley, J. (1988). Perceived effectiveness of international AIDS campaigns. *Health Education Research, 3*(1), 7-17.

Bandura, A. (1977). Self-efficacy: Toward a unifying theory of behavioral change. *Psychological Review, 84*(2), 191-215.

Bandura, A. (1986). *Social foundations of thought and action: A social cognitive theory.* Englewood Cliffs, NJ: Prentice Hall.

Clift, E., & Freimuth, V. S. (1997). Changing women's lives: A communication perspective on participatory qualitative research techniques for gender equality. *Journal of Gender Studies, 6*(3), 289-296.

Flay, B., & Cook, T. (1989). Three models of summative evaluation of prevention campaigns with a mass media component. In R. E. Rice & C. Atkin (Eds.), *Public communication campaigns* (2nd ed., pp. 175-196). Newbury Park, CA: Sage.

Freimuth, V. S., Plotnick, C. A., Ryan, C. E., & Schiller, S. (1997). Right turns only: An evaluation of a video-based, multicultural drug education series for seventh graders. *Health Education & Behavior, 24*(5), 555-567.

Heckman, J. (2000). Turning the focus online. *Marketing News, 34*(5), 15.

Hovland, C., Janis, I., & Kelley, H. (1953). *Communication and persuasion.* New Haven, CT: Yale University Press.

Janz, N. K., & Becker, M. H. (1984). The Health Belief Model: A decade later. *Health Education Quarterly, 11,* 1-47.

Krueger, R. A. (1994). *Focus groups: A practical guide for applied research* (2nd ed.). Thousand Oaks, CA: Sage.

Office of National Drug Control Policy. (1998). *Copy-testing of messages for ONDCP's national youth anti-drug media campaign.* Washington, DC: Author.

Palmer, E. (1981). Shaping persuasive messages with formative research. In R. Rice & W. Paisley (Eds.), *Public communication campaigns* (pp. 227-242). Beverly Hills, CA: Sage.

Petty, R., & Cacioppo, J. (1986). *Communication and persuasion: Central and peripheral routes to attitude change.* New York: Springer-Verlag.

Prochaska, J., & DiClemente, C. (1983). Stages and processes of self change of smoking: Toward an integrative model. *Journal of Consulting and Clinical Psychology, 51,* 390-395.

Rogers, R. (1983). Cognitive and physiological processes in fear appeals and attitude change: A revised theory of protection motivation. In J. Cacioppo & R. E. Petty (Eds.), *Social psychophysiology* (pp. 153-176). New York: Guilford.

Rosenstock, I. (1990). The Health Belief Model: Explaining health behavior through expectancies. In K. Glanz, F. M. Lewis, & B. K. Rimer (Eds.), *Health behavior and health education: Theory research and practice* (pp. 39-62). San Francisco: Jossey-Bass.

Stewart, D. W., & Shamdasani, P. N. (1990). *Focus groups: Theory and practice.* Newbury Park, CA: Sage.

Treiman, E., Freimuth, V. S., Damron, D., Lasswell, A., Anliker, J., Havas, S., Langenberg, P., & Feldman, R. (1996). Attitudes and behaviors related to fruits and vegetables among low-income women in the WIC program. *Journal of Nutrition Education, 28*(3), 149-156.

U.S. Department of Health and Human Services. (1984). *Making health communication programs work: A planner's guide* (NIH Publication No. 84-1493). Bethesda, MD: National Cancer Institute.

U.S. Department of Health and Human Services. (1992). *Making health communication programs work: A planner's guide* (NIH Publication No. 92-1493). Bethesda, MD: National Cancer Institute.

8

A Systems-Based Evaluation Planning Model for Health Communication Campaigns in Developing Countries[1]

Ronald E. Rice
Dennis R. Foote

Systematic evaluation of health and nutrition communication campaigns in less developed countries is of paramount importance because poor health conditions continue to stifle human and national potential, high levels of governmental and individual resources are involved, and the cumulative knowledge about how to design communication interventions effectively in such settings is inconsistent. This chapter presents a systems-theoretic framework for planning evaluations of health communication campaigns in less developed countries, to identify relevant variables and processes, and to facilitate more effective and focused efforts.

AUTHORS; NOTE: We acknowledge the contributions of the following members of the Stanford project team: Carl Kendall, Reynoldo Martorell, Judith McDivitt, Barbara Searle, Leslie Snyder, Peter Spain, and Susan Stone. The U.S. Agency for International Development (USAID) developed the concept of the communication campaigns described herein in the form of the RFP that led to the contract award. The Academy for Educational Development was the project implementer, under Project Director Bill Smith, and Stanford University and Applied Communication Technology were the project evaluators, under Foote. Research was funded through the offices of Education and Health of the Bureau of Science and Technology, U.S. Agency for International Development, under project No. AIDIDSPE-C-0028. Assistance was also generously provided by the USAID missions in Honduras and The Gambia, the Ministry of Public Health in Honduras, and the Ministry of Health, Labour and Social Welfare in The Gambia.

Salmon and Kroger (1992) argue that most campaigns either explicitly or implicitly focus on (a) the individual level rather than the system level and (b) effects of campaigns rather than processes and structures of campaigns (see Chapters 9 and 31, this volume).

Simply stated, systems theory argues that there are common structures and processes operating in phenomena regardless of the research discipline applied (Berrien, 1968; Bertalanffy, 1968; Buckley, 1968). These structures include a system (a set of interacting and interdependent elements, components, or subsystems functioning within a common boundary), some common goal(s), and a surrounding environment (a set of inputs and constraints). A system such as a rural community exists in an initial state in an environment (such as the state of high infant morbidity and mortality in a developing country), obtains or receives (or is prevented from doing so) inputs (such as a health campaign), processes them according to goals and constraints (such as improved health, insufficient water, or cultural norms concerning illness and maternal care), develops (or is prevented from doing so) outputs (such as lower infant mortality or a reorganized health care delivery system), and receives feedback from the environmental actors and elements (such as increased support, political opposition, changed social norms, competition from other systems, and need for maintenance). A system "may exist as a planned, intentionally interrelated set of elements, or as the serendipitous outcome of external forces" and may interact more (open) or less (closed) with its environments (Salmon & Kroger, 1992, p. 133).

Health communication campaigns, for example, are appropriately conceived of systems of influence, both with respect to the multiple media, message, audience, community, and environmental systems and with respect to the campaign organizations and actors as production and political systems (McLeroy, Bibeau, Steckler, & Glanz, 1988; Ray & Donohew, 1990; Salmon & Kroger, 1992; Winett, 1986). Salmon and Kroger note that "only by anchoring change efforts in multiple systems of environmental influence . . . could a health program realistically hope to induce large-scale, enduring change" (p. 136). Campbell, Steenbarger, Smith, and Stucky (1982) applied this systems perspective in evaluating a community counseling project and concluded that taking a systems perspective leads to a widening of the scope of the original evaluation questions, increasing the range of evaluation tools necessary for understanding the system. Rudd, Goldberg, and Dietz (1999) also propose and analyze a comprehensive systems-based approach for sustaining community campaigns. Salmon and Kroger analyze the National AIDS Information and Education Program as both an organizational system and a (campaign) system of influence. Both social marketing and community campaigns implicitly presume an interdependent system of actors, subsystems, environments, resources, and values (see Chapter 27, this volume).

The proposed evaluation planning model (derived to some extent from Suchman's 1967 four-part evaluation model) involves the following stages,

although in an ongoing project, these stages represent processes that are interrelated and interactive: (a) specifying the goals and underlying assumptions of
the project; (b) specifying the process model at the project level; (c) specifying
prior states, system phases, and system constraints; (d) specifying immediate
and long-term intended poststates; (e) specifying the process model at the individual level; (f) choosing among research approaches appropriate to the system; and (g) assessing implications for design. This chapter describes the
model using examples from evaluations carried out on infant health interventions in Honduras and The Gambia.

SPECIFYING THE GOALS AND RELATED PROJECTS

Assessing Behavior Change and Causal Processes in Health Campaigns

Development health communication campaigns, and more specifically infant health and nutrition campaigns, have a considerable history (some of
which is reviewed and referenced by Hornik, 1985, 1988, 1993; see Chapter
14, this volume). The role of early health education interventions was perceived as information provision, without special emphasis on changing
people's behaviors. During the past two decades, projects such as those in
the Philippines, Ecuador, and Nicaragua by Manoff International (Cooke &
Romweber, 1977a, 1977b, 1977c), in Tanzania (Hall & Dodds, 1977; Mahai et
al., 1975), and others have given behavioral outcomes an increasing priority.

The campaigns discussed in this chapter represent the next major step—
paying particular attention to preassessments of the intended audience's needs
and characteristics; to the social, material, and logistical support needed to reinforce behavioral change; to the quality of the message propagated; and to the
causal relationships among components of the intervention and subsystems.

The Honduran and Gambian Projects

One of the major causes of infant mortality in developing countries is
diarrheal disease. It occurs at significant levels in practically every country,
and it is made worse by poor nutrition and bad sanitary conditions (World
Health Organization, 1983). In 1985, there were more than 5 million diarrhea-related infant deaths worldwide (Rohde & Northrup, 1986). Death is typically caused by dehydration—loss of fluids and electrolytes before the child's
natural defenses can defeat the cause of diarrhea. Less acute consequences—
malnutrition and waste of human and material resources—are even more common (CIBA Foundation, 1976).

Since the 1960s, a diverse set of approaches to reducing diarrhea-related infant mortality has been studied, including immunization, improved water
availability, disposal of excreta, weaning education, reduction of infection
through animals and insects, and oral rehydration therapy (ORT) (Ashworth &

Feachem, 1985; Esrey, Feachem, & Hughes, 1985; Feachem, 1986; Feachem, Hogan, & Merson, 1983; Hornik, 1985, 1993). ORT is a comprehensive approach that includes breast-feeding, improved nutrition, and sanitary practices. In addition, an inexpensive oral rehydration solution (ORS) that treats the dehydration by replacing fluids and electrolytes has been developed. ORT-oriented campaigns have significantly decreased diarrhea-related infant deaths in Bangladesh, India, Trinidad and Tobago, Haiti, Nicaragua, and Turkey (World Health Organization, 1983, p. 20) and have improved many aspects of infant health status in these and other countries (Milla, 1985). There are considerable problems associated with ORS, however, such as dangers from improperly mixed solutions, worsening of diarrhea symptoms, and difficulties in distributing ingredients (Hornik, 1985).

In a joint effort to improve prevention and treatment of diarrheal infant mortality, the U.S. Agency for International Development (USAID) and the Ministries of Public Health of Honduras and The Gambia have collaboratively supported a large-scale project in Mass Media and Health Practices. A subsequent USAID-supported project, HEALTHCOM, expanded the approach to more than 20 countries and helped to carry on the effort in Honduras (for comparisons between some HEALTHCOM sites, see Hornik, 1993, McDivitt, Hornik, & Dara, 1994, and Yoder, McDivitt, & Hornik, 1992). In Honduras, ORS (comprising sodium, glucose, potassium, and bicarbonate, called Litrosol) was distributed in packets to be mixed with 1 liter of water. In The Gambia, ORS was mixed at home, with eight bottle caps of sugar, one cap of salt, and three bottles (1 liter) of water, partially due to the expense of ORS packets (more than 10¢, not including internal distribution costs) and partially to avoid production dependencies.

SPECIFYING THE SYSTEM AND ITS COMPONENTS

Figure 8.1 presents an overview of the systems-based evaluation planning model. Taking a systems perspective, this model shows that before any intervention, there exists a prior state (e.g., of the people, their family, their community, the environment, the economy, mortality and morbidity rates, sanitary conditions, and nutritional levels) that is the baseline to which ongoing and final evaluation measurements are compared and constraints existing in the system that affect how the population interacts with the intervention.

The prior state, system constraints, and the intersection of system constraints and intervention inputs interrelate and feed into the process component. For example, perhaps a family learns new approaches to hygiene and wants to perform them but cannot because personal, cultural, or economic conditions prevent them from buying soap or using sufficiently clean water. Thus, system constraints can "block" or transform the progression from process to output.

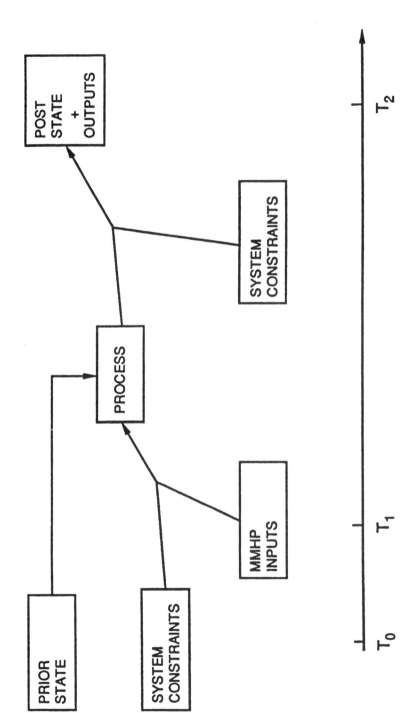

Figure 8.1. System-Based Evaluation Planning Model

The subsequent condition of the goal population constitutes a new or post-state. This poststate, which includes outputs from the process components, consists of the information, attitudes, behaviors, and health status of individuals as well as many of the conditions measured in the prior state component. Many of the values of the variables measured may not have changed; some would not be expected to change. Also, some new aspects of the system may have been introduced, such as new health communication infrastructures, different administrative procedures, or, in the long run, an increase in population growth, leading to a new set of constraints and conditions. Of course, because such interventions occur over time (more than 2 years for the original intensive interventions in both Honduras and The Gambia), this whole model may repeat itself in various phases (five phases in the two original interventions).

Perhaps the most important analytical aspect of an evaluation of a complex campaign is the need to consider, measure, and assess the effect of the major variables that help explain why certain outputs occurred and why certain others did not. These explanations are typically couched in terms of program or theory failure (see Chapter 6, this volume). Broadly, *program failure* results when the program is not or cannot be implemented as planned (such as the use of inappropriate messages or language or dependency on an insufficient distribution system). *Theory failure,* assuming successful program implementation, occurs when one or more of the hypothesized causal links do not occur (such as when people who know the appropriate behavior, understand why it might be to their advantage to adopt it, and have access to the necessary resources nevertheless fail to adopt) or have unexpected effects (such as when greater participation in a campaign-related event is associated with decreased learning).

The likelihood of program and theory failure increases as we move left to right along the process components in Figure 8.1 from more immediate outcomes (such as knowledge levels) to longer term outcomes (such as health status or mortality rates) for three basic reasons. First, it is generally hypothesized that the components are causally related, and thus those subjects who do not choose to, fail to, or are unable to complete one component become unavailable for the remaining components. Second, the cumulative effect of constraints and intervening variables, over which the implementer has no control, is almost certain to decrease the probability of occurrence of the postulated causal processes. Third, even if each component is accomplished, the relative strength of change is stochastic so that the final outcome from many successful components may still be difficult to detect (see Chapter 2, this volume).

SPECIFYING THE PRIOR STATE

The prior state of the environment can be conceptualized as clusters of variables, identified by theoretical processes and prior empirical results, including

1. Community and population variables, such as anthropological, economic, social, and demographic characteristics of the population; health, communication, government, and kinship infrastructures; and cultural beliefs and behaviors that affect MMHP issues

2. Household variables, such as enumeration of household occupants, number of young children, socioeconomic status level or other appropriate measure of wealth and status of household, educational level, and household literacy rate

3. Communication variables, such as access, exposure, usage, and preference for various media; individual literacy; interpersonal communication channels; community volunteer networks; and fieldworkers and medical practitioners

4. Sanitation variables, such as water sources, food preparation practices and facilities, cleaning beliefs and practices, and the "goal" concepts and practices as the primary contents of MMHP messages

5. Information, attitudes, and behaviors relating to child diarrhea, such as causes of diarrhea, response behaviors, relative seriousness of diarrhea, and distinctions among the severity of episodes

6. Nutrition variables, such as dietary recall, feeding patterns at various ages, and maternal and infant nutritional status

7. General health variables, such as health histories, birth and death histories, medicine use, contact with medical and health agents, anthropometric measures, and national decline in health due to economic conditions

8. Child care practice variables, such as caretaker responsibilities, exposure to contamination, conceptions of normal infant development, breast-feeding beliefs and practices, and supplemental feeding beliefs and practices

SPECIFYING SYSTEM PHASES

Fundamental to understanding the evaluation process is the fact that the system, and thus the implementation of the treatments, exists and changes over time— perhaps in phases, even through economic and military upheavals. For example, although the results of the two MMHP projects generally show significant improvements, some measures of health status declined, likely due to the tremendous decrease (26%) in per capita income from 1981 to 1987 in the region due to Central American conflicts (Bell, 1987). Description and analysis of the prior state and system constraints will lead to specification of variables by system phase, identifying when certain interventions should be applied and for which goal populations.

The MMHP campaigns organized their messages in phases according to temporal fluctuations (the rainy and dry seasons affect the type and amount of diarrhea) and a model of cumulative impact. Activities were phased to train health workers at the beginning and to follow a sequence of information, enabling behaviors, and reinforcement in messages for the general population.

Figure 8.2 shows the relative emphasis on prevention versus treatment, and on media versus interpersonal communication, during the five phases in Honduras. During Phase I, prior to the rainy season, the diarrhea rate was low. This phase focused on critical enabling messages identified during the preprogram investigation to establish ORT as standard operating procedure. Training included instruction in ORT. During the rainy season of Phase II, diarrhea rates were high. The central messages here, conveyed by the intensive media intervention, were the purpose, availability, proper mixing, and regimen for ORT. In Phase III, after the rainy season had passed, the intervention messages promoted selected prevention behaviors and maintaining the treatment behaviors. Phase IV was during the next rainy season, during which there was a high rate of diarrhea, so the intervention returned to its treatment focus, with selected prevention messages. In Phase V, after the rainy season had passed, the role of breast-feeding in ORT, and its more general benefits, was emphasized.

SPECIFYING SYSTEM CONSTRAINTS

It is necessary to detect and measure system constraints that may block or transform the progression from inputs to outputs, such as

1. Resource: access to water, heat, soap, medicine, health agents, media, literacy, and ORS packets (e.g., in Honduras, mothers most likely to use ORT were in more rural, less educated, and less wealthy regions, indicating that home ORT filled a need not provided by local health services or resources in poor regions)

2. Cultural: traditional beliefs about causes of diseases, difficulty in distinguishing between bottle and breast-feeding, and notions of privacy in using hygiene facilities (e.g., diarrhea is often viewed as a normal way to purge harmful illnesses such as measles or as unrelated to dehydration; Green, 1986)

3. Medical community: resistance to new treatments, maintenance and extension of training, infrastructure in rural areas, and conflict with traditional rural health actors

4. Environmental: weather, possible epidemics, unintegrated institutional constituencies in various ministries, and discrimination against the rural poor in clinics

5. Input delivery: delays or reductions in broadcasts, insufficient broadcasts, transport difficulties, uneven or restricted ORT materials, legal obstacles to distribution, and insufficient working radios

The pervasiveness of system constraints, even as manifested in how interventions are designed, may well prevent any substantive improvement in the population's health status. Once the linkages between intervention inputs and potential outputs (different system components) are specified theoretically (as in the process component), it becomes crucial to identify distinctions among planned inputs (media, medical practices, ORS packets, etc.), delivery constraints, real inputs, resource and access constraints, and engaged inputs and

154

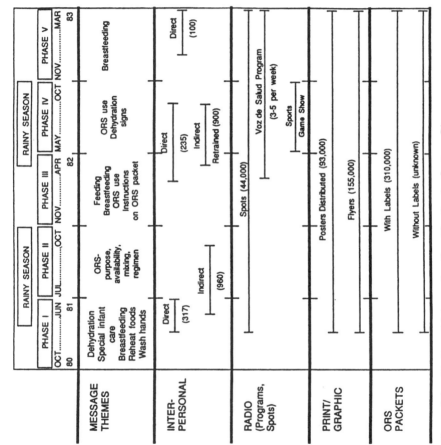

Figure 8.2. Media and Intervention Specification by Systems Phase

final engagement by target individuals (what is perceived as being input by the target audience).

Between the planned intervention inputs and the engagement of such inputs by the goal population lie possible constraints. For example, a series of radio spots with a given frequency of broadcast may be planned inputs, but the broadcasters do not receive the scripts in time or choose not to broadcast all the spots according to schedule; the result is real inputs, which in turn are greater than the inputs actually engaged by the goal population. In The Gambia at the time of the study, 60% of household compounds had at least one working radio receiver. In these compounds, 75% of the women listened to Radio Gambia, which delivered the MMHP spots; therefore, only 45% of the women in the general population could potentially directly engage in processing the campaign's radio messages. Compare this engaged radio input to the 3% literacy rate by individual women, which would prevent any substantial engagement with print messages. Thus, one strategy in the Gambia project was to provide color-coded flyers or wall posters, which were explained and reinforced through radio messages. These engaged inputs must be considered the basis for potential measures of exposure, attention, and recall in analyzing change and poststate measurements, and as such they still do not represent the final basis on which to assess theory failure or success. Thus, tests of program success should use data on planned and real inputs; tests of theory success should use data on real and engaged inputs.

Media Inputs

Each planned media input (such as radio spots) could be coded for goal audience and frequency, region, and station. Specific messages can be coded, by implementation phase, within each specific input. That is, only a few messages in certain media are project inputs in each phase for each subaudience. Therefore, the relative efficacy or recall of those messages, by medium, can be compared to the relative efficacy or recall of different messages, by medium, in later phases. For example, in the Gambia project, the color-coded mixing instruction flyers were the most significant media or print input: Having one at home predicted earlier learning and use of ORT and less forgetting and lack of adoption (Snyder, 1987; also see Griffiths, Zeitlin, Manoff, & Cook, 1983, who report similar results from an Indonesian campaign). Recall of radio spots, however, was most influential only as a reinforcement after the respondent had already learned about ORT. In Honduras, 80% reported that they had a radio, and 85% of these (or 67% overall) demonstrated that they had a working radio. Averaged over several waves, from 9 a.m. to 10 a.m., 19% listened to their radios, and 60% of these reported hearing the campaign spot, representing 12% of the population. From noon to 1 p.m., the percentages were 35%, 81%, and 28%, respectively.

Resource Inputs

The distribution of ORS packets, with associated print material, is considered a planned resource input, which also must be monitored to determine engaged inputs to goal populations. Differential distribution by channel (e.g., commercial and public health outlets) or by geographical region (closer or farther from roads) may prove to be a factor in explaining why intervention efforts were differentially successful in various regions. Constraints to delivery of ORS packets to goal populations can be measured through questionnaire data, but they might also be monitored through delivery invoices or inventory records.

Audience Inputs

Relevant populations other than the goal caretaker-child population—direct contacts such as health workers and physicians and indirect contacts such as volunteer care workers—can be viewed as additional inputs or constraints. Goal audiences can be asked about the interpersonal diffusion channels that may help to spread or resist mass media inputs (Coleman, Katz, & Menzel, 1966; Rogers & Kincaid, 1981; see Chapter 11, this volume). For example, local health workers have been shown to be a significant influence in campaigns to teach correct ORS mixing or to support proper weaning as one approach to reduce diarrhea-related infant deaths (Ashworth & Feachem, 1985; Kumar, Monga, & Jain, 1981).

To assess possible degradation or elaboration of input content, throughout the progression from mass media and medical contacts to the goal caretaker-child population, intervening populations could be measured during the poststate component, during their interaction with the goal audience, and in interviews with health care providers and community leaders. For example, in The Gambia, village health volunteers trained by the health workers were identified by red flags outside their compounds. Local mothers could visit these "red flag volunteers" to learn how to mix the ORS correctly; the volunteers were not supported throughout the campaign by the health workers, however, so this indirect interpersonal channel disappeared.

SPECIFYING IMMEDIATE AND
LONG-TERM PROJECT GOALS

As summarized in Figure 8.3, in the Honduran and Gambian projects, categories of *cognitive* outcomes included attention to—and recognition, recall, and knowledge of—nutritional and preventive behaviors and ORT messages. Categories of *behavior* outcomes included response to diarrheal episode (administration of ORT, taking child to clinics, etc.), infant feeding practices, water purity, and prevention and personal hygiene. Categories of *health* outcomes

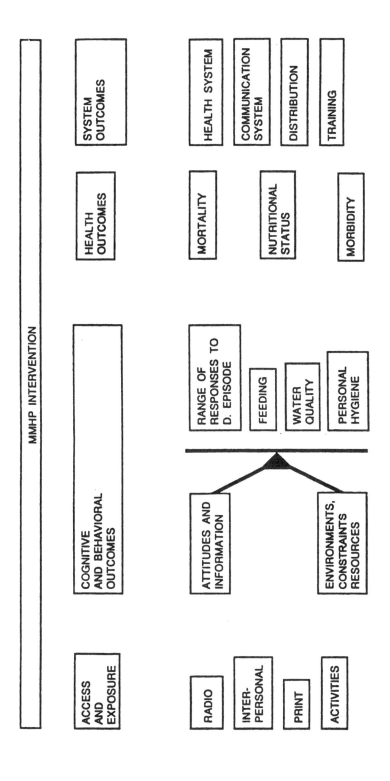

Figure 8.3. Immediate and Long-Term Project Goals

Table 8.1 Selected Results From Evaluations of Honduras ORT Campaign

Variable	Pre: 1981-1982 (%)	Post: 1983-1984 (%)	Long-Term Post: 1987 (%)
Access and exposure			
Has radio in home	77	73	67
Has heard radio spot featuring project characters	59	78	69
Has seen a poster	47		
Has instructional flyer	15	3	
Learning			
Knows product name	49	71	99
Can complete project jingles	50-70	20-83	12-80
Can define dehydration	38	39	22
Learned about ORS from			
Community health workers	29	12	
Nurse, doctor, clinic	39	61	
ORS packet	49	4	
Radio	27	6	
Knows should continue breast-feeding during diarrhea	83	82	
Behavior			
Has tried ORS	0	6	85
Cases treated	9	36	49
Continued breast-feeding during diarrhea	72	98	
Gave more liquid than normal during diarrhea	65	79	
Health status			
Stunting	29	36	
Wasting	1	1	
Deaths under age 5 years involving diarrhea	39	29	

included nutritional status (weight and height relative to international age norms), morbidity (frequency, severity, and duration of diarrhea), and mortality. Categories of *system* outcomes included the institutionalization of ORT in the health system and the communication system (Are the messages incorporated in the content of other development messages and projects?), distribution of ORT in clinics and through community outlets, and incorporation of ORT in national and local training. Table 8.1 summarizes a few selected results from the Honduras project (The Gambia results appear in the second edition of this book).

SPECIFYING THE PROCESS MODEL
AT THE INDIVIDUAL LEVEL

The individual-level process model used in the MMHP projects is derived from three theoretical foundations of health communication campaigns. The Public Health Belief Model considers whether individuals believe they are susceptible, whether the messages are relevant, and whether the individuals have options. Concepts such as self-efficacy, internal information processing, and attitudes are important components of this model (Fishbein & Ajzen, 1975; see Chapters 5 and 12, this volume). The Social Marketing Model emphasizes the identification of markets and audiences and how to place and price a product (see Chapter 27, this volume).

The 12-step communication-persuasion matrix (see Chapter 2, this volume) shows communication variables as inputs (source, message, channel, receiver, and destination factors) and the successive response steps that must be elicited in the public if the communication campaign is to be effective as outputs. Attention (Step 2 in McGuire's matrix) generally can be measured only by the surrogate of recall (Step 8), which lies after the most crucial steps: exposure, attention, reaction, comprehension, yielding, and storing. Evaluation efforts should gather information on some factors affecting these prior stages, such as cultural constraints against yielding to a particular argument about, for example, the amount of liquids a baby can ingest or against comprehension of the distinction between bottle and breast-feeding. Adoption of the advocated message is based on this decision process, but it takes form in the behavior stage (Step 10), which can be measured directly via observations or indirectly by a respondent's report of behaviors or via system measures such as ORT distribution or clinic patient load. Postbehavioral consolidating (Step 12) would take the form of changed cultural, family, or personal norms and behaviors.

Figure 8.4 shows how the MMHP evaluation attempted to monitor or measure some of these individual processes (with selected results in Table 8.1). Each of these steps is accompanied by measurement or monitoring of intervening variables and system constraints that prevent full linkage to the next step and of unforeseen outputs of a prior step.

The application of this evaluation approach has allowed insights into the diagnosis of problems within a given project (program failures) and the design of principles for this type of project (here subsumed as theory failures), such as the following:

1. When emphasis and reinforcement of specific messages are not sustained, initial gains can quickly be lost. For example, in The Gambia, the intervention was vastly reduced in intensity after 1984, and case treatment ratios decreased from 62% to 10% within a few years. Even prior to 1984, it was clear that mothers were not following a simple pattern of adoption followed by sustained use. Snyder (1991), analyzing seven aggregated waves of The Gambia data, showed that use of ORT was

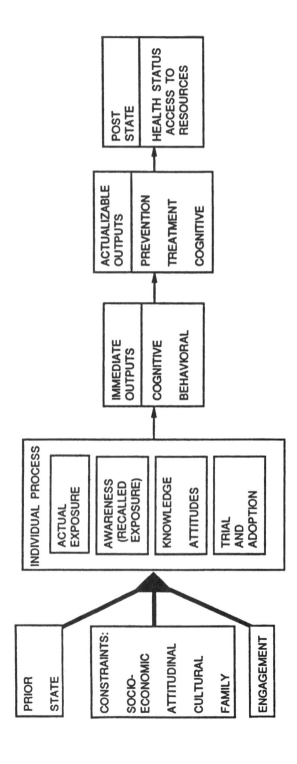

Figure 8.4. Evaluation of Individual Processes, Intervening Processes, and System

maintained by 70% of the initial adopters after 5 months, 50% after 13 months, and only 30% after 21 months. Although only 8% started using ORT and then stopped permanently, 57% started, stopped, and started again. Thus, behavior maintenance should be a major challenge and goal of future campaigns rather than just inducing one-time changes in learning, attitudes, or behaviors.

2. There was considerable difficulty in learning some concepts, such as dehydration, and the benefits of ORT for dehydration rather than for diarrhea. Future interventions will have to consider whether to position such treatments according to the popular views or to teach a scientifically current conception.

3. Learning through different channels, at different times, has different adoption and retention characteristics. The presence of mixing flyers that mothers put in their homes significantly influenced earlier learning about and use of ORT and later forgetting or disadoption of ORT, whereas the recalling of radio messages led to earlier forgetting and disadoption (Snyder, 1991). One explanation is that putting the flyer up was associated with taking action concerning ORT, whereas remembering hearing the message was not necessarily associated with immediate action. When hearing was contemporaneous with learning about ORT or adopting it, then respondents learned earlier and maintained use longer (Snyder, 1991).

CHOOSING AMONG RESEARCH APPROACHES

The MMHP evaluation used six major study groupings that differed markedly from one another in magnitude, study population, and measurement requirements:

1. A longitudinal study (here, monthly to develop sets of measures and observations and to detect sequencing and linkage among process components)

2. A mortality study (in Honduras, an interrupted time series analysis to detect change in mortality due to infant diarrhea in treatment area)

3. An opinion leader and health professional interview study (to elicit assessment of project impact and organizational success)

4. An ethnographic study (to provide more anthropological insights into impacts, customs, and beliefs)

5. An archival study (to assess clinical and hospital measures of infant mortality, morbidity, treatment, etc.)

6. A cost-effectiveness study (to aid in understanding relative payoffs for future programs)

Particular project contexts may lead to emphasis or rejection of one or more of the previously mentioned studies. For example, in Honduras, lack of measurement precision and evidence of marginal returns from changing the media mix or frequency lessened the possibility of a complete cost-effectiveness study.

Because of such often unpredictable constraints, in addition to problems of decreased funding for complete project evaluation, insufficient experimental control, trade-offs between internal and external validity, and the like, triangulation by means of multiple methodologies and data sources is necessary and becoming more prevalent (Heath, Kendzierski, & Borgida, 1982).

IMPLICATIONS FOR DESIGN

Sampling

Issues of sampling and control groups are crucial to any campaign evaluation (Cook & Campbell, 1979; see Chapter 6, this volume). Insights from analysis of the prior state and system constraints, given a set of project goals, will help establish proper sampling frames and units of analysis.

For example, because health delivery infrastructure and broadcast media are typically in place before project intervention, these often establish treatment, and thus sampling, boundaries. Because the objectives of the MMHP evaluation included developing a transnational model of health communication evaluation, the primary objective of sampling was to enable generalizations to the full range of conditions (prior states, inputs, and constraints) represented in developing countries rather than to make possible precise statements about aggregate national levels in a given country.

Particular system contexts and constraints will influence the analytical level. For example, noninstitutional infant care is delivered in the "home"; therefore, all individual variables must be linked to a "home unit." What is a home? In Honduras, a household was defined as a living unit that contains both a place for cooking and a place for sleeping. Thus, in Honduras, 750 mothers were randomly selected from 20 stratified villages. In The Gambia, however, the home is a compound of 10 to 100 people, consisting of physical structures enclosing polygamous multifamily living units. Thus, infant care can never be attributed solely to the attitudes and cognitive and behavioral levels of one individual. Therefore, in The Gambia, 1,029 mothers were sampled from compounds selected randomly from 20 stratified villages.

Control Groups

Because resources for fieldwork are limited, it is crucial to think through carefully the value of mounting data-collection efforts in nontreatment areas (Cook & Campbell, 1979; Suchman, 1967). The Gambia project, which was nationwide from the beginning, had 20 treatment villages receiving multiple measurements, and 8 villages were measured only once (to test for measurement effects); there were no nontreatment controls. In the Honduras project, because the government program rapidly expanded from the pilot site to a national campaign to promote the use of ORT, we could not identify a group outside of the treatment area that had not received some kind of treatment, however minor. Furthermore, because the project effort was not a uniform effort within the pilot region, it was not possible to assign households randomly to treatment conditions. Thus, neither project involved nontreatment groups, but both projects incorporated nonrepeated measures groups to test for measurement influences.

Comparisons Within the Treatment Area

Five sources of data within the treatment area from the study groupings can be used for within-treatment control purposes, as in the Honduras project:

1. Household as its own control: Local interviewers returned for repeated measurements to households that could then serve as their own controls for many variables.

2. Making use of staged implementation: If, because of phases in system constraints, components of the campaign are introduced in different phases in different regions of the treatment area, the study can compare as yet untreated segments of the population within the measurement sample to treated segments.

3. Natural variations in exposure: Because of the vagaries that can be expected in mounting a complex intervention, there will be program failure in some components of the campaign. These variations, if inputs are adequately monitored, can be used for comparison purposes.

4. Self-determination of exposure: Some people will select not to expose themselves to a health campaign because they do not have access to a radio, because they do not choose to talk to health workers, and so on. Although not necessarily comparable, they can be a source of some kinds of information with which to compare exposed respondents.

5. Measurement effects: A smaller sample in both Honduras and The Gambia was interviewed only once or twice across the longitudinal survey for comparison with the larger sample, which may have been sensitized by the multiple interviews. The results, in fact, are slightly more positive for those in the repeated waves than for these treatment effects groups, but both were considerably higher than the baseline figures.

Comparisons With Nontreated Populations

Information about people outside the treatment area can be obtained from several sources, such as archival data, ethnographic studies, other health projects functioning in the region, and standardized data on infant growth and weight (for this project, available from the National Center for Health Statistics). Special one-time studies may assess the level of a belief or practice in a nontreatment area when results in the treatment area are ambiguous.

Table 8.2 Usefulness of Control Data Obtained From Within and Outside the
Treatment Sample

	Outcome		
Source of Control	Cognitive	Behavioral	Health
Within treatment area			
Household as own control	xx	xx	xx
Staged implementation	xx	xx	—
Natural variation in exposure	x	x	x
Self-selected exposure	—	—	x
Measurement effects	xx	x	—
Outside treatment area			
Archival data	—	x	—
Ethnographic studies	xx	x	xx
Data from other studies	x	x	x
One-time studies	xx	xx	—

NOTE: x = source of weak control; xx = source of good control; — = no control comparison is possible.

The Question of Controls in a Longitudinal Study

Table 8.2 summarizes the usefulness of the sources of control data for variables in each of the outcome categories. For example, beliefs, practices, and
levels of knowledge can change quickly on exposure to campaign intervention;
therefore, repeated measures can capture changes in these outcomes between
implementation stages but probably not changes in levels of health status variables, such as changes in mortality due to dehydration.

In the Honduran and Gambian projects, the focus was on infant feeding and
child care practices in traditional communities—practices for which rapid
changes are not expected to occur in the absence of external stimuli. Thus, it
seemed that monitoring other information inputs (via the ethnographic and interview studies) into the treatment villages would be a more efficient way to
evaluate rival explanations for change than collecting measures on control
populations whose comparability is open to doubt. If mothers begin preparing
ORS in the household, this change in behavior can be attributed only to the health
education campaign because it represents the adoption of a new behavior.

A 5-year follow-up survey in both countries of women drawn from equivalent samples, as in the original evaluation, enabled analyses of the long-term
effects and of nationwide historical effects. Table 8.1 provides a few selected
results from these surveys for Honduras.

CONCLUSION

This chapter argued that evaluation of purposive communication projects in less
developed countries has much to gain from the use of a generic planning model

based on a systems approach. Using the example of ORT projects in two developing countries, the model highlights the need to identify and measure seven evaluation components from a systems perspective. The use of such a planning model could not only help guide the development and execution of evaluation efforts but, equally important, also provide a common framework for use in related projects.

NOTE

1. This chapter is revised from the second edition.

REFERENCES

Ashworth, A., & Feachem, R. (1985). Interventions for the control of diarrhoeal diseases among young children: Weaning education. *Bulletin of the World Health Organization, 63*(6), 1115-1127.

Bell, P. (1987, October 18). Central American presidents show real grit in quest for peace. *Los Angeles Times,* p. V1.

Berrien, F. (1968). *General and social systems.* New Brunswick, NJ: Rutgers University Press.

Bertalanffy, L. von. (1968). *General systems theory.* New York: Braziller.

Buckley, W. (Ed.). (1968). *Modern systems research for the behavioral scientist.* Chicago: Aldine.

Campbell, D., Steenbarger, B., Smith, T., & Stucky, R. (1982). An ecological systems approach to evaluation: Cruising in Topeka. *Evaluation Review, 6*(5), 625-648.

CIBA Foundation. (1976). *Symposium 42: Acute diarrhea in childhood.* Amsterdam: Elsevier-Excerpta Medica/North-Holland.

Coleman, J., Katz, E., & Menzel, J. (1966). *Medical innovation: A diffusion study.* New York: Bobbs-Merrill.

Cook, T. D., & Campbell, D. (1979). *Quasi-experimentation: Design and analysis issues for field settings.* Skokie, IL: Rand McNally.

Cooke, T., & Romweber, S. (1977a). *Mass media nutrition education: Vol. 2. Nicaragua* (Final report for USAID Office of Nutrition). New York: Manoff.

Cooke, T., & Romweber, S. (1977b). *Radio, advertising techniques and nutrition education: A summary of a field experiment in the Philippines and Nicaragua* (Final report for USAID Office of Nutrition). New York: Manoff.

Cooke, T., & Romweber, S. (1977c). *Radio nutrition education: A test of the advertising technique: Philippines and Nicaragua.* Unpublished report, Manoff, Washington, DC.

Esrey, S., Feachem, R., & Hughes, J. (1985). Interventions for the control of diarrhoeal diseases among young children: Improving water supplied and excreta disposal facilities. *Bulletin of the World Health Organization, 63*(4), 757-772.

Feachem, R. (1986). Preventing diarrhoea: What are the policy options? *Health Policy and Planning, 1*(2), 109-117.

Feachem, R., Hogan, R., & Merson, M. (1983). Diarrhoeal disease control: Reviews of potential interventions. *Bulletin of the World Health Organization, 61*(4), 637-640.

Fishbein, M., & Ajzen, I. (1975). *Belief, attitude, intention and behavior.* Reading, MA: Addison-Wesley.

Green, E. (1986). Diarrhea and the social marketing of oral rehydration salts in Bangladesh. *Social Science Medicine, 23*(4), 357-366.

Griffiths, M., Zeitlin, M., Manoff, R., & Cook, T. (1983). *Kader evaluation: Nutrition communication and behavior change component, Indonesia nutrition development program.* New York: Manoff.

Hall, B., & Dodds, T. (1977). Voice for development: The Tanzanian national radio study campaigns. In P. Spain, D. Jamison, & E. McAnany (Eds.), *Radio for education and development: Case studies.* Washington, DC: World Bank.

Heath, L., Kendzierski, D., & Borgida, E. (1982). Evaluation of social programs: A multidimensional approach combining a delayed treatment true experiment and multiple time series. *Evaluation Review, 6*(2), 233-246.

Hornik, R. (1985). *Nutrition education: A state of the art review.* Washington, DC: World Bank.

Hornik, R. (1988). *Development communication.* New York: Longman.

Hornik, R. (1993). *Development communication: Information, agriculture, and nutrition in the Third World.* Lanham, MD: University Press of America.

Kumar, V., Monga, O., & Jain, N. (1981). The introduction of oral rehydration in a rural community in India. *World Health Forum, 2*(3), 364-366.

Mahai, B., et al. (1975). *The second follow-up formative evaluation report of the "Food Is Life" campaign.* Dar es Salaam, Tanzania: Institute of Adult Education.

McDivitt, J., Hornik, R., & Dara, C. (1994). Quality of home use of oral rehydration solutions: Results from seven HEALTHCOM sites. *Social Science & Medicine, 38*(9), 1221-1234.

McLeroy, K., Bibeau, D., Steckler, A., & Glanz, K. (1988). An ecological perspective on health promotion programs. *Health Education Quarterly, 15,* 351-377.

Milla, A. (Ed.). (1985). *Annotated bibliography on oral rehydration therapy.* Dhaka, Bangladesh: International Centre for Diarrhoeal Disease Research.

Ray, E., & Donohew, L. (Eds.). (1990). *Communication and health: Systems and applications.* Hillsdale, NJ: Lawrence Erlbaum.

Rogers, E. M., & Kincaid, D. L. (1981). *Communication networks: Toward a new paradigm for research.* New York: Free Press.

Rohde, J., & Northrup, R. (1986). Diarrhea is a nutritional disease. In *Second international conference on oral rehydration therapy* (pp. 30-41). Washington, DC: U.S. Agency for International Development.

Rudd, R., Goldberg, J., & Dietz, W. (1999). A five-stage model for sustaining a community campaign. *Journal of Health Communication, 4*(1), 37-48.

Salmon, C. T., & Kroger, F. (1992). A systems approach to AIDS communication: The example of the national AIDS information and education program. In T. Edgar, M. Fitzpatrick, & V. Freimuth (Eds.), *AIDS: A communication perspective* (pp. 131-146). Hillsdale, NJ: Lawrence Erlbaum.

Snyder, L. (1987). *Learning and acting in a health communication campaign: Teaching rural women to prevent infant dehydration through diarrheal disease control in The Gambia, West Africa.* Unpublished doctoral dissertation, Stanford University, Stanford, CA.

Snyder, L. (1991). Modeling dynamic communication processes with event history analysis. *Communication Research, 18*(4), 464-486.

Suchman, E. (1967). *Evaluative research.* New York: Russell Sage.

Winett, R. (1986). *Information and behavior: Systems of influence.* Hillsdale, NJ: Lawrence Erlbaum.

World Health Organization. (1983). *Third programme report, 1981-1982.* Geneva: World Health Organization, Programme for Diarrhoea Control.

Yoder, P. S., McDivitt, J., & Hornik, R. (1992). Knowledge of oral rehydration and response to diarrhea: A comparison among HEALTHCOM sites. *International Quarterly of Community Health Education, 13*(3), 201-218.

9

Communication Campaign Effectiveness

Critical Distinctions

Charles T. Salmon
Lisa Murray-Johnson

Douglas, Westley, and Chaffee's (1970) article titled "An Information Campaign That Changed Community Attitudes" is frequently cited in review essays as proof that information campaigns can be effective. In Table 4 of their report, the authors show that the campaign was responsible for a net attitude change of 7% in the Treatment community, compared with a net attitude change of 2% in the Comparison community. However, in Table 3, the authors show that the campaign was also responsible for a 12% decline in information gain in the Treatment community compared with a 6% increase in the Comparison community, a finding that is normally neither desirable nor expected from a campaign defined as "effective."

A central concern of communication campaign planners and evaluators during approximately the past 50 years has been to determine whether or not campaigns are "effective." Numerous empirical studies, review essays, and entire books have been devoted to this determination (Backer, Rogers, & Sopory, 1992; Neal & Bathe, 1997; Rossi & Freeman, 1993; Scherer & Juanillo, 1992; Wartella & Middlestadt, 1991; see Chapter 10, this volume). This ongoing effort has been particularly challenging because of two primary obstacles. First, there is no universally accepted standard, nor consensus within the scientific community, regarding what constitutes an effective campaign. Indeed, viewed in one context, a campaign that may appear to be highly effective may, in another context, be interpreted in quite different terms (as with the example presented previously). Second, despite key differences between the two concepts, many campaign evaluators have tended to use the terms "campaign effects" and "campaign effectiveness" interchangeably (Atkin, 1981; Farquhar et al., 1990; Maccoby, Farquhar, Wood, & Alexander, 1977; McGovern et al., 1992; McGuire, 1986; Vartiainen, Paavola, McAlister, & Puska, 1998). The result has been an ambiguous body of research and commentary that provides little potential for valid scientific generalizations about communication campaigns.

The purpose of this chapter is to reconceptualize campaign effectiveness as a multifaceted construct and, in particular, to provide evaluators with guidance for assessing commonly overlooked outcomes of campaigns, whether manifest or latent and intended or unintended.

WHAT CONSTITUTES AN EFFECTIVE CAMPAIGN?

The noted psychologist William James is credited with deriving a formula for calculating either of two enduring pursuits of humankind—"success" or "happiness" (Salmon, 1989). According to the formula, *success,* which is the more relevant concept for this discussion, can be conceptualized as the ratio of achievements divided by expectations. In other words, an achievement or accomplishment is deemed a successful or unsuccessful outcome only relative to what is desired or expected. When the denominator (the expectation) is high, the numerator (the outcome) will have to be of proportionally greater magnitude for it to be judged "a success." Conversely, when the expectation is low, even a much lesser outcome or achievement will be interpreted as successful. (Consider the classic political campaign example of Edmund Muskie, who in 1972 secured the most votes in the New Hampshire primary, but the interpretation of his performance by political and media pundits was that he had not been successful because his margin of victory was not as great as had been expected.)

The relativistic nature of success is particularly appropriate for making sense of the tangle of conflicting results and conclusions regarding the effectiveness of communication campaigns. Advertisers, marketers, internal and external stakeholders, and program staff use different subjective interpretations and criteria to define effectiveness (Rossi & Freeman, 1993). Inevitably, success is a highly relative and indeed idiosyncratic notion defined uniquely by campaign evaluators working in differing historical eras and different topical areas, with different goals and purposes. Because there are literally dozens of ways of analyzing data and presenting and interpreting the same statistical results, different evaluators can interpret the same data as evidence of either campaign effectiveness or ineffectiveness. Thus, in the campaign literature, there are situations such as the following:

- Atkin's (1981) review of the literature cites the Stanford heart disease programs as exemplars of effective campaigns, whereas Haug's (1995) review of the literature concludes that the programs produced little evidence of influencing knowledge, attitudes, or behavior (and hence were not effective).

- Cancion do la Raza, a campaign that achieved 15% exposure and 66% self-reported knowledge gain (which is considered a weak measure in terms of validity), was heralded as very effective (Mendelsohn, 1973); in contrast, the United Nations Information Campaign, a campaign that achieved 83% exposure and 49% recall of the campaign slogan, was labeled a failure (Star & Hughes, 1950).

As evaluation guru Carol Weiss (1997, p. 43) concluded, the rhetoric used to claim "effectiveness" appears to be at the mercy of those who conceptualize and operationalize its meaning.

EXPLICATING CAMPAIGN EFFECTIVENESS

Compounding the difficulty in deriving valid generalizations about campaign effectiveness is the exceedingly broad range of possible campaign outcomes (ranging from individual-level outcomes such as influencing knowledge, attitudes, and behavior to social-level outcomes such as stimulating political action, winning the approval of a community coalition, or placing an item on the media's agenda). Furthermore, different conceptualizations of effectiveness will be used to judge different outcomes as more or less effective by stakeholders representing varied, and often conflicting, interests. The following sections explicate six such conceptualizations: definitional, ideological, political, contextual, cost, and programmatic.

Definitional Effectiveness

The first level of effectiveness pertains to the success that groups have in defining a social phenomenon as a social problem. When a certain condition has been accepted as socially problematic, it reflects the ability of some claims-making organization to get an issue onto various agendas (e.g., media and public) and achieve consensus that one issue is more worthy of political and financial capital than a competitor (Best, 1989; Spector & Kitsuse, 1977). Massive media attention to a small number of cases of Ebola fever compared with the general paucity of media attention to an estimated 16 million cases of diabetes in the United States illustrates this point in a public health context (Harris et al., 1998).

The "selling" of a disease or health problem is thus an integral component of the initial phase of the campaign process because of the inherent limitations on political resources available to fund campaigns. The governmental agenda is limited, for example, in terms of the number of issues for which time, energy, monetary support, and attention are devoted to a health problem. Similarly, mass media outlets are characterized by limitations of time or publication space or both in which to attend to a designated problem. Health advocates are placed in a position of competing with each other, each championing a different health cause and each vying for limited attention and opportunity attention (Hilgartner & Bosk, 1988). Thus, health promoters working in the area of cardiovascular disease, for example, emphasize such claims as "Almost one out of every two Americans will die of cardiovascular disease" as a way of gaining attention. Diseases that kill far fewer people than heart attacks and stroke, such as AIDS or diabetes, must still be positioned in such a way that they are perceived as serious, important, and hence worthy of federal dollars and media attention. The challenge to health communicators is to be effective in this positioning strategy by emphasizing the uniqueness and potential threat of their disease vis-à-vis other diseases that are clamoring for the same limited resources. To the extent that an advocacy group achieves this outcome, it is thus effective in a definitional sense—a type of effectiveness that is often overlooked by evaluators but that is critical to the ultimate success of discrete communication campaigns (see Chapters 1 and 31, this volume).

Ideological Effectiveness

Once a social problem has been constructed, it is concomitantly defined at either the individual or social level of analysis. In most cases, campaigns are designed to modify personal knowledge, attitudes, intentions, and behaviors rather than to modify the political and economic environments in which those attitudes, intentions, and behaviors occur. For example, some social critics contend that the incidence of pregnancy among unwed teenage women constitutes a social problem. To the extent that a group achieves consensus that this is indeed the case, what is the cause or source of this problem? The problem might, by some claimsmakers, be defined at the individual level as due to sexual promiscuity or lack of self-discipline on the part of the teenagers. If this definition were to prevail, a flurry of communication campaigns would result in which women were "educated" on how to avoid unwanted pregnancies. In contrast, the problem might be defined by other claimsmakers at the social level as the lack of social services to accommodate these women and the presence of systemic discrimination against women. If this definition were to prevail, social-level solutions would be deployed, such as enhanced day care, welfare, and other social service programs (see Chapters 4 and 8, this volume).

It is overwhelmingly the case, however, that more often than not health problems are defined at the individual level as problems of lack of knowledge, "poor" attitudes, or lack of "appropriate" behaviors on the part of individuals who seem destined to suffer the consequences of their actions (Tesh, 1988). An example is the Harvard Alcohol Project, which glorified the collaboration among Mothers Against Drunk Drivers, Hollywood producers, and university researchers in advocating the "designated driver" campaign (Montgomery, 1993; see Chapter 21, this volume). Television producers were encouraged to have scriptwriters focus on personal responsibility for drunk driving, as demonstrated by the popular phrase "Friends don't let friends drive drunk." Within 15 months, 62 popular sitcoms and dramas wholeheartedly discussed the concept. To some critics, however, this "effective" effort to implement the designated driver concept failed to address the "real" problem. Alcohol manufacturers and distributors were left untouched by the campaign (and continued to reap public and governmental goodwill in the process), whereas individual drinkers were blamed for irresponsible behavior.

The attempt to "fix" human actions at the individual level is often preferred because campaigns tend to be perceived as ideologically neutral in contrast to systemic solutions, which are often labeled as "partisan" or "political." Communication campaigns are actually no less political than other approaches to social change, but rarely are the hidden assumptions and politics of campaigns considered or debated to the same degree as are proposals for systemic change (see Chapter 25, this volume).

Political Effectiveness

As has been noted elsewhere, health communication represents a highly visible mechanism for demonstrating that a government cares about a particular social problem or issue (Salmon, 1989, 1992). For example, the Stanford Three-Community and Five-City Projects, Minnesota Heart Health Program, Project STAR, and other similar campaigns were large-scale, expensive government grant-sponsored initiatives designed to identify and solve the public health concerns of diet, obesity, physical activity, and drug use. Their massive media messages and community-driven programs created a very visible and public gesture of caring for the health and welfare of constituents. One of the more interesting examples of this occurred a few years ago when the governor of a large midwestern state was being criticized for his lack of attention to AIDS. In response, he budgeted $10,000 and spent the money on a statewide billboard campaign, in which the messages were visible to thousands of motorists. If we beg the question regarding whether the budgeting of $10,000 constituted a meaningful response to AIDS, we would still be confronted with the question of whether that was the best way to spend the money in terms of helping people's lives. Was the campaign effective? In a programmatic sense, the answer is not known; in a political sense, however, the answer is "yes." That is, the visible evidence of government attention to the issue of AIDS diverted criticism from the governor, which very likely was the entire point of the campaign.

In this sense, campaigns constitute a type of symbolic politics (Edelman, 1964). Campaigns are often politically palatable strategies for social change because they resonate with such cherished democratic themes as the value of education, an enlightened populace, a preference for individual-level change through the exercise of free will rather than coercion, and the merits of evolutionary rather than revolutionary change. Indeed, Paletz, Pearson, and Willia (1977) argue that virtually all government public service advertising campaigns portray the federal government as working in a caring and capable manner to solve social problems, thereby inspiring confidence in political institutions while suppressing political participation on the part of citizens. Traditional evaluations, however, will fail to assess political effectiveness unless the sponsor's specific political agenda is known and incorporated into the evaluation study and potential long-term consequences of campaigns, such as political apathy, are studied.

Contextual Effectiveness

When evaluators assess the impact of communication campaigns, they rarely put the results in any kind of context. For example, we might start with the classic distinctions among three different mechanisms of social change offered by Paisley (see Chapter 1, this volume). An *engineering* solution to a social problem typically occurs with the development of a technology or innovation that can alone remedy the problem (such as the introduction of oral or needle inoculation with attenuated polio virus, which has eradicated polio). *Enforcement,* in contrast, typically involves the passage of laws, the use of coercion, or other forms of mandating change (such as seat belt laws, immigration vaccination laws, and mandated child safety protection). The third mechanism, *education,* typically involves modifying knowledge, attitudes, beliefs, or behavior; it is the predominant communication arm of social change.

When evaluating communication campaigns, one needs to take into account the capabilities of the alternatives, engineering and enforcement. If we find, for example, that antidrug public service announcements (PSAs) do not eradicate illegal drug use, we need not instinctively "blame" campaigns or indict them for their ineffectiveness, especially because prior enforcement approaches have often failed. Rather, the focus of the evaluation can instead turn to analyses of why the decision to use communication—instead of engineering or enforcement—was made in the first place and whether or not that decision was an appropriate one. The evaluation should also consider the roles that engineering and enforcement play in influencing the effectiveness of communication or vice versa (as an obvious example, a mandatory seat belt law can have a chance of being effective only if the citizenry is made aware that it exists). Increasingly, various combinations of the three strategies of change are used in unison rather than exclusively, but rarely is this synergy taken into account in most evaluation research.

Cost-Effectiveness

This conceptualization emphasizes whether communication campaigns are more or less cost-effective than other forms of intervention. "Prevention" is a central component of the contemporary health paradigm, as health maintenance organizations and other health service organizations are attempting to reduce costs of medical care by reducing the incidence of individuals' health needs. Communication has become a centerpiece of the prevention movement, which is predicated on the notion that an ounce of prevention is worth a pound of cure. Reflecting this paradigm, for example, the Centers for Disease Control changed its name to the Centers for Disease Control and Prevention (CDC) in an attempt to reposition itself in the federal marketplace. As a result of this repositioning, CDC states that it is no longer merely an organization of disease detectives reacting to mysterious outbreaks of disease but, rather, an organization that engages in proactive prevention activities.

One of the common uses of communication campaigns is to raise awareness of a disease or public health problem and encourage individuals to go to a medical facility for screening and detection. The decision to use campaigns for this purpose, however, must be made very carefully. For example, the incidence of AIDS in the United States is still fairly low (a different issue from its terminal, physical, and social nature). If campaigns heighten anxiety about this disease to the point that millions of people believe that they need to be tested, then several undesirable outcomes can result. First, the public health infrastructure simply is not set up to accommodate massive numbers of individuals requiring screening. Second, allocating more dollars to personnel and materials for testing to handle the increased demand would inevitably lead to fewer dollars available for treatment. Third, because of the relatively low prevalence of the disease, most of the test results would be negative, and thus a great deal of money would be spent on persons who do not have the disease; conversely, fewer dollars would therefore be available for persons who do have the disease and hence are in greater need of the dollars for treatment. Effective campaigns, in this sense, are those that reach the "right" individuals and motivate them to seek appropriate testing and treatment without similarly motivating the "wrong" individuals to do the same. Despite increasingly sophisticated segmentation strategies and techniques, this remains a formidable challenge in any public health intervention.

Cost-benefit analysis has other uses in assessing the effectiveness of communication campaigns. For example, Goldman and Glantz (1998) evaluated the cost-effectiveness of antismoking advertisements in both Massachusetts and California in comparison to the rest of the United States. The 5-year multimedia campaign averaged 50¢ per capita per year in California for an overall reduction of 3.9 packs of cigarettes per capita per year for each campaign dollar spent. In Massachusetts, per capita consumption decreased 1.28 cigarette packs using the same criteria. Goldman and Glantz estimated that given the current trend, overall tobacco sales would decrease by 232 million packs and lead to a sevenfold return for the cost-benefit ratio. The cost saving of this campaign was significant when compared to lifetime insurance and medical costs arising from patients with emphysema and lung cancer, who require continuous and expensive regiments of care. In addition, enhanced quality of life from smoking cessation may contribute to increased earnings over the period of extended life. Thus, the cost-effectiveness of a health intervention can be calculated to include savings in health care resources, diminished opportunity costs, and prolonged life, all of which most campaign evaluations do not address.

Programmatic Effectiveness

Finally, every information campaign is, or at least should be, driven by goals and objectives that specify the nature and degree of impact sought. When campaign performance is measured against these goals and objectives, an assessment of programmatic effectiveness can be made through a direct comparison between objectives and outcomes. This type of effectiveness is described in detail in most standard evaluation research textbooks.

One caveat should be mentioned, however. Critical to the comparison between objectives and outcomes, of course, is awareness of those objectives. For example, PSAs developed by the National AIDS Information and Education Program were designed to encourage individuals to call the National AIDS Hotline, the largest public health hotline in the world. This was done because it was realized that a single 30- or 60-second TV spot could not possibly address all the concerns and questions that an audience member might have about the disease, and that the media message needed to be supplemented by a more interactive interpersonal message. If evaluated in terms of programmatic criteria, the ads were effective because they accomplished what they were designed to accomplish. If evaluated in terms of other criteria applied by outside evaluators not privy to the organization's goals and objectives, however, such as whether the ads influenced a person's behavioral intention to wear a condom, then the ads could (unfairly) be deemed ineffective.

DISTINGUISHING BETWEEN CAMPAIGN EFFECTS AND EFFECTIVENESS

The terms campaign "effects" and "effectiveness" have long been treated as interchangeable and synonymous, at least as used in numerous studies and review essays about campaigns. They are conceptually quite distinct, however. Both represent interpretations of communication outcomes, but they differ in terms of the key dimension of intentionality. For example, a disproportionate amount of research on media effects has focused on antisocial effects, such as children imitating violence in real life after viewing it on television. The imitation of violence would be characterized as evidence of a media effect rather than media effectiveness, however, because it presumably is not the intention of the creators of the media content to induce violent behavior on the part of children watching their show. If a TV show were to adopt entertainment-education (or edutainment; see Chapter 28, this volume) strategies with the specific intention of inducing their viewers to behave in a particular way (e.g., cooperate rather than fight), however, then such a finding would be evidence of both a media effect and media effectiveness. Thus, *effectiveness* constitutes a subset of the larger category of effects—that is, the subset of effects defined in terms of pre-existing goals and intentions. Table 9.1 displays the possible relationships between campaign effects and effectiveness.

Effects and Effectiveness

Cell 1 in Table 9.1 (effects and effectiveness) asks the question, "Can we have a situation in which we have an outcome defined as an effect that we also interpret as evidence of effectiveness?" Consider the case in which the goal of a cardiovascular health campaign is to increase knowledge of heart disease by 10% in a community. If, through pre- and posttests with appropriate comparison communities (see Chapters 6 and 8, this volume), we determine a 10% increase in knowledge, then we conclude that the educational campaign did have an effect and also that it was effective. Although this type of outcome is fairly straightforward and easily understood, the literature on campaigns contains at least as many reports of campaign failure as campaign success.

No Effects, No Effectiveness

Cell 4 in Table 9.1 (no effects and no effectiveness) shows an outcome that we do not recognize as an effect, and the interpretation is a lack of effectiveness. Ineffectiveness has been rationalized as the result of poorly constructed or implemented messages or campaigns, the inability to reach the target audience, lack of inoculation with the campaign message, the inability to produce lasting change in attitudes, knowledge, or behaviors, or all these (Backer et al., 1992; Rossi & Freeman, 1993; Schorr, 1997; see Chapter 7, this volume). Ineffectiveness is a plausible outcome, both in theory and in practice (consider, for example, the titles of studies by Hyman & Sheatsley, 1947, and by Robertson, 1976).

Effect But Not Effectiveness

Whereas Cells 1 and 4 in Table 9.1 are intuitive and commonly alluded to in the campaign literature, Cells 2 and 3 are not. Regarding Cell 3 (effect but not

Table 9.1 Potential Campaign Outcomes: Distinguishing Between Effectiveness
            and Effects

| | *Interpretation That a Given Outcome Constitutes an Effect* | |
Interpretation That a Given Outcome Constitutes Effectiveness	*Yes*	*No*
Yes	1	2
No	3	4

effective), it is plausible to have an outcome judged to be evidence of a campaign's effect but not considered to be evidence of campaign effectiveness. This is an unintended effect because it is not expected in terms of the goals, objectives, and expectations of the campaign planner but is some outcome attributable to the campaign's intervention (and the unintended effect may be positive or negative). Often, campaign planners and evaluators attempt to control for unintended effects by including control communities and additional testing measures. It is not always possible, however, to foresee and mitigate all the different types of unintended effects, such as hysteria or panic, knowledge gaps, discrimination and scapegoating, confusion or misunderstanding or both, and potential boomerang effects. For example, initial AIDS awareness campaigns may have triggered a multitude of unintended effects. Early in the epidemic, policymakers became concerned that these campaigns were inadvertently leading to discrimination against persons with AIDS, unwarranted fear of nonintimate physical contact with persons with AIDS, and stereotyping of social and ethnic groups initially linked to the emergence of this newly diagnosed disease. As a result, subsequent campaigns were developed to address these themes and to allay public concerns that resulted from initial efforts to warn the public of the emerging disease. In general, it is important to note that these outcomes are obviously very important from the standpoint of public policy, and that they merit particular attention from campaign evaluators because of their surprising prevalence (Cho, 1999; Salmon, 1996).

No Known Effect But Effectiveness

Cell 2 in Table 9.1 (no known effect but effectiveness) occurs when there is no evidence of a campaign having any tangible effect, but it is nonetheless judged to be effective. There are two contexts in which this outcome might occur. First, "placement" has long been used as a criterion of effectiveness for publicity and public service efforts. Whereas commercial advertisers "pay" for space and hence are guaranteed control of the placement and timing of their messages in the media, publicity agents and public service campaigners are said to "pray" for space. They must send their materials to media gatekeepers (editors and broadcast news directors) without payment for placement or timing (Wallack, 1989). This publicity model, which serves as the basis of most PSA campaigns, has long relied on the collection of news clippings as evidence that an organization's prayers have been answered—that their messages appeared in the media. This type of evaluation obviously begs the question of whether anyone saw, read, understood, acted on, or remembered the information (whether they are "engaged"; see Chapter 8, this volume), but nevertheless it has endured as an accepted form of campaign evaluation.

The second context is characterized by intense competition. In antismoking campaigns, for example, for which public service campaigners have active adversaries who are attempting to increase their own market share, reinforcement of existing nonsmoking rates rather than actual reduction—or other types of seemingly "null" effects—could be considered a type of victory (and hence effectiveness).

CONCLUSION

As has been noted elsewhere, the search for a definitive answer to the question "Are campaigns effective?" is a search for a minotaur (Salmon, 1989). Neither campaigns nor effectiveness are simple, unidimensional constructs for which there exists conceptual and operational clarity or uniformity. The challenge to the academic community and to program evaluators is to look beyond obvious intended effects and to move beyond mere programmatic evaluation. As a discipline, we have a fairly well-developed body of theory for campaigns but relatively little theory of campaigns (Salmon, 1992). That is, we have a well-stocked arsenal of theories to help us build more sophisticated and powerful interventions, but we have far less understanding of campaigns as a social institution operating in the milieu of sundry social and political forces. Only by broadening the scope of evaluation research and our conceptualization of campaign effectiveness to incorporate such frequently neglected notions as the social construction of health, ideological biases, and conflicting stakeholder agendas can we fully appreciate the role that campaigns play in society and their realistic potential to shape social change.

REFERENCES

Atkin, C. K. (1981). Mass media information campaign effectiveness. In R. E. Rice & W. J. Paisley (Eds.), *Public communication campaigns* (pp. 265-279). Beverly Hills, CA: Sage.

Backer, T. E., Rogers, E. M., & Sopory, P. (1992). *Designing health communication campaigns: What works?* Newbury Park, CA: Sage.

Best, J. (Ed.). (1989). *Images of issue: Typifying contemporary social problems.* Hawthorne, NY: Aldine.

Cho, H. (1999). Unintended effects of fear appeals: The role of stages of change, threat, and efficacy. Unpublished doctoral dissertation, Michigan State University, East Lansing, MI.

Douglas, D., Westley, B. H., & Chaffee, S. H. (1970). An information campaign that changed community attitudes. *Journalism Quarterly, 47,* 479-492.

Edelman, M. (1964). *The symbolic uses of politics.* Urbana: University of Illinois Press.

Farquhar, J. W., Fortmann, S. P., Flora, J. A., Taylor, C. B., Haskell, W. L., Williams, P. T., Maccoby, N., & Wood, P. D. (1990). Effects of community wide education on cardiovascular disease risk factors: The Stanford Five City Project. *Journal of the American Medical Association, 264,* 359-365.

Goldman, L. K., & Glantz, S. A. (1998). Evaluation of antismoking advertising campaigns. *Journal of the American Medical Association, 279,* 772-777.

Harris, M. I., Flegal, K. M., Cowie, C. C., Eberhardt, M. S., Goldstein, D. E., Little, R. R., Wiedmeyer, H. M., & Byrd-Holt, D. D. (1998). Prevalence of diabetes, impaired fasting glucose, and impaired glucose tolerance in U.S. adults. *Diabetes Care, 21,* 518-524.

Haug, M. (1995, August). *Campaigns without effects? A critical examination of the Stanford community studies.* Paper presented at the 12th Nordic Mass Communication Conference, Helsingor, Denmark.

Hilgartner, S., & Bosk, C. L. (1988). The rise and fall of social problems: A public arenas model. *American Journal of Sociology, 94,* 53-78.

Hyman, H. H., & Sheatsley, P. B. (1947). Some reasons why information campaigns fail. *Public Opinion Quarterly, 10,* 412-423.

Maccoby, N., Farquhar, J., Wood, P., & Alexander, J. (1977). Reducing the risk of cardiovascular disease: Effects of a community-based campaign on knowledge and behavior. *Journal of Community Health, 3,* 100-114.

McGovern, P. G., Burke, G. L., Sprafka, J. M., Xue, S., Folsum, A. R., & Blackburn, H. B. (1992). Trends in mortality, morbidity, and risk factor levels for stroke from 1960 to 1990: The Minnesota Heart Survey. *Journal of the American Medical Association, 268,* 753-759.

McGuire, W. J. (1986). The myth of massive media impact: Savagings and salvagings. In G. Comstock (Ed.), *Public communication and behavior* (pp. 175-257). New York: Academic Press.

Mendelsohn, H. (1973). Some reasons why information campaigns can succeed. *Public Opinion Quarterly, 37,* 50-61.

Montgomery, K. C. (1993). The Harvard alcohol project: Promoting the designated driver on television. In T. E. Backer & E. M. Rogers (Eds.), *Organizational aspects of health communication campaigns: What works?* (pp. 178-202). Newbury Park, CA: Sage.

Neal, W. D., & Bathe, S. (1997). Using the value equation to evaluate campaign effectiveness. *Journal of Advertising Research, 37,* 80-85.

Paletz, D. L., Pearson, R. E., & Willia, D. L. (1977). *Politics in public service advertising on television.* New York: Praeger.

Robertson, L. S. (1976). The great seat belt campaign flop. *Journal of Communication, 26,* 41-45.

Rossi, P. H., & Freeman, H. E. (1993). *Evaluation: A systematic approach* (5th ed.). Newbury Park, CA: Sage.

Salmon, C. T. (1989). Campaigns for social "improvement": An overview of values, rationales, and impacts. In C. T. Salmon (Ed.), *Information campaigns: Balancing social values and social change* (pp. 19-53). Newbury Park, CA: Sage.

Salmon, C. T. (1992). Building theory "of" and theory "for" communication campaigns: An essay on ideology and public policy. *Communication Yearbook, 15,* 346-358.

Salmon, C. T. (1996, May). The other side of the coin: A typology of unintended effects of social marketing. Paper presented at the 2nd Annual Social Marketing Conference, Fairfax, VA.

Scherer, C. W., & Juanillo, N. K. (1992). Bridging theory and praxis: Reexamining public health communication. *Communication Yearbook, 15,* 312-345.

Schorr, L. B. (1997). What works and why we have so little of it. In *Common purpose* (pp. 3-21). New York: Anchor.

Spector, M., & Kitsuse, J. I. (1977). *Constructing social problems.* Menlo Park, CA: Cummings.

Star, S. A., & Hughes, H. G. (1950). Report on an educational campaign: The Cincinnati Plan for the United Nations. *American Journal of Sociology, 55,* 389-400.

Tesh, S. N. (1988). *Hidden arguments: Political ideology and disease prevention policy.* New Brunswick, NJ: Rutgers University Press.

Vartiainen, E., Paavola, M., McAlister, A., & Puska, P. (1998). Fifteen year follow-up of smoking prevention effects in the North Karelia youth. *American Journal of Public Health, 88,* 81-85.

Wallack, L. (1989). Mass communication and health promotion: A critical perspective. In R. E. Rice & C. K. Atkin (Eds.), *Public communication campaigns* (2nd ed., pp. 353-367). Newbury Park, CA: Sage.

Wartella, E., & Middlestadt, S. (1991). Mass communication and persuasion: The evolution of direct effects, limited effects, information processing, and affect and arousal models. In L. Donohew, H. E. Sypher, & W. J. Bukoski (Eds.), *Persuasive communication and drug abuse prevention* (pp. 53-69). Hillsdale, NJ: Lawrence Erlbaum.

Weiss, C. (1997). Theory-based evaluation: Past, present and future. In D. J. Rog & D. Fournier (Eds.), *Progress and future directions in evaluation: Perspectives on theory, practice, and methods* (pp. 41-57). San Francisco: Jossey-Bass.

10

How Effective
Are Mediated
Health Campaigns?

Leslie B. Snyder

There has been much debate regarding whether mediated campaigns are effective or not and, if so, how useful they can be in changing behavior. Identification of the conditions under which campaigns have greater effects is valuable for both academics and practitioners. In addition, knowing the percentage of the target audience that a mediated health campaign can reasonably expect to affect given certain conditions would be advantageous when planning and evaluating a health campaign. Such data would help when setting realistic campaign goals, identifying campaigns that have better than average results, choosing message strategies, designing the evaluation, and deciding between different approaches to social change, such as information campaigns, enforcement, or counseling.

Snyder et al. (2000) analyzed the average behavior change in health campaigns as part of the Campaign Meta-Analysis Project. Behavior is often a "bottom-line" outcome for organizations that sponsor health campaigns. Also, because behavior change is more difficult to achieve than awareness, knowledge change, or attitude change (see Chapter 2, this volume), it is a more conservative measure of campaign success.

Meta-analysis, the study of prior studies, is a quantitative approach to synthesizing existing research. It is particularly useful for analyzing literatures in which there are some conflicting conclusions and for analyzing qualitative literature reviews that are in disagreement because the quantitative techniques enable researchers to calculate average results and check for contingent conditions responsible for different findings. In the current meta-analysis, published reports of campaign evaluations were the raw data. Meta-analysis avoided problems related to low power (small sample sizes and effect sizes) that can plague individual evaluations of campaigns because the final pooled sample in the meta-analysis was very large (Flay & Cook, 1989; Snyder et al., 2000; see Chapter 6, this volume).

The methodology consisted of collecting all potentially relevant published studies; discarding studies that did not have complete data or were not, on closer inspection, relevant; coding the data for each campaign, including transforming the reported effects into a common statistic of effect size; computing the average effect size; and testing the influence of various moderators. We found adequate information on 48 health communication campaigns in the United States promoting a wide range of health behaviors (Table 10.1). At this juncture, we included only campaigns that used at least one form of mass media and were community based (rather than school or workplace based). Half of the studies used a quasi-experimental evaluation design with at least one intervention and control community and both baseline and posttest measures; other studies used a pre-post no control, posttest only with control, or partition by exposure design. Because the total number of subjects across all these evaluations was a staggering 168,147, we were able to detect statistically significant effect sizes that were quite low.

The meta-analysis reports the correlation between being in a campaign community (as opposed to a control community) and the amount of short-term behavior change, controlling for moderator variables of interest. The results can also be expressed as the average percentage behavior change in communities with campaigns versus that in communities without campaigns. (The relationship between percentage changed and $\bar{r}$ depends on the variance in levels of the target behavior. When the percentage of people doing the target behavior is very high or very low, variance is low and $\bar{r}$ does not correspond exactly to the average percentage changed. Otherwise, $\bar{r}$ and the average percentage changed are quite similar. For the formulae used, see Snyder et al., 2000.)

OVERALL EFFECT SIZE

Overall, 7% to 10% more of the people in the campaign (intervention) communities changed their behavior than did those in the control communities. When expressed as a correlation, the relationship between community exposure to the campaign and behavior change averaged $\bar{r} = .09$ (Snyder et al., 2000). The effect was not homogeneous across campaigns, however, indicating that there were important differences among moderator variables across campaigns.

Table 10.1 Media Campaigns Used in the Meta-Analysis

Campaign	Key Citation[a]	Behavior	r	Exposure[b] (%)	Message Variable[c]
A Su Salud	McAlister et al. (1992). *American Journal of Health Promotion, 6*, 274-279	Smoking cessation	.20	50	
AIDS Community Demonstration Project	Fishbein et al. (1996). In S. Oskamp & S. C. Thompson (Eds.), *Understanding and preventing HIV risk behavior, safer sex and drug use* (pp. 177-206). Thousand Oaks, CA: Sage	Condom use, vaginal sex, bleach use	.03	43	
AIDS Prevention for Pediatric Life	Santelli et al. (1995). *AIDS Education & Prevention, 7*(3), 210-220	Condom use	.05	64	
America Responds to AIDS	Snyder (1991). *Health Communication, 3*(1), 37-57	Risky sex cessation	.01	17	
California Tobacco Education Media Campaign	Popham (1994). *American Journal of Preventive Medicine, 10*(6), 319-326	Smoking prevention	.03	47	
Cancer Control, Texas Barrio	McAlister et al. (1995). *Journal of the National Cancer Institute Monographs, 18*, 123-126	Mammography screen, Pap smear	.05	42	N, S
COMMIT	COMMIT Research Group (1995). *American Journal of Public Health, 85*(2), 183-191	Smoking cessation	.02	17	
Community Trials Project	Grube (1997). *Addiction, 92*(2), S251-S260	Alcohol sales to minors cessation	.17		N, E
Decreasing binge drinking at college	Haines & Spear (1996). *Journal of the American College of Health, 45*(3), 134-140	Binge drinking cessation	.07	50	

(continued)

Table 10.1 Continued

Campaign	Key Citation[a]	Behavior	r	Exposure[b] (%)	Message Variable[c]
Drinking during pregnancy	Kaskutas & Graves (1994). *American Journal of Health Promotion, 9*(2), 115-124	Limiting drinking	.11	83	
Farm Cancer Control Project	Gardiner et al. (1995). *Journal of Cancer Education, 10*(3), 155-162	Mammography screening	.01	33	S
Five-A-Day for Better Health, California	Foester et al. (1995). *American Journal of Preventive Medicine, 11*(2), 124-131	Fruit and vegetable consumption	.01	17	
Forsyth County Cervical Cancer Prevention	Dignan et al. (1994). *Health Education Research, 9*(4), 411-420	Pap smear	.04	14	S
Freedom From Smoking, St. Louis, Missouri	Wheeler (1988). *Social Science Medicine, 27*(12), 1387-1392	Smoking cessation	.17	84	
Friends Can Be Good Medicine	Hersey et al. (1984). *Health Education Quarterly, 11*(3), 293-311	Supportive behavior	.09	51	
Headstrong	Rouzier & Alto (1995). *Journal of the American Board of Family Practice, 8,* 283-287	Bike helmets	.41		N
Heart to Heart	Goodman et al. (1995). *American Journal of Health Promotion, 9*(6), 443-455	Smoke, exercise, weight, cholesterol, blood pressure	.01	17	
Know When to Say No	Werch et al. (1992). *Journal of Health Education, 23*(6), 364-368	Drinking cessation	.12	99	N
Kentucky rural high blood pressure control	Kotchen et al. (1986). *Journal of the American Medical Association, 255*(16), 2177-2182	Hypertension	.10	13	S

Program	Citation	Topic			N, S
Media-Based Mammography, San Diego	Mayer et al. (1993). *American Journal of Preventive Medicine, 8*(1), 23-29	Mammography screening	.05	44	N, S
Minority smoking cessation, Chicago	Jason et al. (1988). *American Journal of Public Health, 87*(6), 1031-1034	Smoking cessation	.15	53	
MMHP, Minnesota Adult Smoking Prevention	Luepker et al. (1994). *American Journal of Public Health, 84*(9), 1383-1393	Smoking cessation, physical activity	.05	17	
MMHP, Minnesota Youth Smoking Prevention	Perry et al. (1992). *American Journal of Public Health, 82*(9), 1210-1216	Smoking prevention	.09	50	
Minnesota Periodontal Awareness TV campaign	Bakdash (1984). *Northwest Dentistry, 63*(6), 12-17	Dental visits	.13	70	S
Minnesota/Wisconsin adolescent tobacco use	Murray et al. (1994). *Preventive Medicine, 23*(1), 54-60	Smoking prevention	.07	17	
Mpowerment Project	Kegeles et al. (1996). *American Journal of Public Health, 86*(8), 1129-1136	Unprotected anal sex, condoms	.12	87	
Parents magazine intervention	Kishchuck et al. (1995). *Canadian Journal of Public Health, 86*(2), 128-132	Positive, negative interactions with kids	.02	95	N
Preventing baby bottle tooth decay	Bruerd et al. (1989). *Public Health Reports, 104*(6), 631-640	Bottle use cessation	.14	N	
Programma Latino Para Dejar de Fumar	Marin et al. (1994). *American Journal of Preventive Medicine, 10*(6), 340-347	Smoking cessation	.06	45	
Rural CVD program, West Virginia	Farquhar et al. (1997). *American Journal of Health Promotion, 11*(6), 411-414	Wellness	.09		

(continued)

Table 10.1 Continued

Campaign	Key Citation[a]	Behavior	r	Exposure[b] (%)	Message Variable[c]
Seat belt contest	Foss (1989). *American Journal of Public Health, 79*(3), 304-306	Child seat belt use	.09	59	N
Seat belt use	Robertson (1974). *American Journal of Public Health, 64*(11), 1071-1080	Seat belt use	.01	17	
Seat belt use, Elmira, New York	Williams et al. (1987). *Accident Analysis & Prevention, 19*(4), 243-249	Seat belt use	.24		N, E
Seat belt use, Modesto, California	Lund et al. (1989). *Journal of Criminal Justice, 17,* 329-341	Seat belt use	.22		N, E
Seat belts, Virginia	Roberts & Geller (1994). *American Journal of Health Promotion, 8*(3), 172-174	Seat belt use	.16		E
Smoking prevention, California, Prop. 99	Jenkins et al. (1997). *American Journal of Public Health, 87*(6), 1031-1034	Smoking cessation	.04	50	
Smoking prevention in school	Flynn et al. (1992). *American Journal of Public Health, 82*(6), 827-834	Smoking prevention	.10	50	
Smoking: Los Angeles Community Control Center	Danaher et al. (1984). *Addictive Behavior, 9,* 245-253	Smoking cessation	.15	37	
Smoking: VA Hospital Clinic	Mogielnicki et al. (1986). *Journal of Behavioral Medicine, 9*(2), 141-161	Smoking cessation	.19	61	
Stanford Three-Community Study	Fortmann et al. (1981). *American Journal of Clinical Nutrition, 34,* 2030-2038	Diet, weight, cholesterol, fat	.07	50	N

Study	Reference	Topic	Effect	Exposure	Message
Stanford Five-Community Study	Fortmann et al. (1990). *American Journal of Epidemiology*, 132(4), 629-646	Weight, cholesterol, blood pressure, smoking, exercise	.01	60	
Stop Smoking Clinic, New York	Dubren (1977). *Public Health Reports*, 92(1), 81-84	Smoking cessation	.11	50	
Su Vida Su Salud	Saurez et al. (1993). *American Journal of Preventive Medicine*, 9(5), 290-296	Screenings: Pap, mammograms, and breast	.10	34	S
Take a Bite Out of Crime	O'Keefe (1985). *Communication Research*, 12(2), 147-178	Crime prevention	.10	48	
Time to Quit in Buffalo	Cummings et al. (1997). *American Journal of Public Health*, 77(11), 1452-1453	Smoking cessation	.16	99	
VT Drink Calculator Community Education	Worden et al. (1989). *American Journal of Public Health*, 79(3), 287-290	Drinking cessation	.08	81	N
Weight-A-Thon	Wing & Epstein (1982). *Preventive Medicine*, 11, 245-250	Weight loss	.08	50	
Young adolescent smoking behavior	Bauman et al. (1991). *American Journal of Public Health*, 81(5), 597-604	Smoking prevention	.03	14	

SOURCE: Adopted from Snyder and Hamilton (in press).

a. For complete references, see Snyder and Hamilton (in press) or Snyder et al. (2000).

b. Exposure is the percentage of people in the intervention community exposed to the campaign messages minus the percentage in the control community exposed. Studies without measures of exposure are blank.

c. Message variables: N = new information; E = enforcement; S = services.

LESSONS FOR DIFFERENT CONDITIONS

It is easier to promote a new behavior than to persuade people to stop a behavior. Campaigns that promoted the commencement of a new behavior had an average effect size of $\bar{r} = .12$, and approximately 12% of the target population adopted the new behavior. The commencement campaigns promoted seat belt use, exercise, mammography, dental care, condom use, health status screenings, hypertension control, supportive interpersonal behaviors, fruit and vegetable consumption, and crime prevention behaviors.

Behaviors that cessation campaigns were trying to extinguish included smoking, binge drinking, infants sleeping with milk bottle, and sex with risky partners. The average effect size for cessation campaigns was $\bar{r} = .05$, and approximately 5% of the target population changed their behavior.

Prevention campaigns were also more difficult than commencement campaigns. For youth smoking, the only prevention topic represented in the meta-analysis, campaigns had an average effect size of $\bar{r} = .06$, preventing 4% of targeted youth from smoking. The average rate of smoking prevention from media campaigns is similar to those of meta-analyses of traditional school-based youth smoking prevention promotions, which had average change levels of 5% (Rooney & Murray, 1996), and to traditional in-school drug use prevention programs aimed at late elementary grades (such as Project Dare), with an effect size of $\bar{r} = .06$ to .08 (Ennett, Tobler, Ringwalt, & Flewelling, 1994). None of the studies addresses cost-effectiveness, however, which may be the more important criterion for comparisons across outreach techniques.

If there is an enforcement angle to the campaign, it should be publicized (Snyder & Hamilton, in press). Campaigns that used enforcement messages notified people that the authorities would soon be checking people for noncompliance. For example, some seat belt campaigns advertised random road checks by the police (Lund, Stuster, & Fleming, 1989; Roberts & Geller, 1994; Williams et al., 1987). These campaigns had a much higher success rate than earlier seat belt campaigns that did not use enforcement messages (Foss, 1989; Robertson et al., 1974). The average effect size among campaigns that used at least some enforcement messages was $\bar{r} = .17$, or a 17% change. Campaigns that include enforcement messages may be successful because they take advantage of a coercive strategy rather than relying solely on persuasion. More people may change their behavior if they think they might be "caught" than if they think the authorities will not check. Campaigns on topics for which there is no legal ramification for noncompliance could try enforcement by other culturally appropriate authority figures, such as doctors. Research is needed, however, to determine whether enforcement messages are effective at producing behavior only during the time period of enforcement and spot checks.

Campaigns should also prominently feature information that is new to the target audience. The average effect sizes were $\bar{r} = .14$ for campaigns with news (or change in 14% of the population) (Bruerd, Kinney, & Bothwell, 1989;

Rouzier & Alto, 1995; Snyder & Hamilton, in press). Often, by the time public health officials obtain funding for a campaign topic, the formerly new research or behavioral recommendations may be stale news. For example, the Stanford Three-Community Study (Fortmann, Williams, Hulley, Haskell, & Farquhar, 1981; see Chapter 11, this volume) had the advantage of promoting behaviors to reduce risk of heart disease (including diet and weight control) years before it was common knowledge, and it was more successful than later heart campaigns, such as the Stanford Five-Community Study and Minnesota Heart Health Program (Shea & Basch, 1990).

Expect a modest rate of success from campaigns promoting services. The average campaign effect for service promotion campaigns was $\bar{r} = .07$, or 7% change in service utilization. The service promotion campaigns in the study concerned mammography, Pap smears, hypertension treatment compliance, and dental visits.

Everything possible should be done to ensure widespread exposure to the campaign (Hornik, in press). On average, only 40% of the people in the intervention communities were exposed to the campaign. (For cases reporting control community levels of campaign exposure, the measure was the differential between exposure in the intervention and control community.) The percentage of exposed people in the intervention community correlates highly with the campaign effect size (Snyder & Hamilton, in press). This also highlights the need for evaluations to measure levels of exposure in treatment and control communities.

CONCLUSION

The Campaign Meta-Analysis Project studied other potential moderators of campaign effectiveness, including campaign length, messages that use role models, the secular trend (Snyder & Hamilton, in press), campaign topic, the extent of precampaign diffusion of the behavior (Snyder et al., 2000), and evaluation design (Snyder & Hamilton, 1999). Additional issues that need investigation are long-term effects and cost-effectiveness.

REFERENCES

Bruerd, B., Kinney, M. B., & Bothwell, E. (1989). Preventing baby tooth decay in American Indian and Alaska Native communities: A model for planning. *Public Health Reports, 104*(6), 631-640.

Ennett, S. T., Tobler, N. S., Ringwalt, C. L., & Flewelling, R. L. (1994). How effective is drug abuse resistance education? A meta-analysis of project DARE outcome evaluations. *American Journal of Public Health, 84*(9), 1394-1401.

Flay, B. R., & Cook, T. D. (1989). Three models for summative evaluation of prevention campaigns with a mass media component. In R. E. Rice & C. K. Atkin (Eds.), *Public communication campaigns* (2nd ed., pp. 175-195). Newbury Park, CA: Sage.

Fortmann, S. P., Williams, P. T., Hulley, S. B., Haskell, W. L., & Farquhar, J. W. (1981). Effect of health education on dietary behavior: The Stanford Three-Community Study. *American Journal of Clinical Nutrition, 34,* 2030-2038.

Foss, R. D. (1989). Evaluation of a community-wide incentive program to promote safety restraint use. *American Journal of Public Health, 79*(3), 304-306.

Hornik, R. (in press). Public health communication: Making sense of contradictory evidence. In R. Hornik (Ed.), *Public health communication: Evidence for behavior change.* Mahwah, NJ: Lawrence Erlbaum.

Lund, A. K., Stuster, J., & Fleming, A. (1989). Special publicity and enforcement of California's belt use laws: Making a secondary law work. *Journal of Criminal Justice, 17,* 329-341.

Roberts, D. S., & Geller, S. (1994). A statewide intervention to increase safety belt use: Adding to the impact of a belt use law. *American Journal of Health Promotion, 8*(3), 172-174.

Robertson, L. S., Kelley, A. B., O'Neill, B., Wixom, C. W., Eiswirth, R. S., & Haddon, W. (1974). A controlled study of the effect of television messages on safety belt use. *American Journal of Public Health, 64*(11), 1071-1080.

Rooney, B. L., & Murray, D. M. (1996). A meta-analysis of smoking prevention programs after adjustment for errors in the unit of analysis. *Health Education Quarterly, 23*(11), 48-64.

Rouzier, P., & Alto, W. A. (1995). Evolution of a successful community bicycle helmet campaign. *Journal of the American Board of Family Practice, 8,* 283-287.

Shea, S., & Basch, C. E. (1990). A review of five major community-based cardiovascular disease prevention programs. Part II: Intervention strategies, evaluation methods, and results. *American Journal of Health Promotion, 4*(4), 279-287.

Snyder, L. B., & Hamilton, M. A. (1999, August). *When evaluation design affects results: Meta-analysis of evaluations of mediated health campaigns.* Paper presented at the Association for Education in Journalism and Mass Communication annual conference, New Orleans.

Snyder, L. B., & Hamilton, M. A. (in press). Meta-analysis of U.S. health campaign effects on behavior: Emphasize enforcement, exposure, and new information, and beware the secular trend. In R. Hornik (Ed.), *Public health communication: Evidence for behavior change.* Hillsdale, NJ: Lawrence Erlbaum.

Snyder, L. B., Hamilton, M. A., Mitchell, E. W., Kiwanuka-Tondo, J., Fleming-Milici, F., & Proctor, D. (2000). The effectiveness of mediated health communication campaigns: Meta-analysis of differences in commencement, prevention, and cessation behavior campaigns. In R. Carveth & J. Bryant (Eds.), *Meta-analysis of media effects.* Mahwah, NJ: Lawrence Erlbaum.

Williams, A. F., Lund, A. K., Preusser, D. F., & Blomberg, R. D. (1987). Results of a seat belt use law enforcement and publicity campaign in Elmira, New York. *Accident Analysis and Prevention, 19*(4), 243-249.

PART III

Lessons From the Field

11

The Stanford Community Studies

Campaigns to Reduce Cardiovascular Disease

June A. Flora

RATIONALE FOR COMMUNITY CAMPAIGNS

Health behavior and health status are strongly influenced both by biology and by lifestyle, which includes social, cultural, political, and economic factors (Aiken & Mott, 1970; Blum, 1981; Brown, 1984; Flora, Jackson, & Maccoby, 1989; Warren, 1972). The leading causes of death in the United States (cardiovascular disease [CVD] and cancer) are related to lifestyle factors such as diet, exercise, and smoking (U.S. Department of Health and Human Services, 1989). Therefore, a primary premise of the two Stanford community studies was that to be successful, efforts to change behavior must go beyond individuals and include the family, social, and cultural contexts (Farquhar, Fortmann, Flora, & Maccoby, 1991; Kasl, 1980; Shea & Basch, 1990). Furthermore, the Stanford studies aimed to consider the interaction between an individual's thoughts and actions, the physical environment, and social factors. This emphasis on influ-

AUTHOR'S NOTE: This chapter is dedicated to the memory of Nathan Maccoby and his many years of leadership and mentorship in the Stanford studies.

encing the interplay of environmental and personal factors for improving health yielded intervention strategies that occurred in multiple domains of community.

Another premise of the Stanford studies was that all members of the community would benefit from preventive interventions. The reasoning behind this premise is that because the population distribution of many CVD risk factors (e.g., blood cholesterol and blood pressure) is approximately normal, far more people are categorized in the middle range of risk than in the high range (Blackburn, 1997; National Cholesterol Education Program Expert Panel, 1988). Most CVD, therefore, occurs among the many people at moderate risk rather than among the relatively few at high risk (Blackburn, 1983; Puska et al., 1985). Nearly all people in a community are at some level of risk and may benefit from interventions to increase and reinforce healthful behavior (Schooler, Farquhar, Fortmann, & Flora, 1997).

For these two premises, the Stanford community programs focused on multiple audiences, used multiple channels of communication, and targeted multiple cardiovascular health-related outcomes. Furthermore, the timing and placement of individual and environmental change efforts were orchestrated to be mutually reinforcing (Schooler, Flora, & Farquhar, 1993).

THE PROBLEM OF CARDIOVASCULAR DISEASE

In the 1970s and 1980s (as well as in the year 2000), CVDs (fatal and nonfatal heart attacks and strokes) were the greatest cause of premature death and disability in the United States and in most Westernized industrial nations. Approximately one half of all deaths in the United States were attributable to these disorders, with coronary heart disease (CHD) alone accounting for approximately 40% of all deaths (Eliot, 1987). Differential rates of CHD among different countries, however, suggested that there were social and cultural causes for national and community risk and disease rates, such as health behaviors and lifestyles peculiar to the twentieth century and industrialization (Blackburn, 1997; Farquhar, 1987). Lifestyles that include smoking, little or no exercise, diets high in saturated fat and cholesterol, and chronic stress can lead to high blood pressure, high blood cholesterol, and obesity, all of which increase risk of CVD (Farquhar, 1987). It should be noted that these previously high rates of CVD would be found to decline rapidly in the 1970s and 1980s, thus influencing the interpretation of findings of the second Stanford study.

Fueled by these data on CVD, John Farquhar, a Stanford faculty cardiologist and researcher, consulted his social science colleagues such as Nathan Maccoby (at the Institute for Communication Research in the Communication Department at Stanford), known for his research in attitude formation and attitude change. Farquhar asked Maccoby and others at the institute to tell him "how to use the media to change behavior." Farquhar, Maccoby, and another colleague with expertise in biochemistry, Peter Wood, wrote grants to the National Institutes of Health, received funding, and initiated the landmark

Stanford Three-Community Study (TCS). In the late 1970s, the Stanford Five-City Project (FCP) was also funded and implemented (Farquhar, 1978; Farquhar, Fortmann, et al., 1985). This chapter describes the research design, intervention methods, theoretical underpinnings, and final results of the TCS and the FCP.

THE STANFORD THREE-COMMUNITY STUDY

Given a strong rationale for the efficacy of attempting to change the lifestyles of a whole population, the Stanford TCS was funded and mounted in 1971, with full field application in 1972, and extended through 1975. The primary research objective of the TCS was to investigate the influence of a large-scale intervention on the knowledge, attitudes, and risk-related behaviors of the population of two medium-sized communities relative to the change of an untreated matched control community (Farquhar et al., 1977). Specific individual behavior and risk-change objectives included the following:

1. Reductions in plasma cholesterol levels through reduced intake of saturated fat and cholesterol and increased intake of lean meats, nonfat dairy products, complex carbohydrates, and dietary fiber

2. Lowering or controlling blood pressure levels through blood pressure checks, reduced salt intake, reduced weight, increased physical activity, and adherence to medication to control hypertension

3. Declines in cigarette use through prevention of adoption by nonsmokers and through quitting by current smokers

4. Weight loss and control through increased physical activity and reduced intake of fat and calories

5. Increased physical activity, such as walking or participating in some form of aerobic activity 20 minutes per day, three or more times per week

Theoretical Underpinnings

TCS investigators sought to integrate a variety of theories into the fabric of design, implementation, and evaluation of the study. For practical application and long-range planning, these perspectives were integrated into an overall framework that was later formulated as the Communication-Behavior Change (CBC) model (Farquhar, Maccoby, & Solomon, 1984). Table 11.1 presents the steps of the CBC model. The individual change objectives are listed in the right-hand column; the middle column contains the corresponding media functions required to meet those objectives; and the left-hand column reminds us that media products and events must be designed, produced, and distributed in sequence to perform these functions.

Table 11.1 The Health Communication-Behavior Change Model

Communication Inputs	Communication Functions (for the Receiver)	Behavior Objectives (for the Receiver)
Media messages	Gain attention	Become aware
Face-to-face communication	Provide information	Increase knowledge
Community programs	Provide incentives	Increase motivation
and events	Provide models	Learn and practice skills
	Provide training	Take action
	Provide cues to action	Maintain action, practice
	Provide support, self	self-management skills
	management skills	Influence social network members

The CBC model's consideration of knowledge gain, attitude change, and behavior change was influenced by Cartwright's (1949) identification of three psychological processes in behavior change in campaigns: (a) cognitive structures (knowledge), (b) affective structures (motivation), and (c) action structures (behavior). He noted that action structures are typically missing in mass-mediated campaigns. Cartwright concluded that media campaign messages backed up by face-to-face communication improved the likelihood of obtaining changes in behaviors, by cueing action structures, as well as in knowledge and attitudes. Cognitive response theory and studies of persuasion contributed to the ways in which skills were conceptualized in the CBC. For example, Lumsdaine and Janis's (1953) research on methods of resisting persuasive messages through inoculation with two-sided arguments, supported by later work by McGuire (1964) and Roberts and Maccoby (1973), demonstrated that individuals can be inoculated against negative or health-compromising acts of persuasion. Bandura's (1969, 1977) social learning theory emphasized that behavioral skills are often necessary prerequisites for the establishment of healthful habits. Skills can be acquired through observation and guided practice, which increases self-efficacy, provides incentives for health behavior, and gives behavioral feedback. From the standpoint of the target population, this model begins with the individual's current state of knowledge, beliefs, and patterns of behavior. Individuals engage in social comparison processes (Festinger, 1954) to assess the salience and outcomes of others' behavior. Such comparisons, in addition to social norms, attitudes, and behavioral intentions, influence subsequent behavior (Fishbein & Ajzen, 1975). These innovative attitudes and behaviors may then diffuse through interpersonal networks (Katz & Lazarsfeld, 1955; Rogers, 1983). Communication planning depends on assessing the distance between the baseline state of affairs and outcome objectives and determining optimal intervention points based on this information. The health CBC model serves as a general guide for organizing the community intervention task into manageable pieces: illustrating where to begin, establishing short-term objectives, and highlighting necessary prevention messages.

Table 11.2   Knowledge, Behavior, and Risk Factor Outcomes, and Their Data
Collection Periods, of the Three-Community Study

	Gilroy		Watsonville	
Outcome Risk Variable	*Media Only* (n = 363)	*Total* (n = 384)	*Media Plus Instructees* (n = 67)	*Reconstituted Media Only* (n = 384)
Composite CHD risk	S2, S3, S4	S2, S3, S4	S2, S3, S4	S2, S3, S4
Plasma cholesterol	S3, S4	S2, S3, S4	S2, S3, S4	S2, S3, S4
Systolic blood pressure	S2, S3, S4	S2, S3, S4	S2, S3, S4	S2, S3, S4
Smoking	S2	S2, S3, S4	S2, S3, S4	
Dietary cholesterol	S2, S3, S4	S2, S3, S4	S2, S3, S4	S2, S3, S4
Dietary saturated fat	S2, S3, S4	S2, S3, S4	S2, S3, S4	S2, S3, S4
Eggs eaten	S2, S3, S4	S2, S3, S4	S2, S3, S4	S2, S3, S4
Knowledge	S2, S3, S4	S2, S3, S4	S2, S3	S2, S3, S4

SOURCE: Adapted from Farquhar et al. (1977), Maccoby (1980), and Maccoby et al. (1977).
NOTE: S2 = survey at the end of Year 1, after the full campaign; S3 = survey at the end of Year 2, after a reduced campaign; S4 = survey at the end of Year 3, after no campaign.

Research Design

The TCS employed a quasi-experimental design, incorporating surveys of a randomly selected panel of participants aged 35 to 59 years in each of three nonrandomized, agricultural marketing towns in northern California for each of the 3 years. TCS tested the effects of two different types of interventions. In Gilroy, intervention was limited to mass media alone. In Watsonville, a media campaign was supplemented with intensive face-to-face instruction for a randomly selected subset of high-risk residents drawn from the total community sample. In the third community, Tracy, only surveys were conducted for comparison. The application of an intensive intervention to a sample of high-risk participants created three groups for analysis: Watsonville total group, Watsonville media plus intensive instruction group, and Watsonville reconstructed group (mass media-only sample obtained by eliminating intensive instructees) (Farquhar et al., 1977; Meyer, Nash, McAlister, Maccoby, & Farquhar, 1980). Table 11.2 summarizes the conditions, primary measures, and survey schedules.

The TCS Campaign

The TCS education campaign occurred between 1972 and 1975. An English-language campaign was delivered primarily through newspaper columns, television public service announcements (PSAs) and shows, and other print media (such as bus cards, mass-distributed fliers, cookbooks, and health booklets). A Spanish-language campaign involved primarily radio and Spanish-language newspaper doctor's columns and some print (e.g., cookbooks and health booklets). The media campaign began 2 months after the initial baseline survey and continued for 9 months in 1973, was stopped during the second survey, and was then continued for 9 more months in 1974 at a reduced level. The study ended with a third survey 1 year later (Maccoby, Farquhar, Wood, & Alexander, 1977).

The TCS actively incorporated formative and process evaluation (see Chapters 6-8, this volume) into the campaign design and refinement process. Campaign design was an iterative process of audience analysis (using the baseline survey), pilot studies, product pretests, and intervention monitoring. Unobtrusive process evaluation procedures (called "snoops" in the TCS) included interim analysis of newspaper content in both intervention and reference communities, checks on sales data from supermarkets, and observers who rode buses and sat by billboards listening for comments from passersby. This formative and process research ensured that messages were tailored to the cultural experiences, knowledge, and language of the target audiences and effectively implemented.

Results of the TCS

For most risk factor and behavioral outcomes, the media-only town (Gilroy) and the town with media plus face-to-face instruction (Watsonville) showed improvements relative to the no-treatment community (Tracy). The media-plus intervention, however, generally had stronger results than the media-only intervention. The results were consistent with the Cartwright formulation: Mass media supplemented by intensive instruction is likely to be most effective (Cartwright, 1949).

There were successes for media alone, however. In the case of knowledge gain, participants in the media-only condition showed knowledge gains similar to those of participants in the community who received media plus supplementation. In both treatment communities, knowledge gains were significantly greater than in the reference community (Tracy). When only high-risk spouses and participants (who received additional intensive instruction) in the media-plus community were measured, however, their knowledge gains were more than twice those of the residents in the media-only community (Farquhar et al., 1977; Maccoby, 1980; Maccoby et al., 1977).

A primary outcome measure of the TCS study was CHD risk, a composite score that incorporated age, sex, plasma cholesterol, systolic blood pressure, and relative weight (Truitt, Cornfield, & Kannel, 1967). Gilroy, the media-only town, showed a decline similar to that of the Watsonville participants who were not part of the intensive instruction (Watsonville media-only reconstituted). There were greater decreases in risk in Watsonville (media plus town), however, when the participants from Gilroy were compared with the total set of participants in Watsonville. These differences disappeared by the second year of the campaign. All treatment scores were significantly different from the reference community scores at Years 1 and 2 (Farquhar et al., 1977). Some changes were further extended in the third year, despite a reduced educational program (Maccoby, 1980). This was especially true in Watsonville, the community with intensive instruction under a mass media umbrella.

It became evident that certain kinds of behavior associated with risk reduction can be learned through attention to the mass media alone. When behavior change depends primarily on acquiring new knowledge (e.g., improved eating habits), media interventions may be sufficient, whereas other behaviors (e.g., cigarette smoking cessation) required a different constellation of interventions, including interpersonal communication of skills, self-monitoring, and feedback. Media alone were not enough in this instance to sustain behavior change, although they were effective in producing initial behavior changes in smoking behavior.

The results of the TCS can be summarized as primarily a dose-response relationship with significant effects on smoking, blood pressure, cholesterol, and a composite CHD risk reduction of approximately 23% in a cohort sample. Spanish-speaking residents demonstrated proportionately more reductions in CHD than did the Anglo majority (Maccoby et al., 1977). Much of the success of the TCS campaign can be attributed to the quality of the media campaign, which generated acceptance and use of messages. Supplementation of media and interpersonal communication also fostered synergistic interactions among educational inputs (Maccoby et al., 1977).

THE STANFORD FIVE-CITY PROJECT

The TCS results led us to believe that the power of the media could be considerably enhanced if we could devise ways to employ the media to stimulate and coordinate interpersonal instructional programs in natural settings, such as schools, places of work, and community agencies. Thus, one of the main thrusts of the Stanford Five-City Multifactor Risk Reduction project was to involve educating a population of more than 100,000. The following questions helped guide the planning of the FCP:

1. Could we energize existing social networks and organizations in such a way that they would replicate the intensive instruction component of Watsonville?

2. Could we improve the health habits of all members of a community and not just those at high risk?

3. Would the use of mass media be as effective in larger communities as it had been in the TCS?

4. Could we develop effective ways of delivering skills training in such areas as smoking cessation without providing hands-on instructions from experts?

5. Would we be able to develop a model for communitywide risk reduction that would be generalizable to the extent that it could be used, with variations and modifications, elsewhere in the country or indeed the world?

The FCP differed from the TCS in several ways: (a) The age range of the population chosen for surveys was increased from 35 to 59 years in the TCS to 12 to 74 years in the FCP, (b) program objectives included the institutionalization of the educational program, (c) the program included an extensive community mobilization component, and (d) CVD morbidity and mortality (both heart attack and stroke events) were monitored as well as risk factors and behaviors.

Research Design

The FCP was launched in 1978, after 6 months of planning and 1 year of baseline data collection. The 14-year study employed a quasi-experimental research design carried out in five northern California communities. Two communities received the educational intervention, and two served as references, with one community serving only as a morbidity and mortality monitoring control (Farquhar et al., 1985). The total study population was composed of approximately 325,000 individuals, with single community populations varying from 40,000 to 130,000 people. The four education and reference communities were approximately matched with regard to size, employment base, and community demographics (such as education and ethnicity). The two education communities shared a common television and radio market (newspaper markets overlap to a lesser degree), whereas media markets for the reference communities were independent of the education communities.

A series of five cross-sectional surveys of the population combined with five surveys of a panel of individuals (cohorts) constituted the data-collection plan (Farquhar, Maccoby, & Wood, 1985). As Table 11.3 shows, the panel and the independent surveys were implemented in alternate years and conducted in only four of the target communities. The baseline survey served as both the first independent survey and as the first year of the panel. In both the panel and the cross-sectional surveys, data were collected on communication, psychological, behavioral, physical, and physiological variables (Farquhar et al., 1985).

Four Steps to Conducting the FCP Campaign

Problem Identification

Problem identification included updating the scientific justification for a community-based intervention, examining research on the best means to mobilize communities to participate in comprehensive change efforts, and investigating studies of effective intervention strategies. In the case of CVD

Table 11.3 Design of the Stanford Five-City Project

	1978-1979	1979-1980	1980-1981	1981-1982	1982-1983	1983-1984	1984-1985	1985-1986	1986-1987	1987-1988	1988-1989	1989-1990	1990-1991	1991-1992
								Grant Year Date						
Education			1	2	3	4	5	6		Maintenance				
Individual surveys		I-1		I-2		I-3		I-4				I-5		
Cohort surveys		C-1	C-2		C-3		C-4			C-5				
Surveillance cases	X	X	X	X	X	X	X	X	X	X	X	X		
Surveillance work	X	X	X	X	X	X	X	X	X	X	X	X	X	

NOTE: Date locations of individual and cohort surveys are approximate; all except C-2 began at the end of the prior year.

prevention, there continued to be a reasonably good international consensus that risk was determined by powerful cultural forces that may be susceptible to change. It should be noted that the large general declines in CHD that were to occur during the time period of the FCP were not yet documented. Other studies supported the idea that planned social change based on a comprehensive linkage of medical, educational, and media resources had the potential to have favorable effects on CVD. Control of blood pressure, reduction of fat and cholesterol in the diet, increased physical activity, smoking cessation, and maintenance of ideal weight continued to be identified as change objectives for the entire population. Reviews of social science intervention research revealed that studies of systematic school-based health interventions were just beginning to show promising results, group-based interventions were continuing to show strong short-term effects, and physician-based programs were being piloted (Crouch et al., 1986; Fortmann, Sallis, Magnus, & Farquhar, 1985; Killen et al., 1988; Meyer et al., 1980).

Planning

Once the health targets were established, strategies and specific intervention models were identified and planning for intervention began that involved three major activities.

Determining the Theoretical Orientation. The FCP educational goals included achieving a significant reduction in CVD risk in the population and leaving in place a self-sustaining risk-reduction program (for a discussion of sustainability, see Chapter 27, this volume). To achieve these lofty goals, the FCP education program needed to target individuals, social networks (e.g., families and social groups), organizations (health services, restaurants, workplaces, media, and political and religious groups), and the whole community. Although the CBC model (see Table 11.1) was sufficient for individual behavior change, it provided little guidance for social-level interventions.

Community mobilization and adoption principles had been used by other researchers to guide interactions with community agencies, particularly education and health groups and workplaces (Rothman, 1969; see Chapter 27, this volume). These principles were categorized into three distinct models: (a) *consensus development* emphasized the importance of the participation of a wide array of community constituencies throughout the campaign design and community adoption process, (b) *social action* called for strategic actions to mobilize community members to create new social structures via activation of the political process, and (c) *social planning* stressed the use of objective data collected through guidance of experts as the path to achieving systemwide change.

In the FCP, the model selected depended on the stage of the overall campaign (early, middle, or late) and on the objective to be achieved. For example, social action models were useful for developing environmental change strategies (such as developing advocacy and lobbying efforts for creating smoke-free environments and restricting cigarette advertising), whereas consensus development models were important during the process of institutionalizing programs. Social planning, with its attention to data collection and its use of direct and multiplier strategies for change, was most useful as a model of community organization to facilitate campaign planning and implementation.

Selecting Program Implementation Models. Translating theoretical generalizations into intervention actions presented a formidable challenge for FCP campaign designers. Social marketing principles were used to bridge this gap between theory and action (Kotler, 1975; Kotler & Zaltman, 1971; see Chapter 27, this volume). The essential components of social marketing incorporated into FCP design included (a) developing messages, products, and services from the perspective of the focal consumer, thus tailoring theoretic messages to audience subgroups (e.g., for teens, an emphasis on the short-term consequences of smoking, which included bad breath and smelly clothes and hair); (b) planning campaigns as a strategic mix of products (e.g., television public service announcements, printed materials, and curricula), prices (e.g., dollars, time, and energy), places (e.g., libraries, work sites, and schools), and promotions (e.g., events, fliers, and newspaper ads); and (c) using formative research to develop and test the elements of the campaign (Lefebvre & Flora, 1988).

The process of campaign planning for the FCP was composed of four steps. First was the assessment of the status quo (according to the CBC model). Next was the development of theory-based programs designed to move the target audience to a new step in the change process (e.g., skills-based self-help quit smoking kits). Then, these theory-based programs were tailored to individuals' social, cultural, and experiential contexts (e.g., Spanish-language materials, family-based programs, older adult messages, and materials for men and women). Finally, outcomes of these programs were compared, in formative research and midcourse evaluations, to the CBC hierarchy.

Conducting Formative Research. At the time of the FCP, health communication campaigns typically lacked adequate formative evaluation, resulting in a common failure to meet campaign objectives. We aimed to correct this campaign process failure by using extensive formative and process evaluation (see Chapter 7, this volume) through four general categories of formative research in the FCP.

Audience segmentation and individual needs analysis describes a set of data collection and analysis strategies that divides the target audience into homogeneous clusters. These clusters can be classified by cognitive, behavioral, demographic, or lifestyle variables. The segments were then examined to determine their use of various channels of communication, their needs and interests, and appropriate message development (Slater & Flora, 1991).

Organizational needs analysis was composed of three sets of interviews with community leaders, health agencies gatekeepers, and workplace personnel to determine the institutional networks, extent of current incorporation of prevention activities, resources for prevention, and interests in improving prevention services. Based on data from these interviews, individual organizations were incorporated into advisory groups, communitywide institutional programs were developed (e.g., workplace-based exercise, smoking, and weight control programs), and institutional social networks were used to promote and multiply FCP media efforts.

Channel analysis is the investigation of potential uses of media and other communication channels in interventions. Channels in a community can be classified by the nature of their audiences, availability for health messages, accessibility to audience members, and message characteristics (frequency, duration, and intensity) (Flora, Saphir, Schooler, & Rimal, 1997; Lefebvre & Flora, 1988). In the FCP, gatekeepers in each of the media (television, newspapers, newsletters, and radio) were interviewed periodically to determine channel strategies. For example, Spanish-language radio would play and help develop multipart novellas. A TV station preferred its station logo on PSAs and would donate staff and studio time for PSA development. One newspaper would print at no cost, for 5 years, a doctor's column produced by FCP staff.

Message pretesting was an essential component of every product developed by the FCP. The methods of the pretesting varied greatly, from convenience focus groups to individual interviews and experimental trials. The evaluation rigor, time allowed for formative research, and resources dedicated to the effort were related to the importance of the outcome (i.e., behavior change was deemed more important than awareness or knowledge), the expense of the endeavor (e.g., in the 1980s mass mail tip sheets were much more expensive than cooperatively developed TV news series), and the extent to which FCP staff would control the format and content of the program (e.g., FCP was not in total control of programs cooperatively developed with community agencies).

For example, three precampaign formative studies were conducted to develop a weight loss campaign. At that time, there were no published communitywide weight loss interventions, although there were many clinical group programs. The first step in planning an intervention on weight loss and diet was to conduct a community media analysis (e.g., audience reach of television, newspaper, radio, and cable TV). We then analyzed audience use information both from our own baseline data and from Nielsen Media Research rating reports (Nielsen, 1979, 1987) to identify the potential reach, audience specificity, and impact of each media channel. These data were combined with other information on media personnel cooperation, donation of resources, and interest. The second study used FCP baseline data to segment the population and develop target audience profiles by characterizing them by demographics, cognitions (e.g., knowledge, intention, and self-efficacy), attitudes, and health and communication behaviors based on the baseline population survey in the education communities. A third study of information needs was carried out with a subset ($n = 129$) of individuals participating in the baseline survey. In an unstructured interview, participants responded verbally to the question "If you had the chance to talk to an expert about diet and weight loss, what would you ask?" Responses influenced the structure, content, and wording of dietary messages. As a result of this up-front formative research on weight and diet, FCP campaign designers created an integrated set of change materials and messages, such as self-help kits, workplace group-based contests, PSAs, and mass-mailed tip sheets.

Implementation

For campaign implementation to occur, decisions have to be made about the content, sequence, mix, and duration of comprehensive community-based campaigns. These decisions were guided by the campaigns' theoretical foundations (e.g., the CBC model), other published research, and our own formative research. As depicted in the CBC model in Table 11.1, comprehensive risk-reduction campaigns must consider multiple channels of communication, multiple objectives, and multiple targets of change (individuals, networks, organizations, and environments) (Farquhar et al., 1985).

The two treatment communities and the immediately surrounding areas received four or five education campaigns per year. Campaigns were generally carried out in both English and Spanish and were directed at some preselected segment of the total population. Campaigns were conducted four times a year and in general incorporated one or more of the following types of efforts:

1. Media programs included 102 PSAs, 14 television programs, and 11 Spanish radio series disseminated via three television stations and two Spanish- and two English-language radio stations. A weekly doctor's column appeared in English- and Spanish-language newspapers. A total of 166 special features, food columns, news stories, and ads appeared in newspapers. Four mass mailings of print materials (to either all residents or a randomly selected 33%) were conducted. More than 20 different information booklets, skill-development self-help kits, and promotional brochures were developed; more than 1.5 million were distributed (Schooler, Flora, & Farquhar, 1993).

2. Direct education (face-to-face) consisted of more than 800 single and multiple group sessions. We trained teachers and health educators in the community to deliver formal and informal education sessions throughout their interpersonal networks, thus multiplying the effects of the direct education sessions.

3. Workplace programs were a major focus of the second half of the education program. Approximately 90% of all work sites with more than 100 employees partici-

pated in disseminating printed information, offering workshops and classes, sponsoring contests and lotteries, and assessing environmental risks (smoking policy, health food options, and exercise facilities) (Sallis, Hill, Fortmann, & Flora, 1986).

4. Schools, school administrators, teachers, and families were all participants in the FCP education program. Specific curricula on resisting pressures to smoke, eating healthy foods, and increasing exercise were designed for children and adolescents (Flora & Schooler, 1995; King et al., 1988). Parents and teachers were taught how to make changes in their own health and to stimulate changes in their children and students (Flora & Schooler, 1995; Rimal & Flora, 1998).

5. Restaurants, cafeterias, and grocery stores participated in specially designed healthy food programs and menu-labeling programs to influence customers' purchase of low-fat foods (Albright, Flora, & Fortmann, 1990). For example, in one supermarket campaign involving 20 grocery stores, approximately 600,000 nutrition tip sheets were distributed during a 12-week period.

6. Health professional groups, such as physicians, nurses, health educators, counselors, and dietitians, participated in training programs, disseminated print materials, received materials regularly in the mail, and implemented risk-reduction programs in their practices (Fortmann et al., 1985).

7. Contests that provided incentives and competition were used to promote changes in smoking, exercise, nutrition, and weight control (King, Flora, Fortmann, & Taylor, 1987). More than 9,000 individuals participated in these programs both at work sites and in the community at large.

In addition to the implementation of an effective communication campaign, the FCP aimed to promote the institutionalization of components of the program beyond the first 5 years of the media campaign (see Chapter 27, this volume). Long-term maintenance of CVD prevention activities was achieved by applying cooperative learning methods to provide professional development, technical assistance, and other resources to community health educators (Jackson et al., 1994; Schooler et al., 1997).

Evaluation

Each campaign used formative research to plan and test messages (discussed previously), process evaluation to study the application of the intervention (Flora, Jackson, et al., 1989), and summative evaluation to determine the effects of the campaign at individual, organizational, and community levels.

Process Evaluation. Monitoring campaign successes and failures is crucial to the understanding of effects and to the development of future campaigns. FCP process evaluation activities were concentrated into an intervention-monitoring system. Data were collected on the number of messages, the outcome objectives of each message, the risk factor addressed by the message, the potential reach of the message, and the frequency of presentation of the message. This information was combined with a set of standardized variables (e.g., the number of individuals in the community, neighborhood, or county) to develop a set of "constructed reach and impact variables" (Flora et al., 1993).

Using the process monitoring system, we calculated that on average each of the 80,000 adult community residents received more than 900 individual risk-reduction media messages during the 5 years of the campaign. Approximately 70% appeared in newspapers. Television was the next most significant message format (11%), with PSAs accounting for approximately 9% of total messages sent. Examination of dose (the amount of time to use a message, such as 30 seconds for a TV PSA) for various message formats revealed that television PSAs represented at least three times more dose than any other message format. Newspaper columns accounted for the second largest proportion of dose, followed by newspaper ads, radio series, and printed materials such as booklets, self-help kits, and mass-mail tip sheets.

Another analysis considered the proportion of individuals remembering each of the campaign components over the four surveys of the panel (Schooler, Chaffee, Flora, & Roser, 1998; Schooler, Flora, & Farquhar, 1995). Overall exposure was high and increased over time even though, due to limits of the survey, only 30% to 40% of the actual campaign messages sent to community members were measured on the survey. The proportion of TV messages remembered by the education community members increased from 35% in the second time period to 66% by the third assessment. Newspaper message recall also increased, from 43% at Time 2 to 52% by the fourth assessment. Booklets and kits, along with mass-mail print, showed the greatest increases in recall: booklets and kits from 30% at Time 2 to 71% at Time 4 and mass-mail tip sheets from 5% at Time 2 to 74% at Time 4.

Over time, the number of broadcast media messages decreased, and the number of face-to-face messages increased. Furthermore, as the FCP campaign progressed, more skill- and action-oriented messages were sent, whereas the number of CVD awareness messages was reduced.

Outcome Evaluation. The final evaluation of the FCP campaign can be grouped into two types of studies: (a) investigations of main effects, such as behaviors and CVD risk factors, and (b) evaluation of individual programs that occurred during the FCP campaign.

A series of main effects papers, along with a single summary paper, examine in detail the success of the FCP in preventing CVD risk in two communities (Farquhar et al., 1990). Total population risk factor results showed significant reductions favoring education treatment communities for smoking, cholesterol, blood pressure, resting pulse, and CHD risk; there was a greater impact in the cohort surveys compared with the cross-sectional surveys, which showed some late attenuation of large effects on blood pressure. The effects on cholesterol were small and evident most clearly early in the campaign. Although the population-level results of the FCP were less than had been hypothesized and less than those in the TCS, they were sufficient to demonstrate the feasibility of communitywide interventions that can positively affect some CVD risk factor levels in entire communities (Schooler et al., 1997). The FCP outcomes likely were influenced by a variety of factors. Influences included the difficulty of detecting effects in the face of an unanticipated secular trend of greater CVD prevention awareness and declines in CHD rates and large measurement variability that may have compromised the ability to detect significant effects for certain risk factors (e.g., diet). Other factors negatively affecting outcomes might include the relatively short period of time (5 years) allowed for a communication campaign to bring about communitywide behavior change and risk reduction and the education program's relative lack of emphasis on community and institutional policy change.

Within the FCP "mini" campaigns (i.e., separate campaigns were organized every 4 months), there was usually a focal behavioral intervention, such as a quit smoking contest, a new self-help kit, or a workplace program. Most of these focal behavioral interventions were accompanied by experimental or quasi-experimental field evaluations. Studies evaluated components of the mass media effort: a mass-mail self-help program (Maibach, Flora, & Nass, 1991); mass-distributed self-help quit smoking kits and accompanying TV shows (Sallis, Flora, Fortmann, Taylor, & Maccoby, 1985; Sallis et al., 1986); quit smoking contests (King et al., 1987); and the separate effects of newspaper columns, self-help kits, PSAs, and mass-mail tip sheets (Schooler et al., 1993, 1998). Three studies experimentally evaluated the effects of school curricula (Flora & Schooler, 1995; Killen et al., 1988; King et al., 1988). A separate study examined the influence of a restaurant dietary labeling program on sales (Albright et al., 1990). All these studies generally show greater cognitive and behavioral effects than do the populationwide samples, demonstrating that it is easier to change program participants' risk profiles than to engage a sufficient fraction of the community to change the community's risk profile (Fortmann et al., 1995; Schooler et al., 1997). From a phone survey conducted near the end of the FCP, we found that only one third of community adults used educational materials and programs to modify CVD risk factors, illustrating how intervention effects are diluted in surveys of entire communities (Jackson, Winkleby, Flora, & Fortmann, 1991).

Campaign Process Studies. The design of the FCP did not allow comparisons of campaign components, as did the TCS. Thus, a series of studies using statistical techniques for examining different campaign components were undertaken. The campaign process studies led to the following conclusions:

1. The campaign had much greater impact on CVD knowledge during the early years (Farquhar et al., 1990). Furthermore, although everyone learned, those with certain demographic profiles (e.g., education level) and communication habits (e.g., used newspapers and magazines more often) showed greater knowledge gains (Roser, Flora, Chaffee, & Farquhar, 1990; Schooler, Flora, & Farquhar, 1993). Novelty of ideas, information, and programs (such as a free attractive mass-mail tip sheet program) likely contributed to the early increases in knowledge. Increasing secular interest in CVD health, readily available information in the broader communication environment, and perhaps a saturation of FCP messages contributed to the less substantial knowledge gains in the latter half of the campaign.

2. The FCP campaign achieved widespread exposure, which in turn stimulated CVD information seeking and interpersonal discussion. Exposure to the campaign both directly and indirectly (via information seeking and discussion) influenced community members' overall health orientation (a measure combining knowledge, self-efficacy, and health behaviors) (Rimal, Flora, & Schooler, 1999).

3. Many CVD health outcomes were achieved via a cognitively involved process of learning about cardiovascular health, trial behavior, discussion, and self-efficacy enhancement, highlighting the reciprocal nature of the steps in the CBC. This process was stimulated by an interaction between personal knowledge and self-efficacy and campaign components. The process began with early easy access to informative media, breadth media such as PSAs, mass-mail tip sheets, and later use of depth media such as booklets and newspaper health columns (Schooler, Flora, & Farquhar, 1993).

4. The FCP influenced individuals and families. In a study of all FCP survey households with children, we were able to show that the campaign directly influenced the dietary practices of parents and children and that adults influenced children's dietary behavior. Although not always statistically significant, there were also indications that within the FCP, children influenced adults' dietary behavior (Rimal & Flora, 1998).

CONCLUSIONS

An in-depth examination of the two cornerstone community studies, the TCS and the FCP, in the context of a rapid proliferation of community-based campaigns reveals four primary principles. First, the TCS and the FCP were characterized by unique media campaigns and supplementary activities to improve health status. Media were used in comprehensive ways, designed to influence multiple dimensions that shape the health-related behavior of individuals and a community's environment by targeting multiple health problems and focusing on multiple audiences (Flora, Maibach, & Maccoby, 1989; Schooler & Flora, 1997). Second, programs were integrated such that multiple intervention modalities, programs, and messages were linked, and interactions were encouraged such that various interventions might mutually reinforce each other, thus creating the possibility of synergy. Third, the TCS and FCP used theory to guide specific campaign actions in all aspects of development, implementation, and evaluation; used social marketing principles to guide the application of theory; and relied on formative research to guide campaign design. Finally, each of the studies proceeded through a sequence of problem identification, planning, implementation, and evaluation. This sequence of activities led to successes in both the TCS and the FCP.

REFERENCES

Aiken, M., & Mott, P. (1970). *The structure of community power.* New York: Random House.

Albright, C. L., Flora, J. A., & Fortmann, S. P. (1990). Restaurant menu labeling: Impact of nutrition information on entree sales and patron attitudes. *Health Education Quarterly, 17,* 61-77.

Bandura, A. (1969). *Principles of behavior modification.* New York: Holt, Rinehart & Winston.

Bandura, A. (1977). *Social learning theory.* Englewood Cliffs, NJ: Prentice Hall.

Blackburn, H. (1983). Research and demonstration projects in community cardiovascular disease prevention. *Journal of Public Health Policy, 4*(4), 398-421.

Blackburn, H. (1997). Epidemiological basis of a community strategy for the prevention of cardiopulmonary diseases. *Annals of Epidemiology, 7*(Suppl. 7), S8-S13.

Blum, H. (1981). Planning as preferred instrument for achieving social change. In H. Blum (Ed.), *Planning for health: Generics for the eighties* (pp. 39-85). New York: Human Sciences.

Brown, E. (1984). Community organization influence on local public health care policy: A general research model and comparative case study. *Health Education Quarterly, 10,* 205-233.

Cartwright, D. (1949). Some principles of mass persuasion. *Human Relations, 2,* 253-267.

Crouch, M., Sallis, J. F., Farquhar, J. W., Haskell, W. L., Ellsworth, N. M., King, A. B., & Rogers, T. (1986). Personal and mediated health counseling for sustained dietary reduction of hypercholesterolemia. *Preventive Medicine, 15,* 282-291.

Eliot, R. (1987). Coronary artery disease: Biobehavioral factors. *Circulation, 76*(Suppl. 1), 1110-1112.

Farquhar, J. (1987). *The American way of life need not be hazardous to your health* (rev. ed.). Reading, MA: Addison-Wesley.

Farquhar, J., Maccoby, N., & Wood, P. (1985). Education and community studies. In W. Holland, R. Detels, & G. Knox (Eds.), *Oxford textbook of public health* (pp. 207-221). Oxford, UK: Oxford University Press.

Farquhar, J. W. (1978). Community-based model of lifestyle intervention trials. *American Journal of Epidemiology, 108,* 103-111.

Farquhar, J. W., Fortmann, S. P., Flora, J. A., & Maccoby, N. (1991). Methods of communication to influence behaviour. In W. W. Holland, R. Detels, & G. Knox (Eds.),

Oxford textbook of public health (2nd ed., Vol. 2, pp. 331-344). New York: Oxford University Press.

Farquhar, J. W., Fortmann, S. P., Flora, J. A., Taylor, C. B., Haskell, W. L., Williams, P. T., Maccoby, N., & Wood, P. D. (1990). Effects of communitywide education on cardiovascular disease risk factors: The Stanford Five-City Project. *Journal of the American Medical Association, 264*(3), 359-365.

Farquhar, J. W., Fortmann, S. P., Maccoby, N., Haskell, W. L., Williams, P. T., Flora, J. A., Taylor, C. B., Brown, B. W., Solomon, D. S., & Hulley, S. B. (1985). The Stanford Five-City Project: Design and methods. *American Journal of Epidemiology, 122,* 323-334.

Farquhar, J. W., Maccoby, N., & Solomon, D. S. (1984). Community applications of behavioral medicine. In W. E. Gentry (Ed.), *Handbook of behavioral medicine* (pp. 437-478). New York: Guilford.

Farquhar, J. W., Maccoby, N., Wood, P. D., Alexander, J. K., Breitrose, H., Brown, B. W., Haskell, W. L., McAlister, A. L., Meyer, A. J., Nash, J. D., & Stern, M. P. (1977). Community education for cardiovascular health. *Lancet, 1,* 1192-1195.

Festinger, L. (1954). A theory of social comparison processes. *Human Relations, 7,* 117-140.

Fishbein, B., & Ajzen, I. (1975). *Belief, attitude, intention and behavior.* Reading, MA: Addison-Wesley.

Flora, J., Saphir, M., Schooler, C., & Rimal, R. (1997). Toward a framework for intervention channels. *Annals of Epidemiology, 7*(Suppl. 7), S104-S112.

Flora, J., & Schooler, C. (1995). Influence of health communication environments on children's diet and exercise knowledge, attitudes, and behavior. In G. L. Kreps & D. O'Hair (Eds.), *Communication and health outcomes* (pp. 187-213). Cresskill, NJ: Hampton Press.

Flora, J. A., Jackson, C., & Maccoby, N. (1989). Indicators of societal action to promote physical health. In S. B. Kar (Ed.), *Health promotion indicators and actions* (pp. 118-139). New York: Springer.

Flora, J. A., Lefebvre, R. C., Murray, D. M., Stone, E. J., Assaf, A., Mittelmark, M. B., & Finnegan, J. R. (1993). A community education monitoring system: Methods from the Stanford Five-City Project, the Minnesota Heart Health Program and the Pawtucket Heart Health Program. *Health Education Research, 8,* 81-95.

Flora, J. A., Maibach, E. W., & Maccoby, N. (1989). The role of media across four levels of health promotion intervention. *Annual Review of Public Health, 10,* 181-201.

Fortmann, S. P., Flora, J. A., Winkleby, M. A., Schooler, C., Taylor, C. B., & Farquhar, J. W. (1995). Community intervention trials: Reflections on the Stanford Five-City Project experience. *American Journal of Epidemiology, 142*(6), 576-586.

Fortmann, S. P., Sallis, J. F., Magnus, P. M., & Farquhar, J. W. (1985). Attitudes and practices of physicians regarding hypertension and smoking: The Stanford Five-City Project. *Preventive Medicine, 14,* 70-80.

Jackson, C., Fortmann, S., Flora, J., Melton, R., Snider, J., & Littlefield, D. (1994). The capacity-building approach to intervention maintenance implemented by the Stanford Five-City Project. *Health Education Research, 9,* 385-396.

Jackson, C., Winkleby, M. A., Flora, J. A., & Fortmann, S. P. (1991). Use of educational resources for cardiovascular risk reduction in the Stanford Five-City Project. *American Journal of Preventive Medicine, 7,* 82-88.

Kasl, S. V. (1980). Cardiovascular risk reduction in a community setting: Some comments. *Journal of Consulting and Clinical Psychology, 48*(2), 143-149.

Katz, E., & Lazarsfeld, P. (1955). *Personal influence.* New York: Free Press.

Killen, J. D., Telch, M. J., Robinson, T. N., Maccoby, N., Taylor, C. B., & Farquhar, J. W. (1988). Cardiovascular disease risk reduction in tenth graders. *Journal of the American Medical Association, 260,* 1728-1733.

King, A. C., Flora, J. A., Fortmann, S. P., & Taylor, C. B. (1987). Smokers' Challenge: Immediate and long-term findings of a community smoking cessation contest. *American Journal of Public Health, 77,* 1340-1341.

King, A. C., Saylor, K. E., Foster, S., Killen, J. D., Telch, M. J., Farquhar, J. W., & Flora, J. A. (1988). Promoting dietary change in adolescents: A school-based approach for modifying and maintaining healthful behavior. *American Journal of Preventive Medicine, 4,* 68-74.

Kotler, P. (1975). *Marketing for nonprofit organizations.* Englewood Cliffs, NJ: Prentice Hall.

Kotler, P., & Zaltman, G. (1971). Social marketing: An approach to planned social change. *Journal of Marketing, 35,* 3-12.

Lefebvre, R. C., & Flora, J. A. (1988). Social marketing and public health interventions. *Health Education Quarterly, 15,* 299-315.

Lumsdaine, A., & Janis, I. (1953). Resistance to counterpropaganda produced by one-sided and two-sided communication. *Public Opinion Quarterly, 17,* 311-318.

Maccoby, N. (1980). Promoting positive health behaviors in adults. In L. Bond & J. Rosen (Eds.), *Competence and coping during adulthood* (pp. 218-243). Hanover, NH: University Press.

Maccoby, N., Farquhar, J., Wood, P., & Alexander, J. (1977). Reducing the risk of cardiovascular disease: Effects of a community-based campaign on knowledge and behavior. *Journal of Community Health, 3,* 100-114.

Maibach, E., Flora, J. A., & Nass, C. (1991). Changes in self-efficacy and health behavior in response to a minimal contact community health campaign. *Health Communication, 3,* 1-15.

McGuire, W. J. (1964). Inducing resistance to persuasion. In L. Berkowitz (Ed.), *Advances in experimental social psychology* (pp. 191-229). New York: Academic Press.

Meyer, A., Nash, J., McAlister, A., Maccoby, N., & Farquhar, J. (1980). Skills training in a cardiovascular health education campaign. *Journal of Consulting and Clinical Psychology, 48*(2), 129-142.

National Cholesterol Education Program Expert Panel. (1988). Report of the National Cholesterol Education Program expert panel on detection, evaluation, and treatment of high blood cholesterol in adults. *Archives of Internal Medicine, 148*(1), 36-69.

Nielsen, M. R. (1979). *Viewers in profile: July, 1979, Monterey/Salinas, CA.* Chicago: A. C. Nielsen.

Nielsen, M. R. (1987). *1987 Nielsen report on television.* Northbrook, IL: A. C. Nielsen.

Puska, P., Nissinen, A., Tuomilehto, J., Salonen, J. T., Koskela, K., McAlister, A., Kottke, T. E., Maccoby, N., & Farquhar, J. W. (1985). The community-based strategy to prevent coronary heart disease: Conclusions from the ten years of the North Karelia project. *Annual Review of Public Health, 6,* 147-193.

Rimal, R. N., & Flora, J. A. (1998). Bidirectional familial influences in dietary behavior: Test of a model of campaign influences. *Communication Research, 24*(4), 610-637.

Rimal, R. N., Flora, J. A., & Schooler, C. (1999). Achieving improvements in overall health orientation: Effects of campaign exposure, information seeking, and health media use. *Communication Research, 26*(3), 322-348.

Roberts, D., & Maccoby, N. (1973). Information processing and persuasion: Counter-arguing behavior. In P. Clarke (Ed.), *New models for mass communication research* (pp. 269-307). Beverly Hills, CA: Sage.

Rogers, E. (1983). *Diffusion of innovations* (3rd ed.). New York: Free Press.

Roser, C., Flora, J. A., Chaffee, S., & Farquhar, J. W. (1990). Who's listening: Predictors of knowledge in the Stanford Five-City Project. *Public Relations Review, 16*, 61-78.

Rothman, J. (1969). *An analysis of goals and roles in community organization practice.* Englewood Cliffs, NJ: Prentice Hall.

Sallis, J. F., Flora, J. A., Fortmann, S. P., Taylor, C. B., & Maccoby, N. (1985). Mediated smoking cessation programs in the Stanford Five-City Project. *Addictive Behaviors, 10*, 441-443.

Sallis, J. F., Hill, R. D., Fortmann, S. P., & Flora, J. A. (1986). Health behavior change at the worksite: Cardiovascular risk reduction. *Progress in Behavior Modification, 20*, 161-197.

Sallis, J. F., Hill, R. D., Killen, J. D., Telch, M. J., Flora, J. A., Girard, J., Taylor, C. B., & Fortmann, S. P. (1986). Efficacy of self-help behavior modification materials in smoking cessation. *American Journal of Preventive Medicine, 2*, 342-344.

Schooler, C., Chaffee, S., Flora, J. A., & Roser, C. (1998). Health campaign channels: Tradeoffs among reach, specificity, and impact. *Human Communication Research, 24*(3), 410-432.

Schooler, C., Farquhar, J. W., Fortmann, S. P., & Flora, J. A. (1997). Synthesis of findings and issues from community prevention trials. *Annals of Epidemiology, 7*(Suppl. 7), S54-S68.

Schooler, C., & Flora, J. A. (1997). Contributions of health behavior research to community health promotion programs. In D. S. Gochman (Ed.), *Handbook of health behavior research IV: Relevance for professionals and issues for the future* (pp. 285-302). New York: Plenum.

Schooler, C., Flora, J. A., & Farquhar, J. W. (1993). Moving toward synergy: Media supplementation in the Stanford Five-City Project. *Communication Research, 20*, 587-610.

Shea, S., & Basch, C. E. (1990). A review of five major community-based cardiovascular disease prevention programs: Part I. Rationale, design, and theoretical framework. *American Journal of Health Promotion, 4*, 203-213.

Slater, M., & Flora, J. A. (1991). Health lifestyles: Audience segmentation analysis for public health interventions. *Health Education Quarterly, 18*, 221-233.

Truitt, J., Cornfield, J., & Kannel, W. (1967). Multivariate analysis of the risk of coronary heart disease in Framingham. *Journal of Chronic Disease, 20*, 511-524.

U.S. Department of Health and Human Services. (1989). *Health: United States, 1988.* Hyattsville, MD: National Center for Health Statistics.

Warren, R. (1972). *The community in America.* Chicago: Rand McNally.

12

Using Theory to Select Messages in Antidrug Media Campaigns

Reasoned Action and Media Priming

Joseph N. Cappella
Martin Fishbein
Robert Hornik
R. Kirkland Ahern
Sarah Sayeed

This chapter takes on two closely related tasks. First, it describes the large National Youth Anti-Drug Media Campaign (NYADMC) and the efforts to evaluate this program. Then, it focuses on theoretical issues associated with the selection of messages for antidrug campaigns.

THE NATIONAL YOUTH ANTI-DRUG MEDIA CAMPAIGN

In 1997, the Office of National Drug Control Policy (ONDCP) received initial 5-year funding from the U.S. Congress to create "a large-scale paid media cam-

AUTHORS' NOTE: This work was sponsored by Grant 1 ROI DA12356-01 from the National Institute on Drug Abue. The views presented are those of the authors alone.

paign to educate and enable America's youth to reject illegal drugs" (NYADMC, 1998, p. 3)—the National Youth Anti-Drug Media Campaign.

The campaign arose in part as a response to very recent changes in drug use in the United States. Before 1992, long-term trends averaged across all age groups had reported declines. Between 1985 and 1992, the National Household Survey on Drug Abuse (NHSDA) and the Monitoring the Future study (MTF) reported decreases in marijuana, cocaine, and overall drug use during the "past month" (Office of National Drug Control Policy, 1997, p. 9). Since 1979, the decrease in overall drug use had been almost 50%. The average decrease in lifetime marijuana use between 1978 and 1992 was 1.8% per year, according to data from MTF and from NHSDA (Hornik et al., 1999).

After this extraordinary period of change in behavior, the number of marijuana users has been increasing since 1992 (Office of National Drug Control Policy, 1997, p. 11). The University of Michigan's MTF study reports substantial increases among 8th, 10th, and 12th graders in all measures of marijuana use (Johnston, 1996). Simultaneously, there have been steady declines in the percentage of 12th graders who say they disapprove of regular marijuana use and in those who say that regular use is harmful (Johnston, O'Malley, & Bachman, 1996). These trends among adolescents run counter to those in the larger population. In addition, the ONDCP noted in 1997 that antidrug advertising had been in decline since 1995. In the 1980s and early 1990s, antidrug ads had been more numerous (Hornik et al., 1999).

It is to counteract these trends that the NYADMC is directed. The chief goals of the NYADMC are to help young people in the United States prevent drug use (especially drugs of first trial such as marijuana and inhalants) and to encourage occasional users to discontinue use. The campaign's goals and their basis are described in detail in two documents, *The National Drug Control Strategy, 1997* and *The National Youth Anti-Drug Media Campaign: Communication Strategy Statement* (available at *www.ncjrs.org*).

To achieve the campaign's goals, the integrated NYADMC campaign targets two audiences—parents and their children. Schools, churches, and youth leaders will be targeted, but parents are singled out because effective parenting practices are known to be associated with a lowered incidence of substance abuse and other high-risk behaviors (Biglan, Duncan, Ary, & Smolkowski, 1995; Resnick et al., 1997). Also, parents have incomplete knowledge about drug use among young people. Thus, parents are enlisted as sources of influence in the campaign and are also objects of education.

Young people are an equally important target. Three specific age groups have been identified: 9- to 11-year-olds, 12- and 13-year-olds ("tweens"), and 14- to 18-year-olds. The age divisions recognize that it cannot be hoped that antidrug messages that appeal to 9- to 11-year-olds will be effective with older teens. The divisions also take note of the fact that preteens generally have very strong antidrug attitudes and know very few users among their classmates. In the middle school years, antidrug attitudes become less strong, and students are more likely to know classmates who have tried illicit drugs. These trends become more pronounced with older teens. Within all age groups, occasional users and nonusers thought to be at risk for trial are given the greatest attention by the campaign. This marks an implicit decision to focus on those who have the highest likelihood of becoming regular users and to convince them not to do so.

This campaign assumes that the mass media (Internet, radio, television, billboards, magazines, etc.) are the most efficient means of reaching the largest share of the target population with the greatest influence. It further assumes that a campaign cannot be successful unless the audience is exposed to its message (see Chapter 8, this volume). Thus, unlike most prior health campaigns, campaign managers are buying media time and space to present their messages rather than relying on the cooperation of broadcasters and publishers, which is often minimal due to economic considerations. In the first year of the NYADMC campaign (July 1998 to June 1999), the goal was to purchase $150 million of media time and space to reach 90% of teenagers four times per week, 74% of parents three and one half times per week, and 66% of children three times per week (Hornik et al., 1999). The media buys take into account the special preferences of the adolescent age groups, parents, and specific racial and ethnic groups.

Although the specific goals of the campaign might change during the initial 5-year period, the more general goals will remain the same. In the 5-year span of the campaign, the 9- to 11-year-olds will move into and through the period when many young people are first exposed to the temptation of illicit drugs, whereas middle schoolers who have tried drugs face the risk of becoming more frequent users. A successful campaign will find that the strong antidrug attitudes of children and tweens are sustained in reduced drug trial in middle and early high school, whereas drug trial by middle schoolers will be followed by lowered trial or at least lowered likelihood of regular use in high school. The NYADMC has been in the field only since July 1998, consisting of Phase I (media exposure from January 1998 to June 1998 of antidrug ads in 12 markets, with 12 matched markets receiving no paid antidrug ads), Phase II (a national campaign using previous antidrug messages, from July 1998 to early 1999), and Phase III (all new creative content, starting September 1999). Evaluations of the first two phases focused on evidence for exposure to messages and were undertaken by the ONDCP; an independent 5-year evaluation of the third phase began in November 1999.

EVALUATING THE NYADMC

The effectiveness of the NYADMC will be evaluated in part by comparing trends in drug trial and use before, during, and after the campaign, partially through several ongoing surveys. The MTF survey conducted yearly by the University of Michigan from a sample of 8th, 10th, and 12th graders has data dating back to

1976. The NHSDA has archived data on drug use from 1979. The Partnership for a Drug Free America has been conducting its Partnership Attitude Tracking Survey (PATS) on 11th and 12th graders since 1993.

These sources of information about illicit drug use among adolescents, however, are limited in their ability to evaluate the media campaign. An effective evaluation of the NYADMC must be powerful enough to detect small changes in drug use. For example, changes in 12th graders' reported past-month marijuana use registered only 1.8% declines per year from 1978 to 1992. The evaluation must also provide sensitive and valid measures of exposure to the mass media campaign, but neither the NHSDA nor the MTF surveys have given detailed attention to measures of media exposure. Finally, trends and changes in drug use alone cannot be used to explain whether the campaign is effective. They may result from changes in parental practices, adoption of new drug education techniques, changes in community norms, policing practices, drug interdiction at national borders, and saturation of the media market with antidrug advertising.

Thus, in addition to using the annual data provided by MTF, NHSDA, and PATS, the National Institute on Drug Abuse (NIDA) contracted with the Westat Corporation and a team of communication and public health researchers to create a three-pronged evaluation. The first, the National Survey of Parents and Youth (NSPY), is a series of surveys at 6-month intervals over a period of 4 years, begun in November 1999. Each wave will interview approximately 3,350 parents and primary caregivers of young people aged 9 to 18 years. Their children (and wards) will also be interviewed, producing an additional 4,750 interviews every 6 months. The second, the Community Survey of Parents and Youth (CSPY), is a set of annual panel (the same respondents) surveys in one community in each of four regions of the United States carried out over a several-year period. Each community will begin with a baseline of 875 parents and primary caregivers and 1,075 of their children (and wards). Together, the NSPY and CSPY surveys will provide detailed information necessary to evaluate the campaign, including especially drug use, attitudes, and intentions, media exposure and recall, risk factors, family communication patterns, measures of advertising effectiveness, beliefs about the consequences of drug use and trial, and personal efficacy. Finally, current plans call for extended observational and interview research in the four CSPY sites. These will focus on documenting drug- or antidrug-related events and organizational activities in the communities that may not be easily captured by the survey instruments.

USING THEORY TO SELECT ANTIDRUG MESSAGES

The NYADMC will depend on a variety of sources to choose its messages. The Partnership for a Drug Free America, Ogilvy and Mather, and the NYADMC's Behavior Change Expert Panel will bring experience and knowledge of existing theory and research to this process, but they are all working under substantial time pressures to conceptualize, create, test, and broadcast messages. Simultaneously, NIDA has funded a series of studies designed to expand the scientific basis for development of antidrug messages (see Chapters 2, 3, 5, and 7, this volume). The rest of this chapter examines two theoretical perspectives that serve as the basis for one of those studies.

Theories of Behavior and Behavior Change

Information can produce behavior change (Fishbein, Ajzen, & McArdle, 1980). Although it is true that providing people with knowledge about a disease may have little or no impact on their behavior, other types of information about the consequences of performing the behavior, about groups that support behavioral performance, about ways to overcome barriers to behavioral performance, or all three can be effective. Affecting specific behaviors may require influencing only a limited number of variables (Fishbein, 1993, 1995; Fishbein, Bandura, et al., 1992; Fishbein, Chan, et al., 1992). Most of these variables are contained in three theories.

According to the Health Belief Model (Becker, 1974; Rosenstock, Strecher, & Becker, 1994), two major factors influence the likelihood that persons will adopt a recommended preventive health action. First, they must feel personally threatened by or susceptible to a disease with serious or severe consequences. Second, they must believe that the benefits of taking the preventive action outweigh the perceived barriers to (or costs of, or both) preventive action.

According to social cognitive theory (Bandura, 1986, 1989, 1991), there are also two major factors influencing the likelihood that one will take preventive action. First, a person must believe or expect that the benefits of performing the behavior outweigh the costs. Second, the person must have a sense of personal agency, or self-efficacy, that he or she has the skills and abilities necessary for performing the behavior in a variety of circumstances.

The theory of reasoned action (Ajzen & Fishbein, 1980; Fishbein, 1980; Fishbein & Ajzen, 1975) holds that there is one primary determinant of behavior, namely, the person's intention to perform it. This intention is viewed as a function of two determinants—the person's attitude toward performing the behavior (which is based on his or her beliefs about the costs and benefits of performing the behavior) and the person's perception of the social (or normative) pressure exerted on him or her to perform the behavior.

Figure 12.1 presents a theoretical model incorporating these variables. Any given behavior is most likely to occur if one has a strong intention to perform the behavior, if one has the necessary skills and abilities required to perform the behavior, and if there are no environmental constraints preventing behavioral performance (Fishbein, Chan, et al., 1992). If strong intentions to perform the behavior in question have not been formed, the model suggests that there are three primary determinants of intention: (a) the attitude toward performing the behavior, (b) perceived norms concerning performance of the behavior, and (c) one's self-efficacy with respect to performing the behavior. The relative importance of these three psychosocial variables, and thus the appropriate intervention or message, will depend on both the behavior and the population being considered. Thus, before developing interventions to change intentions, it is important to first determine the degree to which that intention is under attitudinal, normative, or self-efficacy control in the population in question.

The model in Figure 12.1 also recognizes that attitudes, perceived norms, and self-efficacy are all functions of underlying beliefs about the (a) outcomes of performing the behavior in question, (b) normative expectations of specific referents, and (c) specific barriers to behavioral performance. Thus, for example, the more one believes that performing the behavior in question will lead to "good" outcomes and prevent "bad" outcomes, the more favorable is one's attitude toward performing the behavior. Similarly, the more one believes that specific others think one should (or should not) perform the behavior in question, and the more one is motivated to comply with those specific others, the more social pressure one will feel (or the stronger the subjective norm) with respect to performing (or not performing) the behavior. Finally, the more one perceives that one can perform the behavior (i.e., has the necessary skills and abilities to do so), even in the face of specific barriers or obstacles, the stronger will be one's self-efficacy with respect to performing the behavior.

The model also shows the indirect role played by more traditional demographic, personality, attitudinal, and other individual difference variables (such as perceived risk) in influencing behavior through their influence on behavioral, normative, or efficacy beliefs or all three.

Applying the Theoretical Model to Illicit Drug Use

There are a variety of different behaviors to consider, each with a different underlying cognitive structure, when thinking about affecting illicit drug use, such as preventing people from starting to use a drug, decreasing or stopping usage altogether, or encouraging them to decide to enter (or not enter) a treatment program.

Changing the target of the action also changes the behavioral criterion and its determinants. For example, trying marijuana is a very different behavior from trying heroin, and one's beliefs about trying drugs in general may be very different from one's beliefs about trying a particular drug. The context of the behavior also defines the behavior of interest. Drugs can be used in many different contexts (e.g., alone at home or with others at a party), and performing a given action in one context is often very different from performing the same action in some other context. Finally, it is important to determine the appropriate time frame. One would expect the beliefs about the consequences of using a particular drug "occasionally" to differ from those about using the same drug "regularly" because they are different behaviors.

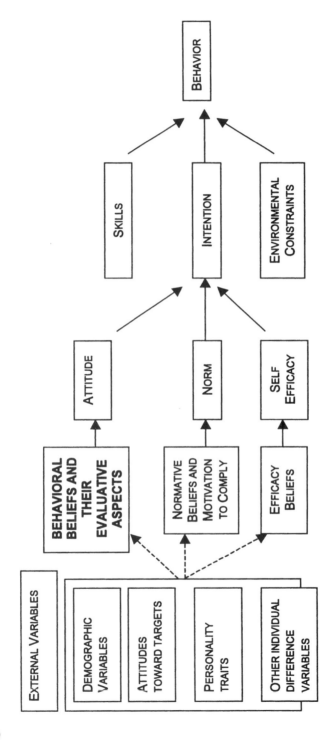

Figure 12.1. An Integrative Theory of Behavior Change

Before developing a behavior change program, it is essential that one identify the relative importance of attitudinal and normative considerations for the intention and population of interest. For example, if a person's intention to perform some behavior is under normative control, little will be accomplished by changing the person's attitude toward performing the behavior. On the basis of findings with regard to cigarette smoking (Fishbein, 1980), one can expect that for illicit drug use the relative importance of attitudes and subjective norms will change dramatically depending on both the behavior in question and the population under consideration. Indeed, although the intention to try a given drug may be under normative control, the intention to stop using that drug may be under attitudinal control.

For example, Albrecht and Carpenter (1976) found that intentions to vote for or sign a petition in opposition to marijuana legalization were slightly more strongly correlated with attitudes ($r = .64$) than with subjective norms ($r = .52$). This difference, however, diminished slightly if one knew one would not get caught ($r = .65$ vs. $r = .62$). Using regression, Bearden and Woodside (1978) found that attitude ($\beta = .45$) was a slightly better predictor of intentions to buy and smoke marijuana than was the social norm ($\beta = .36$). Bentler and Speckart (1979) found that for marijuana use alone, with friends, or at a party, attitude was much more closely related to intentions than was the subjective norm ($\beta = .80$ vs. $\beta = .13$, respectively). Attitudes and subjective norms, however, were equally related to intention to use hard drugs, including cocaine, LSD, and Quaaludes ($\beta = .42$ vs. $\beta = .42$, respectively). Finally, Cook, Lounsbury, and Fontenell (1980) reported that attitude toward the act of smoking marijuana was slightly more strongly correlated with frequency of use than was the subjective norm ($r = .65$ vs. $r = .53$). For amphetamines, however, attitudes and the subjective norm correlated with use at approximately the same levels ($r = .54$ vs. $r = .58$).

Across these studies, intentions to engage in marijuana-related behaviors are fairly consistently more associated with attitudes than with social norms. For harder drugs, the social normative and attitudinal factors have similar associations with intentions. Most of these studies, however, are more than 15 years old and do not focus on the target populations or the behaviors to be addressed by the NYADMC.

Knowing that a given behavior is under attitudinal or normative control is only one step in the process of understanding or attempting to change a person's intention to perform that behavior. To understand or change attitudes and subjective norms, one must first identify their determinants. Also, whereas the theory does point out that these attitudes and norms are based on corresponding salient attitudinal and normative beliefs, it cannot specify the content of these beliefs. Once one has demonstrated that one can predict attitudes and subjective norms from these salient beliefs, one can search for differences in these beliefs among those who do and do not intend to perform the behavior in question. Such an analysis not only provides information concerning the factors influencing a person's decision to perform or not perform the behavior in question but also identifies those beliefs that need to be changed if one wished to produce a change in attitude or subjective norm.

According to the integrative theory of Figure 12.1, then, the messages one should select to achieve behavior change depend on the specific behavior, its context, and whether the behavior is under attitudinal or normative control for the target population. The theory does not consider how or under what conditions the relative weightings of attitudinal or normative control might be changed, nor does it consider how a correlation between a belief (or norm) and an intention might be created (or elevated or depressed). To answer this question, we turn to the theory of "media priming."

Media Priming

Media priming refers to the possibility that messages may affect the relative weights for criteria used in determining an attitude, opinion, or behavior induced by a message.

Research on media priming has been conducted primarily in political communication (Iyengar & Kinder, 1987; Krosnick & Kinder, 1990). For example, overall political popularity of a candidate or office holder is a function of a variety of subsidiary evaluations: performance on inflation, defense, energy, and so on. In other words, the standards for evaluating the leader's performance change as the media coverage activates one standard while suppressing others. The change results not from changing evaluations regarding performance on inflation or defense (specific beliefs about the candidate) but from increased importance (or weight) that this judgment has for overall evaluation of the political leader portrayed. For example, Iyengar and Kinder (1987), in a series of studies on perceptions of the performance of political leaders, found strong effects for priming of economic issues on the ratings of two congressional candidates. They also found that in the Carter versus Reagan presidential race in 1980, Carter's handling of foreign affairs was primed—that is, it was a better predictor of ratings of Carter whether the treatment was positive (handling Camp David accords) or negative (handling of Iraq hostage crisis).

The differences between media priming and persuasion can be demonstrated by an idealized example. Assume that the target behavior for a message is the attitude toward "trying illegal drugs (marijuana) in the next 12 months." Also assume that the vast majority of people in the target population have just two beliefs relevant to the attitude toward this behavior. One is the belief that marijuana trial harms the brain, called Belief A in Table 12.1. The second is the belief that marijuana trial permits acceptance by friends, called Belief B. The first line of Table 12.1 presents the hypothetical baseline situation. For Belief A, the mean level of belief for the population is 3 on a 1 to 5 scale, with 5 representing the judgment that the belief is very likely and 1 the judgment that the belief is very unlikely. For Belief B, the mean is 2 at baseline. The effect of Be-

Table 12.1 Hypothetical Example of Effects of Priming and Persuasion on Attitudes

Condition	Predicted Attitude	Effect (Slope) of Belief A	Effect (Slope) of Belief B	Constant	Mean on Belief A That Marijuana Trial Harms the Brain	Mean on Belief B That Marijuana Trial Permits Acceptance by Friends
Baseline	1.1	−.3	.5	1.0	3	2
If campaign primes Belief A	0.5	−.5	.5	1.0	3	2
If campaign affects mean of Belief A	0.5	−.3	.5	1.0	5	2
If campaign affects and primes Belief A	−0.5	−.5	.5	1.0	5	2

NOTE: The prediction of attitude is based on the following equation: attitude = constant + (slope of A) × (mean of A) + (slope of B) × (mean of B).

lief A on attitude at baseline is captured by its slope of −.3 (the minus sign means that the belief that marijuana harms the brain has a negative impact on attitudes toward trying the drug), whereas the effect of Belief B is .5 and the constant is .5. Then the predicted attitude score would be slightly positive (1.10).

We assume that a message directed at the audience focuses on the single Belief A—that marijuana has harmful consequences for mental functioning. Table 12.1 presents three possible results of such a message. The first is the case of pure message priming. The message has no effect on the mean of any of the beliefs associated with the intention but does have an effect on the slope, and that in turn affects the attitude. By making the "harmful to the brain" belief a stronger predictor of attitude, the attitude changes from 1.1 to 0.5, somewhat less positive than in the no-message situation. In the next case, the campaign affects the mean of the belief but does not prime it—its slope remains unchanged. Again, the attitude is less positive than it was at baseline (1.1 vs. 0.5). Finally, the belief is both primed and its mean changes; the predicted attitude is much less positive than it was at baseline (−0.5 versus 1.1 at baseline). Thus, the attitude (and the subsequent intentions and behavior) can be affected because a respondent is persuaded to believe differently from before and because the respondent pays more attention to the belief (the belief is primed) in developing the attitude.

The theoretical bases for media priming are cognitive activation and changes in accessibility. If media coverage of a particular issue is elevated, that issue is activated cognitively, becomes more accessible, and, as a result, is used as a basis for judgment (Iyengar & Kinder, 1987; Miller & Krosnick, 1996; Price & Tewksbury, 1997). The key empirical indicator of the presence of media priming is the elevated association between the targeted belief and the outcome measure in the presence of elevated media coverage of the issue.

Implicitly, persuasion models such as the theory of reasoned action assume that better quality messages (more credible arguments) will produce more belief change and thus greater change in behavior. Priming theory, however, does not require the assumption of strong arguments. It assumes only that the effects occur if the audience is exposed to an issue and not that the exposure is to a high-quality argument. Although the messages may not directly change beliefs or social norms, they may prime appropriate beliefs and subjective norms, increasing their effect on the attitude toward the behavior and thereby reducing the intention to try or use illegal drugs. This would be an important finding because it would limit the necessity of employing carefully screened messages. It would still be important, however, to be sure that messages did not produce a backlash, targeted the appropriate beliefs and social norms, gained the audience's attention, and were comprehensible.

Priming is primarily concerned with activating specific beliefs through exposure in the media or other communication channels. To deactivate a belief means to avoid discussion or presentation of the belief in mass media. For example, a public service announcement (PSA) might inadvertently activate positive beliefs about the social benefits of marijuana trial while trying to persuade the audience that smoking makes them physically less attractive to romantic partners. In such a case, priming could work to activate the positive beliefs even though this was not the intention of the PSA. Thus, media priming theory suggests both priming the negative consequences and avoiding priming the positive consequences, even if the priming is inadvertent.

Summary

The integrative theory of behavior change (Figure 12.1) implies that changing behaviors is primarily accomplished by changing beliefs and subjective norms. It also implies that the key to changing intention or behavior is to target beliefs or subjective norms that have a high association with the performance of the behavior. Priming theory, however, focuses on the degree of association between behavioral beliefs and attitude (or normative beliefs and subjective norms). It would predict that a campaign that increased the weight of negative consequences or decreased the weight of positive consequences would influence attitudes or social norms and then intentions. Of course, both theories could operate simultaneously. In an antidrug campaign, the integrative theory would try to make the most important negative consequences of drug trial more negative or the most heavily weighted positive consequences less positive to change targets' attitudinal beliefs and subjective norms for change. In the same campaign, priming theory would try to make negative consequences more strongly linked and positive consequences less strongly linked to attitudes, social norms, and intentions.

USING THEORY TO SELECT MESSAGES

In June 1999, a sample of 600 adolescents was surveyed about drug behaviors, attitudes, intentions, and beliefs, derived from the theory in Figure 12.1. The survey included questions about marijuana use and trial. We use these data to illustrate how each of the two theoretical frameworks would lead to different implications for message selection. We examine the roles of five beliefs in predicting attitudes and intentions to use marijuana regularly (which was defined as 10 or more times in the next 12 months). (The results for trying marijuana—that is, once or twice in the next 12 months—are not the same.)

The data were collected by Opinion One, a marketing survey research firm. The sample of 600 adolescents was drawn from 20 malls throughout the United States using lists held by the survey firm. Adults who identified themselves as parents on these lists were contacted to determine if they had a child who was between the ages of 12 and 18 years, and written parental consent for the child to participate was obtained. Participants were asked to come to the mall to fill out a touch-screen survey on a desktop computer. Of all respondents, 25% identified themselves as African American and 71% were Caucasian, whereas the rest did not answer the question about race. Half of the sample was composed of females. The sample split into three equal age groups: 11- to 14-year-olds (34.5%), 15- and 16-year-olds (32%), and 17- and 18-year-olds (34.5%). Forty percent of the sample reported prior use of marijuana, and 14.4% reported use in the past 30 days. Lifetime use (22.9%, 38.4%, and 60.8% for each of the three age groups, respectively; $\chi^2 = 59.7, p < .001$) and use in the past 30 days (9.4%, 11.2%, and 22.6%, respectively; $\chi^2 = 16.2, p < .001$) are significantly higher for older children. Our results on marijuana use correspond well to the 1998 MTF data for 12th, 10th, and 8th graders.

Beliefs and Intentions

The survey asked respondents about 20 beliefs thought to be relevant to their intention to use marijuana regularly in the next 12 months that were derived from an initial list of more than 100 beliefs obtained from previous studies, focus groups, and pretesting. Table 12.2 focuses on five of these beliefs—three negative consequences (including "do worse in school" and "lose ambition"), one of which is more social ("upset parents"), and two positive consequences ("feel dreamy and mellow" and "have a good time with friends"). Table 12.2 presents the mean likelihood of the consequence as judged by the

Table 12.2 Beliefs and Correlations: Marijuana Use 10 or More Times in a 12-Month
Period

Item	Mean (1-5; 1 = Strong Antidrug)	Attitude	Intention	Case
Do worse in school (r)	2.37	.37	.43	Persuasion or priming
Lose my ambition (r)	2.68	.36	.42	Persuasion or priming
Upset parents (r)	1.72	.23	.33	Neither; not movable
Dreamy and mellow	3.65	.11	.06 (ns)	Neither; not important
Good time with friends	3.08	.54	.49	Neither; not plausible

NOTE: Sample size is approximately 400. *ns* = not significant; r = reversed coding so that 1 = very likely.

sample, the correlations between the five beliefs and attitude toward marijuana use in the next 12 months, and intentions to use. Past use of marijuana (ever used and used in the past year) was highly related to both attitudes ($r = .60$ and .43, respectively) and intentions ($r = .60$ and .45, respectively).

Given a focus on changing behaviors, three major considerations must be considered when selecting beliefs to target (Hornik & Wolf, 1999): (a) Is the belief salient to the intention? (b) Are there enough people who do not accept an antidrug belief (who disbelieve a negative consequence or believe a positive consequence) to warrant trying to change it? and (c) Can strong evidence and plausible argument be made to change the belief? Priming theory shares the requirement that an antidrug belief is not universally accepted (b) but does not require that the association already be high or that an argument can be mounted that will bring about change in belief (c). In contrast, priming theory requires that a belief is capable of being primed—that is, that the audience would consider giving greater weight to the belief in determining its attitude, if attention was paid to the belief. Although there is no way to know a priori whether a belief is "prime-able," one criterion for assessing priming potential may be whether it has at least some association (e.g., a correlation of .20 or higher) with the attitude at the start.

Belief Importance

Among the five beliefs presented in Table 12.2, the positive consequence belief ("using marijuana will make me feel dreamy and mellow") has the weakest correlation to intention and attitude. Thus, it is not a good candidate as a target for persuasion. Also, because this belief is a positive consequence of marijuana use, one would not try to prime this positive consequence to give it greater weight in attitude or intention formation. In fact, the campaign should actively avoid priming this belief; inadvertent priming is still priming. The other four beliefs all have moderate to strong correlations to intention and attitude. They all pass the first test on association. The strongest among the remaining four is "have a good time with friends," another positive consequence. The three negative consequences are less strongly weighted, but they are correlated to attitude and intention at modest levels.

Our data produced no example in which a negative consequence was so strongly correlated with attitude or intention that it would become ineligible for priming. If a belief or group of related beliefs was very strongly associated with attitude (e.g., correlations higher than .80), then increasing the correlation would be very difficult. Such a case would eliminate the belief from consideration as a target for priming. The belief would still be eligible for persuasion, however, depending on how it fared on the second criterion—movability.

Room to Move?

Of the four consequences that are moderately related to attitude (and intention), the belief that using marijuana regularly would upset the user's parents is widely accepted as a likely consequence (the mean of 1.72 is between "very likely" and "likely"). Although this negative consequence is linked to adolescents' attitudes and intentions to use marijuana in the next 12 months, targeting this belief as an object of persuasion change in a communication campaign would be ineffective because there is no room to change this belief in the desired direction. Priming is not plausible either, however. Because the vast majority of people believe this consequence strongly, there is little variance in the belief and therefore limited opportunity for association to attitude.

Plausible Argument?

The three remaining beliefs have moderate correlations to attitude and intention and have at least some people who disbelieve the negative consequence and some who believe the positive consequence (i.e., are movable). Of these, the positive belief "have a good time with friends" is most strongly associated with the intention to use marijuana in the next 12 months. Some people believe this consequence is likely, and some believe it is unlikely. It is difficult to envision an argument that could be made to undermine this consequence, however. People choose their own friends, and those intending to use marijuana tend to have friends who use as well. Their experience is that using marijuana with friends is a good time. It will be difficult for a media message to contradict direct experience. Messages suggesting alternative ways to "get high" (i.e., "sensation seeking"; see Chapter 23, this volume) or highlighting negative social consequences of marijuana use do not directly address the "good times with friends" belief. They might affect attitude or intention, but they do not do so by changing or priming the belief that using marijuana leads to having a good time with friends.

The two remaining beliefs are negative consequences for which plausible arguments can be made. They fulfill all three criteria—importance (exhibited as moderate or strong association to attitude and intention), movability, and plausibility. Therefore, priming would imply an increased association, whereas the integrative theory of behavior change would suggest an increased likelihood in believability.

CONCLUSIONS

To be effective, campaign planners must select particular messages, and particular targets for the messages, that will comprise the campaign. Theories such as the integrative theory of behavior change (aimed at changing the beliefs underlying attitudes, social norms, or efficacy) and media priming (aimed at changing the importance of these same beliefs in forming intentions to act) can provide guidance with regard to which beliefs a campaign should target. The integrative theory implies (a) targeting positive and negative consequences that are already important associates of the behavior, (b) targeting positive and negative consequences that are not already completely believed or disbelieved, and (c) targeting positive and negative consequences for which there is strong evidence or for which a strong argument can be built. The theory of media priming implies that negative beliefs that are weakly associated with attitudes can have their linkage strengthened through exposure to messages targeting those beliefs. The strength of the arguments and evidence is less important, according to this theory. The theories cannot determine whether the messages should be rational or emotional, nor which evidence or arguments should be included or excluded. Both theories, however, can provide guidance about which beliefs to target and which to avoid.

REFERENCES

Ajzen, I., & Fishbein, M. (1980). *Understanding attitudes and predicting social behavior.* Englewood Cliffs, NJ: Prentice Hall.

Albrecht, S. L., & Carpenter, K. E. (1976). Attitudes as predictors of behavior versus behavior intentions: A convergence of research traditions. *Sociometry, 39*(1), 1-10.

Bandura, A. (1986). *Social foundations of thought and action: A social cognitive theory.* Englewood Cliffs, NJ: Prentice Hall.

Bandura, A. (1989). Perceived self-efficacy in the exercise of control over AIDS infection. In V. M. Mays, G. W. Albee, & S. F. Schneider (Eds.), *Primary prevention of AIDS: Psychological approaches. Primary prevention of psychopathology* (Vol. 13, pp. 128-141). Newbury Park, CA: Sage.

Bandura, A. (1991). Social cognitive theory of moral thought and action. In W. M. Kurtines & J. L. Gewirtz (Eds.), *Handbook of moral behavior and development* (pp. 45-103). Hillsdale, NJ: Lawrence Erlbaum.

Bearden, W. O., & Woodside, A. G. (1978). Situational and extended attitude models as predictors of marijuana intentions and reported behavior. *Journal of Social Psychology, 106,* 57-67.

Becker, M. (1974). The Health Belief Model and personal health behavior. *Health Education Monographs, 2,* 324-473.

Bentler, P. M., & Speckart, G. (1979). Models of attitude-behavior relations. *Psychological Review, 86*(5), 452-464.

Biglan, A., Duncan, T. E., Ary, D. V., & Smolkowski, K. (1995). Peer and parental influences on adolescent tobacco use. *Journal of Behavioral Medicine, 18,* 315-330.

Cook, M. P., Lounsbury, J. W., & Fontenell, G. A. (1980). An application of Fishbein and Ajzen's attitudes-subjective norms model to the study of drug use. *Journal of Social Psychology, 110,* 193-201.

Fishbein, M. (1980). A theory of reasoned action: Some applications and implications. In H. Howe & M. Page (Eds.), *Nebraska symposium on motivation* (pp. 65-116). Lincoln: University of Nebraska Press.

Fishbein, M. (1993). Introduction. In D. J. Terry, C. Gallois, & M. McCamish (Eds.), *The theory of reasoned action: Its application to AIDS-preventive behavior.* Oxford, UK: Pergamon.

Fishbein, M. (1995). Developing effective behavior change interventions: Some lessons learned from behavioral research. In T. E. Backer, S. L. David, & G. Soucy (Eds.), *Reviewing the behavioral science knowledge base on technology transfer* (NIDA Research Monographs No. 155, pp. 246-261). Rockville, MD: National Institute on Drug Abuse.

Fishbein, M., & Ajzen, I. (1975). *Belief, attitude, intention and behavior: An introduction to theory and research.* Boston: Addison-Wesley.

Fishbein, M., Ajzen, I., & McArdle, J. (1980). Changing the behavior of alcoholics: Effects of persuasive communication. In I. Ajzen & M. Fishbein (Eds.), *Understanding attitudes and predicting social behavior* (pp. 217-242). Englewood Cliffs, NJ: Prentice Hall.

Fishbein, M., Bandura, A., Triandis, H. C., Kanfer, F. H., Becker, M. H., & Middlestadt, S. E. (1992). *Factors influencing behavior and behavior change: Final report—Theorist's workshop.* Rockville, MD: National Institute of Mental Health.

Fishbein, M., Chan, D. K. S., O'Reilly, K., Schnell, D., Wood, R., Beeker, C., & Cohn, D. (1992). Attitudinal and normative factors as determinants of gay men's intentions to perform AIDS-related sexual behaviors: A multi-site analysis. *Journal of Applied Social Psychology, 22*(13), 999-1011.

Hornik, R., Judkins, D., Golub, A., Johnson, B., Maklan, D., Duncan, D., Zador, P., & Cadell, D. (1999). *Evaluation of the National Youth Anti-Drug Media Campaign: Historical trends in drug use and design of the Phase III evaluation.* Unpublished report delivered to the National Institute on Drug Abuse, Rockville, MD.

Hornik, R., & Wolf, K. D. (1999). Using cross-sectional surveys to plan message strategies. *Social Marketing Quarterly, 5,* 34-41.

Iyengar, S., & Kinder, D. R. (1987). *News that matters.* Chicago: University of Chicago Press.

Johnston, L. D. (1996). *Monitoring the Future study* [Press release].

Johnston, L. D., O'Malley, P. M., & Bachman, J. G. (1996). *National survey results on drug use from the Monitoring the Future Study, 1975-1995, Vol. 1* (NIH Publication No. 96-4139). Rockville, MD: National Institute on Drug Abuse.

Krosnick, J. A., & Kinder, D. R. (1990). Altering the foundation of support for the president through priming. *American Political Science Review, 84,* 497-512.

Miller, J. M., & Krosnick, J. A. (1996). News media impact on the ingredients of presidential evaluations: A program of research on the priming hypothesis. In D. C. Mutz, P. M. Sniderman, & R. A. Brody (Eds.), *Political persuasion and attitude change* (pp. 79-99). Ann Arbor: University of Michigan Press.

National Youth Anti-Drug Media Campaign. (1998). *Communication strategy statement.* Washington, DC: Office of National Drug Control Policy.

Office of National Drug Control Policy. (1997). *National drug control strategy: 1997* (Reprint No. 2). Washington, DC: Executive Office of the President.

Price, V., & Tewksbury, D. (1997). News value and public opinion: A theoretical account of media priming and framing. In G. A. Barnett & F. Boster (Eds.), *Progress in communication sciences* (pp. 173-212). Greenwich, CT: Ablex.

Resnick, M. D., Bearman, P. S., Blum, R. W., Bauman, K. E., Harris, K. M., Jones, J., Tabor, J., Beuhring, T., Sieving, R., Shew, M., Ireland, M., Bearinger, L. H., & Udry, J. R. (1997). Protecting adolescents from harm: Findings from the National Longitudinal Study on Adolescent Health. *Journal of the American Medical Association, 278,* 823-832.

Rosenstock, I. M., Strecher, V. J., & Becker, M. J. (1994). The Health Belief Model and HIV risk behavior change. In R. J. Diclemente & J. L. Peterson (Eds.), *Preventing AIDS: Theories and methods of behavioral interventions* (pp. 5-24). New York: Plenum.

13

Public Relations as Communication Campaign

David M. Dozier
Larissa A. Grunig
James E. Grunig

Public relations practitioners and public communication campaigners can learn much from each other. In this chapter, we clarify the conceptual overlap shared by public relations and public communication campaigns and delineate areas in which these two forms of organizational communication differ. We then report findings from the 15-year Excellence Study of public relations and communication management in three nations, highlighting information most applicable to public communication campaigns. In so doing, we put forward the concept of two-way symmetrical communication as an especially ethical and effective orientation for the conduct of public communication campaigns. We close with an exemplar of a symmetrical public relations campaign and a discussion of its implications.

DISTINGUISHING PUBLIC COMMUNICATION AND PUBLIC RELATIONS CAMPAIGNS

In adapting an earlier definition by Rogers and Storey (1987), Rice and Atkin (1989) defined *public communication campaigns* as

> purposive attempts to inform, persuade, or motivate behavior changes in a rela-
> tively well-defined and large audience, generally for noncommercial benefits to

the individual and/or society, typically within a given time period, by means of organized communication activities involving mass media and often complemented by interpersonal support. (p. 7)

Paisley (see Chapter 1, this volume) extended this definition by noting that benefits of public communication campaigns are often driven by *reform* efforts, actions that seek to make life or society or both better, as defined by emerging social values.

Because the intentions of public communication campaigns are to make individuals or society better according to nonuniversal social values, public communication campaigns may be viewed as strategies of social control because one group has taken it on itself to affect the beliefs or behaviors of another group. As Paisley notes (see Chapter 1, this volume), not all public communication campaigns fit nicely under the social control rubric, in which education (communication) is used with engineering and enforcement to bring about desired changes in a target group. Nevertheless, all public communication campaigns seek some change in the target group, often without the true collaboration of those who are targets of the campaign's effects.

Public relations is defined as the management of communication between organizations and publics to build mutually beneficial, reciprocal relationships (Cutlip, Center, & Broom, 1994; Grunig, 1992). Whereas definitions of public communication campaigns focus on goal-directed communication activities aimed at target groups, contemporary definitions of public relations focus on the practice as an emerging professional activity and as a management function in organizations. Indeed, public relations practitioners do manage communication campaigns to bring about changes in target populations. Often in the not-for-profit sector, public relations practitioners seek noncommercial benefits for individuals or society or both (e.g., consider social marketing campaigns; see Chapter 27, this volume). Public communication campaigns are a subset of the organizational responsibilities of such practitioners. In corporate public relations, such noncommercial benefits are sought less frequently. Under the banner of corporate good citizenship, however, even for-profit organizations sometimes execute public communication campaigns in pursuit of noncommercial benefits to individuals and society.

Figure 13.1 provides a schema for delineating key differences and overlaps for public relations and public communication campaigns. Both domains manage communication campaigns that are directed at target populations to bring about some change in knowledge, attitudes, and behaviors in those populations. Regarding public communication campaigns, however, relatively little is known about organizational structure, roles, and culture as variables in the effective execution of such campaigns. Certainly, such campaigns are implemented in some kind of organizational structure composed of stakeholders with purposive intentions to bring about noncommercial benefits to individuals and society. What roles do communicators play in the decision-making pro-

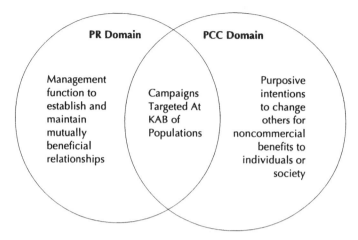

Figure 13.1. A Conceptual Map of the Public Relations and Public Communication Campaign Domains

cesses among the various stakeholders who sponsor such campaigns? Are specific organizational roles clearly delineated? If so, how? To what degree can communicators change the goals and objectives of a campaign? What role does research play in changing the goals and objectives of public communication campaigns? What values drive decisions about campaign strategies?

Whereas only a few studies have examined these questions with regard to public communication campaigns (Guttman, Kegler, & McLeroy, 1996), much research during the past 30 years has explored these questions of structure and values in the public relations domain (Grunig, 1992). When public relations is practiced in an excellent manner, the communication or public relations department has substantial expertise in both communication and social science research. An excellent department is run by a strategic manager who has the support of the organization's dominant coalition that demands (and gets) sophisticated, proactive communication programs from its communication department. Such shared understandings between communicators and other members of the dominant coalition are more likely to occur in organizations with participative organizational cultures.

THE EVOLUTION OF COMMUNICATION
CAMPAIGNS AND PUBLIC RELATIONS

Grunig and Grunig (1992) traced the historical development of four basic models of public relations practices that parallel a similar evolution in public communication campaigns. In its earliest stages (late 1800s), public relations involved the generation of publicity or attracting media attention for the sponsoring organization and issues important to that organization. Such *press agentry,* as Goldman (1948) labeled it, involved the flow of information in one direction—from the organization that sponsored the communication campaign to target populations, usually vaguely defined. Furthermore, the quality and veracity of the information disseminated were questionable. In the early 1900s, a new approach to public relations emerged, emphasizing journalistic standards of new practitioners, often former media reporters. Termed the *public information* model, greater emphasis was placed on disseminating truthful and accurate information, although information harmful to the sponsoring organization sometimes might be withheld. As with the press agentry model, the public information model was concerned largely with the one-way flow of information from the sponsoring organization to various target groups. Arguably, many public communication campaigns still apply a one-way model of information flow (see Chapter 4, this volume). As the other chapters in this volume attest, however, state-of-the-art campaigns employ two-way flows of information.

With the late Edward Bernays as a key advocate, public relations entered a new phase when practitioners coupled social science research methods with traditional information dissemination strategies to create a two-way model of public relations. This phase in the development of public relations parallels the entry of social scientists as stakeholders in public information campaigns. According to Paisley (see Chapter 1, this volume), social scientists became important players in public communication campaigns in the 1940s through a series of important evaluations of such campaigns. As such, social scientists have become stakeholders in public communication campaigns only recently. This is also true for public relations, in which practitioners are skilled at executing media and message strategies but less proficient at social science research techniques needed to close the communication loop (Dozier, 1990).

Bernays's approach to two-way public relations, however, had embedded in it a critical presupposition that one finds embedded in many public communication campaigns—the presupposition of asymmetry. Bernays made this presupposition manifest when he described his research-based, two-way approach to public relations as the engineering of consent (Bernays, 1965). The *asymmetrical presupposition* is the worldview that the sponsoring organization executing a communication campaign has fixed, nonnegotiable objectives; all targeted changes in knowledge, attitude, and behaviors must occur among target populations, which public relations practitioners call publics. Paisley (1989, p. 16) acknowledged this asymmetrical tendency in public communication campaigns when he noted that "most campaigns have mandated objectives that are less amenable to change" than the knowledge, attitudes, and behaviors of target populations. *Two-way asymmetrical public relations* is defined as the use of research and other inputs to design communication programs (campaigns) to bring about changes in the knowledge, attitudes, and behaviors of publics in accordance with the goals and objectives of the sponsoring organization. It is this definition of public relations practices that most closely matches the definitions of public communication campaigns cited elsewhere in this volume.

In public relations, the two-way asymmetrical model poses problems of both an ethical and a strategic nature. Whereas public communication campaigns can invoke good intentions and reformist agendas as rationales for asymmetrical practices, public relations practitioners are not convincing when defending the ethics of many asymmetrical, commercial campaigns. For example, one book highlighting abuses in public relations practices is titled *Toxic Sludge Is Good for You! Lies, Damn Lies and the Public Relations Industry* (Stauber & Rampton, 1995). Because many public relations practitioners hope that their field will be respected someday as a true profession, many have strived to strike a balance between advocacy and ethics. It may seem perfectly ethical to engineer the consent of target populations when the goal of the campaign is to reduce heart disease. When the goal of a communication campaign is to increase public acceptance of environmental damage by manufacturers (e.g., toxic sludge), however, the ethics of asymmetrical presuppositions become more problematic.

A second concern with asymmetry is the strategic issue of effectiveness. Asymmetrical communication campaigns are not as effective as they could be in reaching their goals and objectives. To understand why this might be so, one must understand a fourth model of public relations practices: two-way symmetrical public relations. First delineated as a model by Grunig (Grunig & Grunig, 1992; Grunig & Hunt, 1984), *two-way symmetrical public relations* involves principles of negotiation and dispute resolution, using research as a tool to better understand target populations (publics) rather than to better manipulate them. As originally conceptualized, the two-way models of public relations were viewed as opposite ends of a continuum, ranging from pure domination to pure cooperation. Both theoretical critiques (Murphy, 1991) and an increasing number of empirical studies, however, have resulted in a more fully developed model (Figure 13.2).

The two-way symmetrical model presumes that the relationship between an organization sponsoring a communication campaign and a target population (public) is usefully conceptualized as a mixed motive game (Murphy, 1991). Both the sponsoring organization and the target population seek to further their own interests. Both parties, however, must pursue their interests within the win-win zone. The *win-win zone* is defined as a range of campaign outcomes that both parties regard as sufficiently satisfactory. That is, the outcome does not maximize the desired outcome for either party; the outcome, however, satisfices both.

This conceptual frame from game theory is consistent with many studies (including the Excellence Study) showing that practitioners use both two-way asymmetrical and two-way symmetrical practices simultaneously. The seem-

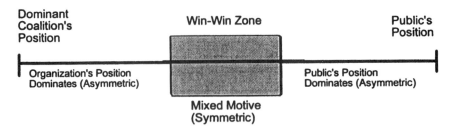

Figure 13.1. The Two-Way Symmetrical Model of Pulic Relations Pracftices

ing contradiction is resolved by nesting asymmetrical practices, which involve the pursuit of short-term tactical advantage, inside the win-win zone. Strategically, these asymmetrical tactics cannot be permitted to undermine an overarching commitment to a long-term symmetrical outcome with which both parties can live. As a boundary spanner, the sophisticated communication manager (with both communication and research expertise) plays a role as the organization's advocate when communicating campaign messages to target populations. In strategic decision-making sessions with the sponsoring organization's dominant coalition, however, the communication manager is an advocate of the publics' interests.

To understand why this fourth model of public relations is especially relevant to public communication campaigns, the concept of representation is useful. Any organization that runs a communication campaign, whether noncommercial or commercial, has a set of shared perceptions of the organization and the organizational environment that its members use to make decisions (White & Dozier, 1992). Optimally, this representation is dynamic, constantly updated by inputs from the environment provided by boundary spanners. As Broom (1986) argued, however, organizations range from those that are relatively closed systems (generally impervious to inputs and internal change) to those that are relatively open (generally responsive to inputs and internal change). Paisley (1989, p. 16) correctly noted that top-down mandates of public communication campaigns make the organization's representation "less amenable to change," placing greater emphasis on the asymmetrical engineering of consent among target populations. As the Excellence Study demonstrates, the two-way asymmetrical model is less effective in achieving objectives than the two-way symmetrical model.

THE EXCELLENCE STUDY

In the 1980s, the International Association of Business Communicators Research Foundation funded a $400,000 study of public relations and communication management in Canada, the United Kingdom, and the United States (the principal investigator was James Grunig, University of Maryland). The purpose of the study was to determine characteristics that contribute to excellent communication departments in organizations and the degree to which such excellence helps organizations achieve their objectives. The study included a quantitative survey (1990-1991) and qualitative case study follow-ups (1994). In the quantitative phase, a stratified, multistage strategy was used to sample for-profit corporations, not-for-profit organizations, government agencies, and trade and professional associations proportionally in each of the three nations. Questionnaires (approximately 100 pages and 1,700 variables per organization) were completed by three sources in each organization: (a) the top communicator, (b) the chief executive officer (CEO) (or other top-ranking manager of the organization), and (c) a purposive sample of regular employees (up to 20 per organization for a total of 4,500). Three hundred twenty-one organizations (some with multiple communication departments) participated in the survey. In 1994, organizations with most excellent and least excellent communication programs (based on the quantitative analysis) were the focus of qualitative case studies, using the long interview to collect data (Grunig, Dozier, & Grunig, 1994). The full methods and findings of the Excellence Study are detailed in Dozier, Grunig, and Grunig (1995) and in Grunig, Grunig, and Dozier (in press).

A Model of Communication Excellence

Derived from the factor analysis of many indexes deemed important to effective communication from prior theorizing and research, the communication excellence model places the knowledge base (expertise) of the communication department at the core of excellent communication. This knowledge base consists of departmental expertise to enact the communication manager role and to execute the two-way models of public relations, both symmetrical and asymmetrical.

The knowledge base is nested within a set of shared expectations between the communication department and the coalition of powerful leaders in the organization that makes strategic decisions, the dominant coalition. These shared expectations include the political support and value placed on communication by the dominant coalition, the kind of role (manager or technician) the dominant coalition wants the top communicator to play, and the kind of model (one-way or two-way and symmetrical or asymmetrical) that the dominant coalition wants the communication department to use in running communication programs. In organizations with excellent communication programs, dominant coalitions expect communication excellence (as described previously), and the communication department shares this expectation and has the expertise to deliver. On the basis of case studies, which allowed analysis of the historical development of excellence in several organizations, these shared expectations create a demand-delivery loop wherein high communication expertise is linked to high expectations from the dominant coalition, leading to excellent communication programs. Excellent communication programs increase the resources and influence of the communication department, which is then even more capable of communication excellence in the future.

Connecting expertise in communication departments to excellent expectations within dominant coalitions is more likely to occur in organizations with participative organizational cultures. Participative organizational cultures are marked by a strong sense of teamwork and shared mission, as reported by a sampling of regular employees in each organization studied. Top management seeks the input from a larger number of organizational constituents when compared to organizations with authoritarian cultures. Although participative organizational cultures provide fertile soil in which strong communication departments can grow, excellence cannot occur without core knowledge in the communication department and shared expectations about communication with the dominant coalition.

Approximately 20 measures of excellence were isolated on a single factor, called the excellence factor. A factor score (excellence score) was assigned to each organization in the study. A key indicator of effectiveness (external to the factor analysis) was the CEO's estimate of return on investment for resources budgeted to the communication department. In organizations with excellence scores in the lowest 10% of those studied, CEOs reported a 146% return on investment ($146 returned for every $100 invested in communication). For organizations that scored in the highest 10% of organizations in the study, however, CEOs reported a dramatic 266% return on investment ($266 returned for every $100 invested in communication). At a programmatic level, top communicators assessed the success of their top three communication programs to achieve their stated objectives. Consistently, organizations with higher excellence scores were more successful at achieving their objectives (Dozier et al., 1995). These findings were also confirmed through case studies of most excellent and least excellent organizations. In summary, the excellence of an organization, including its use of the two-way symmetrical model, is positively associated with achieving program objectives.

The Excellence Study and
Public Communication Campaigns

Among the 321 organizations that participated in the Excellence Study, 18 were isolated as organizations that manage public communication campaigns as defined at the beginning of this chapter. A stipulation of the Excellence Study was that the identities of participating organizations would not be disclosed. In general terms, however, the 18 organizations consisted of 15 not-for-profit organizations and 3 government agencies with clear mandates to administer public communication campaigns. The organizations included those that conduct public communication campaigns to reduce disease risk to various organs of the human body and to reduce the risk of contracting certain

Table 13.1 Two-Way Symmetrical and Two-Way Asymmetrical Items Measuring
Communication Department Expertise

Two-way asymmetrical department expertise (reported by top communicator)

Expertise or knowledge in your communication department to perform these tasks?

　Persuade a public that your organization is right on an issue.

　Get publics to behave as your organization wants.

　Manipulate publics scientifically.

　Use attitude theory in a campaign.

Two-way symmetrical department expertise (reported by top communicator)

Expertise or knowledge in your communication department to perform these tasks?

　Negotiate with an activist public.

　Use theories of conflict resolution in dealing with publics.

　Help management understand the opinions of particular publics.

　Determine how publics react to the organization.

---

life-threatening diseases. Some organizations in this subsample conduct public communication campaigns on behalf of certain age groups, ethnic groups, or persons with certain disabilities. Others conduct campaigns to reduce the consumption of products deemed unhealthy for individuals or harmful to society or both. The three government agencies included in the subsample all conduct campaigns to maintain or improve the quality of the environment (water, air, etc.).

　These 18 organizations were then compared to the remaining 303 organizations with regard to the excellence score (the 20 characteristics of communication excellence isolated through factor analysis). On the basis of the asymmetrical definition of public communication campaigns, we hypothesized that communication departments that run public communication campaigns would have greater asymmetrical expertise and lesser symmetrical expertise than communication departments in other organizations. We also hypothesized that dominant coalitions (as reported by the CEO or other senior manager) in those organizations running public communication campaigns would report higher asymmetrical expectations and lower symmetrical expectations than would dominant coalitions in other kinds of organizations. Tables 13.1 and 13.2 display the items from the top communicator (department expertise) questionnaires and CEO (dominant coalition) questionnaires used to measure these constructs. The normalized symmetrical score was subtracted from the normalized asymmetrical score, generating an asymmetrical difference score, which is the degree to which the asymmetrical model is preferred over the symmetrical model. This was done for both department expertise and dominant coalition expectations.

Table 13.2   Two-Way Symmetrical and Two-Way Asymmetrical Items Measuring
                 Dominant Coalition Expectations

Two-way asymmetrical expectations (reported by CEO)

How do you think the dominant coalition (previously defined) in this organization believes public relations should be practiced?

    In public relations, the broad goal is to persuade publics to behave as the organization wants them to behave.

    Before beginning a public relations program, one should do research to determine public attitudes toward the organization and how they might be changed.

    Before starting a public relations program, one should examine attitude surveys to ensure the organization and its policies are described in ways its publics would be most likely to accept.

    After completing a public relations program, research should be done to determine how effective this program has been in changing people's attitudes.

Two-way symmetrical expectations (reported by CEO)

How do you think the dominant coalition (previously defined) in this organization believes public relations should be practiced?

    The purpose of public relations is to change the attitude and behavior of management as much as it is to change the attitude and behavior of publics.

    Public relations should provide mediation for the organization—to help management and publics negotiate conflicts.

    The purpose of public relations is to develop a mutual understanding between the management of the organization and publics that the organization affects.

    Before starting a public relations program, surveys or informal research should be done to determine how much management and the publics understand each other.

As hypothesized, leaders of organizations running public communication campaigns have higher asymmetrical expectations of their communication departments (Kendall's tau = .08, $N = 277$, $p < .05$) than do the leaders of other organizations. Communication departments in organizations running public communication campaigns have higher levels of expertise to use the asymmetrical model than the symmetrical model (Kendall's tau = .08, $N = 293$, $p < .05$), although in both cases, the effect size is small.

Organizations that run public communication campaigns, however, posted overall excellence scores that did not differ significantly from those of other organizations. In the sample, in fact, organizations running public communication campaigns posted slightly higher overall scores. This was due to the higher than average value placed on communication by dominant coalitions in these organizations (Kendall's tau = .12, $N = 297$, $p < .05$) and to higher levels of manager role enactment by top communicators in organizations running public communication campaigns (Kendall's tau = .09, $N = 295$, $p < .05$).

Conclusions About Excellence and Public Communication Campaigns

The previous findings support the following conclusions that are relevant to public communication campaigns:

1. Leaders of organizations that run public communication campaigns prefer the two-way asymmetrical model rather than the two-way symmetrical model more strongly than do leaders of other organizations in the Excellence Study.
2. Communication departments in organizations that run public communication campaigns have greater asymmetrical expertise and less symmetrical expertise than do communication departments in other organizations.
3. Top communicators in organizations that run public communication campaigns are expected to play the manager role to a greater degree than are top communicators in other organizations.
4. The communication function is more highly valued in organizations that run public communication campaigns when compared to other organizations.

The first two conclusions are consistent with theoretical expectations derived from the asymmetrical presuppositions of public communication campaigns. The last two conclusions are consistent with what one might expect of an organization in which the public communication campaign is its *raison d'être*. Stated succinctly, public communication campaigns excel because of the value they place on well-managed communication, but they are impeded by their own asymmetrical presuppositions.

Discussion

Consider the asymmetrical and symmetrical items in Table 13.1 and Table 13.2 with regard to three scenarios: (a) a communication campaign to reduce heart disease, (b) a communication campaign to encourage women to smoke tobacco, and (c) a communication campaign to promote a "drug-free" America. All three scenarios involve asymmetrical assumptions because program goals were established by the sponsoring organization and are essentially non-negotiable with target populations. These asymmetrical programs differ only in the apparent legitimacy of invoking asymmetrical strategies.

If one is promoting healthy hearts, as did the Stanford Community Studies, getting people at risk of heart disease "to behave as the organization wants them to" seems eminently reasonable. Having the expertise to "manipulate publics scientifically" is implicit in the declaration that the Stanford programs "are prototypes for planned social programs relevant to the prevention of many chronic disease problems *and other social problems* [italics added]" (Flora, Maccoby, & Farquhar, 1989, p. 234; see Chapter 11, this volume).

At the other extreme, consider a second scenario that was once the focus of a public communication campaign (Cutlip, 1994). The issue was the right of women to smoke tobacco in public places and the health issues associated with the consumption of sweets. In 1928, Edward Bernays (arguably the inventor of two-way asymmetrical public relations) devised a publicity campaign to encourage women to reach for a cigarette whenever they craved sweets. He used a network of professional photographers to emphasize the beauty of slenderness, which tobacco would help women achieve. Bernays hired a doctor to review medical findings regarding the deleterious effects of sugar consumption. Encouraging women to smoke, however, required an adjustment in public attitudes toward women who smoke. At the time, strong social taboos discouraged women from smoking in public. Bernays had learned from a psychoanalyst that some women regarded smoking as a symbol of liberation. In 1930, Bernays organized the "torches of freedom" march down Fifth Avenue in New York City, with 10 debutantes lighting and smoking cigarettes in public to protest gender inequality.

Before implementing his public communication campaign, Bernays marshaled scientific evidence on the dangers of sugar and even used primitive psychographic data on the symbolic meaning of smoking tobacco among women. He employed effective media and message strategies (both commercial and noncommercial) to bring about increased freedom for women, and he helped many of them control their weight.

Knowing what we know today about the health risks associated with tobacco, ethical problems with the asymmetrical presuppositions of Bernays's public communication campaign are obvious. Built into the asymmetrical presupposition is an implicit assumption that the organization sponsoring a public communication campaign is omniscient. Even the best laid plans, however, generate unintended consequences. Regarding the use of tobacco, Bernays's public communication campaign achieved short-term objectives of using tobacco to control women's weight and achieve greater equity with men. The unintended health consequences of greater tobacco use among women more than offset any individual or social good of the campaign. (At the time, Bernays was not aware of the health risks that tobacco posed.)

With unintended consequences in mind, consider the third scenario: a public-communication campaign for a drug-free America. The zero tolerance implicit in this reform effort points to one of the most troubling ethical aspects of public communication campaigns. The more righteous and noble sounding the reform, the more asymmetrical such campaigns are likely to become. Asymmetrical communication campaigns become relatively impervious to correction because target populations have no legitimate voice and no advocates among campaign decision makers. Problems with America's so-called "war on drugs" are well documented elsewhere (Bertram, Sharpe, & Andreas, 1996). Unintended consequences include massive federal expenditures, steady erosion of civil liberties, Draconian sentencing laws that flood prisons with perpetrators of victimless crimes, the systematic disruption of agrarian economies in developing nations in which drugs are harvested, long-term environmental damage from the extensive use of herbicides, the inevitable consolidation of organized crime, police corruption, and corruption of the political system. Despite its negligible impact on the availability, price, or consumption of recreational drugs, the war continues. The war on drugs demonstrates two key flaws of well-intended public communication campaigns based on asymmetrical presuppositions: (a) They are less effective at achieving their stated objectives and (b) they have negative, unintended consequences.

AN EXEMPLAR OF A SYMMETRICAL PUBLIC RELATIONS CAMPAIGN

Now consider a fourth scenario—one in which the symmetrical model is used. This campaign involves commercial outcomes, but the symmetrical practices described are equally applicable to public (noncommercial) communication campaigns. This exemplar is a fictional composite of symmetrical practices reported by several organizations in the Excellence Study and operationalizations from public relations theory.

The dominant coalition in this exemplar is a large corporation that decides to launch a major commercial communication campaign to promote a line of low-calorie, low-fat microwave dinners featuring Mexican cuisine entrées. The products and prototype communication campaign materials are market tested in several cities with significant Latino populations. The communication department is involved in the market tests and in the strategic planning for the campaign.

Initial focus group discussions and other ethnographic methods (see Chapter 4, this volume) flag a problem missed by the corporation's (predominantly Anglo) dominant coalition. At the least, the emergent problems could reduce sales; at worst, they could snowball into other areas of corporate concern (consumer boycotts, labor relations, lawsuits, etc.). Formative evaluation (see Chapter 6, this volume) indicates that some people of Latino heritage react negatively to the product line and the communication campaign materials. Some regard the advertisements as "making fun" of Latinos and perpetuating stereotypes. Additional probing indicates that many Latinos believe that their culture is being ripped off by a large, insensitive, and remote corporation. Probing deeper still, formative evaluation indicates that the microwave Mexican entrées represent assimilation and a loss of traditional culture as exemplified through home-cooked meals. The top public relations manager for the company holds a series of meetings with various Latino advocacy groups to develop a better understanding of Latino perspectives and to search for a win-win zone.

The top communicator discovers a complex web of issues that involves her employer and the Latino public. Latino activists point out the absence of Latino employees in the corporation, especially in management positions. They note that the corporation wants to sell Latino cuisine but does not want to give anything to the Latino community. At these meetings, the top communicator acts as spokesperson for the corporation, advocating the company's position while communicating a willingness to negotiate.

The top communicator returns to the strategic planning table with the corporation's dominant coalition, now articulating—even advocating—the various Latino perspectives she has learned. Through careful strategic planning, additional formative evaluation, and more meetings with Latino activists, a five-step, win-win strategy is developed:

1. The advertising and marketing communication strategy is completely revamped to eradicate ethnic stereotypes and invoke positive icons of Latino culture in the United States and in Latin America. Product packaging is redesigned to permit brief stories about important individuals and events in U.S. Latino history. A panel of Latino educators and community leaders is appointed to assist communicators with issues of ethnic sensitivity.

2. The corporation commits itself to aggressively recruit Latino employees, especially in management ranks. A task force composed of corporate managers and community leaders is assigned the task of making affirmative action work. As a first step, several new Latino employees are hired in the communication department.

3. The corporation pledges to divert a fixed percentage of profits from the line of the Mexican cuisine entrées into a Latino Community Development Foundation, with the board of directors reflecting a broad cross section of the Latino community.

4. A separate communication campaign, the "When Time Permits" campaign, is targeted primarily at the Latino community. The campaign uses niche and Spanish-language media advertising and free mailed booklets (in Spanish and English) with special recipes to encourage the preparation of traditional Mexican and Latino dishes using low-fat alternative ingredients "when time permits." Of course, the company's line of microwave entrées is promoted as alternatives when time does not permit.

5. A symmetrical summative evaluation plan is developed. In addition to specific marketing objectives, the summative evaluation also addresses the implementation of the previous four points. Perceptions (understanding) of the corporation in the Latino community are measured in a pretest-posttest design (see Chapters 6 and 8, this volume). Most significantly from the symmetrical perspective, perceptions of the Latino community among the members of the corporation's dominant coalition are also measured in a similar pretest-posttest design. Success of the communication

program is measured, in part, by the degree to which the corporation's dominant co-alition and the Latino community increase their understanding of each other.

Arguably, the first step is consistent with both a two-way asymmetrical and a two-way symmetrical communication campaign. On the basis of research, are messages and packaging being revamped to manipulate or accommodate the Latino community? The answer lies in Steps 2 through 4, which are called action strategies in public relations. *Action strategies* are changes made in an organization's policies, procedures, products, services, and behaviors to build mutually beneficial relations with publics (Cutlip et al., 1994, p. 383). Step 5 incorporates the co-orientation model of evaluation (Broom & Dozier, 1990, p. 83), wherein changes in the corporation and the public are both targets of the communication program and its evaluation. Action strategies and the co-orientation model are tools used in the implementation of symmetrical communication campaigns. In Step 4, note the mixed motive. The corporation encourages traditional home-cooked meals through the When Time Permits campaign. When time does not permit, however, nuke it. Note also that the campaign promotes a public benefit (low calorie and low fat) and a commercial benefit.

How does this commercial communication campaign exemplar inform the design and execution of public (noncommercial) communication campaigns? The key issue is the degree to which campaign goals and objectives are negotiable. A symmetrical public communication campaign treats not just campaign implementation issues but also the campaign goals as negotiable, as coconstructed within the win-win zone. Bryant and Forthofer (2000) clearly stressed symmetry when they advocated active community involvement and participation in health promotion campaigns. If community involvement and participation are reduced to an implementation or compliance-gaining strategy of essentially nonnegotiable campaign outcomes, however, then the campaign is asymmetrical and is less likely to achieve its objectives. The challenge for public communication campaigners is to find the "wiggle room" with funding sources to permit renegotiation of program goals and objectives in concert with target populations.

WHOSE CAMPAIGN IS IT ANYWAY?

The previously described asymmetrical public communication campaigns to fight heart disease, bring about a drug-free America, and liberate women through the public use of tobacco all share one characteristic in common: an invisible client. Regarding public relations, Dozier and Lauzen (2000, p. 19) defined *invisible clients* as "organizations with sufficient resources to hire public relations practitioners." The concept of invisible clients can be more widely applied to public communication campaigns. In the case of Bernays's public communication campaign, the invisible client was the American Tobacco Company, which had hired Bernays to engineer the use of tobacco products among women. Given our historical perspective and our understanding of the harmful effects of tobacco, it is easy to see that the interests of invisible clients do not always coincide with those of target populations. At the other extreme, one can presume that the various invisible clients behind the Stanford Community Studies, such as the National Heart, Lung and Blood Institute, had the best motivations when they funded these prototypic programs of comprehensive, planned social change.

Because public communication campaigns often seek to promote innovations, Rogers's (1983) concern with the *proinnovation bias* in diffusion research—the implication that "an innovation should be diffused and adopted by all members of a social system, that it should be diffused more rapidly, and that the innovation should be neither re-invented nor rejected" (p. 92)—is relevant here. Rogers cut to the heart of the matter when he identified funding by change agencies as one of the two major sources of this bias. Either the change agency approaches the organization that will run the campaign, or the campaign organization seeks out funding from a change agency. Although the innovation (and the public communication campaign that seeks to promote it) may serve the ultimate good of the target (client) population, an important economic relationship already exists between the campaign organization and its invisible client (see Chapter 25, this volume). This creates a conflict of interest whenever the best interests of the target population do not coincide with the interests of the funding source.

Echoing Rogers (1983), Dozier and Lauzen (2000) argued that the economic relationship with invisible clients also leads to a certain myopia, a tendency to see the world through the eyes of invisible clients such as funding sources. Much has been made of the differences between public communication campaigns and commercial communication campaigns. The distinction, however, is more metric than dichotomous. Public communication campaigns, after all, serve to further (or hinder) the career goals of the people who manage them. Reputations of organizations and institutions are enhanced (or tarnished) by the outcomes of public communication campaigns they implement. Up the food chain, funding agencies use successful public communication campaigns that they seek to negotiate a larger slice of the budgetary pie during the next fiscal year. These gains from successful public communication campaigns may not be commercial gains in the strict sense. Public communication campaigns, however, should not be mistaken for pure altruism.

Arguably, two-way symmetrical communication cannot ameliorate all the difficulties that flow from the unequal distribution of resources between organizations and publics (Dozier & Lauzen, 2000). In the context of public communication campaigns, however, the two-way symmetrical model provides an important mechanism of correction for those who might do harm because they are sure they know what is best for someone else. In allowing the target population to negotiate campaign outcomes in the win-win zone of the two-way symmetrical model, public communication campaigns will be more effective at achieving their short-term and long-term objectives. To do so, public communication campaigns need to shift away from engineering consent and toward more flexible goals and objectives that are negotiated in good faith with target populations.

REFERENCES

Bernays, E. L. (1965). *Biography of an idea: Memoirs of public relations counsel Edward L. Bernays*. New York: Simon & Schuster.

Bertram, E., Sharpe, K., & Andreas, P. (1996). *Drug war politics: The price of denial*. Berkeley: University of California Press.

Broom, G. M. (1986, May). *Public relations roles and systems theory: Functional and historicist causal models*. Paper presented at the meeting of the Public Relations Interest Group, International Communication Association, Chicago.

Broom, G. M., & Dozier, D. M. (1990). *Using research in public relations: Applications to program management*. Englewood Cliffs, NJ: Prentice Hall.

Bryant, C. A., & Forthofer, M. S. (2000). Community-based prevention marketing: The next steps in disseminating behavior change. *American Journal of Health Behavior, 24*(1), 61-68.

Cutlip, S. M. (1994). *The unseen power: Public relations. A history*. Hillsdale, NJ: Lawrence Erlbaum.

Cutlip, S. M., Center, A. H., & Broom, G. M. (1994). *Effective public relations* (7th ed.). Englewood Cliffs, NJ: Prentice Hall.

Dozier, D. M. (1990). The innovation of research in public relations practice: Review of a program of studies. In J. E. Grunig & L. A. Grunig (Eds.), *Public relations research annual* (Vol. 2, pp. 3-28). Hillsdale, NJ: Lawrence Erlbaum.

Dozier, D. M., with Grunig, L. A., & Grunig, J. E. (1995). *Manager's guide to excellence in public relations and communication management*. Mahwah, NJ: Lawrence Erlbaum.

Dozier, D. M., & Lauzen, M. M. (2000). Liberating the intellectual domain from the practice: Public relations, activism, and the role of the scholar. *Journal of Public Relations Research, 12*(1), 3-22.

Flora, J. A., Maccoby, N., & Farquhar, J. W. (1989). Communication campaigns to prevent cardiovascular disease: The Stanford community studies. In R. Rice & C. Atkin (Eds.), *Public communication campaigns* (2nd ed., pp. 233-252). Newbury Park, CA: Sage.

Goldman, E. F. (1948). *Two-way street: The emergence of the public relations counselor*. Boston: Bellman.

Grunig, J. E. (Ed.). (1992). *Excellence in public relations and communication management*. Hillsdale, NJ: Lawrence Erlbaum.

Grunig, J. E., & Grunig, L. A. (1992). Models of public relations and communication. In J. E. Grunig (Ed.), *Excellence in public relations and communication management* (pp. 285-325). Hillsdale, NJ: Lawrence Erlbaum.

Grunig, J. E., & Hunt, T. (1984). *Managing public relations*. New York: Holt, Rinehart & Winston.

Grunig, L. A., Dozier, D. M., & Grunig, J. E. (1994). *Phase II: Qualitative study.* San Francisco: International Association of Business Communicators Research Foundation.

Grunig, L. A., Grunig, J. E., & Dozier, D. M. (in press). *Excellent public relations and effective organizations: A study of communication management in three countries.* Mahwah, NJ: Lawrence Erlbaum.

Guttman, N., Kegler, M., & McLeroy, K. R. (1996). Health promotion paradoxes, antinomies and conundrums. *Dissertation Abstracts International, 55,* A407.

Murphy, P. (1991). The limits of symmetry: A game theory approach to symmetric and asymmetric public relations. In J. E. Grunig & L. A. Grunig (Eds.), *Public relations research annual* (Vol. 3, pp. 115-131). Hillsdale, NJ: Lawrence Erlbaum.

Paisley, W. (1989). Public communication campaigns: The American experience. In R. Rice & C. Atkin (Eds.), *Public communication campaigns* (2nd ed., pp. 15-41). Newbury Park, CA: Sage.

Rice, R. E., & Atkin, C. K. (1989). Trends in communication campaign research. In R. Rice & C. Atkin (Eds.), *Public communication campaigns* (2nd ed., pp. 7-11). Newbury Park, CA: Sage.

Rogers, E. M. (1983). *Diffusion of innovations* (3rd ed.). New York: Free Press.

Rogers, E. M., & Storey, D. (1987). Communication campaigns. In C. Berger & S. Chaffee (Eds.), *Handbook of communication science* (pp. 817-846). Newbury Park, CA: Sage.

Stauber, J., & Rampton, S. (1995). *Toxic sludge is good for you! Lies, damn lies and the public relations industry.* Monroe, ME: Common Courage Press.

White, J., & Dozier, D. M. (1992). Public relations and management decision making. In J. E. Grunig (Ed.), *Excellence in public relations and communication management* (pp. 285-325). Hillsdale, NJ: Lawrence Erlbaum.

Strategic Communication for International Health Programs

Phyllis Tilson Piotrow
D. Lawrence Kincaid

During the past half century, international health communication programs have gradually moved from a primarily individual educational effort to a more market-oriented approach, more responsive to communities and to individuals as participants and as consumers. In the process, health communication programs have adopted and adapted many strategic concepts from the expanding fields of commercial enterprise, political campaigning, and mass media. During the past two decades, family planning and population programs have replaced agriculture-based extension programs as leaders in development communication. They have been followed by increasing emphasis on nutrition (Hornik, 1998), child health through immunization and oral rehydration (Graeff, Elder, & Booth, 1993; Seidel, 1992), maternal health (Griffiths, Moore, & Favin, 1991), and preventing the spread of HIV/AIDS and other infectious diseases (Edgar, Fitzpatrick, & Freimuth, 1992; Liskin, Church, Piotrow, & Harris, 1989).

Because the source of behavior change or healthy behavior in the field of reproductive health, as well as in the care of infants and children, rests with the individual, the family, and the community, these programs have highlighted the need for effective communication directly to individuals and communities

AUTHORS' NOTE: We acknowledge the support of the U.S. Agency for International Development for financial assistance and encouragement for the programs described in this chapter.

and for improved communication between health care providers and their clients. Moreover, as reproductive health programs have attracted larger resources from government donors (Conly & Speidel, 1993), institutions and individuals worldwide have been stimulated to refine strategic communication models and to experiment with new ways of designing, implementing, and evaluating health promotion campaigns. Paradoxically, the developing countries of Asia, Africa, and Latin America have often been at the forefront of these efforts, despite low levels of literacy, lack of easy access to media, generally limited private sector and poor-quality government sector services, discrimination against women, and a whole array of cultural and religious constraints. This chapter summarizes elements of strategic health communication today and provides examples from programs in Asia, Africa, and Latin America.

MAKING COMMUNICATION
PROGRAMS MORE STRATEGIC

Some of the early family planning programs, such as the Taichung Experiment in Taiwan (Freedman & Takeshita, 1960) and the Mothers Clubs in the Republic of Korea, used innovative and effective communication strategies (Park, Chung, Han, & Lee, 1973; Rogers & Kincaid, 1981). Generally, however, the first family planning communication programs had notable weaknesses: (a) lack of a strategic design or plan identifying specific, measurable goals to be achieved and the means to achieve them; (b) a disconnect between the communication campaigns and many of the service delivery programs because it was assumed that those exposed to the campaign would immediately seek out services without additional encouragement or support; (c) very general messages intended to appeal to an undifferentiated public with such slogans as "A Small Family Is a Happy Family"; (d) lack of concern for pretesting of messages and media with intended audiences; (e) little attention to well-articulated models of behavior change that could guide communication programs in developing appropriate content and sequences for messages and activities; and (f) failure to formulate precise indicators and to use available research and evaluation designs to measure the impact and appropriateness of any communication interventions, including message content or media channels (Piotrow, Kincaid, Rimon, & Rinehart, 1997; Rogers, 1973; Schramm, 1971).

Currently, social programs worldwide are recognizing that communication—with policymakers, clients, the public, and health care providers—is not a spare wheel, to be used when programs break down, but rather a steering wheel that can guide the direction of people's thinking, community norms, informed individual choice, and therefore service programs (Fraser & Restrepo-Estrada, 1999; Piotrow et al., 1997; Piotrow & Rimon, 1999; Piotrow, Treiman, Rimon, Yun, & Lozare, 1994). This trend was reinforced a decade ago when leading demographers began to make the case that the demographic transition toward lower fertility was prompted more by ideational factors than by economic factors, as had previously been supposed (Cleland & Wilson, 1987; Freedman, 1987). *Ideation* is defined as new ways of thinking that diffuse in a society by means of social interaction. Additional analyses of data and a deeper understanding of individual and community changes indicated that ideational factors, communication networks, cultural and religious norms, and other influences more social in nature than economic, and highly dependent on channels of communication, were required to explain behavior change (Bongaarts & Watkins, 1996; Kincaid, 2000a, 2000b; Kincaid, Figueroa, Underwood, & Storey, 1999; Rogers, 1995; Rogers & Kincaid, 1981; Valente, 1995).

STRATEGIC HEALTH COMMUNICATION TODAY

Strategic communication is based on a combination of facts, ideas, and theories integrated by a visionary design to achieve verifiable objectives by affecting the most likely sources and barriers to behavioral change with the active participation of stakeholders and beneficiaries. Facts are obtained from formative research with all those involved, which ideally uncovers the most likely sources and barriers to change. To achieve the greatest impact, the messages designed to produce those changes should be based on valid theories that explain and predict how the communication objectives corresponding to those changes can be achieved. Good ideas are derived from bright and talented people. The specification of verifiable objectives makes it possible to evaluate the ultimate impact of the campaign and to determine why and how the communication worked. Finally, all the elements of a successful communication campaign should be integrated by a creative vision that instills a sense of coherence and dynamic energy and builds in strong community participation. This is increasingly the approach chosen by governments and private sector donors who seek to achieve a significant impact among large populations.

The concept of strategic communication encompasses a wide variety of public health interventions, including community mobilization, client-centered counseling, social network interventions, social marketing, entertainment-education by means of TV or radio dramas and music, provider promotion, public policy, behavior change communication, advocacy, personal and community empowerment, public relations, mass media information dissemination, and so forth, including any type of communication process that leads to behavior change. The specific health problem and the analysis of the population determine which types of strategies and which messages and activities are most appropriate for different communities.

There are at least 10 key elements of strategic communication. They are

1. **Science and research based:** A science- and research-based approach to communication requires both accurate data and relevant theory. It begins with formative or preliminary research and adequate data to define a specific health problem, identify feasible solutions to the problem, and describe the intended

population or audience (Scriven, 1972; see Chapters 6 and 7, this volume). Formative research is used to improve project design. Strategic communication also depends on appropriate social science models or theories of behavior change, which might include (a) stages of change or diffusion theories (McGuire, 1981; Piotrow et al., 1997; Prochaska, DiClemente, & Norcross, 1992; Rogers, 1995; Valente, 1995), (b) cognitive theories (Bandura, 1986; Fishbein & Ajzen, 1975), (c) emotional response theories (Clark, 1992; Zajonc, 1984), (d) social process and influence theories (Friedkin, 1998; Kincaid, 1987, 1988, 2000b; Latané, 1981; Moscovici, 1976; Nowak, Szamjre, & Latané, 1990; Rogers & Kincaid, 1981), and (e) mass media theory (Gerbner, 1977; Gerbner, Gross, Morgan, & Signorelli, 1980). A science-based approach also includes an implementation program to put interventions into practice, a research design sufficiently rigorous to test hypotheses in the field and measure changes in behavior resulting from specific interventions, and the evaluation and documentation of results to determine whether and how they have been achieved (Rogers & Storey, 1987).

2. **Client centered:** A client-centered approach calls for substantial message pretesting and audience research (both qualitative and quantitative), including focus groups, interviews, surveys, and psychographic research (Mitchell, 1983). Audience research makes it possible to segment audiences based on relevant characteristics and then design engaging but often different messages for diverse groups. A client-centered approach can offer practical support to clients, for example, by making client-provider communication more convenient, less time-consuming, and more polite. It also implies more strategic changes that affect the balance of power in service programs, such as encouraging increased community participation, allowing clients to choose their own methods or treatment or even to set priorities for health services and to sustain individual behavior changes over time (Moser, 1993; Pariani & Van Arsdol, 1991; see Chapters 4 and 13, this volume).

3. **Benefit oriented:** Perhaps the most important single element in strategic health communication is to emphasize the desires and constraints of specific clients, potential clients, or segmented audiences (for example, young, sexually active males or older married women with children) rather than general benefits or the goals and objectives of policymakers or service providers (Ries & Trout, 1981). This benefit—whether quality, convenience, affordability, or whatever—becomes the vision or creative design of the program—the image that everyone will have of the program.

4. **Service linked:** Health promotion campaigns should increasingly identify and promote the specific sites, providers, brand name products, and even means of access that can help individuals meet their needs as do social marketing campaigns (Andreasen, 1995). The audience needs to know what to do and where to find any help that is needed. Campaigns should reinforce *individual self-efficacy* (i.e., the ability to resolve a problem oneself) or *collective self-efficacy* (i.e., the ability of a community to assert its will) by clearly linking the desired result with the actions needed to achieve it (Bandura, 1986).

5. **Entertainment-education focused:** Mass media are spreading throughout the world, bringing new topics, new information, and new forms of entertainment to new audiences. Between 1975 and 1995, for example, the number of radio receivers in the developing world increased from approximately 230,000 to more than 1 million, and the number of television sets increased from approximately 50,000 to more than 700,000 (International Broadcasting Audience Research Library/ British Broadcasting Company, 1996). Strategic communication in the mass media, in addition to "street" and "folk" media, uses entertainment to attract audience attention, to tell a compelling story, to create role models, to show the consequences of wise or foolish behavior, and, above all, to provide an emotional impact that helps clients remember and internalize the advice that is given (Coleman & Meyer, 1990; Jato et al., 1999; Kaiser Family Foundation, 1996; Lozare et al., 1993; Rimon et al., 1994; Robinson & Lewis, 1999; Singhal & Rogers, 1999; Storey, Boulay, Karchi, Heckert, & Karmacharya, 1999; see Chapter 28, this volume). Entertainment-education is important to strategic communication due to the "nine p's": *pervasive,* meaning it reaches almost everyone; *popular,* meaning everyone likes it; *passionate,* meaning it evokes emotions; *personal,* meaning people identify with characters in entertainment; *participatory,* meaning people often become actively involved in following entertainment figures and situations; *persuasive,* meaning individual role models and consequences of behavior can be convincingly portrayed; *practical,* meaning the entertainment industry already exists and can readily incorporate health themes in ongoing work in a cost-effective manner; *profitable,* meaning high-quality production can draw commercial sponsorship and produce revenue; and *proven effective* through ongoing research (Piotrow et al., 1997).

6. **Professionally developed:** Currently, nongovernmental organizations and ministries of health contract for the skills of communication professionals such as market researchers, advertising agencies, community mobilizers, radio and television producers, theatrical directors, script writers, and performers. Ironically, although the pursuit of quality in service delivery and in health care management is highly valued, a double standard is sometimes applied to communication materials. Instead of being praised, attractive, top-quality communication products in public campaigns are sometimes criticized as "glitzy," "slick," or "wasteful." In fact, the most wasteful and counterproductive materials are those that are unattractive or convey the impression that health products and programs are not as valuable as other consumer products or services.

7. **Advocacy linked:** Advocacy occurs on two interrelated levels—personal and political. *Personal advocacy* occurs when current and new adopters of a behavior acknowledge their change and encourage family members and friends to adopt similar behavior. In this sense, advocacy is the last stage of individual behavior change because it confirms the change publicly and reduces the likelihood of discontinuing the behavior. *Political or policy advocacy* occurs when individuals from the grassroots to the decision-making level speak out in support of specific policies or programs that facilitate the change. Officials and community leaders

especially have access to the mass media by means of press conferences, talk shows, and official site visits that are covered by journalists. They can not only endorse the goals of a particular project but also call for public policy changes to remove barriers and facilitate change, publicly mention the names of local health centers and providers, hand out awards for national recognition, and even adopt the recommended health behavior themselves on national or local television and radio. The two levels of advocacy reinforce one another. When community members offer public testimonials in support of certain health behaviors, local and national leaders are more likely to appreciate those policies and programs that will facilitate the behavior and to remove the barriers against it. If no one advocates a behavior or policy publicly, the rate of change is likely to be much slower. Therefore, strategic communication programs should create ample opportunities for advocacy, not only in families and social networks but also in community events and media (see Chapter 31, this volume).

8. **Expanding to scale:** A strategic communication program must be able to scale up to reach ever larger populations and areas. The era of small pilot projects is ending. Continuing, extensive, and cumulative exposure to multiple media increases the probability of beginning and continuing use of modern family planning (Jato et al., 1999; Kincaid et al., 1999).

9. **Programmatically sustainable:** The experience of the corporate world confirms that continuing advertising and public relations are an essential part of consumer communications (see Chapter 13, this volume), just as continuing service delivery is an essential part of health care. Every year, new segments of the population become eligible for information and services as its members age and mature and enter new stages in the life cycle. Moreover, as service programs become more complex, focusing on client-centered care, informed choice, and gender balance, the need for an ongoing communication component and the skills and capacity to manage it all increase.

10. **Cost-effective:** Finally, strategic communication needs to examine the bottom line. Because donors constantly ask "Are communication programs financially sustainable?" strategic communication has to respond by persuading its audience at an ever-decreasing cost per person reached. Donors and long-term planners are beginning to ask, "Where can additional funds be allocated with greatest effect to achieve and sustain healthy behavior?" (Behrman & Knowles, 1998; Robinson & Lewis, 1999). Strategic communication programs can be a very good investment, but the burden of proof is on the field to document the impact and returns.

STRATEGIC HEALTH COMMUNICATION AT WORK: FIVE EXAMPLES

The previously discussed 10 components of modern strategic communication are illustrated to varying degrees in five recent international reproductive health communication programs, summarized in Table 14.1. Figure 14.1 shows the logos from the campaigns.

Table 14.1 Elements of Strategic Communication in Five Communication Programs, 1986 to 1999

	Country				
	Bolivia	*Philippines*	*Bangladesh*	*Egypt*	*Uganda*
Elements of strategic communication					
Science based	+	+ +	+	+	+
Client centered	+	+ +	+	+	+
Benefit oriented	+ +	+ +	+	+ +	+ +
Service linked	+ +	+	+ +	+ +	+ +
Entertainment focused	+ +	o	+ +	+ +	+
Professionally developed	+ +	+ +	+ +	+ +	+
Advocacy linked	+ +	+	o	+	+
Expanding to scale	+ +	+ +	+	+ +	+
Programmatically sustainable	+	+	+	+	+
Cost-effective	*NA*	+	*NA*	+ +	*NA*
Verifiable objectives					
Exposure	+ +	+	+ +	+ +	+
Logo recognition	+ +	+ +	+ +	+ +	+
Increases in					
Knowledge	+ +	+ +	+	o	+
Clinic attendance	+	*NA*	+	*NA*	+ +
Use of family planning	+ +	+	+	+	+ +
References	Valente et al. (1996) Saba and Valente (1999)	Kincaid (2000a) Kincaid et al. (1998) Rimon (1998)	Hasan (1998) Kincaid et al. (1999) Whitney, Kincaid, and de-Fossard (1999)	Brancich and Under-wood (1998) CAPMAS (1998) Saffitz, Hess, and Al-Alfi (1998) Robinson and Lewis (1999)	Delivery of Improved Services for Health (1999) Lettenmaier (1999)

NOTE: Demographic and health surveys from each of the five countries during the past two decades provide data on some of the indicators, especially use of family planning, sources, and method.
o = negligible; + = moderate; + + = substantial; *NA* = data not available.

Bolivia: The Las Manitos logo and slogan (Reproductive health is in your hands) remind people to improve their own health.

Philippines: "If you love them, plan for them." Family planning is positioned as a sign of love for children and a means to protect them.

Bangladesh: "Take services. Stay well." The Green Umbrella symbol stands for a range of integrated health services all available under one roof.

Egypt: The Gold Star symbol identifies quality reproductive health services at local clinics that meet national standards.

Uganda: The Green Flower under the Rainbow shows people where family planning, HIV/AIDS, and other health services are available.

Figure 14.1. Strategic Communicatio: Examples of Logos From Developing Country Programs

Bolivia

Reproductive health campaigns in Bolivia offer a good example of a strategic health communication program with strong political and advocacy overtones. Before these activities began in the mid-1980s, family planning was a taboo issue in Bolivia. In the early 1970s, a dramatic film essentially accused U.S. Peace Corps volunteers of encouraging forced sterilization and denying appropriate health care to Bolivian peasants. (Evidence was never found to document these charges.) As a result, family planning was condemned, health centers were closed, and program leaders were sent to jail. In the mid-1980s, however, a complete turnabout in policies and programs began based on extensive audience analysis. Research had shown that there was increasing interest and curiosity in Bolivia about health and population issues and great concern regarding high infant and maternal mortality. As a result of these findings, 10 discussion meetings were held in 1986 and 1987 among 700 policymakers and influential citizens to discuss the pros and cons of family planning. The result was a consensus to support family planning as a way to reduce maternal and infant mortality and to provide couples with safe and acceptable choices. These meetings were followed by radio spots in the three largest cities and distribution of print materials. Audiocassettes for long-distance buses played family planning health messages with popular music, comedy, and entertainment. A private health care center promoted its services. This first campaign aroused no opposition and resulted in a more than 70% increase in new family planning clients at the clinics of the private organization (Saba & Valente, 1999).

A second, more extensive multimedia campaign beginning in 1994 used a pretested logo depicting a baby's hand clinging to a parent's finger with the slogan "Reproductive health is in your hands." This emphasized both the voluntary nature of all family planning services, dispelling any lingering fears of coercion, and the ability of men and women to secure help for reproductive health problems (Saba & Valente, 1999; Valente et al., 1996). A third campaign beginning in 1996 strengthened the self-efficacy theme as more clinics began to offer family planning services and social marketing programs offered condoms and, later, oral contraceptives commercially. The phrase "[Reproductive health is] now much closer to you" was added to the original slogan. The third campaign used dramatic TV episodes and testimonials to highlight the benefits of family planning in reducing maternal mortality and preventing unsafe abortions.

These campaigns together succeeded in doubling the country's modern contraceptive prevalence rate from 12.2% of married women of reproductive age in 1989 to 25.2% in 1998. Modern contraceptive methods became more prevalent than traditional ones, with intrauterine device use increasing from approximately 5% to 11%. The program gradually went to scale, beginning in one city and moving to three and then to a fourth large urban area (Saba & Valente, 1999).

The latest step in the strategic campaign series (1998-1999) is the Lilac Tent project designed to reach rural areas of Bolivia not easily accessible by radio and television with three lilac-colored tents housing videos, live music, theater, dance groups, mimes, games, puppet shows, print material, and interactive learning devices. Each tent operates in coordination with local political leaders, health providers, schoolteachers, students, and performers in the community. It provides advocacy opportunities for local services. It seeks sustainability with support from the army for transportation, from the United Nations Population Fund for extension to additional villages, and from local communities and groups eager to participate in the programs. At the personal level, it stimulates young people and spouses to discuss family health issues between themselves, to seek services together, and to be assisted by trained providers. The need for the services is now endorsed by political leaders and parties, demonstrating that personal appeals and political advocacy can reinforce one another (Saba & Valente, 1999).

Philippines

In the Philippines, the opposition of the Catholic Church to modern contraceptive methods has posed a constant challenge for family planning promotion. To meet the concerns of clients and would-be clients identified through focus groups, the campaign developed a logo of two children skipping along and a slogan, "If You Love Them, Plan for Them," honoring the Philippine belief in children as central to the family. The aim of family planning, therefore, is not so much to avoid having children as to provide the opportunity to care for each child better by planning for each appropriately (Kincaid, 2000a; Rimon, 1998).

The campaigns were designed in three phases: (a) the repositioning of family planning as "love of children," (b) the presentation of health providers as better trained and caring, and (c) promotion of specific contraceptive methods as safe and effective through testimonials. The term *hiyang* or "suitable for you," often heard in focus group discussions, was used to counteract the argument that modern contraceptives are unnatural or artificial. The campaign was launched after the logistics system was in place and the health providers were trained to provide improved services. Throughout the 3-year period, the communication materials were designed, packaged, and tested by professional marketing, research, and advertising agencies (Kincaid, 2000a; Rimon, 1998).

Services were widely promoted in a range of mass media through radio spots, billboards, print materials, and appropriate media news and references. Simultaneously, the campaign integrated community events and stimulated interpersonal, and especially interspousal, communication as part of the overall strategy. The benefit of family planning for families and children was consistently emphasized. During a 3-year period (1993-1996), these communication programs helped to increase modern contraceptive use from 25% to 30%. After the campaign, women who perceived modern contraceptives as *hiyang* were twice as likely to adopt and use these methods. The approval rating for the logo and the "If You Love Them, Plan for Them" message was 99.9% (National Statistics Office, 1999). The Department of Health adopted the logo as the new symbol for the family planning program. Also, social marketing programs provided oral contraceptives and condoms, which were also promoted in various ways. From 1988 to 1999, contraceptive prevalence increased from 36.1% to approximately 50%, and use of modern methods, especially oral contraceptives, increased from 21.6% to 32.4% (National Statistics Office, 2000).

Bangladesh

The Green Umbrella campaign illustrates how an effective visual symbol can communicate the idea of integrated services and the important concept of preventive services as protection for the whole family (Hasan, 1998; Kincaid, 1999; Whitney, Kincaid, & deFossard, 1999). After extensive audience research, the Green Umbrella logo, with its slogan "Take Services, Stay Well," was introduced to dramatize the new orientation of the primary health care programs from a door-to-door delivery system toward more fixed-site facilities able to provide a range of family planning, reproductive health, and maternal and child health services. Launched with great fanfare and a parade through the streets of the capital city of Dhaka, the Green Umbrella was soon recognized by 52% of the population (Hasan, 1998).

The Green Umbrella logo and its message were reinforced through an entertainment-education TV serial in late 1997 in which a charming fieldworker, Bokhul, traveled with her green umbrella to different villages and different families to provide needed family planning supplies and health advice to mothers with young children. Approximately 79% of the urban population and 65% of the rural population with access to TV watched *Shabuj Shathi*. A nationally representative cross-sectional survey of 10,500 women showed that married women who watched the TV drama were more likely to use a modern contraceptive (53%) than were those who did not watch (38%) (Hasan, 1998; Kincaid, 1999; Whitney et al., 1999). Moreover, those who watched *Shabuj Shathi* gained substantial knowledge of HIV/AIDS, childhood diseases, and nutrition, and they were more likely to visit a health and family planning service facility and use a modern contraceptive. Interestingly, none of the other available sources of information—watching TV, listening to radio, or visit by health worker—or demographic factors had a comparable impact on HIV/AIDS knowledge (Kincaid, 1999). Moreover, a follow-up series, *Shabuj Chhaya,* beginning in January 2000, generated more than 200,000 letters after only three episodes—convincing proof of the reach of entertainment-education and mass media even in Bangladesh.

Egypt

In Egypt, the Gold Star Program is an example of a strongly service-linked, client-oriented program. It was initiated by the Ministry of Health in 1992 to increase client visits to ministry clinics. The ministry and medical experts began by identifying 101 indicators of high-quality services, such as that family planning clinic sessions must occur in an area of privacy and comfort; new clients must be provided with information about approved, available methods; running water must be available; and observations from any physical examination must be recorded in the client's medical record (Ministry of Health, 1994). For several years, health care providers and their supervisors were extensively trained to offer services following these standards. When training was complete, clinics were visited and assessed every quarter. Those that passed the 101 indicators with a satisfactory score for two successive quarters were eligible to receive a bright Gold Star emblem to place outside and inside the clinic. This simple image and symbol of quality was widely publicized and well-recognized and understood by most clients (Central Agency for Public Mobilization and Statistics, 1998; Saffitz, Hess, & Al-Alfi, 1998). The certification of a Gold Star clinic is an important community event in which local leaders, health officials, and the media play a prominent role. Between 1992 and 1997, the percentage of family planning users who sought services from Ministry of Health clinics increased from 30% to 40%. Between 1995 and 1997, the country's overall contraceptive prevalence rate increased from 48% to 55% (Brancich & Underwood, 1998).

Uganda

In Uganda, a series of strategically designed communication campaigns contributed to an increase in the contraceptive prevalence rate from 12.6% in 1995 to 18.6% in 1997 (Lettenmaier, 1999). The campaigns also contributed to a 50% increase in condom use among men and a 55% increase in the number of monthly client visits at 75 sentinel health facilities (Lettenmaier, 1999). The Uganda project, known as Delivery of Improved Services for Health (DISH), is closely linked to service facilities. Seven different campaigns have essentially promoted existing family planning services, addressed HIV/AIDS prevention, sexually transmitted diseases (STDs) and maternal health services, and HIV testing and counseling services. Up to 90% of the clients in these services recognize the program logo—a rainbow over a yellow flower—and know at least two services (such as family planning and immunization) available at health facilities displaying the symbol (DISH, 1999).

The benefits to clients, explored through preliminary focus groups and other research, are promoted in various ways, such as "Plan today and enjoy tomorrow," "Safer sex or AIDS," and "Take control of your life," emphasizing the individual benefits of safer sex practices. The Uganda program also used a unique form of entertainment-education—sports. The Men's Challenge Cup comprised a series of promotional activities for the campaign against STDs that took place during the 6-week-long 1998 World Cup Tournament and helped produce the largest number of (STD) client visits ever recorded in the 75 sentinel health facilities (Lettenmaier, 1999). Sports activities have a unique ability to reach an important male audience, to obtain advocacy by sports heroes, and to be almost entirely sustainable through support from commercial donors.

Uganda's DISH program initially focused on 10, and then 12, districts and has not yet gone to scale nationally. Mass media components such as the prize-winning radio program *Choices* and TV spots, serials, print materials, community activities, drama performances, and bicycle rallies, however, have all reached a national audience. To date, Uganda's campaigns and approach to HIV/AIDS—which calls for continuing public campaigns, political advocacy, information, and condom distribution—have been the most successful in Africa in reducing the rates of HIV/AIDS prevalence, perhaps by as much as half.

NEW CHALLENGES FOR THE 21ST CENTURY

There are at least six areas that will probably receive much more attention in the 21st century.

1. *Communicating effectively with young people,* who are known for their risk-taking propensities and lack of concern regarding future hazards (HIV/AIDS and unwanted pregnancy), will require that young people participate actively in the design of strategic communication as, for example, the youth advisory groups did with the radio Youth Variety Show in Kenya (Krenn, Kiragu, & Sienche, 1998).

2. *Linking community mobilization and media advocacy* will become increasingly important to avoid the fragmentation of these complementary efforts and to strengthen community norms that support health behavior (Bracht, 1998; see Chapter 27, this volume).

3. *Promoting specific health behaviors within a comprehensive integrated program* will call for phasing in or layering different messages so that they do not compete with one another.

4. *Increasing advocacy and managing controversy effectively* will occupy a large part of managers' time—including organizing coalitions, recruiting credible experts, citing appropriate data, mobilizing sympathetic spokespeople, making changes where necessary, and, most important, responding promptly to criticism—to highlight important health issues, to stimulate informed public debate, and to encourage spousal and family discussion of reproductive health issues.

5. *New developments in communication technology* are creating exciting opportunities for strategic communication in health (Rice & Katz, 2001; see Chapters 29 and 30, this volume). An example of the new technology at work in health communication is the SCOPE (Strategic Communication Planning and Evaluation) software, available on a CD-ROM (Bailey & Khan, 1998). Developed by the Johns Hopkins Center for Communication Programs, SCOPE leads users step by step through the process of developing a strategic communication program, including analysis, strategy, development and pretesting, implementation, evaluation, and planning for sustainability. SCOPE includes relevant data on reproductive health problems, audiences, and channels of communication for more than 20 different countries and in six languages, and it is used in 2- to 4-week intensive workshops, in classrooms, and in distance learning courses over the Internet.

6. *Health communication programs will be under increased pressure to evaluate and document* their impact, cost-effectiveness, and sustainability (Behrman & Knowles, 1998; Robinson & Lewis, 1999; see Chapters 2, 6, and 10, this volume) despite the multiple problems inherent in evaluating national communication campaigns (Valente, 1997; Yoder, Hornik, & Chirwa, 1996; see Chapter 8, this volume).

A FUTURE BRIGHT BUT CHALLENGING

The future is bright but challenging for health communication and especially for strategic national or regional communication programs that seek to change individual and community health behaviors on a large scale. As improved understanding and treatment reduce mortality from many causes, the so-called lifestyle diseases or behavior-based health hazards, such as STDs, HIV/AIDS, tobacco-induced lung cancer, cardiovascular disease, drug abuse, excess fertility, and accidents, will account for an increasing proportion of all mortality and morbidity. Even other major sources of mortality, such as malaria and tuberculosis, can be better addressed by changing individual and community knowledge, attitudes, and behavior through strategic communication programs. The challenge is clear, and the tools are available.

REFERENCES

Andreasen, A. (1995). *Marketing social change: Changing behavior to promote health, social development, and the environment.* San Francisco: Jossey-Bass.

Bailey, M. S., & Khan, O. (1998). *SCOPE: A software tool incorporating processes for strategic planning.* Paper presented at the annual meeting of the American Public Health Association, Washington, DC.

Bandura, A. (1986). *Social foundations of thought and action.* Englewood Cliffs, NJ: Prentice Hall.

Behrman, J. R., & Knowles, J. C. (1998). Population and reproductive health: An economic framework for policy evaluation. *Population and Development Review, 24*(4), 697-737.

Bongaarts, J., & Watkins, S. C. (1996). Social interactions and contemporary fertility transitions. *Population and Development Review, 22*(4), 639-682.

Bracht, N. (Ed.). (1998). *Health promotion at the community level: New advances* (2nd ed.). Thousand Oaks, CA: Sage.

Brancich, C., & Underwood, C. (1998). Egypt's Gold Star Quality Program wins clients and communities. In *Communication impact, 4.* Baltimore, MD: Johns Hopkins University, Center for Communication Programs.

Central Agency for Public Mobilization and Statistics (CAPMAS). (1998). *The Gold Star Campaign: Findings from the post-test survey conducted among Egyptian men and women.* Unpublished manuscript.

Clark, M. S. (Ed.). (1992). *Emotion and social behavior.* Newbury Park, CA: Sage.

Cleland, J., & Wilson, C. (1987). Demand theories of fertility transition: An iconoclastic view. *Population Studies, 41,* 5-30.

Coleman, P. L., & Meyer, R. C. (1990). *Entertainment for social change. Proceedings of the Enter-Educate Conference.* Baltimore, MD: Johns Hopkins University, Center for Communication Programs.

Conly, S. R., & Speidel, J. J. (1993). *Global population assistance: A report card on the major donor countries.* Washington, DC: Population Action International.

Delivery of Improved Services for Health, Pathfinder International and MEASURE Evaluation Project. (1999). *Uganda delivery of improved services for health evaluation surveys 1997* (Technical report). Chapel Hill: University of North Carolina, Carolina Population Center.

Edgar, T., Fitzpatrick, M. H., & Freimuth, V. S. (Eds.). (1992). *AIDS: A communication perspective.* Hillsdale, NJ: Lawrence Erlbaum.

Fishbein, M., & Ajzen, I. (1975). *Belief, attitude, intention and behavior: An introduction to theory and research.* Reading, MA: Addison-Wesley.

Fraser, C., & Restrepo-Estrada, S. (1999). *Communication for development.* London: Tauris.

Freedman, R. (1987). The contribution of social science research to population policy and family planning program effectiveness. *Studies in Family Planning, 18*(2), 57-82.

Freedman, R., & Takeshita, J. (1960). *Family planning in Taiwan: An experiment in social change.* Princeton, NJ: Princeton University Press.

Friedkin, N. E. (1998). *A structural theory of social influence.* New York: Cambridge University Press.

Gerbner, G. (1977). *Mass media policies in changing cultures.* New York: Wiley.

Gerbner, G. L., Gross, L., Morgan, M., & Signorelli, N. (1980). The mainstreaming of America: Violence Profile No. 11. *Journal of Communication, 30,* 10-27.

Graeff, J. A., Elder, J. P., & Booth, E. M. (1993). *Communication for health and behavior change: A developing country perspective.* San Francisco: Jossey-Bass.

Griffiths, M., Moore, M., & Favin, M. (1991). *Communicating safe motherhood: Using communication to improve maternal health in the developing world* (Working paper). Arlington, VA: John Snow International, MotherCare Project.

Hasan, K. (1998). *National media survey 1998*. Dhaka, Bangladesh: ORG-MARG Quest, sponsored by Bangladesh Center for Communication Programs, Johns Hopkins University, Social Marketing Company, and UNICEF.

Hornik, R. C. (1998). *Development communication: Information, agriculture and nutrition in the Third World*. New York: Longman.

International Broadcasting Audience Research Library/British Broadcasting Company. (1996). *World radio and television receivers*. London: Author.

Jato, M. N., Simbakalia, C., Tarasevitch, J. M., Awasum, D. N., Kihinga, C. M. B., & Mungu, E. N. (1999). The impact of multimedia family planning promotion on the contraceptive behavior of women in Tanzania. *International Family Planning Perspectives, 252*(2), 60-67.

Kaiser Family Foundation. (1996). *The uses of mainstream media to encourage social responsibility: The international experience*. Report prepared by Advocates for Youth for the Henry J. Kaiser Family Foundation, Menlo Park, CA.

Kincaid, D. L. (Ed.). (1987). *Communication theory: Eastern and Western perspectives*. New York: Academic Press.

Kincaid, D. L. (1988). The convergence theory of communication: Its implications for intercultural communication. *International and Intercultural Annual, 7*, 280-298.

Kincaid, D. L. (1999). *Impact of the Shabuj Shathi television drama of Bangladesh: Key findings*. Unpublished report. Johns Hopkins University, Center for Communication Programs.

Kincaid, D. L. (2000a, June). *Mass media, ideation, and behavior: A longitudinal analysis of contraceptive use change in the Philippines*. Paper presented at the annual meeting of the International Communication Association, Acapulco, Mexico.

Kincaid, D. L. (2000b). Social networks, ideation, and contraceptive behavior in Bangladesh: A longitudinal analysis. *Social Science and Medicine, 50*, 215-231.

Kincaid, D. L., Figueroa, M. E., Underwood, C. R., & Storey, J. D. (1999, March). *Attitude, ideation, and contraceptive behavior: The relationship observed in five countries*. Paper presented at the annual meeting of the Population Association of America, New York.

Krenn, S., Kiragu, K., & Sienche, C. (1998). Advocacy and mass media: A winning combination for Kenyan youth. In *Communication impact, 2*. Baltimore, MD: Johns Hopkins University, Center for Communication Programs.

Latané, B. (1981). The psychology of social impact. *American Psychology, 36*, 343-365.

Lettenmaier, C. (1999). Uganda communication campaigns spur integrated health programs. In *Communication impact, 6*. Baltimore, MD: Johns Hopkins University, Center for Communication Programs.

Liskin, L., Church, C. A., Piotrow, P. T., & Harris, J. A. (1989). AIDS education—A beginning. In *Population reports, L-8*. Baltimore, MD: Johns Hopkins University, Center for Communication Programs.

Lozare, B. V., Hess, R., Yun, S. H., Gill-Bailey, A., Valmadrid, C., Livesay, A., Khan, S. R., & Siddiqui, N. (1993, November). *Husband-wife communication and family planning: Impact of a national television drama*. Paper presented at the annual meeting of the American Public Health Association, San Francisco.

McGuire, W. J. (1981). Theoretical foundations of campaigns. In R. E. Rice & W. J. Paisley (Eds.), *Public communication campaigns* (pp. 41-70). Beverly Hills, CA: Sage.

Ministry of Health. (1994). *Standards of service for quality improvement programs monitoring system.* Cairo: Author.

Mitchell, A. (1983). *The nine American lifestyles.* New York: Macmillan.

Moscovici, S. (1976). *Social influence and social change.* London: Academic Press.

Moser, C. O. (1993). *Gender planning and development: Theory, practice and training.* London: Routledge.

National Statistics Office, Department of Health (Philippines), and Macro International, Inc. (1999). *National demographic and health survey 1998.* Manila: National Statistics Office/Macro International.

National Statistics Office of the Philippines. (2000, January 3). *Family planning survey* (as reported by Agence France Presse).

Nowak, A., Szamjre, J., & Latané, B. (1990). From private attitude to public opinion: A dynamic theory of social impact. *Psychological Review, 97*(3), 362-376.

Pariani, S., & Van Arsdol, M. D., Jr. (1991). Does choice make a difference to contraceptive use? Evidence from East Java. *Studies in Family Planning, 22*(6), 384-390.

Park, J. P., Chung, K. K., Han, D. S., & Lee, S. B. (1973). *Mothers clubs and family planning in Korea.* Seoul: Seoul National University, School of Public Health.

Piotrow, P. T., Kincaid, D. L., Rimon, J. G., II, & Rinehart, W. E. (1997). *Health communication: Lessons from family planning and reproductive health.* Westport, CT: Praeger.

Piotrow, P. T., & Rimon, J. G., II. (1999). Asia's population and family planning programmes: Leaders in strategic communication. *Asia Pacific Population Journal, 14*(4), 73-90.

Piotrow, P. T., Treiman, K. A., Rimon, J. G., II, Yun, S. H., & Lozare, B. V. (1994). *Strategies for family planning promotion* (World Bank Technical Paper No. 223). Washington, DC: World Bank.

Prochaska, J. O., DiClemente, C. C., & Norcross, J. C. (1992). In search of how people change: Applications to addictive behaviors. *American Psychologist, 47*(9), 1102-1112.

Rice, R. E., & Katz, J. (Eds.). (2001). *The Internet and health communication.* Thousand Oaks, CA: Sage.

Ries, A., & Trout, J. (1981). *Positioning: The battle for your mind.* New York: McGraw-Hill.

Rimon, J. G., II. (1998). Philippines communication outreach accelerates family planning use in 1993-1998. In *Communication impact, 3.* Baltimore, MD: Johns Hopkins University, Center for Communication Programs.

Rimon, J. G., II, Treiman, K. A., Kincaid, D. K., Silayan-Go, A., Camacho-Reyes, M. S., Abejuela, R. M., & Coleman, P. L. (1994). *Promoting sexual responsibility in the Philippines through music: An enter-educate approach* (Occasional Paper Series No. 3). Baltimore, MD: Johns Hopkins University, Center for Communication Programs.

Robinson, W., & Lewis, G. (1999). *Developing a cost-effective framework for analyzing family planning IEC program interventions.* Unpublished paper. Johns Hopkins University, Center for Communication Programs.

Rogers, E. M. (1973). *Communication strategies for family planning.* New York: Free Press.

Rogers, E. M. (1995). *Diffusion of innovations* (4th ed.). New York: Free Press.

Rogers, E. M., & Kincaid, D. L. (1981). *Communication networks: A new paradigm for research.* New York: Free Press.

Rogers, E. M., & Storey, J. D. (1987). Communication campaigns. In C. Berger & S. Chafee (Eds.), *Handbook of communication science* (pp. 817-846). Newbury Park, CA: Sage.

Saba, W., & Valente, T. (1999). Bolivia's lilac tent: A first in health promotion. In *Communication impact, 5.* Baltimore, MD: Johns Hopkins University, Center for Communication Programs.

Saffitz, G., Hess, R., & Al-Alfi, S. (1998). *The Gold Star Campaign process evaluation report.* Baltimore, MD: Johns Hopkins University, Center for Communication Programs.

Schramm, W. (1971). Communication in family planning. *Studies in Family Planning, 7,* 1-43.

Scriven, M. (1972). The methodology of evaluation. In C. H. Weiss (Ed.), *Evaluating action programs: Readings in social action and education* (pp. 123-136). Boston: Allyn & Bacon.

Seidel, R. (1992). *Results and realities: A decade of experience in communication for child survival.* Washington, DC: HEALTH-COM, Academy for Educational Development.

Singhal, A., & Rogers, E. M. (1999). *Entertainment-education: A communication strategy for social change.* Mahwah, NJ: Lawrence Erlbaum.

Storey, J. D., Boulay, M., Karchi, Y., Heckert, K., & Karmacharya, D. M. (1999). Impact of the integrated radio communication project in Nepal, 1994-1997. *Journal of Health Communication, 4,* 271-294.

Valente, T. W. (1995). *Network models of the diffusion of innovations.* Cresskill, NJ: Hampton.

Valente, T. W. (1997). On evaluating mass media's impact [Letter]; and Hornik, R., & Yoder, P. S. [Reply to letter]. *Studies in Family Planning, 28*(1), 170-172.

Valente, T. W., Saba, W. P., Merritt, A. P., Fryer, M. L., Forbes, T., Perez, A., & Beltran, L. R. (1996). *Reproductive health is in your hands: Impact of the Bolivia National Reproductive Health Program Campaign* (IEC Field Report No. 4, Spanish-English edition). Baltimore, MD: Johns Hopkins University, Center for Communication Programs.

Whitney, E., Kincaid, D. L., & deFossard, E. (1999). Bangladesh TV serial promotes integrated services. In *Communication impact, 7.* Baltimore, MD: Johns Hopkins University, Center for Communication Programs.

Yoder, P. S., Hornik, R., & Chirwa, B. A. (1996). Evaluating the program effects of a radio drama in Zambia. *Studies in Family Planning, 27*(4), 188-203.

Zajonc, R. B. (1984). On the primacy of affect. *American Psychologist, 39*(2), 117-123.

PART IV

A Campaign Sampler

15

Singing the (VD) Blues[1]

Bradley S. Greenberg
Walter Gantz

For the past few years, media throughout the world have been discussing and reporting the AIDS problem on news programs, talk shows, telethon fund-raisers, PSAs and dramas, newspaper and magazine stories, even novels, often advocating the use of condoms and clean needles, both graphically displayed. What effect is this coverage having on its audiences? Are we more informed or more compassionate? Are we more willing to talk openly with friends, lovers, and other loved ones about the disease and its impact on our own behaviors? Our study on the classic TV show *VD Blues* gives us a good sense of the answers to such questions.

VD Blues achieved notoriety in the early 1970s because it was the first television program to deal candidly with the largely "unmentionable" topic of venereal disease. At that time, the program was too strong for the commercial networks; it aired several times on public television. With a healthy mix of songs and humorous skits and the inclusion of frank words such as "syphilis" and "gonorrhea," *VD Blues* declared war on the taboo and poked fun at the medical establishment. The fast-paced variety show used a popular talk show host (Dick Cavett) to lead the proceedings, well-known actors and actresses to portray bumbling doctors, deadly germs, and frightened lovers, and popular singers and rock music groups to drive the messages home. It was, as one reviewer put it, "educational entertainment, a sort of Sesame Street for the sexually active" (Resnik, 1972).

Motivated by the unique approach of the program, a research project was formulated and conducted in 1974. The conceptual framework was that of "taboo topics," issues that people are not comfortable talking about, such as terminal illness, homosexuality, and sexually transmitted diseases. These were messages that Rogers (1972) had referred to as "extremely personal and private in nature" and that Gantz (1975) had defined as "situations in which a behavior should not be performed and/or communicated about." The research question focused on the extent to which public, mediated discussions of taboo topics would stimulate interpersonal conversations. It was our contention that the mass media could intervene effectively, that this television production would increase knowledge, increase the perception of personal knowledge-ability, reduce inhibitions that limit talk about VD, and enhance the impor-tance of the topic by increasing its visibility. To examine these hypotheses, we conducted a field survey and a controlled experiment.

FIELD SURVEY

The night after the program was aired in the Lansing, Michigan, area, telephone interviews were completed with 923 adults. Of the sample, 15% said they had watched the show the previous evening or in its first local showing several months earlier; this gave us 135 viewers to analyze. Compared to nonviewers, viewers were younger, more educated, and tended to have more prior media-based information about VD, and they tested more highly on the knowl-edge questions used. Specifically, they were more knowledgeable about rela-tively complex issues; for example, they could identify more ways in which VD can and cannot be transmitted, and they could identify more long-term effects associated with those diseases. Furthermore, their perceptions of being informed were positively correlated with actual information level.

Although viewers did not differ from nonviewers in terms of how much they would be embarrassed if someone wanted to talk to them about VD, there were sharp differences in the number of situations in which these groups thought it would be "okay to talk about VD." Given seven possible contexts (e.g., be-tween marital partners, with parents, with friends, or using different media), 93% of the viewers said that six or seven of these contexts were okay, compared with 77% of the nonviewers.

Finally, a set of exposure variables (seeing the show the previous night or earlier, reading about VD, and seeing or hearing other shows) was significantly correlated with the dependent measures of knowledge and tabooness.

EXPERIMENT

Subjects were 102 undergraduates; half were shown the program and half were not (26 who had already seen the show were omitted from the analyses). In addi-tion to the survey hypotheses, a new proposition examined the subjects' judg-ment of the seriousness of the VD problem as an agenda-setting issue. This was confirmed by the results, as 85% of the viewers said that the VD problem was "quite" or "very" serious, compared with 50% of the nonviewers. Viewers scored higher on a summative knowledge index across a variety of knowledge items. Nonviewers scored substantially better on one subindex that asked for symptoms identifying VD. Since the program stressed that people often could not tell if they had VD, viewers may have believed there were fewer clear symptoms associated with it.

There were no discernible differences between viewers and nonviewers for three measures of the perceived communicative tabooness of VD—how comfortable others their age would be discussing VD, how comfortable they themselves would be, and whether or not it was right to broadcast radio and television programs about VD. This nonfinding may be attributed to college students' willingness to talk about almost anything.

IMPLICATIONS

This single hour-long show stimulated awareness, knowledge, and concern about a serious problem. Given that three fourths of the viewers in our survey had seen the show fully 3 months before they were interviewed, the survey results were a severe test of our propositions and these outcomes.

Results with regard to the alleviation of communicative tabooness were less marked, perhaps because the topic was less taboo to talk about than we had assumed. In the survey sample, less than a majority said they felt uneasy with the issue and, in the college experiment, a ceiling effect limited movement to more openness. There also may have been a methodological problem in that a survey that focuses on such an issue may itself induce less tabooness in talking about the issue. Given that those aware of the show (whether they had seen it or not) may already have been more receptive to talking about VD, it would have been useful to compare this group with those unaware. Even more appropriate would be assessments of the magnitude of topic or issue tabooness prior to broadcast of *VD Blues* as well as after exposure.

Over the years, *VD Blues* has been considered a model for programming efforts designed to promote health issues. Since we did not measure reactions to the show itself (e.g., the perceived appropriateness of the skits and songs), we cannot speak directly about the impact of the straightforward but entertaining manner in which VD information was presented in the program. To our knowledge, however, no data collected since that effort suggest that the persuasive punch delivered by information programs is reduced when the program makes use of attention-grabbing presentation techniques.

With *VD Blues* as a guide, we conclude that a concentrated media presentation focused on particular health issues is likely to result in heightened awareness, knowledge, and salience of health issues such as AIDS as well as increased and more at-ease interpersonal communication about them.

NOTE

1. This chapter is reprinted from the second edition.

REFERENCES

Gantz, W. (1975). *The movement of taboos: A message-oriented approach.* Unpublished manuscript.

Resnick, H. (1972, October 14). Putting VD on public TV. *Saturday Review,* pp. 33-38.

Rogers, E. M. (1972). *Taboo communication and social change: Family planning in Asia, and some suggested modifications in the classical diffusion model.* Paper presented to the Department of Human Communication, Rutgers University, New Brunswick, NJ.

16

The McGruff Crime Prevention Campaign[1]

Garrett J. O'Keefe
Kathaleen Reid-Martinez

The "Take a Bite Out of Crime" campaign was developed in the late 1970s to promote public involvement in crime prevention activities. The campaign was initiated under the sponsorship of the Crime Prevention Coalition, a group of government, private, and not-for-profit agencies, with the major media components of the program produced by the Advertising Council. Major objectives included (a) generating a greater sense of individual responsibility among citizens for reducing crime; (b) encouraging citizens to take collective preventive actions and to work more closely with law enforcement agencies; and (c) enhancing crime prevention programs at local, state, and national levels.

The Ad Council's volunteer agency for the campaign, Dancer Fitzgerald Sample, designed the media materials around an animated trench-coated dog, McGruff, who called on citizens to help "take a bite out of crime" by making their homes more secure, by taking more precautions when outdoors, and by working together with their neighbors in neighborhood/block watch programs. Importantly, the highly publicized national media campaign was supplemented by a full range of locally promoted supplemental activities throughout the country by law enforcement agencies, community groups, and businesses. The first media messages were disseminated via television, radio, newspapers, magazines, billboards, and posters in late 1979. Hundreds of thousands of supplemental brochures and related materials containing more specific information also were distributed.

Evaluating the McGruff campaign's effectiveness (O'Keefe, 1985, 1986) presented several noteworthy conceptual and methodological problems, most related to the necessarily scattershot nature of media campaigns reliant on public service advertising. Because public service announcements (PSAs) are disseminated on largely unpredictable schedules convenient to individual media sources, optimal evaluative designs using controlled exposure patterns are virtually impossible. As a "next best" option, a two-phase design was used in which (a) interviews with a national probability sample of 1,200 adults were carried out 2 years into the campaign, and (b) a panel sample of 426 adults in three representative cities were interviewed just prior to the campaign's onset and again 2 years later.

The campaign's impact was measured in terms of the extent to which it increased citizens' competency, in terms of (a) awareness of preventive techniques, (b) attitudes that they could make a positive difference, (c) sense of personal capability or efficacy in helping prevent crime, (d) concern about crime, and (e) engagement in preventive behaviors.

The campaign had fairly widespread penetration. More than half of the national sample said they had seen or heard at least one of the McGruff PSAs by late 1981. Most had seen them on television, and exposure was well distributed across demographic groups and across citizens with widely varying perceptions, attitudes, and behaviors with respect to crime. Substantial selectivity was found in attention patterns, with the more attentive likely to be more generally prevention competent. Respondents indicated a largely favorable response, with the PSAs viewed as effective, likable, and worth mentioning to others. Approximately one fourth of the respondents said that they had learned something new from the PSAs, and nearly half said they had been reminded of things they had forgotten. Almost half reported the ads had made them more confident about protecting themselves and more positive about the effectiveness of citizen prevention efforts. Lesser impact was found for overall concern about crime and sense of individual responsibility. Approximately one fourth reported taking specific actions as a consequence of PSA exposure, mainly in improved household security and cooperating with neighbors, the two main themes of McGruff to that point.

The panel sample confirmed the previous findings with respect to information gain and attitude change, and it offered particularly strong evidence of behavioral change. The campaign-exposed group reported significantly greater activity in nearly all behaviors specifically advocated by the PSAs, with no such changes found for nonadvocated behaviors. These findings held when potentially confounding variables (e.g., exposure to other crime-related media stimuli and direct victimization experience) were controlled for.

Opportunity for action appeared to be one influence on effects (e.g., women spending more time at home showed more gains in neighborhood cooperation). Importantly, behavioral change at times occurred without corresponding cognitive or attitudinal change, particularly among citizens who already believed themselves more at risk. These results challenge traditional hierar-chy-of-effects models (i.e., cognitive effects precede attitudinal ones, which precede behavioral ones) (see Chapter 2, this volume). Those less at risk, how-ever, indicated greater cognitive and attitudinal changes. In some cases, attitu-dinal change was not uniformly associated with cognitive change.

Recommendations for subsequent campaigns include paying greater atten-tion to community-based prevention efforts and the role of interpersonal com-munication. Exceptionally careful handling of fear arousal in crime prevention campaigns is also mandated because the situation is one in which the mere mention of the topic can stimulate concern. More precise audience targeting is also required, not only in terms of demographics but also by psychological ori-entations toward crime and communication-related variables. One group with particular needs is the elderly, and subsequent formative research on crime-re-lated and communication habits of aged persons revealed several distinctive campaign strategies for approaching them.

A 1992 national survey of responses to the campaign indicated that it had continued to gain in popularity and impact during the previous decade, likely as a result of keeping a focused vision for the popular McGruff character, while simultaneously disseminating novel, distinct messages that were tied to chang-ing crime patterns and trends throughout the years, maintaining public interest (O'Keefe, Rosenbaum, Lavrakas, Reid, & Botta, 1996).

NOTE

1. This chapter is adapted from the second edition.

REFERENCES

O'Keefe, G. (1985). "Taking a bite out of crime": The impact of a public information campaign. *Communication Research, 12*(2), 147-178.

O'Keefe, G. (1986). The "McGruff" national media campaign: Its public impact and future implications. In D. Rosenbaum (Ed.), *Community crime prevention: Does it work?* Beverly Hills, CA: Sage.

O'Keefe, G. J., Rosenbaum, D. P., Lavrakas, P. J., Reid, K., & Botta, R. A. (1996). *"Taking a Bite out of Crime": The impact of the National Citizens' Crime Prevention media campaign.* Thousand Oaks, CA: Sage.

17

Smokey Bear[1]

Ronald E. Rice

Each year, approximately 5 million acres of land in the United States are ravaged by wildfires. In central, southern, and eastern regions, almost all wildfires are caused by people or by equipment operated by people. This tremendous national problem has been countered with one of the most famous of all campaigns—the Smokey Bear campaign (Morrison, 1996).

The Forest Service's Cooperative Forest Fire Prevention Program began in 1942, as part of the wartime response to potential wildfires caused by enemy bombing, and to the shortage of firefighter personnel. The newly formed Wartime Advertising Council ("Wartime" was dropped after World War II ended) created a media campaign kit. The first poster's message was "Careless Matches Aid the Axis—Prevent Forest Fires." The idea of using a bear as the symbol of forest fire prevention was conceived by representatives of the Foote, Cone, and Belding advertising agency and the Forest Service. Smokey's first poster, by Walt Disney, appeared in 1944, replacing the initial poster featuring Disney's "Bambi." The 1945 poster, by the noted animal illustrator Albert Staehle, had Smokey in dungarees and a ranger's hat, pouring water on a campfire, with the message, "Smokey Says: Care Will Prevent 9 Out of 10 Forest Fires." The slogan "Remember, Only You Can Prevent Forest Fires" was developed by Foote, Cone, and Belding in 1947. There have been many Smokey posters since then (Haverkamp & Schamel, 1994); 28 of them are used to tell Smokey's story at the web site *www.odf.state.or.us/Smokey/SMOKEY.HTM*.

Smokey became a living symbol in 1950 when a black bear cub, badly ᵉd, was rescued from a forest fire in New Mexico and housed in the Na- l Zoo until his death in 1977. A second bear represented Smokey until his death in 1990. The symbol of Smokey Bear became so well-known that it was legally protected by Congress in 1952 (though there have been recent legal challenges), and it provides yearly royalties for the Smokey Bear campaign. A Smokey Bear Junior Forest Ranger Program, begun in 1953, mails an official fire prevention materials kit to the millions of children who write to Smokey Bear Headquarters; it had to get its own zip code in 1966 to handle the hundreds of cards and letters received each day.

The Ad Council (which implements nearly three dozen campaigns) and its business and advertising community supporters continued to work in cooperation with the Forest Service and the Association of State Foresters on the Smokey Bear campaign. Once the Ad Council approves a campaign, it requests an ad agency from the American Association of Advertising Agencies to handle the campaign by contributing creative talent and message production. During the 1970s, approximately $50 million was allocated annually to the Smokey Bear campaign. In 1979 alone, more than $1 million worth of materials were produced and distributed, involving mailings to thousands of television and radio stations (representing 4 billion electronic media impressions) and messages placed for free (estimated at a total commercial value of over $55 million) in thousands of newspapers and magazines, along with numerous billboards. Smokey has frequently appeared on a Rose Parade float, as a Macy's Thanksgiving Day Parade balloon, and at other festivals and fairs.

There has been no comprehensive evaluation of the Smokey campaign, and it would be difficult to pinpoint specific effects of a nationwide campaign over such a long period. We can point to some suggestive evidence, however, as well as some areas for improvement. Acreage lost through wildfires has decreased substantially from the 30 million per year before the program began in 1942 to less than 5 million. The estimated resource savings during the first 30 years of the Smokey Bear campaign amounted to $17 billion, but the annual program budget is half a million dollars, not including Ad Council donations. A public awareness survey conducted in 1976 showed a near-universal 98% aided recall awareness of Smokey Bear (AHF Marketing Research, 1976).

What are some of the reasons for this high visibility and potential success? Clearly, Smokey Bear is both an engaging and a fairly credible source used consistently as a symbol of the fire prevention concept. The extremely large exposure through multiple media outlets, made possible by the Ad Council's continuing support (O'Toole, 1992; see also *www.adcouncil.org/current_camp/ body_fire_prevention.html*), has provided extensive coverage for more than 50 years (Ronk, 1994; "Smokey," 1994)—a longer period of time than for any other PSA-based campaign. The original slogan—"Only You Can Prevent Forest Fires"—attempts to involve the audience member personally, especially relevant because of the large percentage of fires caused by humans (often out of carelessness or ignorance, but all too frequently intentionally). Other strategies in some of the Smokey Bear campaign materials include emotional appeals (showing burned animals) and personal values (such as maintaining recreational opportunities and natural environments). Smokey Bear is also generally present at school fire prevention programs and fairs, generating both excitement and campaign identity among children and adults alike, supplementing the media campaign with interpersonal communication.

The challenge, however, is to continue to increase the allocation of resources to wildfire prevention, educate the public, and change behavior under complex conditions with little maintenance. Some recent efforts included Forest Service personnel contact with campers and tourists entering forest areas, discussions with small groups of students in fire prevention school programs, local media coverage of wildfire conditions, and displays and exhibits at fairs and forest entry sites. Smokey even has his own web site, *www. smokeybear. com*, with games and discussion lists for kids.

As suburbanites expand their residential areas into the countryside, and as more people visit forest areas every year, they bring with them urban habits and minimal knowledge about forest conditions that contribute to the large number of preventable wildfires. The very longevity of Smokey Bear may also work against its effectiveness: The theme of "Only You Can Prevent Forest Fires" assumes the campaign is well-known enough that specific knowledge and behaviors will be activated by these words. Every year brings new children into schools and new visitors into forest areas who have never been exposed to specific information or behavioral models about fire prevention, however. Thus, when prompted, they are highly aware of Smokey, but they seldom recall Smokey or know what to do to prevent wildfires during their annual vacations or weekend walks in the woods. Indeed, the study cited previously found a very low unaided awareness of Smokey Bear in the general population—only 7% (AHF Marketing Research, 1976). Therefore, despite the tremendous contributions of the media community and the very real successes of the Smokey Bear campaign, there is much work to be done in the area of forest fire prevention.

NOTE

1. This chapter is revised from the second edition, in which it appeared as a short adaptation of a chapter from the first edition by Eugene F. McNamara, Troy Kurth, and Donald Hansen.

REFERENCES

AHF Marketing Research. (1976). *Forest fire prevention: An awareness and attitudes study.* New York: Author.
Haverkamp, B., & Schamel, W. (1994). Fire prevention posters: The story of Smokey Bear. *Social Education, 58*(3), 165-168.

Morrison, E. (1996). *Guardian of the forest: A history of Smokey Bear and the coopera-tive forest fire prevention program* (3rd ed.). Alexandria, VA: Morielle Press.
O'Toole, J. (1992). Smokey Bear: The Advertising Council's oldest customer [Special issue]. *Fire Management Notes, 53/54,* 14.
Ronk, T. (1994). Smokey Bear 1944-1994. *Missouri Conservationist, 55*(8), 4-7.
Smokey: The bear essentials of fire prevention. (1994). *Smithsonian, 24*(10), 59.

18

Littering

When Every Litter Bit Hurts[1]

Robert B. Cialdini

The classic public service announcement against littering begins with a shot of a majestic-looking American Indian paddling his canoe up a river that carries the scum and trash of various forms of industrial and individual pollution. (Ignore, if you can, the recently revealed fact that the Indian actor was an Italian from Brooklyn.) After coming ashore near the littered side of a highway, the Indian watches as a bag of garbage is thrown, splattering and spreading along the road, from the window of a passing car. The camera pans up from the refuse at his feet to the Indian's face, on which a tear is running down his cheek, and the slogan appears "People Start Pollution, People Can Stop It." According to the Keep America Beautiful Organization, this public service announcement (PSA) is the single most memorable and effective message ever sent to the American public against litter and pollution; everyone they talk to about littering recalls the ad. *TV Guide* ("The Fifty Greatest," 1999) rated this as the "16th greatest TV commercial of all time."

Despite the fame and recognition value of this spot, it may contain aspects that may be less than optimal and perhaps even counterproductive in their impact on viewers' littering behavior. In addition to the laudable (and conceivably effective) recommendation in the ad urging viewers to stop littering, there is an underlying theme that many people do litter: Debris floats on the river and lies at the roadside, trash is tossed from automobiles, and we are told that "people start pollution."

Thus, the creators of the spot may well have pitted two kinds of norms against each other: *prescriptive* norms (involving perceptions of which behaviors are societally approved) and *popular* norms (involving perceptions of which behaviors are typically performed). A longstanding research tradition in social psychology indicates that both kinds of norms motivate human action (Deutsch & Gerard, 1955). In the process of communicating that littering is contrary to prescriptive norms, the PSA also may have communicated the undercutting message that littering is consistent with popular norms. Theoretically, it would have been preferable to have presented the message in a way that allowed the two types of norms to work in concert.

One such possibility is suggested by research conducted by my students and me. We knew from previous research (Krauss, Freedman, & Whitcup, 1978) that people littered less into a clean area than into a dirty one. We reasoned that a subject who saw someone litter would become focused on the issue of whether people normally litter in the situation; consequently, the subject would examine the state of the environment more intently than usual to determine what people normally did there. Finding a littered area, the subject would be more likely than ever to litter; finding a clean area, however, he or she would be less likely than ever to litter.

We conducted a study in which individuals found handbills placed on their windshields when they returned to their cars in a parking garage. Before getting to their cars, however, they witnessed someone else (an experimental confederate) who either dropped one of the fliers on the ground while walking by or who simply walked by, carrying no such flier. Beforehand, we had either littered the parking area with fliers, paper cups, candy wrappers, and the like or had removed all litter from it. We then watched from a hidden vantage point to see what subjects did with the fliers they found on their cars. The results confirmed our expectations in two respects. First, in the no-littering condition, a clean environment received less litter than a dirty one (7 of 50 subjects vs. 11 of 34, $p < .05$). Second, in the littering condition, this difference was substantially enhanced (2 of 31 vs. 13 of 24, $p < .001$). We think that these results occurred because witnessing someone else littering focused our subjects on the issue of what other people do in the situation.

It is this latter finding that would appear to have the greater applied value. Take, for example, its implications for the antilittering spot. The creators of the ad described previously seem to have been correct in their decision to show an instance of someone (the passing motorist) actively littering into the environment, but they may have been mistaken in their decision to use an already littered environment because this combination of conditions produced the greatest littering in our study. (For a subsequent analysis and discussion of this proposition, see Cialdini, Reno, & Kallgren, 1990.)

Were we to advise the Keep America Beautiful organization on how to revise the PSA, then, it would be to make the procedurally small but theoretically meaningful modification of changing the depicted environment from trashed to clean. Of course, it would be unwarranted to assume from our data that this ad has been negative in its overall impact on the public's littering actions. Because it is so moving and memorable a piece, it has likely been a strong positive force. Nonetheless, our data suggest that (a) even classic PSAs may contain unintended elements that could undermine optimal effectiveness, and (b) formative research should be conducted before expensive PSA production to detect and help eliminate such unfavorable elements.

In addition to this particular high-profile PSA, the larger antilittering campaign of the 1970s presented many other messages in various channels. On the basis of 30% to 50% decreases in the amount of observed litter in numerous locales throughout the country during this period, the Keep America Beautiful organization's campaign appears to have been notably successful overall. Due to a combination of prominently placed messages and a receptive audience willing to invest the small extra effort to dispose of litter properly, this campaign rates as one of the most effective in recent history.

NOTE

1. This chapter is adapted from the second edition.

REFERENCES

Cialdini, R. B., Reno, R., & Kallgren, C. (1990). A focus theory of normative conduct: Recycling the concept of norms to reduce littering in public places. *Journal of Personality and Social Psychology, 58*(6), 1015-1026.

Deutsch, M., & Gerard, H. (1955). A study of normative and informational social influences upon individual social judgment. *Journal of Abnormal and Social Psychology, 51*, 629-636.

The fifty greatest TV commercials of all time. (1999, July 3-9). *TV Guide*, 2-34.

Krauss, R., Freedman, J., & Whitcup, M. (1978). Field and laboratory studies of littering. *Journal of Experimental Social Psychology, 14*, 109-122.

19

The Strategic Extension Campaigns on Rat Control in Bangladesh[1]

Ronny Adhikarya

A strategic extension campaign in Bangladesh, organized and implemented in 1983 and 1984, produced massive behavior change among farmers in adopting methods to reduce the prevalence of and damage caused by rats (Adhikarya & Posamentier, 1987). As in many Asian countries, rats in Bangladesh were destroying large amounts of grain, about 10% of the standing wheat crop yearly, and damaging physical structures such as irrigation systems, wiring, and buildings. Farmers had taken little action because the responsibility for such problems had traditionally been placed in the hands of government, inexpensive rodenticides were not easily available, and there was little cultural precedent for village and community collaboration in controlling rats.

In the 1983 wheat farmer campaign, target behavioral outcomes included taking action on full-moon nights (to encourage farmers to take coordinated if not collaborative action, so that rats would not just be driven from one farm to the next); flooding, digging, or smoking out rats; simultaneous planting; keeping fields clean; and using a new, ready-made rat bait.

The target audience was segmented according to different levels of knowledge, attitudes, and practices concerning rat control. The logo on all campaign materials emphasized individual responsibility for rat control. Positioning of the messages included religious appeal (using a Moslem quote that killing rats is virtuous), fear arousal, awareness of the extent of damage, guilt appeal (relating farmers' inaction to resulting food shortages and child starvation), and a ridicule appeal (posters showing rats laughing at farmers trapped instead of rats) that served as a discussion point.

Radio spots and posters provided general information and motivational messages. Extensive training sessions were conducted to motivate and educate the campaign workers on their specific tasks before the campaign. Interpersonal support was provided by extension fieldworkers, who conducted small group discussions, field demonstrations, and training sessions. Teachers, children, and agricultural supply retailers were also used to augment the extension workers. For example, motivational comics were distributed by teachers and were taken home by schoolchildren to discuss with their (farmer) parents, most of whom are illiterate. This component was complemented by an essay contest for schoolchildren on their parents' problems with rats, requiring family and community discussion of the topic. Posters and leaflets explaining the proper application of the rat control methods were distributed to agricultural products dealers. Over a half million motivational posters, instructional posters, comic sheets, and leaflets, numerous radio spots and television programming segments, and nearly a quarter million ready-made rat bait packets were involved in the campaign. As has been found in other health campaigns, posters were ranked by the extension workers as the most effective input (see Chapter 8, this volume).

The percentage of wheat farmers who conducted rat control jumped from 10% to 32% following the 1983 campaign. Surveys showed that, compared to the farmers who did not use rat control techniques, damage was reduced by 26% for farmers who used control measures other than the ready-made bait, but 56% for those who used the ready-made bait. A total of $40,000 U.S. was spent on operational expenses and bait (with a per-farm family unit cost of $.004), while the estimated net gain from increased wheat production was more than $834,000.

The 1984 campaign attempted to solve some problems uncovered by the 1983 evaluation, such as a lower adoption by farmers with smaller plots who lived in districts that received secondary coverage, and flawed message designs in posters and other media. The new campaign was directed to farmers of all crops, and it supplemented extensive media use with interpersonal channels (such as pesticide and seed dealers, and community leaders) to encourage specific and effective rat control actions. Similarly large numbers of media, interpersonal, and bait inputs were involved as in the 1983 campaign.

After the 1984 campaign, the proportion of wheat farmers who conducted rat control rose from 32% to 40%, and the rat control practice by all kinds of farmers jumped from 49% to 67%. By providing equal campaign treatment to the districts that had received primary or secondary treatment in the 1983 campaign, the 1984 campaign achieved equal levels of adoption of rat control practices (40%) in both types of districts. Similarly, the adoption rate by large farmers rose from 47% before the campaigns to 58% after 1983, and to 72% after

1984; the figures for small farmers were 41%, 41%, and 63%, respectively. Cost-benefit results from the 1984 campaign were similar to the 1983 figures.

Several implications follow. First, the concept of conducting and systematically evaluating a multimedia campaign in developing countries is not only feasible, but effective and necessary. Second, the application of strategic planning concepts and techniques is extremely useful, especially for identifying systematic problems, formulating and targeting campaign objectives, segmenting target audiences, selecting multimedia mixes, designing messages, and developing and packaging materials. Third, the conceptual framework for strategic multimedia campaign development can be operationalized effectively if the campaign process starts with a knowledge, attitude, and practice (KAP) survey (such as focus groups and sample surveys) to identify target audiences' reasons for the nonadoption of the recommended technology.

The Agricultural Education and Extension Service of the United Nations Food and Agricultural Organization has translated the lessons from this series of campaigns (Adhikarya & Posamentier, 1987) into a series of workshops, training sessions, and campaign materials that have led to replications of this process in a wide variety of countries and problems: integrated weed management and rodent control in Malaysia, lime-sowing rice cultivation in Liberia, pest surveillance in Thailand, and land preparation, tick-borne disease control, and golden snail control in other countries.

NOTE

1. This chapter is reprinted from the second edition, in which it appeared as a short version of the chapter from the first edition.

REFERENCE

Adhikarya, R., & Posamentier, H. (1987). *Motivating farmers for action: How strategic multi-media campaigns can help*. Eschborn, Germany: Deutsche Gesellschaft fur Technische Zusammenarbeit.

20

Mass Campaigns in the People's Republic of China During the Mao Era[1]

Alan P. L. Liu

From the consolidation of political power in the early 1950s by the Chinese Communists under Mao Zedong, until his death in 1976, the People's Republic of China (PRC) conducted more than 74 national mass campaigns (Cell, 1977). Late in this revolutionary and formative period, word began spreading about both the massiveness and the apparent success of such campaigns. The mobilization of an entire nation toward some social conditions, mixed with minimal information about them, lent an air of mystique to the PRC campaigns.

These campaigns typically served one of several purposes: (a) class struggle campaigns designed to introduce a new institution (such as land reform) while simultaneously repudiating the resisting forces, (b) denunciation of purged political figures, (c) support for the study of particular political doctrines, (d) emulation of model workers or institutions, (e) familiarization of the public with new policies, (f) countering inappropriate public opinion, and (g) general information campaigns (such as birth control, antispitting, or snail eradication).

In general, most mass campaigns followed the model Mao used in mobilizing troops during the 1930s and 1940s: Policies, goals, and mechanisms were decided by top leaders, and mass communication and involvement were used to implement and institutionalize them. This approach was accomplished through the pervasive control by the Communist Party and the state bureaucracy of all levels of government as well as mass organizations such as trade unions, women's associations, and youth leagues. A typical campaign involved the following stages (see Liu, 1981, for more detail).

(1) A separate ad hoc organization was established and devoted solely to the campaign, headed by a well-known government figure, in order to accentuate the importance of the campaign, to ensure a high degree of homogeneity in communication, to increase participation of people from various circles, and to overcome the inherent inflexibility and inertia of the bureaucracies. (2) A special group of "activist" campaign workers was trained, selected primarily on the basis of political reliability and experience in a special line of work. This stage was used to broaden the impact of a policy rapidly. (3) Several "testing points," a kind of audience survey or formative evaluation, were selected. For example, testing points in the 1956-1958 birth control campaign found that while there was a large demand for birth control information, older people resisted the idea, rural women felt that bearing children was their natural lot, and men and women wanted separate exhibits. (4) A "key point" application typically followed, which was the methodical execution of the campaign in a region where the target problem or disease was especially common. Once the key point campaign had been refined and appeared successful, and could be used as an administrative and visible model, the full campaign was activated throughout a "plane," such as county, province, or the nation.

(5) During the plane stage, all available communication media were fully brought to bear: "folk" media such as posters, blackboards and bulletin boards, folk plays, and songs, in addition to radio, movies, and newspapers. However, interpersonal communication was emphasized in the form of group and mass meetings (except where small meetings were more appropriate, such as in the birth control campaign, because public discussion about sex ran counter to Chinese custom). Face-to-face persuasion was especially favored, through processes such as "recollection and comparison" (in which a person is asked to recall "past suffering" and compare that with the "present improvement in living conditions"), "reckoning of accounts" through statistics (e.g., in the birth control campaign, information about birthrates, effects on productivity, extent of child-bearing illness, child expenses, and social welfare expenses), "airing complaints" (in which hardships that need to be overcome are recounted), and the use of individuals as positive and negative models in support of the campaign and as instances for others to make public their support.

Various social science principles were mirrored in these stages: (a) the human relations principle that communication between hierarchical levels and participation in decision making increases perceived commitment and satisfaction; (b) the two-step flow model, whereby opinion leaders and personal influence diffuse persuasive communications initially delivered through mass media; (c) cognitive dissonance and memory models, which propose that persuasion is more effective if the audience role-plays and improvises the message; and (d) conflict-arousal theory, which suggests that addressing conflicts in the mind of the audience may increase the persuasive effect of a communication.

Obstacles were often inherent in many of these campaigns: (a) Because there was only one central government-controlled media delivery channel, resistance by local or regional media gatekeepers could stifle campaign efforts; (b) the basis for much of this campaign approach, the mobilization of the Red Army in the 1940s, may have been an inappropriate foundation for designing communications with the mass public; (c) often the objective reality experienced by the local audiences contradicted the models used in a campaign; (d) the frequent and institutionalized use of group meetings eventually took on a ritualistic and mechanical nature that reduced their novelty and effectiveness; (e) much of rural China was still isolated from the media; (f) genuine participation and involvement by the masses were often missing; and (g) campaign goals often were excessively unrealistic.

Some campaigns were very successful, however, such as the third family planning campaign begun in 1968 (Aird, 1978; Whyte & Gu, 1987). The desired goal was a two-child family in urban areas and three in rural areas, through the use of contraception, abortion, and sterilization; current policies encourage one-child families in urban areas. The primary persuasive mechanism was to eliminate traditional (Confucian) values such as early marriage, large families, preferences for sons, and privacy in family matters. Rational arguments included a reduced need for large families because of lower mortality rates and state-provided security for old age; sexual emancipation, so that daughters were as valuable as sons; the personal economic benefits of fewer children; and the disruption to the planned economy of high birthrates (Aird, 1978). Concrete economic strategies included incentives and sanctions in the areas of taxes, child allowances, education, and job placement. Although the official position in the early 1970s was that birth control was voluntary, a wide range of coercive activities has been reported, ranging from conversational house visits by leading cadre members through public denunciations to involuntary sterilizations (Aird, 1978; Pear, 1988). This third campaign was an astounding success: The national birthrate dropped from 6.1 in 1955 to 2.3 in 1980. Births of a third or more child, as a percentage of all births, dropped from 62% in 1970 to 20% in 1985 (Whyte & Gu, 1987).

In general, however, it appears that the effectiveness of some of even the most famous PRC campaigns disappeared as soon as concentrated government support was removed, or were never successful in the first place—such as the Tachai Brigade, a demonstration farm touted as a successful economic innovation from 1963 through 1978. One of the philosophic insights that might be derived from the failure of these campaigns is that, perhaps unfortunately, emphasizing collective (community or national) benefits at the cost of individual sacrifice cannot be the primary basis of enduring social change. China, as well as other countries, continues to deal with this fundamental tension.

NOTE

1. This chapter is reprinted from the second edition, in which it appeared as a short adaptation of the chapter from the first edition.

REFERENCES

Aird, J. (1978). Fertility decline and birth control in the People's Republic of China. *Population and Development Review, 4*(2), 225-254.

Cell, C. (1977). *Revolution at work.* New York: Academic Press.

Liu, A. P. L. (1981). Mass campaigns in the People's Republic of China. In R. E. Rice & W. Paisley (Eds.), *Public communication campaigns* (pp. 199-223). Beverly Hills, CA: Sage.

Pear, R. (1988, August 6). Chinese who shun 1-child plan get asylum. *New York Times.*

Whyte, M., & Gu, S. (1987). Popular response to China's fertility transition. *Population and Development Review, 13*(3), 471-493.

21

The Designated Driver Campaign

Jay A. Winsten
William DeJong

Using a designated driver is a simple strategy for avoiding driving after drinking. A couple or group of friends selects one person to abstain from alcohol and be responsible for driving, with the others free to drink or not as they choose. The designated driver concept has been heavily promoted by the Harvard Alcohol Project (HAP), a national media campaign launched in 1988 by the Harvard School of Public Health's Center for Health Communication. Working with the cooperation of leading television networks and Hollywood production studios, the campaign's thrust is to promote an emerging social norm that the driver should abstain from alcohol (Winsten, 1994).

Although lobbying of the U.S. entertainment industry to include prosocial messages in television programs and films has been common during the past 25 years, this strategy was given new impetus by the HAP (Montgomery, 1990). Highly publicized, the HAP is the first such project to enjoy the full support of Hollywood, including every major production studio, the television networks, and major trade organizations (e.g., the Academy of Television Arts and Sciences, the Screen Actors Guild, and the Writers Guild of America, West).

MEDIA STRATEGIES

The HAP's media strategies include dialogue placement in top-rated network series, prime-time public service announcements (PSAs) sponsored by the major television networks, and major news coverage. Estimated by one industry expert to have a value of more than $100 million, the designated driver campaign has had the frequency and reach of a major commercial advertising campaign (Winsten, 1994).

Messages consistent with the HAP's agenda have appeared in more than 160 entertainment programs (e.g., *Beverly Hills 90210* and *Cheers*), including both dialogue and the display of designated driver posters developed by the HAP (e.g., "The Designated Driver Is the Life of the Party"). In an episode of *Growing Pains,* for example, a central character's new boyfriend dies in an alcohol-related traffic crash. Collectively, the programming has served to demonstrate the advantages of planning ahead to choose a designated driver.

In 1988, the ABC, CBS, and NBC television networks began to broadcast their own designated driver PSAs. Among the three networks, messages were aired approximately 20 times per week during the December 1988 holiday season, mostly during prime time (DeJong & Winsten, 1990). Between 1987 and 1992, more PSAs were developed on the use of designated drivers than on any other subject related to impaired driving (DeJong & Atkin, 1995). In one set of CBS spots, for example, different actors read the following script: "Before you go out, decide who is going to drive and stick to the plan. The designated driver doesn't drink."

The networks continue to air designated driver messages, albeit far less frequently. Each December, President Bush and then President Clinton cut a PSA for the campaign, which is a traditional time for anti-drunk driving media messages. In recent years, the president's message has been run during the holiday season on ABC, CBS, NBC, Fox, UPN, WB, and 45 cable networks.

A critical challenge faced by entertainment lobbyists is how to keep their issue before entertainment executives, given the infrequent access they will normally have to them. The HAP found several innovative ways to maintain awareness of the designated driver message in Hollywood, including high-profile articles in *The New York Times* and *Variety,* an entertainment industry trade publication. The project director (Winsten) also wrote about the campaign in a journal published by the Writers Guild of America, West. At the Guild's 1989 awards dinner, the back of the drink tickets read "Not for Designated Drivers."

During the campaign's first year, HAP held a reception for production studio executives, producers, and actors at Spago, a trendy West Hollywood restaurant owned by celebrity chef Wolfgang Puck. The invitation sent to the guests was itself an important reminder of their commitment to the campaign. News coverage of the event by Los Angeles television stations and *Entertainment Tonight,* a nationally syndicated television show, also helped maintain the campaign's visibility.

Advertising for the campaign included a donated billboard on Sunset Boulevard to thank Hollywood for its contributions to the campaign and a paid print advertisement in *Emmy* magazine, published by the American Academy of Television Arts and Sciences at the time of its annual Emmy Awards ceremony.

Especially innovative was a Los Angeles-based media campaign during Labor Day weekend in 1989. With the cooperation of the local media, this minicampaign included radio PSAs and editorials, hourly reminders by radio traffic reporters to use a designated driver, a promotional billboard on Sunset Boulevard, and aerial advertisements over area beaches. News coverage in *Variety* and *The Malibu Times* enhanced the weekend campaign's visibility in Hollywood. In 1990, a similar effort was undertaken on Martha's Vineyard, a popular summer resort for Hollywood executives and celebrities.

CAMPAIGN IMPACT

A Gallup survey in September 1988, 2 months prior to the campaign's start, found that 62% of all respondents said that they and their friends use a designated driver all or most of the time. In early 1989, following the holiday period campaign blitz, this percentage increased to 66%. By mid-1989, it increased to 72%, a statistically significant increase compared to the precampaign figure. This upsurge was largely due to male respondents, whose use of designated drivers increased from 54% prior to the campaign to 71% by mid-1989 (DeJong & Winsten, 1990).

In a 1993 survey sponsored by the National Highway Traffic Safety Administration (NHTSA), 74% of all survey respondents said that people should not be allowed to drive if they have been drinking any alcohol at all (NHTSA, 1995). Comparable results were also reported in NHTSA's 1995 survey, thus showing wide acceptance of a social norm that the driver should not drink (NHTSA, 1996).

REASONS FOR SUCCESS

Would-be imitators have been inspired by the Harvard project, but several factors point to its limitations as a model for other health promotion efforts.

First, HAP's director was afforded access to top Hollywood executives through the direct intervention of Dr. Frank Stanton, former president of CBS and, at the time, a member of Harvard's Board of Overseers, and Grant Tinker, the former president of NBC who had recently returned to Hollywood to run a new television production company. The most successful lobbying efforts have been set up by industry insiders or greatly assisted by them and have used those personal connections as a basis for private discussions with individual producers (Montgomery, 1989). Obviously, few public health advocates can rely on this kind of insider support, and most will find access extremely difficult to achieve.

Second, the designated driver concept has several important features that distinguish it from other public health topics and make it a more attractive theme for producers and network executives. First, Mothers Against Drunk Driving and other advocacy groups had already aroused public concern about the drunk driving problem. Thus, the role of the television industry could be accurately described as one of reinforcing an emerging trend rather than "engineering" a new one.

Third, the designated driver message, by emphasizing individual responsibility to prevent drunk driving, meets the television industry's need to do something positive while not alienating the alcohol industry, on which broadcasters depend for a significant portion of their advertising revenue. In general, the television industry is more likely to focus on politically noncontroversial subjects or solutions—an important limitation (Montgomery, 1990).

Fourth, the designated driver message can be easily incorporated into programming on a routine basis, especially because scenes involving alcohol use are a staple of television programming (Gerbner, 1990). All that is needed is for a character to ask, "Who's the designated driver tonight?" In contrast, the introduction of other public health topics (e.g., drug abuse, AIDS, teenage pregnancy, and organ transplantation) represents a more radical departure from standard programming fare. These health issues lend themselves to dramatic treatment, but only in special episodes or programs. A small number of such programs should not be viewed as a tool for bringing about substantial change over the long term.

CONTROVERSIES

Despite its widespread public acceptability and use, the designated driver strategy was criticized by some public health advocates. A chief concern was that having a designated driver might encourage excessive drinking by the driver's passengers.

In fact, a 1993 survey of more than 17,000 U.S. college students established that the designated driver campaign has had a net beneficial effect (DeJong & Winsten, 1999). Among drinkers, 1,908 students who could be classified as heavy drinkers reported not drinking heavily the last time they served as a designated driver. At the same time, only 1,031 students who normally would not be classified as heavy drinkers reported drinking heavily the last time they rode with a designated driver.

Other critics worried that a systematic effort to influence public opinion and behavior through entertainment programming was an abuse of concentrated media power. It is true that the content of prime-time network shows is determined by a relatively small number of producers, but these individuals passionately guard their independence. Each producer was free to include dialogue about the use of designated drivers or not. It should also be noted that the HAP was funded through grants from private foundations. More worrisome are

Hollywood lobbying projects funded through federal government contracts, such as the antidrug media campaign launched in 1998 by the Office of National Drug Control Policy (Forbes, 2000; see Chapter 12, this volume).

CONCLUSION

The use of designated drivers is now a well-established strategy for avoiding impaired driving. This strategy can be used in conjunction with other approaches for discouraging driving after drinking, including the states' adoption of key policies such as reducing the legal per se limit to .08% blood alcohol concentration, expanding the use of sobriety checkpoints, and imposing administrative license revocation. As part of a comprehensive strategy to combat impaired driving, the states should also adopt policies and programs that will serve to prevent excessive alcohol consumption by young people in general and not just drivers (DeJong & Hingson, 1998).

REFERENCES

DeJong, W., & Atkin, C. K. (1995). A review of national television PSA campaigns for preventing alcohol-impaired driving, 1987-1992. *Journal of Public Health Policy, 16,* 59-80.

DeJong, W., & Hingson, R. (1998). Strategies to reduce driving under the influence of alcohol. *Annual Review of Public Health, 19,* 359-378.

DeJong, W., & Winsten, J. A. (1990). The Harvard Alcohol Project: A demonstration project to promote the use of the "designated driver." In M. W. B. Perrine (Ed.), *Proceedings of the 11th International Conference on Alcohol, Drugs and Traffic Safety* (pp. 456-460). Chicago: National Safety Council.

DeJong, W., & Winsten, J. A. (1999). The use of designated drivers by U.S. college students: A national study. *Journal of American College Health, 47,* 151-156.

Forbes, D. (2000, January 13). *Prime-time propaganda* [On-line]. Available: *www.salon.com/news/feature/2000/01/13/drugs.index.html.*

Gerbner, G. (1990). Stories that hurt: Tobacco, alcohol, and other drugs in the mass media. In H. Resnik, S. E. Gardner, R. P. Lorian, & C. E. Marcus (Eds.), *Youth and drugs: Society's mixed messages* (pp. 53-127). Rockville, MD: U.S. Department of Health and Human Services, Office for Substance Abuse Prevention.

Montgomery, K. C. (1989). *Target: Prime time.* New York: Oxford University Press.

Montgomery, K. C. (1990). Promoting health through entertainment television. In C. Atkin & L. Wallack (Eds.), *Mass communication and public health: Complexities and conflicts* (pp. 114-128). Newbury Park, CA: Sage.

National Highway Traffic Safety Administration. (1995). *National survey of drinking and driving attitudes and behavior: 1993.* Washington, DC: Author.

National Highway Traffic Safety Administration. (1996). *National survey of drinking and driving attitudes and behavior: 1995.* Washington, DC: Author.

Winsten, J. A. (1994). Promoting designated drivers: The Harvard Alcohol Project. *American Journal of Preventive Medicine, 10*(Suppl. 1), 11-14.

22

RU SURE?

Using Communication Theory to Reduce Dangerous Drinking on a College Campus

Linda C. Lederman
Lea P. Stewart
Sherry L. Barr
Richard L. Powell
Lisa Laitman
Fern Walter Goodhart

Dangerous drinking is a serious social issue on college campuses today. For example, Wechsler, Davenport, Dowdall, Mooykens, and Castillo's (1994) national study of drinking among college students found that 44% of the respondents reported a recent episode of dangerous drinking (defined as five or more drinks in one sitting for males and four or more drinks for females). This problem is exacerbated because students consistently overestimate the percentage of their peers who engage in dangerous drinking. Thus, one of the most

AUTHORS' NOTE: Funding for this campaign was provided, in part, by the U.S. Department of Education Safe and Drug Free Schools Program, the New Jersey Higher Education Consortium on Alcohol and Other Drug Prevention, the Rutgers University Health Services, and the Rutgers University Department of Communication.

successful approaches to reducing dangerous drinking has been a social norms approach based on changing students' misperceptions of the prevalence of dangerous drinking on campus (Berkowitz & Perkins, 1987; Haines, 1993; Jeffrey & Negro, 1996).

Rather than examining drinking behavior in isolation, a prevention campaign based on reconceptualizing dangerous drinking as socially situated experiential learning considers drinking in the context of the social interactions naturally occurring among students (Lederman & Stewart, 1999). In these relationships, students are learning about the social cachet of drinking. They engage in drinking behaviors because they believe everybody else does so. Thus, drinking dangerously is used as a way to meet the need to belong, to maintain relationships, and to share a topic of conversation.

THEORETICAL FOUNDATIONS

Communication theory argues that communication is the process through which social institutions and the norms and customs embedded in these institutions are created and maintained (Lederman, 1998; Mannis & Meltzer, 1967; Ruben & Stewart, 1997). Individuals' attitudes, beliefs, and behaviors (here, drinking related) can be examined in relation to one another and as the product of the interpretive processes of the individual within the sociocultural community.

Experiential learning theory argues that a person has an experience, reflects on that experience, draws some conclusions about the lessons to be drawn from that experience, and then uses those lessons as part of his or her basis for reactions to future experiences (Dewey, 1929; Kolb, 1984; Lederman, 1992). For example, students who engage in risky sexual behavior while drinking do not perceive themselves as outcasts in their social circles because, in their everyday "experience," their behaviors are the norm as they perceive them (Burns, Ballou, & Lederman, 1991; Burns & Goodstadt, 1989).

Social norms theory asserts that students measure themselves against others in assessing the appropriateness or acceptability of their own behaviors (Haines & Spear, 1996). Often, however, these measures are based on false understandings of what is normative or misperceptions of others' behavior, such as the notion that everyone drinks excessively in college. Social norms theory is employed in prevention campaigns by collecting data on the extent of misperceptions, successfully communicating this information to a targeted campus population, assisting them to understand the discrepancies between fact and myth, and making salient new behaviors and norms associated with the facts instead of the myths (Berkowitz & Perkins, 1987; Haines, 1993; Jeffrey & Negro, 1996).

Thus, according to this model, in their interactions with one another, college students' drinking is reconceptualized as socially situated experiential learning.

THE RU SURE? CAMPAIGN

We designed the RU SURE? campaign to encompass all facets of this model. The project consisted of three phases (baseline data collection, campaign activities, and evaluation) and the following components:

- Gathering baseline data and norming dangerous drinking on campus: A Personal Report of Student Perceptions survey revealed that two thirds of students had three or fewer drinks the last time they drank, and that one of five students does not drink at all (Lederman et al., 1998).

- Design and implementation of a media campaign: Two primary mediated messages were developed for the RU SURE? campaign: the Top Ten Misperceptions at Rutgers and the RU SURE? logo and message. The Top Ten Misperceptions included three alcohol misperceptions accompanied by a norming message (e.g., "Everyone who parties gets wasted," with the answer that two thirds of RU students stop at three or fewer drinks) as well as seven humorous statements (e.g., "It's easy to find a parking space on campus") to get students engaged with the message process. The RU SURE? logo consists of four beer mugs with the last one containing the message "RU SURE?" and an additional line, "Yes, 3 or fewer. We got the stats from you!" to reinforce the fact that the data were collected from students. These messages have been disseminated in the campus newspaper and on posters, t-shirts, pens, and other artifacts. Preliminary intercept interviews with the target population (first-year students living in residence halls) indicate that 84% of respondents can accurately recall the campaign message.

- Curriculum infusion: Students in undergraduate communication courses have been used to design or pilot test or both all messages, posters, and logos for the print campaign. Two purposes are served by this approach. First, because these students are part of social networks that exchange information about this issue, working with them on the campaign leads to even greater dissemination of accurate information about dangerous drinking on the campus and the misperceptions. Second, students are highly credible sources of information for other students and about how messages work for them, so this approach designs messages in the voice of the students.

- Web site design and development: A web site (*www.scils.rutgers.edu/chi*) has been used to disseminate the misperceptions message and to gather additional data (see Chapter 29, this volume). Initial analysis of data gathered from this site shows a high level of awareness of the misperception messages.

- Interpersonally based experiential prevention strategies: Given our focus on college drinking as socially situated experiential learning, we believe that a misperceptions campaign cannot be truly effective in changing behavior without an interpersonal component to the message delivery. Thus, we have included an experiential component that includes groups of advanced undergraduates working with first-year students living in residence halls. The focus of this effort is RU

SURE? Bingo, in which students complete a bingo card by finding other students who fit particular characteristics (e.g., born in a large city, do not drink, and can recall the misperceptions messages). This activity allows students to have fun and interact interpersonally with other students, it reinforces the misperceptions messages, and students model and learn the social skills that they might otherwise believe they need alcohol to facilitate.

- Public relations campaign: A public relations campaign emphasizing the actual norms of college drinking has resulted in extensive coverage in the student newspaper, an article in the *New York Times,* and interviews on CNN and several New Jersey television stations.

- Community coalition: A partnership has been formed with local merchants and civic leaders to address issues of dangerous drinking by college students in the community. The focus of this effort has included a health educator communicating the misperceptions message to this group and community efforts to ensure that underage students will not be served alcohol (see Chapter 27, this volume).

- Ongoing assessment: All aspects of the campaign are being subjected to ongoing assessment. Data have been gathered throughout the campaign to determine its effectiveness both in raising awareness of this issue on campus and in affecting students' behavior, by means of students' self-reports on the surveys and by environmental data (such as the amount of alcohol-related vandalism in the residence halls). Additional data collection and analysis will reveal the extent to which these misperceptions have changed and the resultant influence on drinking behavior.

CONCLUSIONS

The goal of this campaign is to create a university environment in which students are aware of actual norms of students' drinking behavior, know that everyone does not have to drink to fit in, and understand that those who choose to drink can do so moderately and still be socially attractive.

REFERENCES

Berkowitz, A. D., & Perkins, H. W. (1987). Current issues in effective alcohol education programming. In J. S. Sherwood (Ed.), *Alcohol policies and practices on college and university campuses* (pp. 69-85). Washington, DC: National Association of Student Personnel Administrators.

Burns, D., Ballou, J., & Lederman, L. (1991). *Perceptions of alcohol use and policy on the college campus: Preventing alcohol/drug abuse at Rutgers University* (Research Report No. 1). New Brunswick, NJ: Rutgers University, Center for Communication and College Health Issues.

Burns, D., & Goodstadt, M. (1989). *Alcohol use on the Rutgers University campus: A study of various communities.* Unpublished U.S. Department of Education Fund for the Improvement of Post Secondary Education (FIPSE) conference paper.

Dewey, J. (1929). *Experience and education.* New York: Harper.

Haines, M. P. (1993). Using media to change students' norms and prevent alcohol abuse: A tested model. *Oregon Higher Education Alcohol & Drug Coordinating Committee, 1*(2), 1-3.

Haines, M. P., & Spear, S. F. (1996). Changing the perception of the norm: A strategy to decrease binge drinking among college students. *Journal of American College Health, 45,* 134-140.

Jeffrey, L. R., & Negro, P. (1996). *Contemporary trends in alcohol and other drug use by college students in New Jersey.* Unpublished manuscript, New Jersey Higher Education Consortium on Alcohol and Other Drug Prevention Education.

Kolb, D. (1984). *Experiential learning: Experience as a source of learning.* Englewood Cliffs, NJ: Prentice Hall.

Lederman, L. C. (Ed.). (1992). *Communication pedagogy: Approaches to teaching undergraduate courses in communication.* Norwood, NJ: Ablex.

Lederman, L. C. (Ed.). (1998). *Communication theory: A reader.* Dubuque, IA: Kendall Hunt.

Lederman, L. C., & Stewart, L. P. (1999, November). *Reconceptualizing college drinking as socially situated experiential learning.* Paper presented at the meeting of the National Communication Association, Chicago.

Lederman, L. C., Stewart, L. P., Kennedy, L., Laitman, L., Powell, R., & Goodhart, F. (1998). *Self report of student perceptions: An alcohol awareness measure* (Research Report No. 1). New Brunswick, NJ: Rutgers University, Center for Communication and College Health Issues.

Mannis, J. G., & Meltzer, B. (1967). *Symbolic interaction: A reader in social psychology.* Boston: Allyn & Bacon.

Ruben, B. D., & Stewart, L. P. (1997). *Communication and human behavior.* Boston: Allyn & Bacon.

Wechsler, H., Davenport, A., Dowdall, G., Mooykens, B., & Castillo, S. (1994). Health and behavior consequences of binge drinking in college. *Journal of the American Medical Association, 272*(21), 1672-1677.

23

Sensation Seeking in Antidrug Campaign and Message Design

Philip Palmgreen
Lewis Donohew
Nancy Grant Harrington

During the past 15 years, with the aid of a series of grants from the National Institute on Drug Abuse, we have developed an approach to audience targeting and message design that successfully addresses the vexing problem of reaching and persuading individuals to avoid risky and unhealthy behaviors. The approach, called SENTAR, revolves around sensation seeking as a particularly potent risk factor for drug use and other unhealthy behaviors and is theoretically based on an activation model of information exposure (Donohew, Lorch, & Palmgreen, 1998; Donohew, Palmgreen, & Duncan, 1980). In SENTAR, sensation seeking is used at three critical stages in media campaign design: (a) segmenting or targeting the at-risk audience, (b) designing messages that are effective with this audience, and (c) placing these messages in program contexts that are attractive to the target audience. The result is a coherent and parsimonious theoretical framework that guides intervention strategies from inception to delivery and meshes well with many other theoretical approaches to prevention.

AUTHORS' NOTE: The research reported here was supported by Grants DA03462, DA05312, and DA06892 from the National Institute on Drug Abuse.

SENSATION SEEKING

Sensation seeking is a personality trait associated with the need for novel, complex, ambiguous, and emotionally intense stimuli. It is a moderate to strong predictor of use of a variety of drugs and earlier onset of use across long developmental time spans. The trait has a high heritability factor and many biochemical correlates (Zuckerman, 1979, 1994).

High sensation seekers (HSSs) also have distinct and consistent preferences for particular kinds of messages based on their needs for the novel, the unusual, and the intense (Donohew, Lorch, & Palmgreen, 1991; Zuckerman, 1979, 1994). HSSs (above the median on the sensation-seeking scale) greatly prefer messages that elicit strong sensory, affective, and arousal responses. Such messages tend to be novel, dramatic, emotionally powerful or physically arousing, graphic or explicit, unconventional, fast paced, or suspenseful (Palmgreen et al., 1991). Low sensation seekers (LSSs) prefer lower levels of these features.

Several of our experiments have shown that high sensation value (HSV) messages, and antidrug public service announcements (PSAs) embedded in HSV programming, were more effective than low sensation value (LSV) messages on outcomes such as free and cued recall, attention, attitude toward cocaine, intention to use cocaine, and calling an antidrug hotline (Donohew et al., 1991; Everett & Palmgreen, 1995; Lorch et al., 1994).

APPLICATIONS OF SENTAR

The Alternatives to Drugs Campaign

Our prior research was then applied in a televised antidrug PSA campaign conducted in Lexington, Kentucky (Palmgreen et al., 1995). The campaign was targeted at young adults and older teens through paid and donated advertising and included five PSAs developed through formative research with HSS members of this audience. The spots concluded with an appeal to call a hotline for more information about alternatives to drug use.

More than 2,100 calls to the hotline were received during the 5-month campaign, a relatively large number from a small market and narrowly defined target audience. More than 73% of the callers were above the population median on sensation seeking, as determined by surveys of hotline callers and the general population of 18- to 25-year-olds in Lexington (the age of most of the callers). Other surveys indicated that most HSSs were reached frequently by the PSAs. A postcampaign survey revealed that sensation seeking and drug use influenced exposure to the two most-aired PSAs. For both PSAs, HSS users of illicit drugs in the past 30 days displayed the highest recall certainty (either "fairly certain" or "very certain" they had seen the PSA), followed closely by the small group of LSS users (whose use status apparently made the PSAs salient) and then the HSS nonusers, another very important group to reach in a prevention campaign. Trailing these groups by a substantial margin was the large group of LSS nonusers, the segment least at-risk. Reported frequency of exposure was related to sensation seeking and drug use in a similar fashion.

The Two-Cities Campaigns

A recent study of the impact of SENTAR campaigns involved a controlled interrupted time-series design to evaluate the effectiveness of televised HSV antimarijuana PSA campaigns targeted at HSS adolescents in Lexington, Kentucky, and Knoxville, Tennessee (Palmgreen, Donohew, Lorch, Hoyle, & Stephenson, in press). Televised antimarijuana PSAs, designed and developed through formative research, were aired with high media reach and frequency (using a combination of paid and donated time) from January through April 1997 in Lexington. Similar campaigns were conducted from January through April 1998 in both Lexington and Knoxville. Beginning 8 months prior to the first Lexington campaign and ending 8 months after the 1998 campaigns, personal interviews (computer-assisted, with self-administration of sensitive items) were conducted in the home with 100 randomly selected students per month in each county (total $N = 6,371$). The population cohort followed was in the 7th through 10th grades initially.

Full sample medians were employed to separate the Knoxville and Lexington monthly samples into groups of HSSs and LSSs. Time-series regression analyses indicated that all three campaigns actually reversed upward developmental trends in 30-day marijuana use among HSS adolescents ($p <$ .002 for each campaign). For example, 30-day use among Knoxville HSSs increased in a linear fashion from 16.6% initially to 33.0% during the 20-month precampaign period and then decreased approximately 9 points to 24% from the start of the campaign to the completion of data gathering 12 months later. The decrease in the proportion of HSSs using marijuana was 26.7%. The first Lexington campaign also reversed a strong upward trend in 30-day use among HSSs. Perhaps because Lexington HSSs were higher than their Knoxville counterparts on most drug risk factors and lower on most drug protective factors, the upward development trend resumed about 6 months after the campaign. This trend, however, was also reversed by the second or "booster" Lexington campaign, and marijuana use continued to decline until the completion of data gathering. As expected, LSSs exhibited low use and no campaign effects.

The strong impact of these campaigns may be partly attributed to the use of well-tested social and behavioral theories related to drug abuse prevention and message design and also to careful message and channel targeting. The campaigns also achieved levels of exposure (85% of HSS adolescents reached three times/week) considered substantial but not overwhelming by ad agency standards. We believe that much of the credit is due, however, to the application of SENTAR principles.

SUMMARY OF SENTAR PRINCIPLES

The following principles summarize the SENTAR approach to the prevention of substance use and other risky behaviors: (a) Use the sensation-seeking trait as a major segmentation variable, (b) conduct formative research with HSS members of the target audience, (c) design prevention messages high in sensation value to reach HSSs, and (d) place campaign messages in HSV contexts (e.g., dramatic, novel, and often unconventional TV programs preferred by HSSs).

These principles are being applied in the Office of National Drug Control Policy's (ONDCP) 5-year National Youth Anti-Drug Media Campaign. Although the campaign is a multimedia effort, its central component is dissemination of televised PSAs targeted at at-risk tweens and teens, with sensation seeking an important factor in determining those "at-risk." Campaign messages are developed based on social science theory and on information from HSS focus groups. Ad agency personnel are also being guided by specific communication objectives and a sensation-seeking "brief" for developing HSV messages. Finished messages are then tested with HSS adolescents via a randomized control group methodology. The large campaign evaluation study funded by the National Institute on Drug Abuse is employing sensation seeking as a contingent and predictor variable, as is the ad tracking survey conducted by ONDCP as part of its process evaluation.

The SENTAR approach is not restricted to illicit drug abuse prevention, however. Sensation seeking is also related to alcohol use (Donohew et al., 1999) and tobacco use (Clayton, Cattarello, & Walden, 1991), risky sex, crime, deviance, drinking and driving, and speeding (Donohew et al., 2000; Newcomb & McGee, 1991; Zuckerman, 1994). It is also very likely related to a wide range of other risk behaviors. These principles, of course, should be used in conjunction with other proven cognitively oriented theoretical frameworks, such as social cognitive theory, the Health Belief Model, and the theory of reasoned action. The SENTAR approach reminds us to also consider fundamental affective and sensory needs in defining our target audiences and in developing the messages and campaign strategies to reach them most effectively.

REFERENCES

Clayton, R. R., Cattarello, A., & Walden, K. P. (1991). Sensation seeking as a potential mediating variable for school-based prevention intervention: A two-year follow-up of DARE. *Health Communication, 3*(4), 229-239.

Donohew, L., Lorch, E. P., & Palmgreen, P. (1991). Sensation seeking and targeting of televised anti-drug PSAs. In L. Donohew, H. E. Sypher, & W. J. Bukoski (Eds.), *Persuasive communication and drug abuse prevention* (pp. 209-226). Hillsdale, NJ: Lawrence Erlbaum.

Donohew, L., Lorch, E. P., & Palmgreen, P. (1998). Applications of a theoretic model of information exposure to health interventions. *Human Communication Research, 24,* 454-468.

Donohew, L., Palmgreen, P., & Duncan, J. (1980). An activation model of information exposure. *Communication Monographs, 47,* 295-303.

Donohew, L., Zimmerman, R., Cupp, P. S., Novak, S., Colon, S., & Abell, R. (2000). Sensation seeking, impulsive decision-making, and risky sex: Implications for risk-taking and design of interventions. *Personality and Individual Differences, 28,* 1079-1091.

Donohew, R. L., Hoyle, R. H., Clayton, R. R., Skinner, W. F., Colon, S. E., & Rice, R. E. (1999). Sensation seeking and drug use by adolescents and their friends: Models for marijuana and alcohol. *Journal of Studies on Alcohol, 60,* 622-631.

Everett, M. W., & Palmgreen, P. (1995). Influences of sensation seeking, message sensation value, and program context on effectiveness of anticocaine public service announcements. *Health Communication, 1,* 225-248.

Lorch, E. P., Palmgreen, P., Donohew, L., Helm, D., Baer, S. A., & Dsilva, M. U. (1994). Program context, sensation seeking, and attention to televised anti-drug public service announcements. *Human Communication Research, 20*(3), 390-412.

Newcomb, M. D., & McGee, L. (1991). Influence of sensation seeking on general deviance and specific problem behaviors from adolescence to young adulthood. *Journal of Personality and Social Psychology, 61,* 614-628.

Palmgreen, P., Donohew, L., Lorch, E. P., Rogus, M., Helm, D., & Grant, N. (1991). Sensation seeking, message sensation value, and drug use as mediators of PSA effectiveness. *Health Communication, 3*(4), 217-227.

Palmgreen, P., Donohew, L., Lorch, E. P., Hoyle, R. H., & Stephenson, M. (in press). Television campaigns and sensation seeking targeting of adolescent marijuana use: A controlled time-series approach. In R. Hornik (Ed.) *Public health communication: Evidence for behavior change.* Hillsdale, NJ: Lawrence Erlbaum.

Palmgreen, P., Lorch, E. P., Donohew, R. L., Harrington, N. G., Dsilva, M., & Helm, D. (1995). Reaching at-risk populations in a mass media drug abuse prevention campaign: Sensation seeking as a targeting variable. *Drugs and Society, 8,* 29-45.

Zuckerman, M. (1979). *Sensation seeking: Beyond the optimal level of arousal.* Hillsdale, NJ: Lawrence Erlbaum.

Zuckerman, M. (1994). *Behavioral expression and biosocial bases of sensation seeking.* New York: Cambridge University Press.

24

The Cumulative Community Response to AIDS in San Francisco

James W. Dearing

Practitioners and scholars trying to encourage community-level change are in the midst of a paradigm shift from social psychology to social ecology. The traditional approach of communication campaigns is based in the social psychological idea that success is defined by individual-level behavior change. The social ecology approach to understanding and studying community improvement is based in the idea that social change occurs because of complementary and reinforcing information circulating through social and organized systems that constitute a community. Such community-level campaigns aim multiple positively related interventions at multiple levels of impact within a given geographic area (Goodman, Wandersman, Chinman, Imm, & Morrissey, 1996). Because this approach to community change seeks to mimic the everyday cumulative way that social influence occurs, the co-occurrence of concomitant campaigns carried out in the same geographic area can produce community-level effects even without coordination. Consider the case of San Francisco and HIV prevention.

Compared with other U.S. cities, San Francisco's population is liberal and progressive and has, since the 1849 Gold Rush, displayed a "live and let live" philosophy with tolerance for diverse lifestyles. In 1974, police harassment of

AUTHOR'S NOTE: This study is based on research funded by the U.S. Agency for Health Care Policy and Research Grant 5R01H0760-02.

gay men was halted by the city government. This "coming of rights" was important for the already large gay and lesbian population of the city. Word spread rapidly that San Francisco was a place where gays could publicly declare their sexual orientation without fear of reprisal. Then HIV and AIDS struck at the heart of this liberation.

Beginning in 1978, the estimated number of new HIV infections per month in San Francisco increased dramatically, reaching an apex of nearly 500 new infections a month in late 1981 (Brookmeyer & Gail, 1994). Then, beginning in 1982, the number of estimated new infections decreased just as rapidly, averaging fewer than 50 new infections per month by 1985 (San Francisco Department of Public Health, 1999). Part of this decrease can be attributed to new infections reaching a high saturation plateau—nearly half of gay men older than the age of 26 were infected by the late 1980s. The scope and rapidity of behavior change in the city, however, was unparalleled in the history of medicine (Kolata, 1994). What else accounts for this communitywide shift in behavior?

There can be little doubt that high uncertainty about the then mysterious epidemic, rumors about its causation, symptoms, and seriousness, as well as communication with and observation of sick friends led individuals to take precautions to protect their health. Just as certainly, however, the number of new HIV infections decreased precipitously and then continued to decline because of the diffusion and effects of innovative organized prevention activities (Coates & Stryker, 1994; Fineberg, 1988).

Organized prevention activities to combat HIV and AIDS in San Francisco progressed through three eras (Rogers et al., 1995). From 1981 to 1987, a handful of nonprofit organizations received contracts from the city to communicate messages to and build skills among gay men, especially whites, whom the epidemic first hit hardest. These organizations, such as the San Francisco AIDS Foundation, grew rapidly and came to coordinate the work of thousands of volunteers, many of whom were infected with HIV. During the 1984 and 1985 fiscal year, the three largest of these organizations provided more than 80,000 hours of social support and counseling, responded to more than 30,000 telephone inquiries, and distributed 250,000 pieces of AIDS-related literature (Dearing & Rogers, 1992). By 1987, 7,000 men had taken part in a small-group communication intervention based in the living rooms of gay men, the STOP AIDS Project (Wohlfeiler, 1997). Extensive local coverage of the epidemic and its ramifications by mass media and the gay press—along with a politically efficacious affected subpopulation, responsive elected officials, and a proactive city department of public health—had pushed the issue of AIDS to the top of the media, public, and policy agendas in San Francisco by 1984 (Dearing & Rogers, 1996; see also Chapter 1, this volume).

Following the viral spread of HIV, prevention entered a second era in 1988. Many small, community-based organizations in San Francisco pressured the city into funding their diverse programs for prevention, education, and outreach. This so-called "revolution of 1988" saw the birth of hundreds of HIV prevention programs that resulted in uncoordinated waves of prevention messages for some unique populations, especially those for which funding was readily available. Competition between community-based organizations for audiences and funding was fierce (Broadhead & Margolis, 1993). One stock-taking in 1993 counted 401 organizations offering AIDS-related services in the city, 212 of which were prevention focused (Dearing et al., 1996).

In 1994, a third era of HIV prevention began. The city's department of public health began to strongly encourage collaboration among prevention providers, leading to consortia formed primarily on the basis of channels of communication. Coordination of prevention efforts was also driven by federal policy tied to funding (Dearing, Larson, Randall, & Pope, 1998). Now, organized communication about HIV and AIDS is routinized for both prevention and care information (whereas there has been a steep decrease in the number of new cases, the number of people in the city living with AIDS continues to increase), making information seeking easier. Organizations created in response to the disease have become institutionalized. In 1997, the University of California at San Francisco unveiled the largest AIDS research institute outside the U.S. National Institutes of Health, with 1,000 researchers conducting basic laboratory research, clinical trials of treatments, HIV prevention campaigns, and AIDS policy analyses.

The largely successful experience in San Francisco with HIV prevention speaks to the positive causal influence that a comprehensive community response—even one that is disorganized for years—can have on a public health crisis through the decentralized diffusion of new information, new attitudes, new behaviors, and new community norms that are all (at some base level) mutually reinforcing and thus act cumulatively to tip a community over a critical mass of change (see Chapter 27, this volume). Campaign stakeholders in San Francisco learned by doing through stops and starts, through periods of great and terrible uncertainty, much of it characterized by partial information, interorganizational turf battles, and carrot-and-stick prompting to encourage greater efficiency and effectiveness of public communication campaign activities. *Social capital,* resources embedded in community social structure (Lin, 1999), was accessed and mobilized in response to HIV through interpersonal and interorganizational action. Mass media channels were flooded with anti-HIV messages; the most effective campaigns targeted at unique populations emphasized trust building between change agents and clients prior to placing emphasis on prevention messages (Dearing et al., 1996).

Overall, the community's capacity to deal with problems, in terms of citizen participation and leadership, skills, resources, social and interorganizational networks, a shared sense of community and its collective history, power, and critical reflection, was certainly demonstrated if not strengthened. Influential people in San Francisco's gay community spoke and wrote about the need for preventive action; individuals adopted behavioral changes, especially fewer sexual partners and safe sex; and these influential and individual actions were reinforced by the cavalcade of organized campaigns that served to reinforce opinions about an already salient and obtrusive topic, thus altering the city's social ecology through new community norms and dramatically reduced HIV infection rates.

REFERENCES

Broadhead, R. S., & Margolis, E. (1993). Drug policy in the time of AIDS: The development of outreach in San Francisco. *Sociological Quarterly, 34,* 487-522.

Brookmeyer, R., & Gail, M. H. (1994). *AIDS epidemiology. A quantitative approach.* New York: Oxford University Press.

Coates, T. J., & Stryker, J. (1994, May 5). *HIV prevention: Looking back, looking ahead.* Keynote address presented at the 1994 Charles C. Shepard Award Ceremony, U.S. Centers for Disease Control and Prevention, Atlanta.

Dearing, J. W., Larson, R. S., Randall, L. M., & Pope, R. S. (1998). Local reinvention of the CDC HIV prevention community planning initiative. *Journal of Community Health, 23*(2), 113-126.

Dearing, J. W., & Rogers, E. M. (1992). AIDS and the media agenda. In T. Edgar, M. A. Fitzpatrick, & V. S. Freimuth (Eds.), *AIDS: A communication perspective* (pp. 173-194). Hillsdale, NJ: Lawrence Erlbaum.

Dearing, J. W., & Rogers, E. M. (1996). *Agenda-setting.* Thousand Oaks, CA: Sage.

Dearing, J. W., Rogers, E. M., Meyer, G., Casey, M. K., Rao, N., Campo, S., & Henderson, G. M. (1996). Social marketing and diffusion-based strategies for communicating with unique populations: HIV prevention in San Francisco. *Journal of Health Communication, 1,* 343-363.

Fineberg, H. V. (1988). Education to prevent AIDS: Prospects and obstacles. *Science, 239,* 592-596.

Goodman, R. M., Wandersman, A., Chinman, M., Imm, P., & Morrissey, E. (1996). An ecological assessment of community-based interventions for prevention and health promotion: Approaches to measuring community coalitions. *American Journal of Community Psychology, 24*(1), 33-61.

Kolata, G. (1994, February 16). AIDS in San Francisco hit peak in '92, officials say. *New York Times,* p. A8.

Lin, N. (1999). Building a network theory of social capital. *Connections, 22*(1), 28-51.

Rogers, E. M., Dearing, J. W., Rao, N., Campo, M. L., Meyer, G., Betts, G. J. F., & Casey, M. K. (1995). Communication and community in a city under siege: The AIDS epidemic in San Francisco. *Communication Research, 22*(6), 664-678.

San Francisco Department of Public Health. (1999). *Quarterly AIDS surveillance report* (AIDS cases reported through September 1999). San Francisco: Author.

Wohlfeiler, D. (1997). Community organizing and community building among gay and bisexual men: The STOP AIDS Project. In M. Minkler (Ed.), *Community organizing and community building for health* (pp. 230-243). New Brunswick, NJ: Rutgers University Press.

25

America's Sacred Cow

Matilda Butler

A survey of print ads, conducted by Video Storyboard Tests, named it the most popular print campaign of the year. Stuart Elliott, advertising columnist for the *New York Times,* called it one of the 10 best campaigns of the year. It is a pop culture icon. Its posters are collected by teenagers. It has spawned a club with more than 40,000 members. It has been the source of spoofs and parodies on television and in magazines. Yes, it is the "Milk. Where's Your Mustache?" campaign.

WHY A CAMPAIGN FOR MILK?

Although milk consumption shows modest increases during the 1979 to 1997 period for which data are available (increasing from 21.9 billion pounds to 23.3 billion pounds) (Blisard, Blayney, Chandran, & Allshouse, 1999), per capita consumption has declined (from 31 gallons per year in 1970 to 24 gallons in 1996). Because of this decline, Congress, at the urging of the dairy lobby, provided for a national program for the promotion of dairy products in the Dairy and Tobacco Adjustment Act of 1983. In 1990, Congress passed the Fluid Milk Promotion Act and established a national program for the promotion of fluid milk under the aegis of the U.S. Department of Agriculture (USDA). This program is funded by a 20¢ per hundred weight assessment on milk processors who market more than 500,000 pounds of milk per month. Although there have been several campaigns funded by these two acts, the most famous are the "Milk Mustache" campaign managed by the National Fluid Milk Processors Promotion Board and the "Got Milk?" campaign initially developed and managed by the California

Milk Processor Board and later licensed to Dairy Management, Inc. and the
MilkPEP (Processor Education Program) Board for national distribution (and
ranked as the 13th greatest commercial of all time by *TV Guide* ["The Fifty
Greatest," 1999]).

MILK MUSTACHE CAMPAIGN FOCUS AND STRATEGY

In 1994, Bozell Worldwide was selected by the National Fluid Milk Processor
Promotion Board as the advertising agency to develop its campaign to increase
per capita milk consumption. At the beginning of this process, a study commissioned by the milk processors indicated that people were drinking less milk
because of concern about fat and a belief that low-fat milk products contained
fewer nutrients. In addition, the research showed that mothers ages 25 to 49 had
the greatest influence on family milk consumption.

With this research in hand, Bozell began the creative work of designing the
campaign. First, they allocated most of the $37 million to magazine advertise-
ments for maximum impact. By becoming a major, and in some cases the largest, advertiser in a magazine, they could increase the impact by asking for, and
getting, additional coverage of milk products in the magazine's editorial content. Second, they selected only magazines read by women ages 25 to 44.
Finally, they focused on a fairly simple message—interesting facts that would
present milk in a new way.

How should the message be presented? Early in the process, two decisions
were made in addition to using only magazines: (a) Use only a small amount of
text and (b) create a poster-style campaign that, by its striking visual, would
generate readership. Eventually, the creative staff at Bozell developed a campaign that showed ordinary people with milk mustaches and four lines of text
on each poster initially following the formula of the first and last lines providing information about the person and the middle two lines presenting a nugget
of information about milk (Schulberg, 1998).

The Fluid Milk Processors Promotion Board liked the campaign but asked if
celebrities could be used. With this final element in place, the Milk Mustache
campaign was born. Annie Leibovitz, well-known for her photo portraits in
Rolling Stone and *Vanity Fair,* signed on as the photographer. The first five ads
appeared in 58 publications on Valentine's Day 1995 and featured Lauren
Bacall, Naomi Campbell, Christie Brinkley, Vanna White, and Joan Rivers. At
the end of the first year, two men appeared in ads (Steve Young and Billy Ray
Cyrus).

With perceived campaign success, the budget was doubled the following
year to reach additional magazine audiences. Milk-mustached personalities
continued to provide the iconic portraits. Appeals were made to specific subgroups (e.g., teenage females and teenage males) by varying the message content, the choice of personalities, and the magazine. Bozell used events and pop
culture to create new advertising opportunities. For example, the 1997 Super

Bowl XXXI resulted in two ads, one showing the quarterbacks of the two Super Bowl teams, Brett Favre and Drew Bledsoe, before the game and the other showing the winning quarterback Brett Favre the following morning. The popularity of television shows such as the *Simpsons, Friends,* and *Everybody Loves Raymond* created opportunities to showcase their stars in ads.

Campaign Content: Which Milk?

One goal of the Milk Mustache campaign is to promote low-fat and nonfat milk by ensuring that the target audience learns that lower fat products have the same nutrients as whole milk. An analysis of the 81 ads covering the 1995 to 1998 period in *The Milk Mustache Book* (Schulberg, 1998), however, does not indicate a major emphasis of this goal. Of the 68 ads with copy, 60% (41) made no mention of specific milk type, 22% (15) mentioned no-fat/skim milk, 12% (8) mentioned low-fat/1% milk, and 6% (4) mentioned reduced-fat/2% milk. Sixty ads had analyzable themes. Two can be classified as major because they represent 87% of the theme content: calcium in milk (47%, 28 ads) and nine essential nutrients/protein in milk (40%, 24 ads). The two minor themes accounting for the remaining 13% of the theme content were milk is superior to sports drinks (8%, 5 ads) and clinical science ("studies suggest that . . .") (5%, 3 ads). Fifty-seven percent of these themes were associated with ads making no specific reference to milk type.

Campaign Outcomes

The Milk Mustache ads are the core of a generic advertising campaign designed to increase industrywide sales of milk. Has the campaign been successful? Yes, maybe, and no.

Yes

Bozell's campaign has been successful with the Fluid Milk Processors Promotion Board and its members. They have not only continued to fund the campaign but also increased the yearly budget from an initial level of approximately $37 million to a steady state of approximately $110 million. The campaign has caught the imagination of the press, which has written extensively about the engaging ads. The campaign has been popular with celebrities, who want to be associated with the campaign even though they are paid only $25,000, a token amount for famous personalities. The campaign has been successful in expanding from poster-based magazine ads to complementary components, such as the 100-city Milk Mustache mobile tour, the formation of Club Milk with more than 40,000 children members, the milk mustache birthday party planner, an Internet initiative with *iVillage.com/milk* (*http://www. ivillage.com/milk*) to help women change their nutritional habits (the site carries the campaign theme by including an interactive milk mustache tool that lets users draw a mustache on a printable scanned picture), a consumer hotline, informational brochures on milk-related topics, a MilkPEP Internet site, milk mustached dairy-category managers in grocery trade publications, the 2000 Fame Game in-store promotion, and yearly SAMMY (Scholar Athlete Milk Mustache of the Year) contests for scholarship prizes. In a single month, additional coverage of the Milk Mustache ads on *Entertainment Tonight, VH-1 News,* and *Good Morning America* and in *Newsweek* and newspapers reached more than 63 million consumers (*dairyinfo.com,* 1999). Finally, the campaign has changed knowledge about milk. Roper Starch Worldwide conducted research before the start of the campaign and then 1 year later. An additional 14% of those surveyed recognized that milk could be low in fat, an additional 15% knew skim milk could be high in calcium, and an additional 17% correctly stated that skim milk was high in vitamin and minerals (Milk and Dairy Beef Quality Assurance Center, 1996).

Maybe

When interviewed in 1998, Kurt Graetzer, executive director of the Milk Processor Education Program, stated that people's attitudes toward milk had changed and that milk was now perceived as "cool and contemporary" (Maurstad, 1998), but no evidence was provided.

No

The Milk Mustache campaign has not changed behaviors adequately to increase per capita milk consumption, although the campaign may have helped to halt the decline in consumption. This information is derived from models built by the Department of Agriculture's Economic Research Service indicating that fluid milk sales increased due to the additional advertising expenditures from the combined 1984 and 1993 acts—an additional 8.1 billion pounds of fluid milk were sold during the 1984 to 1997 period than would have been sold without the advertising (Blisard et al., 1999).

PUBLIC CAMPAIGN, INDUSTRY CAMPAIGN, AND COMPANY CAMPAIGN

An increasing number of campaigns and promotions seek to establish or exploit a connection between food products and health. *Public service* campaigns are exemplified by the National Cancer Institute's campaign to eat five daily servings of fruits and vegetables to reduce cancer risk. *Company promotions* are exemplified by Welch's "Fighter, Defender, Protector" promotion to drink grape juice for its antioxidant and anticlotting benefits. *Industry campaigns* are hybrids that sometimes are more like public service campaigns and sometimes more like company campaigns. Some industry campaigns, such as those undertaken by The Century Council with funds from five major distillers, are willing to forego some sales to ensure that the public is aware of problems that can be associated with using the product. The Milk Mustache message, however, is couched in the objective language of a public service campaign but is aligned with the usual promotion goal of increasing sales.

Most of us grew up hearing "Drink your milk." School lunches included milk. Elementary school nutrition was taught with materials provided by dairy councils. Milk is a sacred cow in American nutrition, and this status has helped the Milk Mustache campaign.

Who speaks out against any of these campaigns? Public service campaigns do not usually create controversy. No one argues about the goals of the Smokey Bear, Every Litter Bit Hurts, Take a Bite Out of Crime, or Just Say No campaigns (see these samplers in this volume). The Milk Mustache campaign, however, has raised objections from four quarters. First, animal rights groups have staged protests at Milk Mustache mobile sites, displaying photographs of the treatment of dairy cows and their offspring. Second, the science behind the nutrition messages is part of an ongoing medical research debate. It has not been determined that dairy calcium helps to prevent osteoporosis; indeed, some research indicates that the highest rates of osteoporosis occur in nations with the highest levels of dairy consumption. It is also argued that high intake of animal protein raises blood acidity to levels that must be neutralized by calcium drawn from bones, and that milk's magnesium-to-calcium ratio is four times lower than the ratio needed for optimal calcium metabolism (Gaby, 1994; Germano, 1999; Robbins, 1987). Third, the lack of adequate data to evaluate the outcomes, and the use of sole-source contracts, was highlighted in late 1998 (and again on February 11, 1999) by the Department of Agriculture's Office of Inspector General ("IG," 1998), which noted that the 1984 and 1993 acts mandate independent studies to determine the campaign's impact.

The fourth and most significant protest comes from the Physicians Committee for Responsible Medicine (PCRM), which in April 2000 filed a petition with the Federal Trade Commission stating that the Milk Mustache ads violate federal advertising guidelines for health-related product claims (*pcrm.org*, 2000a). In a previous confrontation with the dairy lobby in Washington, D.C., the PCRM secured a change in the USDA Dietary Guidelines, causing them to state that soymilk is on a par with cow's milk as a calcium source (*pcrm.org*, 2000b). According to the April 2000 PCRM petition, the Food and Drug Administration (FDA) guidelines for health claims directed that "to ensure calcium and osteoporosis claims will not mislead those individuals within the population for whom relatively higher calcium intake over a lifetime offers no apparent benefit to their bone health," subpopulations clearly at risk must be identified. These FDA-defined subpopulations exclude males of any age, any racial group other than Asians and Caucasians, or women older than their bone-building years. The PCRM specifically criticized the promotion of milk to African Americans, a large percentage of whom are lactose intolerant.

CONCLUSION

Campaign planners who rely on outcomes data to judge campaign effectiveness will find limited value in this engaging industry campaign because the public relations and marketing organizations responsible for the campaign are not releasing outcomes data—and in fact may be relying on secondary measures and anecdotal data rather than true campaign evaluations. In addition, the use of health claims in food promotion can be problematic if there are responsible and well-publicized contrary views. Finally, public sensitivity to health claims is affected by media critiques of major campaigns such as this.

REFERENCES

Blisard, N., Blayney, D., Chandran, R., & Allshouse, J. (1999). *Analysis of generic dairy advertising, 1984-1997* (Technical Bulletin No. 1873). Washington, DC: U.S. Department of Agriculture.

Dairyinfo.com. (1999). *www.dairyinfo.com/check/hl0899.html.*

The fifty greatest TV commercials of all time. (1999, July 3-9). *TV Guide,* 2-34.

Gaby, A. R. (1994). *Preventing and reversing osteoporosis.* Rocklin, CA: Prima.

Germano, C., with Cabot, W. (1999). *The osteoporosis solution: New therapies for prevention and treatment.* New York: Kensington.

IG: Milk board not doing a body good. (1998, October 6). *CongressDaily/A.M.* [On-line serial]. Available: www.govexec.com/dairy/fed/1098/100698t.htm.

Maurstad, T. (1998, May 4). Shilled MILK: Mass of mustaches has soaked into our collective consciousness. *Dallas Morning News,* p. 1C.

Milk and Dairy Beef Quality Assurance Center. (1996, August). Milk mustache campaign moves into second phase. *DQA Quest* [On-line serial]. Available: *www.dqacenter.org/quest/96/aug961.htm.*

pcrm.org. (2000). The "milk mustache" ads are all wet: PCRM takes it to the Federal Trade Commission. *http://www.pcrm.org/news/milk_mustache_complaint.html.*

pcrm.org. (2000b). Soymilk makes the grade with federal diet panel: Controversial lawsuit gets credit, says physicians group. *http://www.pcrm.org/news/health000211.html.*

Robbins, J. (1987). *Diet for a new America.* Walpole, NH: Stillpoint.

Schulberg, J., with Hogya, B., & Taibi, S. (1998). *The milk mustache book.* New York: Ballantine.

26

The Nazi Antitobacco Campaign

Robert Proctor

The Nazis conducted cruel and unusual experiments against concentration camp victims. Nazi doctors organized the world's first campaign to murder the physically and mentally handicapped, first by gas chamber and then by starvation and lethal injection. Nazi medical crimes are legendary, involving forcible sterilization, euthanasia, abusive experimentation, and so on.

The Nazis, however, also launched the world's most aggressive anticancer campaign, encompassing bans on carcinogens in food and water, restrictions on the use of asbestos and other carcinogens in the workplace, and novel dietary and chemical therapeutics (Proctor, 1999). German physicians were in fact the first to come to the conclusion that smoking was the major cause of lung cancer—a little-known fact obscured by postwar prejudices. Although the 1950s are often considered the beginning of tobacco health research (Doll & Bradford Hill, 1950; Kevles, 1996), pioneering studies were performed in Germany in the 1930s and 1940s, resulting in the world's first broad medical consensus that smoking is the major cause of lung cancer. This recognition was fostered by a national political climate stressing the virtues of racial hygiene and bodily purity. In the Nazi worldview, tobacco was a genetic poison; a cause of infertility, cancer, and heart attacks; a drain on financial resources and public health; and a threat to the "maternal organism."

Tobacco had been suggested as a cause of cancer of the lip in the 18th century, but smoking remained a relative luxury throughout the 19th century. Therefore, as recently as World War I, lung cancer was still an extreme rarity.

(Today, of course, it is the world's most common cause of cancer death.) Smoking became more popular toward the end of the 19th century, following the introduction of mechanized cigarette rolling, tobacco advertising, and state promotion or monopoly of cigarettes to generate revenues. In the 20th century, cigarettes were provided with rations to the soldiers of World War I. The introduction of milder types of tobacco and flue curing made it easier to inhale, encouraging a shift away from pipes and cigars and allowing the smoke to be drawn deeper into the lungs, delivering a much higher dose of tar, nicotine, and other noxious substances.

The cancer consequences were profound, as lung cancer rates exploded. Although there were many other suspected causes (influenza, automobile exhaust, occupational exposures, chest X rays [Herz, 1930], World War I chemical warfare agents, and even racial mixing), cigarettes began to come under suspicion in the 1920s, especially through the work of Fritz Lickint, a Dresden physician who in 1929 published some of the first statistical evidence linking lung cancer and the "golden weed." His monumental *Tabak und Organismus* (1939, with 1,200 pages reviewing 8,000 studies) chronicled an extraordinary range of ills—from cancer to miscarriages—derived from smoking or chewing tobacco (as well as from "passive smoking," a term he introduced).

Germany's tobacco and alcohol temperance movements from the 1920s were strengthened by the rise of National Socialism. Nazi rule was generally welcomed by the antialcohol and antitobacco forces, but it is important not to overlook Hitler's personal aversion. A former heavy smoker in his youth, Hitler later claimed that Germany might never have achieved its present glory as a fascist state if he had continued to smoke. One could argue that Germans were able to make such strong claims against tobacco because they had never experienced Prohibition and therefore did not suffer, during the 1930s and 1940s, the backlash against tobacco moralism felt by American physicians.

In the Nazi era, tobacco was said to hinder the military prowess of the German soldier and also to cause automobile accidents, prompting criminal penalties for accidents caused by driving "under the influence" (of cigarettes). Tobacco was also said to cause spontaneous abortions, which was especially disturbing to Nazi authorities, who placed a premium on boosting Germany's birthrate. Tobacco was also blamed for creating an addictive allegiance to a foreign, filthy, and "unnatural" substance in an era when both mind and body were supposed to belong to the führer.

Legal sanctions began to be put into place in 1938 and 1939, with bans on smoking in the Luftwaffe, the post office, and the National Socialist German Workers' Party and for all uniformed police and SS officers while on duty. Tobacco rationing coupons were denied to pregnant women, and restaurants and cafes were barred from selling cigarettes to female customers. A July 1943 law made it illegal for anyone under 18 years of age to smoke in public. Advertisements implying that smoking possessed "hygienic values" were barred, as were images depicting smokers as athletes, sports fans, or automobile drivers.

The Reich Institute for Tobacco Research in Forchheim, near Karlsruhe, perfected methods to remove nicotine from tobacco and cigarettes. By 1940, fully 5% of the entire German harvest was "nicotine-free tobacco." Research was also launched into the psychology and psychopharmacology of smoking: Dozens of preparations (from oral to injectable), along with hypnotism, were available to assist people in quitting smoking, and various forms of psychological counseling were provided at dozens of tobacco counseling stations established throughout the Reich.

German antitobacco activism culminated in 1940 and 1941, encouraged by the success of the early military campaigns and the euphoric effort to find "final solutions" for Germany's problems. The most important antitobacco research institution—Jena's Institute for Tobacco Hazards Research—was established in April 1941 by a 100,000 Reichsmark grant from Hitler's Reichskanzlei. Karl Astel, director of the new institute, was also president of Thuringia's Office of Racial Affairs and president, since the summer of 1939, of the University of Jena. Astel was not only a vocal anti-Semite and high-ranking SS officer but also a militant antismoker and teetotaler who banned smoking at the University of Jena and the institute.

Astel's antitobacco institute promoted both medically informed propaganda—including the production of an antismoking film—and politically informed scientific work. The most intriguing work of the institute was Schairer and Schoeniger's 1943 paper on experimental lung cancer epidemiology—the most convincing, and scientifically rigorous (standardized not just for age, sex, and, of course, race but also for health), demonstration up to that time that people with lung cancer were far more likely to smoke than the "control population" with other kinds of cancer.

I do not want to exaggerate Nazi success in combating tobacco: Tobacco consumption increased dramatically during the first 7 years of Nazi rule— evidence that whatever propaganda may have been launched against the habit seems to have had little or no effect on consumption, at least in these early years. One argument has been put forward that people smoked—or listened to jazz or went to "swing" dance parties—as a kind of cultural opposition to Nazi macho asceticism. Nazi tobacco activists were well aware of the American backlash against Prohibition, and they used this to caution against a total ban on cigarettes.

As the war dragged on, in fact, the campaign did lose much of its steam. Wartime urgencies led a military physician in 1944 to write that "only a fanatic" would withhold a drink or a smoke from a soldier trying to calm his nerves after the horrors of battle. Also, the campaign really never had the priority of, for example, the destruction of the Jews. Effects to link Jews and tobacco in 1940 and 1941 were short-lived and aroused some high-level protests. Hitler was asked to adjudicate the issue, and although he sided with the antitobacco forces, antitobacco propaganda was muted after the summer of 1941. This is also approximately the time that the tobacco industry launched its own medical institute, the Tabacologia Medicinalis, to counter antitobacco science and pro-paganda, foreshadowing the later fight between the American tobacco indus-try's propaganda offices and the American health authorities. One interesting difference between the German and American cases is that in Germany under the Nazis, the industry's propaganda office was required to close as a threat to German health and well-being.

Why was the campaign not more successful? The rapid economic recovery in the first 6 years of Nazi rule boosted the average German's purchasing power, and tobacco companies took advantage of the boom to promote their product. Tobacco also provided an important source of revenue for the national treasury. In fact, by 1941, national income from tobacco taxes and tariffs was in excess of nearly 2 billion Reichsmarks. Also, 200,000 Germans were said to owe their livelihood to tobacco.

German tobacco consumption did begin to decline after the second or third year of the war, as bombing raids began to cut into finished supplies. A 1944 survey of 1,000 servicemen found that although the proportion of soldiers smoking had increased since the start of the war, the total consumption of to-bacco had actually decreased by approximately 14%. Postwar poverty further cut consumption. Shortages became so severe that American authorities de-cided to ship tobacco, free of charge, into Germany as part of the Marshall Plan (which shifted German tobacco tastes from the traditionally favored black to-bacco to the milder, blond Virginian blend from American companies).

After the war, Germany lost its position as home to the world's most aggres-sive antitobacco science and policy. Hitler, of course, was dead, but many of his antitobacco underlings had lost their jobs, committed suicide, or were other-wise silenced. Also, the taint of Nazism pervaded even the anticancer efforts.

My goal has not been to fabricate banalities (e.g., that "good can come from evil") or to rescue any honor from this era. Nor has it been to argue that today's antitobacco efforts have fascist roots, or that public health measures are in principle totalitarian (in contrast to some in the popular press who have used this historical research to denounce the antismoking movement as fascist "nicoNazis"). Rather, I think it is important to recognize that just as the routine practice of science is not incompatible with the routine exercise of cruelty, so too the dictatorial and eliminative aspirations of fascism are not necessarily at odds with the promotion of public health, at least for certain portions of the population. There surely is more to the story than "medicine gone mad" (Caplan, 1992).

REFERENCES

Caplan, A. L. (Ed.). (1992). *When medicine went mad: Bioethics and the Holocaust.* Clifton, NJ: Humana Press.
Doll, R., & Bradford Hill, A. (1950). Smoking and carcinoma of the lung. *British Medical Journal, 2,* 739-748.

Herz, F. (1930). Hat das Lungenkarzinom an Haufigkeit zugenommen. *Medizinische Klinik, 26,* 1666-1669.

Kevles, D. J. (1996, May 12). Blowing smoke. *New York Times Book Review,* p. 1.

Lickint, F. (1939). *Tabak und organismus.* Stuttgart: Hippocrates Verlag.

Proctor, R. N. (1999). *The Nazi war on cancer.* Princeton, NJ: Princeton University Press.

Schairer, E., & Schoniger, E. (1943). Lungenbrebs und tabakverbrauch. *Zeitschrift fur Krebsforschung, 54,* 261-269.

PART V

New Approaches and Current Challenges

27

Community Partnership Strategies in Health Campaigns

Neil Bracht

Two decades of experience in conducting community health promotion campaigns have produced a growing consensus about the importance of active community involvement and collaboration in the design and implementation of local projects. Successful campaign partnership approaches build on the principles of community organization theory that promote the planned involvement and contribution(s) of community citizens, leaders, and organizations. Commitment of campaign planners and professionals to community empowerment and capacity building not only adds to the material and human resources needed for any given campaign but also increases the likelihood that campaign results endure beyond the campaign or project period (Thompson & Winner, 1999). Many private foundations and governmental funding programs now require community involvement protocols as part of the grant application and intervention process. The goal is to increase local decision making and build the capacity for ongoing responsibility for community change. As Green (1990, p. 41) notes, community-based health promotion efforts attempt to "put the control over the determinants of health where it belongs . . . with the people."

This chapter reviews lessons learned from numerous community studies and experiences that have employed a community involvement orientation. The global nature of the health promotion movement offers a rich base for understanding the common strategies and the pitfalls involved in mobilizing a community's participation in health campaigns (Mittelmark, 1999). Not all campaigns achieve intended results. Not all citizen participation structures are effective. The following are some of the questions that arise: What are the best approaches to achieve real partnership? What organizing structures (e.g., coalition and lead agency) work best to promote local decision making? How is social change theory integrated into actual practice in the field? How are variables such as community empowerment and capacity building measured? How can communities sustain campaign effects? These and related questions will be discussed within a five-stage community intervention model. The model illustrates how a community-based campaign process unfolds, develops, and sustains intended objectives. Exemplars used in this five-stage process will be drawn principally from the health promotion field, but it should be readily apparent that the general principles and strategies of community organization can be applied to almost any type of community change or campaign focus.

The chapter discusses four major themes: (a) community collaboration, (b) community change theory, (c) a five-stage model of basic strategies in planning and organizing at the community level, and (d) a summary of lessons learned and future research implications.

COMMUNITY COLLABORATION: PERSPECTIVES ON PARTNERSHIP APPROACHES

Examined broadly, the concept of *citizen participation* is a fundamental aspect of civic life and democratic tradition. Active citizen involvement in various social, political, and cultural developments reflects the expectations and aspirations that naturally arise in human societies. Numerous examples of community improvement are initiated through civic action and volunteer effort (sometimes with and sometimes without professional input). When disparate community resources and talents are mobilized for a specific campaign goal, the larger community can be energized for action using all institutional sectors (e.g., media; schools; work sites; and government, business, and civic groups). This intersectorial integration allows for the incorporation of campaign goals throughout several sectors of daily community life. Mittelmark (1999, p. 3) noted, "The social and physical environments at the communitywide level have significant influence on the well-being of individuals who live in the community and who, in turn, influence their environment, thus the well-being of others."

In keeping with the goal of community empowerment and capacity building, many community-based projects use lay volunteers and leaders to deliver campaign interventions. Lasater et al. (1984) showed how church groups could be involved in heart health campaigns. Veblen-Mortenson et al. (1999) illustrate the use of local citizens as advocates in enforcing alcohol sale ordinances for minors. Approximately 50% of Americans volunteer annually ("Review and Outlook," 1999). This citizen pool is an enormous resource of talent and energy and has been used to achieve many of the goals of the health promotion movement. Breslow (1999, p. 11) refers to this movement as "a modern international movement that emerged out of the historical need for a fundamental change in strategy to achieve and maintain health." Citizen contributions are an essential part of this change.

This paradigm shift to communitywide or population-based models of intervention has fostered hundreds of community health promotion and research projects. Mittelmark (1999) completed a comprehensive survey of these many diverse projects and found that community organization strategies are common to most. Another common focus is the importance placed on community analysis prior to campaign implementation. As Fortmann et al. (1995, p. 578) from the Stanford group caution, "There is an urgent need to understand communities better, particularly how communities differ in health status and in their readiness and resources to change health status." Factors to be included in a comprehensive community analysis will be discussed in more detail in Stage 1 of the community intervention model.

The use of community-based organizations and associations to assist in broad public health work, of course, is not a new phenomenon (see Chapter 1, this volume). Starting in the late 1800s, block committees of local mothers were organized in support of early maternal and child health clinic goals (e.g., Hull House in Chicago). The National Citizens' Committee on Prevention of Tuberculosis worked closely with public health professionals to combat infectious diseases in the early 1900s. The National Mental Hygiene movement of the 1930s was a citizen-based group that was instrumental in achieving important reforms in the treatment of the mentally ill. Today, hundreds of voluntary health and social reform groups (e.g., The American Cancer Society and Mothers Against Drunk Driving) bring outstanding volunteer resources to community improvement programs. Internationally, nongovernmental organizations play a similar role in providing citizen input and leadership. One of the pioneering community-based studies to reduce heart disease, the North Karelia Project in Finland (Puska et al., 1985), used the local voluntary heart association as a major partner in conducting the campaign to inform the citizens of very high rates of heart-related mortality in the region. Other groups in agriculture and food processing were also involved. Successful multisectorial interventions depend on cooperation among many partners and stakeholders of the community.

Today, as our understanding of specific social, behavioral, and environmental determinants of population health increases, so also does our appreciation of the importance of broader public and private resources and collaborations required to reduce the burden of chronic illness. Bracht (1999) summarized many of the important (but unfortunately largely negative) national and international health indices (e.g., lower life expectancies, increasing rates of alcoholism, smoking and violence among youth, and millions of AIDS orphans in Africa) that call for immediate and sustained prevention and health promotion efforts. Community-led efforts in addition to strong national budgetary sup-port will be crucial in the next decades to stem and, it is hoped, reverse these trends. Key to such successful efforts is the application of tested social change theories and processes.

COMMUNITY CHANGE THEORY: INTERDISCIPLINARY APPLICATIONS

Figure 27.1 shows Thompson and Kinne's (1999) synthesis of various change theories (e.g., organizational, environmental, and behavioral). The community system "box" in the diagram is the focus of discussion in this chapter, but the dia-gram's reference to the larger external environment box of pivotal events (e.g., loss of sustaining industry in the region, secular trends such as changes in smok-ing norms, or policy influences such as the national managed care movement) can also have dramatic changes on local community life. War, dislocation, and natural disasters are other examples. Often, spontaneous events can occur (civil rights sit-ins in the 1960s and political scandals) that exert considerable pressure for change or reform efforts (Pilisuk, McCallister, & Rothman, 1996).

Whether planned or unplanned, change efforts can produce unintended (of-ten negative) consequences (see Chapter 9, this volume). In one smoking ces-sation campaign in the upper Midwest, adult smokers who stopped smoking (chemically verified) during a community contest period became eligible for a prize drawing that included an all-expenses-paid family vacation trip to Ha-waii. Some teenagers in the study community were instrumental in convincing nonsmoking parents to take up smoking and then quit and become eligible for the contest prize(s). This was not exactly the desired intention of the health promoters who framed the stop smoking intervention.

A unifying construct in the application of social change theory to popula-tion health is the view of the community as a dynamic system in which change or alteration in one segment or institutional sector of the community will influ-ence one or more other sectors. As mentioned earlier, the health promotion movement generally targets multiple sectors (churches, work sites, schools, etc.) of the entire community system to maximize intervention dissemination throughout the broader population. Of course, enhanced marketing or organiz-ing strategies can simultaneously occur in selected sectors (e.g., special out-reach efforts and involvement of Hispanic churches in the religious sectors of a city). In fact, these special activities may be critical to overall program success and durability of program effects. For example, in the Lee County, Florida, Community Breast Screening Project (Worden et al., 1994), a local community group, Partners in Health, was able through continued fund-raising events ($50,000-$80,000 per year) to provide no-cost diagnostic services to lower-income women. Through these initiatives, local empowerment was enhanced and local access to services was improved.

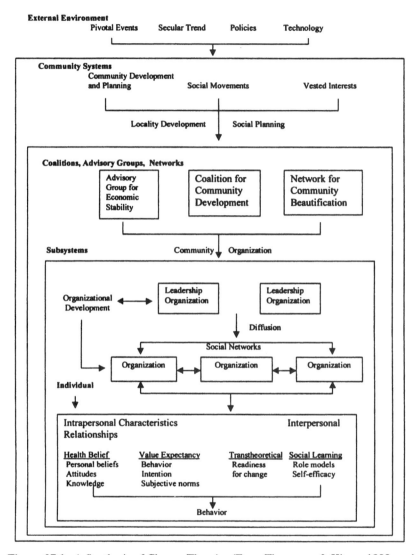

Figure 27.1. A Synthesis of Change Theories (From Thompson & Kinne, 1999, p. 41)

Many of the earlier health promotion projects focused on behavioral change outcomes only (e.g., smoking cessation). The overall results have been mixed (Koepsell, Diehr, Cheadle, & Kristal, 1995; Kottke, 1995; Mittelmark, 1999; Seedhouse, 1997; Shea & Basch, 1990). Recent social advocacy strategies (e.g., stronger enforcement of penalties for proven illegal tobacco or alcohol sales to minors) have offered alternative strategies. Increasingly, both behavioral and social advocacy approaches are being combined in community campaigns.

Another trend is to combine social marketing with community campaigns. Smith (2000) argues that the social marketing approach involves four primary domains (Goldberg, Fishbein, & Middlestadt, 1997; Middlestadt, Schechter, Peyton, & Tjugum, 1997). The first is a philosophy of exchange, in which consumers (or at-risk populations, campaign audiences, etc.) enter into a fair arrangement with providers and campaign sponsors so that both meet their needs. This means that campaign designers must understand these needs and construct messages and interventions that provide exchange value rather than impose their values or presume what constitutes a satisfying exchange. The second is an ongoing, iterative research strategy because needs, subgroups, and external conditions change over time. The third is the "marketing mix," or the appropriate emphasis on the combination of the "4 P's," including product benefits (perceptions, uses, and attributes), price (including all individual, social, and institutional barriers to change), and place (the infrastructure and social system enabling or preventing one from engaging the service, product, or behavior, including training, sales, and advice) (Bryant, Forthofer, Brown, Landis, & McDermott, 2000, p. 64). The fourth is promotion, including not just the traditional campaign message but also user education, interpersonal support, public relations, and conferences, provided through appropriate channels and media. Finally, social marketing emphasizes the importance of positioning the message, product, or service within the context of competing messages, products, services, attitudes, fears, expectations, and norms (such as from friends or advertisements advocating cigarette smoking) and oriented toward relevant and changing audience segments.

More research will be required in the next decade to determine the overall effectiveness of these "newer" combined approaches. (For additional discussion on effectiveness and evaluation of campaign results, see Chapters 6-8 and 31, this volume.)

Finally, in measuring the results of social change efforts, Thompson and Kinne (1999) provide an additional challenge to the next generation of researchers:

> Existing community projects pay little attention to norm and value change and seldom measure such change. . . . The lack of empirical attention paid to changing community norms can be partially attributed to the lack of comprehensive theories explaining how such change occurs. (p. 30)

Ways to accelerate norm change will be especially vital to future health promotion efforts. For example, the increasing number of road rage incidents throughout the United States will most likely be altered only through a persuasive and carefully crafted campaign to reverse aggressive auto driving behaviors and improve speed limit enforcement. Such a campaign (pilot programs are currently under way) will most likely need to combine policy initiatives (e.g., improved highway flow mechanisms and wider deployment of new video monitoring mechanisms) with behaviorally based education and safety messages. The basic strategies employed for campaigns such as this and others are described in the following section.

BASIC STRATEGIES IN ORGANIZING COMMUNITY CAMPAIGNS: A FIVE-STAGE MODEL

Here, we discuss the key aspects of community mobilization and campaign implementation using a five-stage model. A detailed description of the model and the many activities associated with each stage is provided by Bracht, Kingsbury, and Rissel (1999). Here, we highlight the key factors and tasks in each stage, beginning with the first and extremely important phase of community analysis. It should be noted that these stages are overlapping, and some tasks may need to be repeated in later stages. For example, planning tasks for durability of effort should begin in the analysis phase, but progress and finalization of plans need to be assessed in the maintenance and dissemination stages as well.

The combined principles from community-based campaigns and social marketing are being applied to community-based prevention marketing (CBPM) projects such as the University of Florida's Prevention Research Center's program to prevent initiation of smoking and alcohol consumption among middle school students in one county (Bryant et al., 2000). This project team essentially helps bring together and train community partners and coalitions in social marketing concepts and practices. The community's advisory committee, however, mobilizes the community; determines and assesses the resources, contexts, and problems; conducts formative evaluation; develops objectives; chooses the methodologies and interventions; develops a tracking system and dissemination plan; and, to some extent, conducts the evaluations.

Stage 1: Key Tasks in Conducting a Community Analysis

Commitment to community participation in campaigns requires a knowledge of the assets, capacity, and history of a local community. Although all communities share certain definable functions (e.g., social participation and social control), a careful mapping of the community (McKnight, 1988) brings forth the unique qualities, norms, and modes of organization in each community. It is this uniqueness (of both assets and possible deficiencies) that provides the basis for an informed community involvement approach—one that realistically matches goals with citizen readiness, expectations, and resources. Analysis is a critical first step not only in shaping the design of campaign interventions but also in adapting implementation plans to unique community characteristics (e.g., rural vs. urban). The product of community analysis is a dynamic community profile that blends health and illness statistics with demographic, political, and sociocultural factors. A good example is provided by Worden et al. (1994), who discuss the Lee County Breast Screening Program.

Key Task 1: Define the Community

Community is a term that has different meanings and interpretations. Some define community as a psychological bond or relationship that unites individuals in a common goal or experience. Others use community in the geographic or physical sense as a space with political or economic boundaries. Geographical space alone, however, does not tell us all we need to know about community membership. Hillery (1955) studied 94 definitions of community and found that 73% of the definitions agreed that social interaction, area, and common ties were frequently found features.

Rissel and Bracht (1999) discuss the implications of using differing conceptual approaches to the study of the community. Campaigns often focus on geographic localities (towns or neighborhoods) or special population subgroups. Clarity about target audience, geographical boundaries, and so on must be achieved early and in consultation with local representatives. If more than one community in a region is to be involved, patterns of cooperation and commerce among the communities may need special analysis. In some community projects, adjacent towns may lie in different state jurisdictions, thus complicating intervention messages (e.g., information ads on nonsmoking ordinances may differ).

Key Task 2: Initiate Data Collection

Community analysis requires the collection and analysis of a wide range of data to achieve a comprehensive profile of the campaign area or target group. Table 27.1 summarizes these various data needs and the likely sources of such information. Citizens and local organizations are directly involved in this study process. Some of the information required may have already been compiled locally or is available from past community projects in the area. The degree of cooperation in gathering data by local people and organizations is a first indication of community readiness.

Key Task 3: Assess Community Capacity and Readiness for Change

A primary assessment focus in communitywide health promotion programs is the study of social institutions or organizational sectors (education, health, recreation, business and labor, etc.). Knowledge about these institutions is crucial in understanding community resources and the possibilities for coordinating communitywide programs of health action. Leadership persons are often

Table 27.1 Summary of Community Analysis Components and Typical Data Sources

Analysis Question	Typical Data Sources
General community characteristics, structure, and history What are the relevant geographic features? What are its unique concerns, social and health-related community agendas, and recent civic actions?	Wide range of social and economic sources, such as census information, economic development and social service data, and historical and other social indicators
Health-wellness outcomes assessment What are the levels of ill health and disability? Are there any indicators of wellness?	Epidemiological measures; past health or quality of life studies, and regional and national health data sources, including regional or state health departments
Health risk profile What are the behavioral, social, and environmental risks to the population or special subgroups or both?	Local health screening surveys or past risk factor studies from state or national sources and registries; behavioral risk factor telephone surveys
Community health promotion survey What programs, resources, skills, and provider groups already exist? What is the level of participation in these programs? What possibilities exist for collaboration? In what areas is there a need to develop or expand?	Current community inventories used to develop database through contacts with local informants; health departments, local medical clinics and hospitals, and nongovernment organizations
Specialized studies What special target groups or gatekeepers exist? Can they facilitate diffusion of program messages? What do these groups want to do? Who are the people who can help or hinder the project?	Systematic surveys or key informant interviews of special target groups, interviews with organization officials and reputed influentials, and leadership surveys

SOURCE: Rissel and Bracht (1999, p. 65).

the source of this information, and their willingness to cooperate is another indicator of community support and readiness for program initiation. Rissel and Bracht (1999) discuss techniques and approaches used to study leadership patterns.

Community readiness for change can be measured by a combination of factors, including past history of cooperative community action, degree of support and enthusiasm among community influentials for current project, willingness to commit organizational resources, the local skill level (e.g., quit smoking counseling) of lay citizens and professionals available for use in the campaign, and the presence of motivated advocates or visionaries supporting the project.

Stage 2: Key Tasks in Design and Initiation of a Campaign

The design aspects for a collaborative community campaign begin to emerge. A core planning group of citizens and professionals will usually begin the process of establishing a more permanent organizational structure (e.g., coalition) to elicit or coordinate broader citizen support and involvement. This group's responsibilities may also include calling public attention to the data analysis and identified community needs, writing a mission statement, and selecting a community-based project coordinator. Some preliminary decisions will likely have to be made about campaign objectives and initial intervention design(s). Later, these decisions will be approved by the permanent citizen organization.

Key Task 1: Develop an
Organizational Structure for Collaboration

There are several alternative structures for organizing community involvement and participation, including advisory board, coalition, lead agency, and informal network. Thompson (1999) discusses the pros and cons of these various structures. Sometimes, existing agencies or coalitions can be used as collaboration structures for campaigns, thus avoiding the start-up time required for new organizations.

The type of structure chosen should be based on community factors such as culture and history of change efforts, past decision-making styles, and any competing events or programs. Final choice of organizational structure usually rests with the community and its representatives. Some funding agencies, however, often prescribe in advance the community structure most preferred or recommended (e.g., coalition). This can be risky because one model seldom fits all communities. An important lesson learned from earlier demonstration projects is that citizen-based structures are dynamic, and organizational patterns often evolve into new or modified arrangements.

Coalitions (membership of several community groups or health organizations or both) have become increasingly popular structures for implementing community health promotion efforts. This model was used successfully in the 17-state American Stop Smoking Intervention Study (ASSIST) smoking control project of the National Cancer Institute (1996). *Coalition* has been defined as an organization of individuals representing diverse organizations, factions, or constituencies who agree to work together to achieve a goal.

Coalitions often form in response to a specific issue or legislative goal. The major advantage of the coalition is that it involves a breadth and diversity of membership that may occasionally make for strange bedfellows but can cut across ideologies and constituencies to achieve results not attainable by more narrowly focused groups. Bracht et al. (1999) reviewed the literature on coali-

Table 27.2 Factors and Skills Important to the Effectiveness of Partnerships and Coalitions

Factor/Skill	*Definition*
Leadership	The extent to which state and local coalitions have one or more members who are well respected and experienced in organizing group activities, garnering resources, facilitating discussion, motivating others, negotiating, and recruiting new members
Management	The extent to which state and local coalitions have the expertise to effectively manage the meeting logistics, resources, and operations of the coalition
Communication	The degree to which written and verbal communication among state coalition members, committee and task force members, staff, and individuals outside the coalition has been clear, timely, and effective
Conflict resolution	The degree to which friction and tensions arising from turf issues, different personalities, or competing interests of coalition members have been effectively resolved
Perception of fairness	The extent to which state and local coalition members perceive that they are being treated equitably and the different organizations in the coalition are contributing their fair share in terms of resources or work or both
Shared decision making	The degree of influence that state and local coalition members have in determining the policies and actions of the statewide coalitions, and the amount of authority coalition representatives have to make decisions on behalf of the organizations they represent
Perceived benefits versus costs	The degree to which individual members and member organizations on state and local coalitions believe the time they have served has been worthwhile

SOURCE: Bracht, Kingsbury, and Rissell (1999, p. 96).

tion effectiveness and found the functions listed in Table 27.2 to be important to overall coalition productivity. Leadership was the most frequently mentioned asset required to bring about coalition effectiveness. Because territorial issues often surface, organizers must also be skilled in conflict resolution strategies. For additional information about this and other aspects of coalition functioning, see Butterfoss, Goodman, and Wandersman (1993), Dluhy and Kravitz (1990), and Koh (1996).

Key Task 2: Increase Community Participation and
Membership in Organization

The core planning group will be contacting individuals to assess interest in serving on task forces or the executive committee of the new organization. The experience and skill of a paid coordinator or community organizer are frequently used in health promotion programs. The person employed for this purpose must understand how change occurs in communities and must be knowledgeable about local history and values. A local resident or professional is generally preferred. Past experience in facilitating organizational collaboration, including good management skills, is critical. Experience in volunteer deployment is also desired.

Key Task 3: Early Intervention Design and Plans

During this phase of work, collaboration between community groups and outside professionals usually begins on intervention goals and design. A review of data collected from the analysis stage is a good beginning point for such deliberations. A heart disease prevention intervention(s) will require a close examination of prevalence and incidence data. What do people know about heart attacks and their causes? Are professionals well versed in preventive approaches? What should be the focus of intervention work (e.g., nutrition education, exercise, smoking cessation, or rapid treatment)? A task force of citizens and professionals can usually develop a preliminary plan within 2 or 3 months. The plan should also include a preliminary evaluation or monitoring strategy. Pirie's (1999) helpful guide to evaluation strategies in health promotion may be useful here for citizen groups to review. Later, the intervention goals and objectives will need the approval and support of the wider community group as mentioned previously.

Stage 3: Campaign Implementation

Implementation turns theory and ideas into action, translating design into effectively operating programs. Organizations and citizens are mobilized and involved in the planning of a sequential set of activities that will accomplish campaign objectives. Written intervention action plans with specific timelines have been shown to be a critical forerunner of successful change efforts (Fawcett et al., 1995). Intervention cost estimates should be included in the plan, along with monitoring and feedback strategies. The key element in this stage is the determination of priority intervention activities and the focusing of efforts for maximum impact. On the basis of experience from other community projects, it has been learned that some community members may want to rush the intervention implementation process. There is a tendency to want to "jump in with both feet" and to get the project going. Organizers need to channel enthusiasm, helping task forces and work groups to select, evaluate, and plan for best practices in implementation. Although such "delays" can dampen the enthusiasm of more action-oriented volunteers, it is probably better to have to deal with this motivational issue than to see interest and commitment to the project "dampened" by early reports of negative results of interventions caused by poorly operationalized and delivered campaign strategies.

Key Task 1: Clarify Roles and Responsibilities of All Partners

Complex community campaigns require the coordinated effort of many people and resources. Role clarification at the outset is essential if the project is to unfold smoothly and systematically. For example, in a community stop smoking campaign, how will the role of the local heart association be coordinated with the ongoing antismoking activities of the American Lung Association? A written understanding of the intervention role(s) is often helpful, especially in large coalition-led programs.

A formal process, called responsibility charting (explained in detail by Bracht, 1999, p. 99), helps participants to review approximately 30 tasks associated with campaign implementation—such as determine goals and priorities, community and public relations, staff hiring, design evaluation strategies, and plan for durability—and decide on which person or group will be accountable for completion of required activities.

Key Task 2: Provide Orientation and Training

Effective citizen and volunteer involvement usually requires some level of additional training and skill development. For example, special classes in smoking cessation techniques for community professionals may be in order. Such training adds to community capacity building and also enhances the likelihood of the durability of ongoing campaign and community objectives.

Key Task 3: Refine the Intervention Plan to the Local Situation

No matter how good an intervention looks on paper or how successful it was reported in the literature, when it is implemented in a community it must speak that community's language (Vincent, Clearle, Johnson, & Sharpe, 1988). The approaches and messages must be acceptable to the community. For example, Ramirez (1997) and colleagues developed a most useful training manual on mass media messages and community outreach for minority groups. Their work shows how to better integrate community values into the programs, materials, and messages of the campaign.

Key Task 4: Generate Broad Citizen Participation

Throughout the implementation process, continuing efforts to reach out to people and encourage their participation are required. Special attention to ways of involving minority communities may be needed if there is a history of noninclusion or lack of participation in health projects. Interviews with key community minority participants will help in this process and shed light on current or past difficulties with trust or collaboration or both (Kone & Sullivan, 1998).

Stage 4: Program Maintenance Consolidation

During this stage, the citizen organization should be developing a solid foundation and acceptance in the community. Problems in implementation (e.g., media misses coverage of certain key events) will obviously have been encountered, but an indicator of community capacity building will be the ability to overcome and improve future intervention activities. Campaign program elements should be more fully incorporated into the established structures of the community (e.g., exercise programs become a regular part of work site culture). Task forces of the local citizen organization need to reassess past efforts and determine any new tasks or directions of the program.

Key Task 1: Maintain High Levels of Volunteer Effort

Turnover of volunteers and even of paid staff is to be expected in multiyear projects. To counteract this, one needs to establish a plan to identify, recruit, and involve new people in the project on an ongoing basis. Seek out new members. New sources of energy and commitment can be helpful to volunteers who may be experiencing some "burnout" characteristics. Florin and Wandersman (1990) found that participation was more prevalent in people who were concerned about their neighborhood, had more experience in community leadership, and believed that other competent colleagues could be engaged to reach project goals. Peer support and morale are critical factors in group cohesion and continued participation. Appreciation letters to volunteers, celebratory luncheons, and training retreats are ways of enhancing volunteer morale and commitment to the project.

Key Task 2: Continue to Integrate
Intervention Activities Into Community Networks

Integration of intervention activities into established community structures creates a broad context for the acceptance and adoption of health-promoting behaviors and norms. In a Midwest heart disease prevention project, local churches initiated a monthly "exercise Sunday" project into their routine service schedule. The project encouraged families to leave the car at home and walk, bike, or jog to church. Key influentials and stakeholders often assist in this kind of organizational adoption and integration of programs. For more discussion of this process, see Rissel, Finnegan, and Bracht (1995).

Stage 5: Dissemination and Durability

In this last stage, the strategic dissemination of information on project results and the finalization of plans for durability of intervention efforts are the key considerations. Communities and citizens need to receive clear, succinct messages describing what has been accomplished and what continuing effort may be required. Such messages are reinforcing when community influentials and decision makers, as opposed to professional experts, are involved in their presentation. How this dissemination process occurs is a basic element of a durability plan along with a vision for future programming.

Key Task 1: Reassessment of
Campaign Activities and Outcomes

Final results of campaigns may not always be available in time for citizens and communities to act on future directions. Process or formative evaluations that have been done during the campaign (e.g., participation rates in health-risk screening programs) can help assist the project group in reassessing interventions that have worked and those that have experienced difficulty. Steps in implementation can be retraced and analyzed. A "report to the community" should be drafted and submitted to the overall citizen group for review and comment. When complete, this report on campaign results becomes the foundation of a durability plan. The CBPM project team discussed earlier is evaluating the CBPM approach (Bryant, 2000). The process evaluation is assessing the feasibility of the elements, community perceptions of the value of the elements, and the extent to which the project is being managed in accord with community-based research and action. The impact evaluation is assessing changes in community competence, durability and sustainability, control and social capital, the use of social and prevention marketing in other community problems, and the extent to which the smoking prevention objectives are met. The results will be used to redesign the CBPM model and processes.

Key Task 2: Refine the Durability Plan

Essentially, the citizen group needs to address several important questions: What has been accomplished to date and what do citizens desire to continue? What is the vision of the project for the future? What human resources would be required to continue interventions or modifications of same? Are any new skills required for the future and what kinds of trainings might be required to finalize community capacity for maintaining such efforts? Finally, what kind of citizen structure will work for the future? The process of answering these questions may take several weeks or months, so it should be started as soon as possible.

Key Task 3: Update the Community Analysis

Part of durability planning may require updating the community analysis and profile. This involves searching for changes that have occurred in leadership, resources, and organizational relationships in the community. Key community members, opinion leaders, and organizations in a community will change over time. Reviewing these changes may point to a need for new collaborators and for efforts to recruit new board and task force members. On the basis of this new review of resources, programs are modified, expanded, abandoned, or all three. Thompson (1999) developed a strategic planning model to be used by communities that wish to develop a detailed plan for durability of project effort.

SUMMARY OF LESSONS LEARNED AND FUTURE RESEARCH IMPLICATIONS

As community health promotion programs have proliferated and expanded nationally and internationally, a common set of essential planning and organizing tasks has emerged from these community mobilization and implementation experiences. Programs in dissimilar locales and with different goals encounter common concerns that must be anticipated and planned for. The following are the most common issues and tasks that occur: (a) selecting broadly representative community participants, (b) establishing an effective organizational partnership structure, (c) achieving campaign mission clarity and realistic objectives, (d) identifying community assets and resistance factors, (e) establishing evaluation and tracking mechanisms early, (f) managing and reinforcing volunteer involvement, (g) conducting ongoing training and skill(s) development, (h) recruiting a community organizer or facilitator with appropriate competencies and experience, and (i) securing resources for the durability of campaign effect(s). All these factors have been discussed within the five-stage model.

The participatory community approach to campaigns in health promotion seeks to stimulate and fuse citizen energies, interests, and resources into a collective response for change. Often, this is done in collaboration with professional or research groups, but the decision-making role of community groups should remain paramount. The theories and principles of community organization and empowerment are central to this approach. The lessons learned about citizen and community participation in health promotion draw from a wide range of national and international studies and experiences (Thompson,

Corbet, Bracht, & Pehacek, 1993). Key factors that seem to contribute most to successful citizen mobilization and community collaboration include the following:

1. There must be an early commitment of project leaders to partnership and community development approaches.
2. Decision-making authority of citizen groups should be clearly defined. Resources to carry out designated roles and functions must be available, adequate, and include skill development training opportunities.
3. A strong volunteer management and training program must be in place at the start of a campaign. This includes regularly scheduled performance assessments, clearly stated time commitments, and planned recognition and celebratory events.
4. There must be timely use of conflict resolution strategies when disagreements occur regarding project goals, research objectives, or implementation issues.

These lessons learned have implications for future research directions. Some have been mentioned earlier, such as the challenge to invest more scholarly investigation into community norm(s) change and to the evaluation of mixed strategies that combine both behavioral change and advocacy and policy change. Concern was also raised about the need to improve community analysis methods to better define populations at-risk and target limited resources. In addition, improvement in qualitative measures (Mitchell & Radford, 1996) must continue, along with special emphasis on community empowerment indices (Minkler & Wallerstein, 1997). Labonte (1993) believes that qualitative forms of documentation are often more appropriate and ethically consistent forms of accountability in community or partnership development work. Integrating qualitative and quantitative measures of accountability will remain a central challenge to community-based research (MacNair, 1998). On the basis of the lessons of the past two decades of community studies, Fortmann et al. (1995) recommend that

> the emphasis of future studies should shift from whether communitywide change is possible to improving methods of community organization and health education, reaching diverse subpopulations that are at high risk, incorporating ongoing efforts into health care and other social structures and maintaining regulatory and environmental changes that enhance the effects of health education. (p. 580)

REFERENCES

ASSIST Working Group on Durability. (1996). *Turning point for tobacco control: Toward a national strategy to prevent and control tobacco use.* Rockville, MD: Prospect Associates.

Bracht, N. (Ed.). (1999). *Health promotion at the community level: New advances* (2nd ed.). Thousand Oaks, CA: Sage.

Bracht, N., Kingsbury, L., & Rissel, C. (1999). A five stage community organization model for health promotion: Empowerment and partnership strategies. In N. Bracht (Ed.), *Health promotion at the community level: New advances* (2nd ed., pp. 83-104). Thousand Oaks, CA: Sage.

Breslow, L. (1999). Foreword. In N. Bracht (Ed.), *Health promotion at the community level: New advances* (2nd ed.). Thousand Oaks, CA: Sage.

Bryant, C., Forthofer, M., Brown, K. Mc., Landis, D., & McDermott, R. (2000). Community-based prevention marketing: The next steps in disseminating behavior change. *American Journal of Health Behavior, 24*(1), 61-68.

Butterfoss, F., Goodman, R., & Wandersman, A. (1993). Community coalitions for prevention and health promotion. *Health Education Research: Theory and Practice, 8*(3), 315-330.

Dluhy, M., & Kravitz, S. (1990). *Building coalitions in the human services.* Newbury Park, CA: Sage.

Fawcett, S. B., Paine-Andrews, A., Francisco, V. T., Schultz, J. A., Richter, K. P., Lewis, R. K., Williams, E. L., Harris, K. J., Berkley, J. Y., Lopez, C. M., & Fisher, J. L. (1995). Using empowerment theory in collaborative partnerships for community health and development. *American Journal of Community Psychology, 23,* 677-697.

Florin, P., & Wandersman, A. (1990). An introduction to citizen participation, voluntary organizations, and community development: Insights for empowerment through research. *American Journal of Community Psychology, 18*(1), 41-53.

Fortmann, S., Flora, J., Winkleby, M., Schooler, C., Taylor, C., & Farquhar, J. (1995). Community intervention trials: Reflections on the Stanford five-city experience. *American Journal of Epidemiology, 142,* 576-586.

Goldberg, M., Fishbein, M., & Middlestadt, S. (Eds.). (1997). *Social marketing: Theoretical and practical perspectives.* Mahwah, NJ: Lawrence Erlbaum.

Green, L. (1990). Contemporary developments in health promotion: Definitions and challenges. In N. Bracht (Ed.), *Health promotion at the community level* (pp. 29-44). Newbury Park, CA: Sage.

Hillery, J. (1955). Definitions of community: Areas of agreement. *Rural Sociology, 20*(2), 118-127.

Koepsell, T., Diehr, P., Cheadle, A., & Kristal, A. (1995). Invited commentary: Symposium of community intervention trials. *American Journal of Epidemiology, 142,* 594-599.

Koh, H. (1996). An analysis of the successful 1992 Massachusetts tobacco tax initiative. *Tobacco Control, 5,* 220-225.

Kone, A., & Sullivan, M. (1998). *The community interview project: Promoting collaboration between communities and researchers.* Seattle, WA: King County Department of Public Health.

Kottke, T. (1995). Community-based heart disease prevention: The American experience. In P. Puska, J. Tuomilehto, A. Nissinen, & E. Vartiaianen (Eds.), *The North Karelia Project: 20 year results and experiences* (pp. 331-343). Helsinki: National Public Health Institute.

Labonte, R. (1993, July/August). Community development and partnerships. *Canadian Journal of Public Health, 84*(4), 237-240.

Lasater, T., Abrams, D., Artz, L., Beaudin, P., Cabrera, L., Elder, J., Ferreira, A., Knisley, P., Peterson, G., Rodrigues, A., Rosenberg, P., Snow, R., & Carleton, R. (1984). Lay volunteer delivery of a community-based cardiovascular risk factor change program: The Pawtucket experiment. In J. D. Matarazzo, S. H. Weiss, J. A. Herd, N. E. Miller, & S. W. Weiss (Eds.), *Behavioral health: A handbook of health enhancement and disease prevention* (pp. 1166-1170). New York: Wiley.

MacNair, R. (Ed.). (1998). *Research strategies for community practice.* Binghamton, NY: Haworth.

McKnight, J. (1988). *Mapping community capacity.* Evanston, IL: Northwestern University, Center for Urban Affairs and Policy Research.

Middlestadt, S., Schechter, C., Peyton, J., & Tjugum, B. (1997). Community involvement in health planning: Lessons learned from practicing social marketing in a context of community control, participation, and ownership. In M. Goldberg, M. Fishbein, & S. Middlestadt (Eds.), *Social marketing: Theoretical and practical perspectives* (pp. 291-312). Mahwah, NJ: Lawrence Erlbaum.

Minkler, M., & Wallerstein, N. (1997). Improving health through community organization and community building. In K. Glanz, F. M. Lewis, & B. K. Rimer (Eds.), *Health behaviour and health education: Theory, research and practice* (2nd ed.). San Francisco: Jossey-Bass.

Mitchell, T., & Radford, J. (1996). Rethinking research relationships in qualitative research. *Canadian Journal of Community Mental Health, 15*(1), 49-59.

Mittelmark, M. (1999). Health promotion at the community-wide level: Lessons from diverse perspectives. In N. Bracht (Ed.), *Health promotion at the community level: New advances* (2nd ed., pp. 3-28). Thousand Oaks, CA: Sage.

Pilisuk, M., McCallister, J., & Rothman, J. (1996). Coming together for action: The challenge of contemporary grassroots community organizing. *Journal of Social Issues, 52*(1), 15-37.

Pirie, P. (1999). Evaluating community health promotion programs: Basic questions and approaches. In N. Bracht (Ed.), *Health promotion at the community level: New advances* (2nd ed., pp. 127-134). Thousand Oaks, CA: Sage.

Puska, P., Nissinen, A., Tuomilehto, J., Salonen, J. T., Koskela, K., McAlister, A., Kottke, T., Maccoby, N., & Farquhar, J. (1985). The community-based strategy to prevent coronary heart disease: Conclusions from the ten years of the North Karelia Project. *Annual Review of Public Health, 6,* 147-193.

Ramirez, A. (1997). *En accion training manual* (NIH Publication No. 97-4260). Bethesda, MD: National Cancer Institute.

Review and outlook. (1999, December 17). *Wall Street Journal,* p. 17.

Rissel, C., & Bracht, N. (1999). Assessing community needs, resources and readiness: Building on strengths. In N. Bracht (Ed.), *Health promotion at the community level: New advances* (2nd ed., pp. 59-71). Thousand Oaks, CA: Sage.

Rissel, C., Finnegan, J., Jr., & Bracht, N. (1995). Evaluating quality and sustainability: Issues and insights from the Minnesota Heart Health Program. *Health Promotion International, 10*(3), 199-207.

Seedhouse, D. (1997). *Health promotion: Philosophy, prejudice and practice.* Chichester, UK: Wiley.

Shea, S., & Basch, C. (1990). A review of five major community-based cardiovascular disease prevention programs. Part I: Rationale, design, and theoretical framework. *American Journal of Health Promotion, 4,* 202-213.

Smith, W. (2000). Social marketing: An evolving definition. *American Journal of Health Behavior, 24*(1), 11-17.

Thompson, B., Corbett, K., Bracht, N., & Pehacek, T. (1993). Lessons learned from the mobilization of communities in the Community Intervention Trial for Smoking Cessation (COMMIT). *Health Promotion International, 8,* 69-83.

Thompson, B., & Kinne, S. (1999). Social change theory: Applications to community health. In N. Bracht (Ed.), *Health promotion at the community level: New advances* (2nd ed., pp. 29-46). Thousand Oaks, CA: Sage.

Thompson, B., & Winner, C. (1999). Durability of community intervention programs: Definitions, empirical studies and strategic planning. In N. Bracht (Ed.), *Health promotion at the community level: New advances* (2nd ed., pp. 137-154). Thousand Oaks, CA: Sage.

Veblen-Mortenson, S., Rissel, C., Perry, C., Forster, J., Wolfson, M., & Finnegan, J., Jr. (1999). Lessons learned from project Northland: Community organization in rural communities. In N. Bracht (Ed.), *Health promotion at the community level: New advances* (2nd ed., pp. 105-117). Thousand Oaks, CA: Sage.

Vincent, M., Clearle, A., Johnson, C., & Sharpe, P. (1988). *Reducing unintended adolescent pregnancy through school-community educational interventions: A South Carolina case study.* Atlanta: U.S. Department of Health and Human Services, Public Health Service, Centers for Disease Control.

Worden, J., Mickey, R., Flynn, B., Costanza, M., Vacek, P., Skelly, J., Lloyd, C., Landis, D., Myer, D., & Noonan, M. (1994). Development of a community breast screening promotion program using baseline data. *Preventive Medicine, 23,* 267-275.

28

The Entertainment-Education Strategy in Communication Campaigns[1]

Arvind Singhal
Everett M. Rogers

This chapter summarizes lessons learned about the use of entertainment-education in communication campaigns dealing with family planning, gender equality, HIV prevention, and environmental conservation. A communication campaign (a) intends to achieve specific effects, (b) in a relatively large number of individuals, (c) within a specified period of time, and (d) through an organized set of communication activities (Rogers & Storey, 1987).

THE ENTERTAINMENT-EDUCATION STRATEGY

The entertainment-education strategy abrogates the needless dichotomy in almost all mass media content—that mass media programs must either be entertaining or educational (Fischer & Melnik, 1979; Singhal & Rogers, 1989). *Entertainment-education* is the process of purposely designing and implementing a media message to both entertain and educate to increase audience members' knowledge about an educational issue, create favorable attitudes, and change overt behavior (Singhal & Rogers, 1999). Entertainment-education seeks to capitalize on the popular appeal of entertainment media to show individuals how they can live safer, healthier, and happier lives (Piotrow, Kincaid, Rimon, & Rinehart, 1997; Singhal & Brown, 1996).

If implemented correctly, the entertainment-education strategy can offer important advantages to development officials of national governments, broadcasting networks, educators, commercial sponsors, and audiences. The entertainment-education strategy often provides an opportunity for an educational message to pay for itself. Thus, commercial and social interests can both be met.

THE RISE OF ENTERTAINMENT-EDUCATION

The idea of combining entertainment with education goes as far back in human history as the timeless art of storytelling. For thousands of years, music, drama, dance, and various folk media have been used in many countries for recreation, devotion, reformation, and instructional purposes. "Entertainment-education," however, is a relatively new concept in that its conscious use in radio, television, comic books, and popular music has received attention only in the past few decades (Singhal & Rogers, 1999; Valente, Kim, Lettenmaier, Glass, & Dibba, 1994).

In radio, the earliest well-known illustration of the entertainment-education strategy occurred in 1951 when the British Broadcasting Corporation began broadcasting *The Archers,* a radio soap opera that carried educational messages about agricultural development (*The Archers* is still broadcast and addresses contemporary educational issues such as HIV/AIDS prevention and environmental conservation). The entertainment-education strategy in television was discovered more or less by accident in Peru in 1969 when the television soap opera *Simplemente María* was broadcast (Singhal, Obregon, & Rogers, 1994). The main character, María, a migrant to the capital city, worked during the day and was enrolled in adult literacy classes in the evening. She then climbed the socioeconomic ladder of success through her hard work, strong motivation, and skills with a Singer sewing machine. *Simplemente María* attracted very high audience ratings, and the sale of Singer sewing machines boomed in Peru. So did the number of young girls enrolling in adult literacy and sewing classes. When *Simplemente María* was broadcast in other Latin American nations, similar effects occurred. Audience identification with María was very strong, especially among poor, working-class women: She represented a Cinderella role model for upward social mobility.

Inspired by the audience success and the unintentional educational effects of *Simplemente María,* Miguel Sabido, a television writer-producer-director in Mexico, developed a methodology for entertainment-education soap operas. Between 1975 and 1982, Sabido produced seven entertainment-education television soap operas that helped motivate enrollment in adult literacy classes, encourage the adoption of family planning, and promote gender equality (Nariman, 1993). Sabido's entertainment-education soap operas were also commercial hits for Televisa, the Mexican television network, earning audience ratings equivalent to those of Televisa's other soap operas.

The idea of combining education with entertainment in the mass media has since resulted in more than 100 projects in 50 countries, spurred by the efforts of institutions such as Population Communications International, a nongovernmental organization headquartered in New York City, and Johns Hopkins University's Population Communication Services. The entertainment-education strategy has been widely re-created by creative media professionals in television, radio, film, print, and theater. For example, Dr. Garth Japhet in South Africa developed the long-running "Soul City" mass media campaign, providing an entertainment-education model for health promotion that is advocated by the European Union and United Nations agencies such as UNICEF and UNAIDS.

KEY ELEMENTS IN AN ENTERTAINMENT-EDUCATION CAMPAIGN

An entertainment-education campaign includes several integrated sets of activities.

Creating a Moral Framework and Values Grid

Prior to launching an entertainment-education intervention, a "moral framework" of the specific educational issues to be emphasized in an entertainment-education intervention and a values grid for the educational messages are created. The moral framework is usually derived from a nation's constitution, its legal statutes, or documents such as the United Nations' *Declaration of Human Rights,* to which the country is a signatory. For instance, a constitutional right expressed as "All citizens will have an equal opportunity for personal and professional development" provides the moral basis to produce media messages about gender equality. The values grid, in turn, is derived from the moral framework and contains various positive and negative statements, such as "It is good to send a girl child to school" and "It is bad to not send a girl child to school." The values grid specifies the exact behavior changes that are to be encouraged or discouraged in the entertainment-education project such as a soap opera. It also constitutes a formal statement signed by government, religious, and media officials pledging their support of the educational values promoted in the intervention. For example, Sabido asked Catholic Church leaders in Mexico to help develop the values grid for his telenovela about family planning.

Formative Evaluation Research

Formative evaluation is a type of research that is conducted while an activity, process, or system is being developed or is ongoing to improve its effectiveness (Rogers, 1986, p. 193; see Chapters 6-8, this volume). Research-based information about the characteristics, needs, and preferences of a target audience can sharpen the design of entertainment-education. For example, a formative evaluation survey in Tanzania in 1992 found that many adults, including those using the rhythm method of contraception, did not know the days in the women's menstrual cycle when fertility was most likely. Correct information was then provided in a radio soap opera, *Twende na Wakati (Let's Go With the Times)* (Rogers et al., 1999).

Theory-Based Message Design

The messages for the entertainment-education intervention are designed on the basis of various theories of behavior change. For example, Bandura's (1977, 1997) social learning theory is often used; it states that learning can occur through observing media role models, and that this vicarious learning usually is more effective than direct experiential learning.

Sabido's entertainment-education soap operas in Mexico had three types of role models: (a) those who support the educational value (positive role models), (b) those who reject this value (negative role models), and (c) those who change from negative to positive behavior (transitional role models) during the soap opera's broadcasts. Transitional characters start out as negative role models or at least are unsure about adopting the desired behavior. When transitional characters change their attitudes and behaviors toward the educational value, their transformation is reinforced and explained in the epilogues (which are brief statements by a prestigious individual who connects the episode to individuals' lives). Each time a positive role model or a transitional character performs the socially desirable behavior (such as adopting family planning), he or she is rewarded immediately in the storyline. Each time a negative role model performs a socially undesirable behavior, he or she is immediately punished. For example, in the Tanzanian radio soap opera, *Twende na Wakati,* Mkwaju (literally "walking stick") is a negative role model for sexual responsibility; he is a truck driver who is promiscuous, sleeps with commercial sex workers, and contracts AIDS. He is punished by losing his prestigious job, his family, and eventually his life (Rogers et al., 1999). When transitional characters change their behavior, audience members may be influenced to follow their lead.

Multimedia Broadcasts and Campaign Activities

The effects of entertainment-education are greater when various supplementary activities are part of an integrated communication campaign. For instance, in the late 1980s, Johns Hopkins University's Population Communication Services used rock music songs to promote sexual responsibility among teenagers in the Philippines, and the songs were accompanied by print and broadcast advertisements, personal appearances by the two singers, label buttons urging "Say No to Sex," posters, and a telephone hotline ("Dial-a-Friend"). These messages constituted a coordinated communication campaign rather than just a popular song featuring lyrics with an educational message. Although the cost and effort invested in a total campaign are greater than those for just the entertainment-education message, the synergy of the communication campaign elements often leads to greater effects in changing human behavior (Piotrow et al., 1997).

Process and Summative Evaluation

Entertainment-education campaigns can be strengthened through such process evaluation activities as analysis of audience individuals' letters (the epilogue-giver usually encourages audience members to write letters), monitoring of clinic data (e.g., to track family planning adoption), and content analysis of the entertainment-education messages (to determine if the scripts are consistent with the moral framework and the values grid). Feedback can thus be provided in a timely manner to entertainment-education producers for appropriate midcourse corrections. Summative evaluation research can measure the effects of the entertainment-education campaign on audience behaviors (see Chapter 6, this volume). Often, multimethod triangulation is employed to ascertain effects. For example, an entertainment-education radio soap opera, *Tinka Tinka Sukh* (*Happiness Lies in Small Pleasures*), in Hindi-speaking India was evaluated by a field experiment (using pre-post, treatment-control audience surveys), content analysis of the episodes and viewers' letters, and a case study of one village in which the program had strong effects (Papa et al., in press).

SOUL CITY:
AN ENTERTAINMENT-EDUCATION EXEMPLAR

Soul City is an exemplary, ongoing entertainment-education campaign in South Africa. In the late 1980s, Dr. Garth Japhet, a young medical doctor, was assigned to a rural health clinic in South Africa's Natal Province.[2] While treating poor, rural patients, Japhet realized that South Africa harbored "developing" country health problems in a "developed" country environment: HIV prevalence among adult South Africans was high (approximately 10%), and young children in rural areas often died of diarrhea. This dismal health record existed despite a highly developed mass media system in South Africa: Approximately 70% of South Africans regularly watch television, 93% regularly listen to radio, and 50% regularly read newspapers and magazines (Community Agency for Social Enquiry [CASE], 1995).

Japhet noted that the health promotion activities in the South African media were inadequate and mainly slogan based. There was a Tuberculosis Day, an AIDS Day, a Malaria Day, and so on. Such health promotion efforts lacked *sustainability,* the degree to which the effects of a program continue after the intervention ends. Research did not play an important role in health promotion. Although South Africa had a robust advertising industry, lessons from advertising and social marketing were not being applied in health communication campaigns. Furthermore, institutional partnerships between the media, the government, and the private sector did not exist for health promotion; the health ministry usually implemented programs in a top-down manner. Japhet also realized that despite a wealth of mass media talent and resources, there was little indigenous drama on South African television or radio.

In 1992, Japhet established Soul City, a nongovernmental organization whose mission was to harness the mass media for promoting good health. Intuitively, he realized that for media-based health promotion interventions to be sustainable, they had to be popular, attract the highest possible prime-time audience, and be of top-notch quality. He also realized that the institutional partnerships between government, media, private corporations, and donor agencies had to be designed so as to be "win-win"—that is, commercial and social interests could both be honored. Therefore, entertainment-education was placed at the core of Soul City's health promotion strategy. Research, both formative and summative, was to undergird this entertainment-education focus: "It is research that distinguishes 'edu-tainment' from pure entertainment" (Japhet & Goldstein, 1997b).

Soul City is a unique example of entertainment-education in that it represents a series of integrated, ongoing mass media activities, year after year. Each year, a series of mass media interventions is implemented, including the flagship *Soul City,* a 13-part prime-time television drama series that runs for 3 months and promotes specific health education issues. Simultaneously, a 60-episode radio drama series is broadcast daily (Monday through Friday) during prime time in eight South African languages. Although the story in the radio drama is different from that of the television program, the health issues and topics addressed in it are the same. Once the television and radio series are broadcast, 2.25 million health education booklets, designed around the popular TV series' characters, are distributed free of cost to select target audience groups. The booklets are serialized by 12 major newspapers.

The first *Soul City* television series, broadcast in 1994, focused on maternal and child health and on HIV prevention and control. The second series, broadcast in 1996, focused on HIV and tuberculosis prevention, housing and urban reform, alcohol abuse, and domestic violence. The third series, broadcast in 1997, dealt with HIV prevention and control, alcohol and tobacco abuse, and domestic violence. Finally, the fourth series, broadcast in 1999, focused on violence against women, AIDS and youth sexuality, hypertension, and personal finance and small business management. Issues of national priority other than health (e.g., housing reform and entrepreneurship) are also woven into the *Soul City* storyline.

Audience Popularity

How popular are the Soul City mass media interventions? The *Soul City* television series emerged as the number one rated television drama series in South Africa (Japhet & Goldstein, 1997b). The prime-time radio series in eight languages also earned very high audience ratings. The Soul City year-long health campaign reaches an estimated half (more than 20 million) of South Africa's population, including 8 million adults.

By using a multimedia approach, Soul City helps build a campaign atmosphere that is sustained throughout the year. Each medium reinforces the popularity of the *Soul City* television series while appealing to a somewhat different target audience. For instance, television reaches urban viewers, whereas radio broadcasts reach rural listeners. Furthermore, each medium reinforces the health education messages of the others in a synergistic process. For instance, booklets and newspapers provide more detailed information on a health topic than is possible on television or on radio. Such a multimedia strategy helps facilitate the brokering of media partnerships: "Print wants to be involved because television is involved; radio wants to come aboard because print is on board" (Japhet & Goldstein, 1997b).

Soul City recognizes that overt behavior change is facilitated when audience members talk to one another, as has been found for other entertainment-education interventions (Rogers et al., 1999). Therefore, after the television and radio series are broadcast, several campaign activities are implemented to keep people talking. High-quality education packets, produced cooperatively by curriculum specialists and creative designers, are targeted to adult and youth populations nationwide. The adult packet includes the health education booklet (mentioned previously), comic books that are based on the story of the television series, audiotapes of the comic books, *Soul City* posters, and a facilitator's guide to maximize impact. The youth packets, in keeping with audience needs, are geared toward building life skills competencies and consist of a comic book based on the television series and also four workbooks that address issues of personal responsibility, self-identity, personal relationships, and so on. They also include a facilitator's guide for use in high schools. The credibility of the Soul City "brand name," and the popularity of its media programs, is harnessed in additional initiatives such as the "Soul City Search for Stars" (to recruit talent for the next year's television and radio series), the "Soul City Health Care Worker of the Year" (to recognize outstanding outreach workers), and "Soul Citizens" (recognizing outstanding youth who engage in community development activities). In addition, Soul City has struck a partner relationship with 12 journalists, representing the most influential South African newspapers, who regularly publish health education features derived from Soul City's activities. By carrying out these multiple health promotion activities, Soul City has emerged as a highly credible brand name in South Africa, a reputation it uses to its advantage (Japhet, 1999).

The Soul City health promotion strategy rests on producing high-quality media materials. The best scriptwriters, actors, cartoonists, and producers are hired and paid at market rate or better. The *Soul City* television series is broadcast at 8 p.m., a prime-time slot during which one third of South Africa's population is tuned in (in contrast, the non-prime-time educational slots on South African television earn ratings of only 2% or 3%). Japhet (as quoted in Japhet & Goldstein, 1997b) explained, "So our media materials have to not just compete with the best. . . . They have to be the best."

The ongoing, year-by-year nature of Soul City's health promotion activities provides several advantages. Soul City's media interventions serve as a resource for various health and development groups in South Africa to piggyback issues of national priority without reinventing the research-production-partnership wheel, as happens when each new health or development initiative is launched. More important, by broadcasting a recurrent television and radio series, Soul City avoids the problem of *audience lag,* the time taken to build a sizable and dedicated audience for a new media program. A highly watched *Soul City* television series in a previous year ensures a large audience at the beginning of the following season. The second, third, and fourth *Soul City* series (broadcast in 1996, 1997, and 1999, respectively) earned high audience ratings from the beginning (Japhet, 1999).

Evaluation Research

Formative and summative research are key to designing and evaluating Soul City's mass media interventions. Formative research is conducted to identify health issues of national priority and to ensure that the mass media interventions can be backed up at the ground level by the needed infrastructure. Summative research procedures include gathering ratings and viewership data and conducting before and after national and regional sample surveys to determine the effects of the television, radio, and print interventions. Summative research evaluation reports show that the Soul City mass media interventions spur high levels of interpersonal communication among audience members, increasing knowledge about health issues, promoting more positive attitudes toward them, and contributing to behavior change on the part of audience members (CASE, 1995; Japhet & Goldstein, 1997a). For instance, in 1994, during the first year of the Soul City campaign, more than 1 million black South African adults reported changing their high-risk behavior, inspired by the media role models (CASE, 1995).

The total cost incurred by Soul City for 1 year of multimedia materials, including the 13-episode *Soul City* television series, the 60-episode radio series in eight local South African languages, 2.25 million booklets, plus marketing, advertising, and public relations activities, is $3.5 million. How is this money raised? Approximately 25% is provided by the South African government, 25% by international donor agencies such as the European Union and

UNICEF, 25% by corporations such as British Petroleum and Old Mutual, and the remaining 25% by the broadcast media. The key reason for Soul City's effectiveness is these partnerships with government, media, corporate, and donor agencies: "Partnerships make this intervention possible. . . . The more you work together, the more people understand the intervention, and the stronger the partnership gets. . . . Also, the expertise of the technical production staff improves" (Japhet & Goldstein, 1997b). Japhet aptly calls this process "the cycle of positive reinforcement" (Japhet & Goldstein, 1997b).

Soul City is mostly a research and management organization. It coordinates the activities of its various corporate, government, media, and donor partners. Its employees do not directly produce, direct, or publish its health communication materials. They commission them from professionals, and through research they ensure high quality. Soul City owns the media messages that are produced (and thus any aftermarket and syndication sales), and it pays the bills. This role gives it the power to "veto" a product if it does not meet high standards.

The reach of Soul City extends beyond South Africa. In partnership with UNICEF, which considers the Soul City experience as a "best practice," Soul City materials are distributed in neighboring Botswana, Zimbabwe, Lesotho, Swaziland, Namibia, and Zambia. Research evaluations show that the Soul City materials are highly popular in these countries, and audiences find them to be culturally shareable (Japhet & Goldstein, 1997b; Singhal & Svenkerud, 1994). African countries such as Nigeria, Ghana, and Malawi have also requested Soul City materials for local use.

THE ETHICS OF ENTERTAINMENT-EDUCATION

The entertainment-education strategy involves several ethical dilemmas (Brown & Singhal, 1990, 1998; Cambridge, McLaughlin, & Rota, 1995). *Ethics* is a branch of philosophy concerned with the principles of right or wrong in human conduct. Entertainment-education implementers are somewhat unique in the development community in that they question whether or not what they are doing is ethical (see Chapter 2, this volume). Rarely do agricultural extension agents worry about the ethics of introducing a new breed of rice. Equally rare is for health workers to worry about the ethics of promoting immunization of children. Most implementers of development projects assume their work is good; the ethical criticisms typically come from outsiders.

Entertainment-education implementers have taken several proactive steps regarding ethics. For instance, Miguel Sabido establishes a moral framework for an entertainment-education program to ensure that the values it promotes are enshrined in the country's constitution and its legal statutes. A program's values grid, signed by various stakeholders (government officials, commercial sponsors, religious leaders, and broadcast media officials), provides support for the scriptwriters concerning the program's educational content. The use of local writers and creative teams helps to ensure that the program is culturally sensitive and incorporates local language. The use of subject matter specialists to review program scripts ensures that the technical information provided in the program is accurate. The depiction of positive and negative role models, and realistic consequences of their behaviors, allows the audience to draw its own conclusions rather than being preached to in a didactic manner. Furthermore, the conduct of formative and summative evaluation research helps practitioners (a) analyze the target audiences' needs and aspirations, (b) produce relevant and user-friendly media materials, and (c) understand the intended and unintended effects of the entertainment-education intervention. Entertainment-education practitioners, however, must be mindful of important ethical dilemmas (Brown & Singhal, 1990, 1998).

The Prosocial Development Dilemma

The foremost ethical problem concerning the entertainment-education strategy centers around a fundamental question: Is it right to use the mass media as a persuasive tool to foster social change? It is virtually impossible to produce "value-free" entertainment messages. Whether or not it is ethical to produce an entertainment-education message depends on the nature of the behavior being promoted, who decides that a certain behavior is prosocial or not, and what effects the promotion of a certain behavior is likely to have on an audience. The educational issues promoted by past entertainment-education have mostly been of unquestionable value, such as HIV prevention. Who would want individuals to contract HIV/AIDS? The prosocial content is constructed in line with the moral and values guidelines, so this ethical question is much ameliorated.

The Prosocial Content Dilemma

The prosocial content dilemma centers around the problems of distinguishing between prosocial and antisocial content. What may be construed as "prosocial" by certain audience members might be perceived as "antisocial" by other audience individuals. For example, proabortion groups, which support a woman's choice in controlling her reproductive behavior, consider a media message about abortion to be prosocial. Antiabortion groups, which support the rights of the unborn fetus, consider such messages to be antisocial. In fact, just such a conflict erupted in 1972 when Norman Lear's "Maude" chose to have an abortion instead of bearing an unwanted birth (Montgomery, 1989). Labeling an issue as prosocial versus antisocial obviously involves a value judgment on the part of the message source. By conducting audience needs assessment and designing messages in line with the moral framework, this ethical question is appropriately addressed.

The Audience Segmentation Dilemma

Another ethical issue concerning the use of entertainment-education programs is associated with targeting educational messages to a particular audience segment or geographical area (Brown & Singhal, 1998). *Audience segmentation* fine-tunes messages to fit the needs of the targeted audience (see Chapter 7, this volume). For instance, media messages about family planning in developing countries are usually targeted to fertile-aged couples. Such segmentation, however, may alienate other important audience segments, such as adolescents, sexually active singles, and others who believe that they too could benefit from contraceptive messages.

Using treatment and control areas in the field experiment to evaluate the effects of *Twende na Wakati* in Tanzania led to blocking radio broadcasts for 2 years (1993 to 1995) in the Dodoma control region (comprising 3 million people). Individuals living in this control area may have had unwanted pregnancies and may have contracted HIV during this 2-year period—events that otherwise could have been prevented (Rogers et al., 1999). The ethical problems of audience segmentation that occur in field experiments need to be recognized and dealt with. For instance, an interrupted time-series design, which does not have a control, might be preferable to a field experiment. In Tanzania, *Twende na Wakati* was broadcast for 2 years (1995-1997) in the Dodoma region, where it had strong effects that were similar to those that occurred previously in the treatment area.

The Oblique Persuasion Dilemma

The entertainment-education strategy takes a somewhat oblique route to audience persuasion in that education is "sugarcoated" with entertainment, in part to break down individuals' learning defenses to the educational message. Audiences might think that they are being entertained, whereas they are being educated subtly about a prosocial issue. Most audiences, however, realize that entertainment-education messages are just that—both educational and entertaining (Rogers et al., 1999; see Chapter 2, this volume, in which it is argued that putting educational messages within a program is probably much more effective than placing them in ads or public service announcements).

The Sociocultural Equality Dilemma

How can one provide equal educational treatment to various audience segments that differ in socioeconomic status? Equality means regarding each social and cultural group with the same importance (Gudykunst & Kim, 1984, p. 5). Achieving sociocultural equality through entertainment-education is especially important in a socioculturally diverse country such as India. The *Hum Log* (*We People*) television soap opera, within the limits of the patriarchal social system of India, confronted viewers' traditional beliefs about women's status in Indian society. The viewers' ethnicity, linguistic background, and gender, however, were found to be important determinants of beliefs about gender equality (Singhal & Rogers, 1989). Subservience of women is still considered to be acceptable in many Indian households. Such is not the case throughout all parts of India, however. When an entertainment-education message does not give equal play to different voices, it presents an ethical dilemma for certain groups that believe that their views are not represented.

The Unintended Effects Dilemma

Another ethical dilemma of entertainment-education is unintended effects. Audience members actively negotiate the meanings that they perceive when processing an entertainment-education text. Entertainment-education program designers cannot ensure that all audience members will read the text in exactly the way that was intended (Sherry, 1997). The "Archie Bunker" effect is an example of such an oppositional reading of negative role models. Usually, only a small portion of the audience members display the Archie Bunker effect (Vidmar & Rokeach, 1974). For example, 1% of the male audience of *Twende na Wakati* in Tanzania perceived Mkwaju, the promiscuous truck driver, as a positive role model for their behavior, contrary to the intent of the program's designers (see also Chapter 9, this volume).

CONCLUSIONS

The entertainment-education approach may be a promising communication strategy for behavior change because much evaluation research has reported strong effects (Nariman, 1993; Piotrow et al., 1997; Singhal & Rogers, 1999). Many interventions use the entertainment-education strategy as one part (usually the centerpiece) of a communication campaign. This approach has been widely used in the nations of Latin America, Africa, and Asia. Evidence that entertainment-education can be effective in an industrialized nation is provided by Soul City in South Africa. To date, however, applications of the entertainment-education strategy in the United States have been few. This strategy can be used flexibly, on a local level (rather than in a nationwide intervention) or as one component in a multimedia campaign.

Most entertainment-education projects to date have concerned health-related education issues such as family planning or HIV/AIDS prevention. Less frequently, the entertainment-education strategy has been used to encourage enrollment in adult literacy programs, environmental protection, and gender equality, suggesting that this communication strategy can be used for an even wider range of educational issues. MTV's "Rock the Vote" campaign is an example.

Here, we argued for the potential of the entertainment-education strategy and discussed ethical aspects concerning its use. We suggest that entertainment-education can be a useful component of communication campaigns.

NOTES

1. This chapter is based on Singhal and Rogers (1999).

2. This case draws on an audiotape recording of a presentation given by Japhet and Goldstein (1997b) on Soul City at the Second International Conference on Entertainment-Education and Social Change in Athens, Ohio, on May 7, 1997. This audiotape was produced and distributed by RoSu Productions, Inc. (Columbus, OH). We thank Ms. Sue Goldstein (personal communication, September 3, 1998) for clarifying various aspects of Soul City.

REFERENCES

Bandura, A. (1977). *Social learning theory.* Englewood Cliffs, NJ: Prentice Hall.

Bandura, A. (1997). *Self-efficacy: The exercise of control.* New York: Freeman.

Brown, W. J., & Singhal, A. (1990). Ethical dilemmas of prosocial television. *Communication Quarterly, 38*(3), 268-280.

Brown, W. J., & Singhal, A. (1998). Ethical guidelines for promoting prosocial messages through the popular media. In G. Edgerton, M. T. Marsden, & J. Nachbar (Eds.), *In the eye of the beholder: Critical perspectives in popular film and television* (pp. 207-223). Bowling Green, OH: Bowling Green State University Popular Press.

Cambridge, V., McLaughlin, E., & Rota, J. (1995, May). *Entertainment-education and the ethics of social intervention.* Paper presented to the International Communication Association, Albuquerque, NM.

Community Agency for Social Enquiry. (1995). *Let the sky to be the limit: Soul City evaluation report.* Johannesburg, South Africa: Jacana Education.

Fischer, H., & Melnik, S. R. (Eds.). (1979). *Entertainment: A cross-cultural examination.* New York: Hastings House.

Gudykunst, W. B., & Kim, Y. Y. (1984). *Communicating with strangers.* Reading, MA: Addison-Wesley.

Japhet, G. (1999). *Edutainment: How to make edutainment work for you.* Houghton, South Africa: Soul City.

Japhet, G., & Goldstein, S. (1997a). Soul City experience. *Integration, 53,* 10-11.

Japhet, G., & Goldstein, S. (1997b, May 7). *The Soul City experience in South Africa.* Audiotape recording of a presentation made to the Second International Conference on Entertainment-Education and Social Change, Athens, OH. Columbus, OH: RoSu Productions.

Montgomery, K. C. (1989). *Target: Prime time.* New York: Oxford University Press.

Nariman, H. (1993). *Soap operas for social change.* Westport, CT: Praeger.

Papa, M. J., Singhal, A., Law, S., Pant, S., Sood, S., Rogers, E. M., & Shefner-Rogers, C. L. (in press). Entertainment-education and social change: An analysis of parasocial interaction, social learning, collective efficacy, and paradoxical communication. *Journal of Communication.*

Piotrow, P. T., Kincaid, D. L., Rimon, J., II, & Rinehart, W. (1997). *Health communication: Lessons from family planning and reproductive health.* Westport, CT: Praeger.

Rogers, E. M. (1986). *Communication technology.* New York: Free Press.

Rogers, E. M., & Storey, D. (1987). Communication campaigns. In C. Berger & S. Chafee (Eds.), *Handbook of communication sciences* (pp. 817-846). Newbury Park, CA: Sage.

Rogers, E. M., Vaughan, P. W., Swalehe, R. M. A., Rao, N., Svenkerud, P., & Sood, S. (1999). Effects of an entertainment-education radio soap opera on family planning in Tanzania. *Studies in Family Planning, 30*(3), 193-211.

Sherry, J. (1997). Prosocial soap operas for development: A review of research and theory. *Journal of International Communication, 4*(2), 75-101.

Singhal, A., & Brown, W. J. (1996). The entertainment-education communication strategy: Past struggles, present status, future agenda. *Jurnal Komunikasi, 12,* 19-36.

Singhal, A., Obregon, R., & Rogers, E. M. (1994). Reconstructing the story of "Simplemente María," the most popular telenovela in Latin America of all time. *Gazette, 54*(1), 1-15.

Singhal, A., & Rogers, E. M. (1989). Pro-social television for development in India. In R. E. Rice & C. Atkin (Eds.), *Public communication campaigns* (2nd ed., pp. 331-350). Newbury Park, CA: Sage.

Singhal, A., & Rogers, E. M. (1999). *Entertainment-education: A communication strategy for social change.* Mahwah, NJ: Lawrence Erlbaum.

Singhal, A., & Svenkerud, P. (1994). Pro-socially shareable entertainment television programs: A programming alternative in developing countries. *Journal of Development Communication, 5*(2), 17-30.

Valente, T. W., Kim, Y. M., Lettenmaier, C., Glass, W., & Dibba, Y. (1994). Radio promotion of family planning in The Gambia. *International Family Planning Perspectives, 20,* 96-100.

Vidmar, N., & Rokeach, M. (1974). Archie Bunker's bigotry: A study in selective perception and exposure. *Journal of Communication, 24*(1), 36-47.

29

A Web-Based Smoking Cessation and Prevention Program for Children Aged 12 to 15

David B. Buller
W. Gill Woodall
John R. Hall
Ron Borland
Bryan Ax
Melissa Brown
Joan Marquardt Hines

After many years of declining tobacco use, recent data show that the number of children who smoke is increasing (Flay, 1993; U.S. Department of Health and Human Services [DHHS], 1994). Moreover, children who smoke do not enroll in smoking cessation programs in large numbers, and programs attempting to increase cessation, as opposed to preventing the uptake of smoking, have generally failed (Prince, 1995).

In response to this increase in smoking and campaign failure, our research group, representing a collaboration between the AMC Cancer Research Center in Denver, Colorado, the University of New Mexico, the University of Arizona,

AUTHORS' NOTE: This project is funded by Grant CA78206 from the U.S. National Cancer Institute.

and the Anti-Cancer Council of Victoria in Australia, created a web-based health communication program titled *Consider This* to reduce smoking among adolescent children aged 12 to 15 (Grades 6-9). It is in this age range when many children first try smoking. The program features are based on theories of health behavior, persuasive communication, and education and research identifying factors associated with the uptake of tobacco by youth. In this chapter, we review trends in tobacco use by children and the current state of tobacco prevention in the United States. Then, we describe the planning and production of the program, from initial conceptualization to identification of relevant theoretical principles and production of multimedia activities within the program for various groups of smoking and nonsmoking adolescents. We conclude with a brief description of the procedures for evaluating the program's effectiveness.

RECENT TRENDS IN U.S. TOBACCO USE AND TOBACCO CONTROL

Recent data from U.S. government surveys of youth reveal an alarming trend toward increasing tobacco use among teens. From 1991 to 1997, the U.S. Centers for Disease Control and Prevention's (CDC) Youth Risk Behavior Survey, conducted for children in Grades 9 through 12, detected an increase in current cigarette smoking, with the rate of frequent smoking at 32% of youth, although the prevalence of lifetime smoking and proportion of children reporting smoking before age 13 remained stable during this period (CDC, 1998; DHHS, 1998). From 1991 to 1995, the Monitoring the Future survey, funded by the National Institute on Drug Abuse, showed that cigarette smoking by 8th and 10th graders increased by 34% (Johnston, O'Malley, & Bachman, 1995).

The increases in youth smoking are especially troubling in light of two facts. First, smoking by adults declined and stabilized at 25% of the adult population during the 1990s (DHHS, 1994). Second, efforts to reduce smoking in the United States received substantial resources during this decade. The U.S. government provided funding to state health departments to promote community tobacco control efforts through the National Cancer Institute's American Stop Smoking Intervention Project and its successor, the Centers for Disease Control and Prevention's IMPACT program. The Robert Wood Johnson Foundation also provided support to states for local tobacco control programs through its Smokeless States Initiative. Five states—Arizona, California, Florida, Massachusetts, and Oregon—applied additional taxes to the sale of cigarettes and used portions of the proceeds from these new taxes to fund large tobacco prevention and cessation programs. Some of the state-level programs were not fully implemented until late in the decade, however, leaving little time to reverse the unfavorable trends in tobacco use.

Data from California, Florida, and Oregon showed that the tobacco control programs supported by these taxes had modest positive effects as long as substantial resources were devoted to the programs. For example, per capita consumption of cigarettes (estimated from tobacco sales) declined faster in California and Oregon than in the nation as a whole in the first few years following the implementation of their programs (1989-1996 and 1996-1998, respectively) (CDC, 1999a; Pierce et al., 1998). Although some of this success may be due to nonprogram influences such as higher cigarette prices due to new excise taxes, surveys in California showed greater reductions in smoking prevalence after the tobacco control program began. From 1998 to 1999, during which the state of Florida initiated an intensive statewide tobacco control campaign targeted toward youth, smoking prevalence among middle school students (Grades 6-8) declined by 3.5% and that among high school students (Grades 9-12) declined by 2.2%. Additional findings from Florida showed that reductions occurred among both boys and girls in middle school and among girls in high school and were largest among non-Hispanic white children. The use of cigars among middle school boys and the use of smokeless tobacco by both boys and girls in middle schools also declined (CDC, 1999b).

Studies in California, however, showed that early successes with adults declined in magnitude from 1993 to 1996 at the same time that funding for antitobacco programs declined, with the decline in per capita consumption slowing and the reduction in smoking prevalence flattening or trending upwards compared to the period from 1989 to 1993 (Pierce et al., 1998). Other analyses showed close associations between the introduction of a media campaign and reduction in tobacco consumption in California (Glantz, 1993; Goldman & Glantz, 1998), although the effects on children in Grades 4 through 12 were mixed (Popham et al., 1994).

In the past decade, several studies have tested methods of promoting communitywide tobacco control. The most notable of the communitywide studies was the Community Intervention Trial for Smoking Cessation (COMMIT) sponsored by the National Cancer Institute. It randomized 22 communities to either an intervention condition—a program to increase the capacity of communities to address smoking issues in four channels (health care providers, work sites, cessation resources and services, and public education) aimed at reducing smoking by light to moderate smokers—or a control condition and followed them for 4 years. There were no differences between intervention and control communities in cessation rates among smokers, however (COMMIT Research Group, 1995).

Two recent efforts at developing school-based tobacco use prevention yielded some success. An approach teaching middle and high school students life skills to promote personal responsibility, resistance to social influences to smoke, and a nonsmoking norm have reduced the rate of smoking by children in the test schools (Botvin, 1996). Similarly, a curriculum addressing the combination of normative and informational social influence to smoke and physical consequences of smoking reduced the use of cigarettes and smokeless tobacco (Sussman, Dent, Burton, Stacy, & Flay, 1995). Cessation programs designed to convince children to quit smoking once they have begun, however, have had little success (Prince, 1995; Sussman et al., 1995). This lack of success may stem from the fact that smoking by many adolescents is often sporadic—a few times a week or a month—and may not be viewed as a problem by children, thus producing less motivation to quit. Sporadic smoking also does not match the model of regular, addicted smoking assumed by many adult cessation programs that have sometimes been translated for children. Fear of revealing their early smoking to parents, teachers, and other adults may be another reason why early adolescent smokers hesitate to enroll in smoking cessation programs.

It is too early to tell whether the alarming trends in tobacco use will be reversed as the new century commences, but there have been some positive indications, at least in areas in which intense communitywide campaigns have been conducted. Unfortunately, California, Arizona, and Florida have experienced budget reductions that have reduced the intensity of their campaigns (Balbach & Glantz, 1998) and, at least in California, apparently resulted in smaller reductions in smoking (Pierce et al., 1998). It has been speculated that cigarettes were aggressively marketed to children during the 1990s, which can counter the effects of tobacco control campaigns (Botvin, 1997).

It is hoped that these circumstances will change with the recent settlement of the civil lawsuit brought by 46 states, 5 territories, and the District of Columbia against the U.S. tobacco industry (Table 29.1). Many terms of the settlement will restrict the ability of tobacco companies to market tobacco products to children, counter claims about the health hazards of using tobacco products, and lobby against legislation and rules to reduce youth access and consumption of these products. Settlement funds will support a national campaign to reduce youth smoking and use of other tobacco products and research to identify effective prevention and cessation strategies and monitor use of tobacco products. In addition, Phillip Morris has offered to fund the purchase and distribution of the Life Skills tobacco prevention curriculum created by Botvin (1979-1998) to schools through a grant program.

THE CONSIDER THIS SMOKING
CESSATION AND PREVENTION PROGRAM

The Consider This web-based smoking cessation and prevention program was conceived in early 1997 with the primary aim of convincing adolescents experimenting with cigarettes to stop smoking before they become addicted to nicotine. Preventing initiation of smoking by nonsmokers was a secondary aim. The international investigative team was composed of researchers with experience in several fields, including communication sciences, psychology, health education, computer-based education, tobacco and substance abuse prevention for

Table 29.1 Key Terms in the 1998 Settlement Between the States and the Tobacco Industry

Creates a charitable foundation funded by $250 million and a national public education fund for tobacco control funded by $1.45 billion from the tobacco industry: The foundation will use these funds to conduct a nationwide, sustained advertising and education program to reduce youth smoking; develop, disseminate, and test counteradvertising campaigns; fund research into factors that influence youth smoking and substance abuse; and track and monitor youth smoking and substance abuse

Bans the use of cartoons in advertising, promotion, packaging, or labeling of tobacco products; outdoor and transit advertising of tobacco products; distribution and sale of apparel and merchandise with brand-name tobacco logos; gifts from tobacco companies without proof of age; payments to promote tobacco products in movies, television shows, theater productions or live performances, live or recorded music performances, and videos and video games; brand-name sponsorship of events with a significant youth audience or team sports and sponsorship of events at which the paid participants or contestants are underage; and tobacco brand names for stadiums and arenas

Limits tobacco advertising outside retail establishments to 14 square feet, tobacco companies to one brand-name sponsorship per year, and the distribution of free tobacco samples to facilities or enclosed areas in which the operator ensures no underage person is present

Prohibits targeting youth in tobacco advertising, promotions, or marketing and tobacco industry actions aimed at initiating, maintaining, or increasing youth smoking

Prohibits tobacco companies from opposing proposed state or local laws or administrative rules intended to limit youth access to and consumption of tobacco products

Prohibits tobacco companies from jointly contracting or conspiring to limit or suppress information about health hazards from using their products, research into smoking and health, and research into the marketing or development of new products and from making material misrepresentations regarding health consequences of smoking

Requires tobacco companies to open and maintain for 10 years a web site with all documents produced in state and other smoking and health-related lawsuits

Disbands the Council for Tobacco Research, the Tobacco Institute, and the Council for Indoor Air Research

Limits pack sizes to 20 cigarettes

Requires the tobacco industry to pay to the states a total of $206 billion from 2000 to 2025 (payments range from $25 billion to California and New York to $16.5 million to the North Marianas territory), with upfront payments of nearly $13 billion, and a payment of $8.61 billion to a strategic contribution fund to be allocated to the states reflecting their contribution toward resolution of the state lawsuits youth, cessation counseling for adults, and statistical analysis. The program was developed within a two-phase research project funded by a grant from the National Cancer Institute. The first phase included formative research into adolescents' early smoking patterns and the production and beta testing of the multimedia web-based program. The second phase included a randomized evaluation of the program's effects on students in Grades 6 through 9 from school districts in Denver, Albuquerque, and Tucson and a demonstration of program feasibility in other community organizations serving children.

The Consider This web program was designed to deliver information and persuasive messages about tobacco use directly to adolescents aged 12 to 15 in a semiprivate on-line environment. (For the remainder of the chapter, we refer to this target group as adolescents, children, or users.) The content is presented in a user-centered, nonjudgmental tone to promote honesty about smoking experiences. The communication approach used in the program assumes that discussion of smoking issues grounded in the current experiences and thoughts of the children will be more effective than an approach that treats all children as if they do not smoke. Some of the interactive features of programs created for the World Wide Web are used to obtain information from children about their smoking experience and their personal characteristics so that content is adjusted to match communication and skill building to adolescents' experiences with cigarettes. Program features are based on social cognitive theory, theories of persuasive communication and education, and research identifying factors associated with the uptake of tobacco by youth.

The Consider This web site features six 50-minute modules. The first unit contains an introduction to the entire web site and reviews procedures for its use. The web site is described as a program that is intended to discuss skills that adolescents need to take charge of their lives. The next three units discuss information related to key social skills that influence behavior—media literacy, relationship development and management, and addiction recognition and stress management. These are taught in sessions discussing how the media, people around them, and their own mind and body influence decisions to behave one way or another. The final two units provoke reassessments of current smoking behaviors. One unit illustrates the application of decision-making skills to tobacco use, teaches skills for implementing decisions, and provokes values clarification related to tobacco use. The final unit focuses on strategies for resisting influences to smoke. It shows how some apparent pressures to smoke are really more like social rituals, but that some apparently innocent depictions of smoking in the media are designed to influence their decisions through biasing norms and providing role models for smoking.

In addition to the content units, the web site contains a discussion area in which users can post e-mail messages to debate issues raised in each unit or to ask questions related to tobacco use and cessation. This is intended to provide more personalized feedback to users. Also, a series of hypertext links is displayed with each unit to explore more information on the topics in the unit and is available to users throughout subsequent units. Finally, there are suggested assignments related to each unit to provide additional instructional opportunities for evaluating user performance. Thus, the Consider This web site acts as an integrated communication environment, enhancing and reinforcing concepts and skills through several channels, with the 50-minute units as the core of the web site. Figure 29.1 provides a site map of the Consider This web site.

Application of Theories of Health Behavior Change, Communication, and Persuasion

On the basis of principles of social cognitive theory (Bandura, 1986), we developed vivid sequences, occasionally featuring attractive peer models, that engage adolescents' attention. Actors create positive outcome expectancies and self-efficacy expectations for tobacco cessation. Several messages aim to correct often inaccurate tobacco use norms held by adolescents.

Persuasive message strategies were created based on several theories of communication and persuasion. From our previous use of language expectancy theory in formulating sun safety messages for families (Buller et al., in press; Burgoon, 1995), psychological reactance theory (Brehm & Brehm, 1981), and postdecisional regret models (Kahneman & Tversky, 1982), we created messages that should avoid producing psychological reactance in children. In general, messages use moderate language intensity and inductively styled persuasive arguments when provoking children to reassess their decisions to smoke. For example, adolescents consider key personal values and are asked whether or not smoking fits well with those values. In contrast, with children who report they are considering quitting, we use messages with high language intensity that reinforce their decision to quit (Buller, Borland, & Burgoon, 1998). Children who indicate that they are progressing toward quitting also receive messages specific to their stage of quitting (e.g., think about quitting or actually quitting). This is loosely based on the transtheoretical model (Prochaska, DiClemente, & Norcross, 1992; Velicer et al., 1993), which is used to place people in different stages in the process of behavior change and adjust intervention strategies for stage.

We also use messages with high language intensity to tell children who say they enjoy smoking that they are at high risk for nicotine addiction. High-intensity language can increase the sense of danger (Burgoon, 1995). We argue that these children should quit smoking before they are addicted, and that they are at very high risk of becoming addicted if they do not stop now. Children who smoke regularly and are probably addicted to nicotine are directed to web resources outside of our program. For children experimenting with cigarettes, decisions to stop are assumed to be driven by consumptive rather than addictive processes, and messages reinforce decisions to quit following postdecisional regret theory (Kahneman & Tversky, 1982) and advice on resisting pressures to relapse.

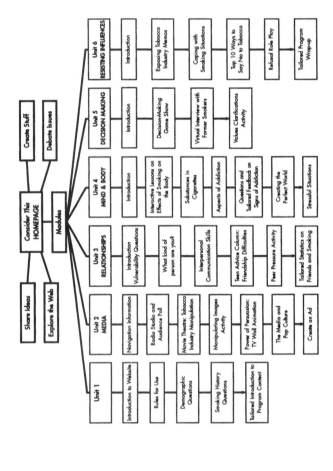

Figure 29.1. Site Map of the Consider This Web Site

Finally, the instruction on resisting influences to smoke goes beyond traditional training in refusal skills and teaches adolescents about strategies for avoiding group conformity pressures and for maintaining positive relationships when refusing to smoke. Users are also shown that some media depictions of smoking outside of direct advertising are designed to model smoking and increase beliefs that smoking is normative. Refutational activities are provided to produce inoculation against common prosmoking arguments (McGuire, 1964; Pfau & Van Brockern, 1994).

Application of Education Paradigms

The Consider This web program follows three educational paradigms to structure learning: revelatory, conjectural, and emancipatory (Clayden & Wilson, 1988). In the *revelatory* paradigm, learning occurs when meeting challenges, exploring options, and making decisions that overcome challenges. Children choose paths and explore what is hidden and gradually emerges in modules using game-like exercises. On the basis of the *conjectural* paradigm, in which learners not only explore the content but also actually change the nature of it or its underlying parameters, we deploy simulations in which adolescents make choices and the effects of alternative choices are revealed. The *emancipatory* paradigm is reflected in the use of hypertext links to related ideas (Briggs, Ramesh, Romano, & Latimer, 1994-1995; Graziadei & McCombs, 1994-1995). These allow learners to explore multiple levels of information.

WEB PROGRAM PRODUCTION

Content and Unit Development

At the beginning of production, we reviewed existing smoking prevention (Botvin, 1979-1998; Project TNT Staff, 1998; Victorian Smoking and Health Program, 1989) and cessation programs for youth (Alvaro & Salazar, 1998; American Lung Association of Minnesota, 1989). We also reviewed research on smoking initiation for adolescents, paying special attention to those aimed at our target ages (12- to 15-year-olds) (Meijer, Branski, Knol, & Kerem, 1996) and those reaching experimental smokers (Friedman, Lichtenstein, & Biglan, 1985; Nichter, Nichter, Vuckovic, Quintero, & Ritenbaugh, 1997). We also reviewed research on differences in the smoking habits of adolescents based on race and ethnicity (Landrine, Richardson, Klonoff, & Flay, 1994; Robinson, Klesges, Zbikowski, & Glaser, 1997; Sussman, Dent, Flay, Hansen, & Johnson, 1987), gender (Presti, Ary, & Lichtenstein, 1992; Wang, Fitzhugh, Turner, & Fu, 1997), and socioeconomic status (Conrad, Flay, & Hill, 1992;

Radziszewska, Richardson, Dent, & Flay, 1996). Bibliographic databases were searched by topic (youth smoking, etc.) and names of authors who are known for their extensive research in this field (e.g., Botvin, Flay, and Sussman). A large amount of research on youth smoking and prevention-based programs was identified; little, however, focused on experimental smokers or on smoking cessation programs for children.

An initial conceptual set of six program units was developed: (a) introduction to decision making, (b) media literacy, (c) relationship formation, (d) stress and anxiety management, (e) decision-making skills, and (f) resistance to persuasion. A plan for each program unit was prepared containing a description of the unit goals and aims, key principles or topics to be addressed, and a list of educational curriculum standards that the content of each unit fulfilled (based on national health education standards and the national communication education standards for Grades 6-9). Media production specialists developed practical procedures for formatting scripts so that they contained all the relevant production information, including description of content and narration, graphics, animation, sound and special effects, video elements, and additional instructions to explain each unit.

Initial scripts were developed by the investigators and project staff that contained the information needed by graphic designers, animators, and multimedia programmers to produce the first prototype of the web-based tobacco control program. All scripts went through a procedure of internal and external reviews, revisions, and modifications. Students in middle and high school read the scripts and made suggestions for unit revisions to make them more novel, appealing, relevant, and age appropriate to users in their peer group. As a result of this process, all scripts have been revised extensively.

Multimedia Programming and Production

A primary production objective was to maximize the level of interactivity at the Consider This web site. A host of interactive activities was created, ranging from users in a radio studio booth answering phone calls for an imaginary radio talk show to giving children the opportunity to create their own perfect world as they think about ways to reduce stress. These activities actively use audio narration, sound effects, and music to captivate users in a multisensory fashion. A variety of software applications for multimedia programming, graphics, audio and video editing, and digital compression were used to produce the program. Finally, the Consider This web site is managed on the server using Microsoft FrontPage and an SQL database that contains information on users' tobacco use and personal characteristics. The entire web site runs on common Internet browser software available on Windows and Macintosh computer platforms that supports the various audio, video, and graphics plug-ins.

Despite some limitations, the use of the web environment for this program is superior to a CD-ROM format. The web provides easier cross-platform compatibility for both Macintosh and Windows operating systems, both of which are common in schools. Maintenance is also simplified by using the web because revisions can be handled simply and quickly on the web server.

Finally, the web provides new and unique opportunities for interaction that CD-ROM-based programs do not. Adolescents at different sites in different states can interact and share ideas with each other from within the web site and, in this way, contribute to a larger community of their peers. They can also use the site as a portal to access additional health-related information by following links included within the site. The web gives them on-line, anonymous opportunities to discuss smoking prevention and cessation with other adolescents.

Tailoring Unit Content

The Consider This program content, activities, and graphics are tailored to address certain needs of various populations of children within the targeted age ranges. We gathered information on knowledge, attitudes, and behaviors related to tobacco from adolescents in Grades 6 through 9 by using surveys and focus groups. We were especially interested in discovering how factors implicated in the uptake of smoking differed between children based on ethnicity, gender, and smoking history.

Although we included some alterations in the program to reflect race and ethnicity and gender differences based on our preprogram research, via the inclusion of a variety of images of children, most of the adjustments in the content respond to differences in the smoking behavior of the users. Analyses of the survey responses from adolescents showed pronounced differences based on prior smoking experience and vulnerability to future smoking. These variables produced seven categories of children for which we adjusted web site content: (a) stable never-smoker, (b) unstable never-smoker, (c) vulnerable never-smoker, (d) invulnerable former smoker, (e) vulnerable former smoker, (f) current experimenter, and (g) regular smoker.

For children who have never smoked, persuasive messages aim to alert them that they will probably encounter opportunities to smoke and advocate that they learn resistance strategies. For former smokers, messages reinforce their decisions not to smoke. If either nonsmokers or former smokers indicate that they would smoke in the future, the web site content also attempts to make them reevaluate this desire, opt instead not to smoke, and learn skills to resist influences to smoke. In contrast, messages for experimental smokers direct them to review how they began smoking, clarify the relationship of smoking to their personal values, consider stopping smoking, and learn to recognize and understand social pressures to smoke and strategies to resist them. If users are regular smokers whose consumption is determined by nicotine addiction, they receive information geared toward convincing them to consider stopping smoking and are directed to web and other cessation resources to help them actually quit and cope with withdrawal symptoms. For both experimenters and regular smokers, messages are intended to keep the perceived dangers of smoking high by alerting them to signs of their increasing addiction and to convince them that they can and must take action to reduce these dangers.

We also found that rebelliousness, perceived social and personal smoking norms, and perceived benefits of smoking are higher among more regular smokers, so we use statements that avoid reactance with more regular smokers and provide content that challenges their perceptions that smoking is normative and has benefits. The values clarification activities were based on motivational interviewing, a nonconfrontational dyadic clinical intervention technique that has been successful in reducing substance abuse behavior (Lawendowski, 1998). The Consider This web program also includes content to correct the perceived norms for smoking (i.e., perceptions of how many children like them and how many adults smoke). Illustrating that their smoking is inconsistent with adolescents' core values and that their perceptions of smoking norms are inaccurate is intended to motivate adolescents to reassess their smoking behavior, reduce their ambivalence toward their smoking, and provoke decisions to stop (see also Chapter 22, this volume).

All this tailoring is determined by having adolescents respond to on-line questions and write their responses to the SQL database. In early units, we pose questions on gender, ethnicity, and smoking history and adjust content for whether a child has smoked cigarettes and, if so, how often. In the third and fourth units, we ask additional questions about susceptibility to future smoking, the presence of friends who smoke, and signs of nicotine addiction and tailor messages on these variables. In the last two units, we address unique messages to all seven groups of children.

EVALUATING THE CONSIDER THIS WEB PROGRAM

The Consider This web program is being evaluated with children enrolled in Grades 6 through 9 in 30 middle schools from school districts in Denver, Albuquerque, and Tucson that are enrolled in a pair-matched randomized pretest-posttest control group field experiment. Children from schools in Australia are also enrolled in the field trial because many trends in tobacco use in Australia are similar to those in the United States (Australian Department of Health and Aged Care, 1999). Exposure to the web site is ensured by training teachers how to use the web program and having them implement the Consider This web site as part of the curriculum during normal class periods using the schools' computers and Internet access service. The primary outcome measure is 30-day prevalence of smoking. Exposure to the Consider This web program is assessed through the SQL database on the web server using unique user identifications and passwords assigned by the researchers.

Implementing the Consider This web program in school classrooms ensures exposure to the program and helps provide a well-controlled assessment of program effects. The web program, however, can also be used by other community groups that provide health, social, and Internet services to children. A group of such organizations makes the Consider This web program available to their child clients. We monitor their efforts to market the program and the amount of program usage at these organizations to demonstrate feasibility in nonschool environments.

CONCLUSION

The World Wide Web provides new ways for communicating with children about smoking and other high-risk behaviors and represents one of the exciting new opportunities in tobacco control. This new medium, which marries computer functionality with audio and visual stimuli, offers unique features unavailable for public campaigns in traditional mass media. Web programs are addressable, which allows users to seek information they desire and to provide information that can be used to adjust content for their needs and circumstances. The asynchronous nature of the web means that web programs and resources can be available when users want them. These features, however, require that people be motivated to "use" the web programs. Motivation can be both a barrier and a facilitator of effective communication and behavior change via the web. Thus, it is unreasonable to believe that the use of the web per se will improve smoking cessation and prevention programs. On-line features that allow one to develop expert systems that adjust communication to make it relevant to the characteristics and experiences of each child, however, hold promise for improving our current approaches to tobacco control with children.

REFERENCES

Alvaro, E. M., & Salazar, Z. (1998). *Arizona smokers' help line youth diversion program.* Tucson: University of Arizona, Arizona Program for Nicotine and Tobacco Research.

American Lung Association of Minnesota. (1989). *Tobacco-free teens.* St. Paul: Author.

Australian Department of Health and Aged Care. (1999). *Australia's national tobacco campaign: Evaluation report, Vol. 1.* Canberra, ACT: Australian Government Printing Service.

Balbach, E. D., & Glantz, S. A. (1998). Tobacco control advocates must demand high-quality media campaigns: The California experience. *Tobacco Control, 7,* 397-408.

Bandura, A. (1986). *Social foundation of thought and action: A social cognitive theory.* Englewood Cliffs, NJ: Prentice Hall.

Botvin, G. J. (1979-1998). *Life skills training: Promoting health and personal development.* Princeton, NJ: Princeton Health Press.

Botvin, G. J. (1996). Substance abuse prevention through life skills training. In R. D. Peters & R. J. McMahon (Eds.), *Preventing childhood disorders, substance abuse, and delinquency* (pp. 215-240). Thousand Oaks, CA: Sage.

Botvin, G. J. (1997). Preventing adolescent cigarette smoking. *Developmental and Behavioral Pediatrics, 18,* 47-48.

Brehm, S. S., & Brehm, J. W. (1981). *Psychological reactance: A theory of freedom and control.* San Diego, CA: Academic Press.

Briggs, R. O., Ramesh, V., Romano, N. C., & Latimer, J. (1994-1995). The exemplar project: Using group support systems to improve the learning environment. *Journal of Educational Technology Systems, 23,* 277-291.

Buller, D. B., Borland, R., & Burgoon, M. (1998). Impact of behavioral intention on effectiveness of message features: Evidence from the Family Sun Safety project. *Human Communication Research, 24,* 433-453.

Buller, D. B., Burgoon, M., Hall, J., Levine, N., Taylor, A., Beach, B., Melcher, C., Buller, M. K., Bowen, S., Hunsaker, F., & Bergen, A. (2000). Using language intensity to increase the success of family intervention to protect children from ultraviolet radiation: Predictions from language expectancy theory. *Preventive Medicine, 30,* 103-114.

Burgoon, M. (1995). Language expectancy theory. In C. R. Berger & M. Burgoon (Eds.), *Communication and social influence processes* (pp. 29-52). East Lansing: Michigan State University Press.

Clayden, G. S., & Wilson, B. (1988). Computer-assisted learning in medical education. *Medical Education, 22,* 456-476.

COMMIT Research Group. (1995). Community intervention trial for smoking cessation (COMMIT): I. Cohort results from a four-year community intervention. *American Journal of Public Health, 85,* 183-192.

Conrad, K. M., Flay, B. R., & Hill, D. (1992). Why children start smoking cigarettes: Predictors of onset. *British Journal of Addiction, 87,* 1711-1724.

Flay, B. R. (1993). Youth tobacco users: Risks, patterns, and control. In J. Slade & C. T. Orleans (Eds.), *Nicotine addiction: Principles and management* (pp. 365-384). New York: Oxford University Press.

Friedman, L. S., Lichtenstein, E., & Biglan, A. (1985). Smoking onset among teens: An empirical analysis of initial situations. *Addictive Behaviors, 10,* 1-13.

Glantz, S. A. (1993). Changes in cigarette consumption, prices, and tobacco industry revenues associated with California's proposition 99. *Tobacco Control, 2,* 311-314.

Goldman, L. K., & Glantz, S. A. (1998). Evaluation of antismoking advertising campaigns. *Journal of the American Medical Association, 279,* 772-777.

Graziadei, W. D., & McCombs, G. M. (1994-1995). The 21st century classroom-scholarship environment: What will it be like? *Journal of Educational Technology Systems, 24,* 97-112.

Johnston, L. D., O'Malley, P. M., & Bachman, J. G. (1995). *National survey results on drug use from the Monitoring the Future study, 1975-1994: Vol. 1. Secondary school students.* Rockville, MD: National Institute on Drug Abuse.

Kahneman, D., & Tversky, A. (1982). The psychology of preferences. *Scientific American, 246,* 160-173.

Landrine, H., Richardson, J. L., Klonoff, E. A., & Flay, B. R. (1994). Cultural diversity in the predictors of adolescent cigarette smoking: The relative influence of peers. *Journal of Behavioral Medicine, 17,* 331-346.

Lawendowski, L. A. (1998). A motivational intervention for adolescent smokers. *Preventive Medicine, 27*(5, Pt. 3), A39-A46.

McGuire, W. (1964). Inducing resistance to persuasion. In L. Berkowitz (Ed.), *Advances in experimental social psychology* (Vol. 1, pp. 191-229). New York: Academic Press.

Meijer, B., Branski, D., Knol, K., & Kerem, E. (1996). Cigarette smoking habits among school children. *Chest, 110*, 921-926.

Nichter, M., Nichter, M., Vuckovic, N., Quintero, G., & Ritenbaugh, C. (1997). Smoking experimentation and initiation among adolescent girls: Qualitative and quantitative findings. *Tobacco Control, 6*, 285-295.

Pfau, M., & Van Brockern, S. (1994). The persistence of inoculation to promote resistance to smoking initiation among adolescents. *Communication Monographs, 59*, 213-230.

Pierce, J. P., Gilpin, E. A., Emery, S. L., White, M. M., Rosbrook, B., & Berry, C. C. (1998). Has the California tobacco control program reduced smoking? *Journal of the American Medical Association, 280*, 893-899.

Popham, W. J., Potter, L. D., Hetrick, M. A., Muthen, L. K., Duerr, J. M., & Johnson, M. D. (1994). Effectiveness of the California 1990-1991 tobacco education media campaign. *American Journal of Public Health, 10*, 319-326.

Presti, D. E., Ary, D. V., & Lichtenstein, E. (1992). The context of smoking initiation and maintenance: Findings from interviews with youth. *Journal of Substance Abuse, 4*, 35-45.

Prince, F. (1995). The relative effectiveness of a peer-led and adult-led smoking intervention program. *Adolescence, 30*, 187-194.

Prochaska, J. O., DiClemente, C. C., & Norcross, J. C. (1992). In search of how people change: Applications to addictive behaviors. *American Psychologist, 47*, 1102-1114.

Project TNT Staff. (1998). *Project TNT: Towards no tobacco use.* Santa Cruz, CA: ETR Associates.

Radziszewska, B., Richardson, J. L., Dent, C. W., & Flay, B. R. (1996). Parenting style and adolescent depressive symptoms, smoking, and academic achievement: Ethnic, gender, and SES differences. *Journal of Behavioral Medicine, 19*, 289-305.

Robinson, L. A., Klesges, R. C., Zbikowski, S. M., & Glaser, R. (1997). Predictors of risk for different stages of adolescent smoking. *Journal of Consulting and Clinical Psychology, 65*, 653-662.

Sussman, S., Dent, C. W., Burton, D., Stacy, A. W., & Flay, B. R. (1995). *Developing school-based tobacco use prevention and cessation programs.* Thousand Oaks, CA: Sage.

Sussman, S., Dent, C. W., Flay, B. R., Hansen, W. B., & Johnson, C. A. (1987). Psychosocial predictors of cigarette smoking onset by white, black, Hispanic, and Asian adolescents in southern California. *Morbidity and Mortality Weekly Report, 36*(Suppl. 4), 11S-16S.

U.S. Centers for Disease Control and Prevention. (1998). Tobacco use among high school students—United States, 1997. *Morbidity and Mortality Weekly Report, 47*, 229-233.

U.S. Centers for Disease Control and Prevention. (1999a). Decline in cigarette consumption following implementation of a comprehensive tobacco prevention and education program—Oregon, 1996-1998. *Morbidity and Mortality Weekly Report, 48*, 140-143.

U.S. Centers for Disease Control and Prevention. (1999b). Tobacco use among middle and high school students—Florida, 1998 and 1999. *Morbidity and Mortality Weekly Report, 48,* 248-253.

U.S. Department of Health and Human Services. (1994). *Preventing tobacco use among young people: A report of the Surgeon General.* Washington, DC: Government Printing Office.

U.S. Department of Health and Human Services. (1998). *Youth risk behavior survey 1997 CD ROM.* Atlanta, GA: U.S. Department of Health and Human Services, Public Health Service, Centers for Disease Control and Prevention, National Center for Chronic Disease Prevention and Health Promotion, Division of Adolescent and School Health.

Velicer, W. F., Prochaska, J. O., Bellis, J. M., DiClemente, C. C., Rossi, J. S., Fava, J. L., & Steiger, J. H. (1993). An expert system intervention for smoking cessation. *Addictive Behaviors, 18,* 269-290.

Victorian Smoking and Health Program. (1989). *Be smart—Don't start: A smoking prevention education program resource for teachers.* Carlton South, VIC, Australia: Author.

Wang, M. Q., Fitzhugh, E. C., Turner, L., & Fu, Q. (1997). Social influence on southern adolescents' smoking transition: A retrospective study. *Southern Medical Journal, 90,* 218-222.

30

Using Interactive Media in Communication Campaigns for Children and Adolescents

Debra A. Lieberman

Interactive media offer a sharp contrast to traditional persuasional approaches to campaigns. Whereas mass media direct predominantly one-way messages at audiences, interactive media teach via participation and by individualized responses to each user's input. Campaign designers using interactive media can focus on experiential interventions instead of persuasive message construction. With interactive media, we can conceptualize a campaign and develop goals and methods that have not previously been feasible on a large scale. Although no two people are likely to experience any campaign the same way, with interactive media the choices are theirs, and the system's responses to each person are unique. These experiences are enhanced by the interpersonal communication channels that interactive media also offer.

Campaign designers are only beginning to tap the potential of interactive media, as new concepts, theories, and applications are being developed in this field. Already, however, a small body of research, evaluation studies, and campaign experiences from the field has shown us what works and what does not.

AUTHOR'S NOTE: I thank Ron Rice, Chuck Atkin, and Steve Chaffee for helpful comments on previous drafts of the manuscript. Research on the health education video games discussed in this chapter was funded in part by the National Institutes of Health, the National Institute of Diabetes and Digestive and Kidney Diseases (Grant 2R44 DK44402-03) and the National Institute of Allergy and Infectious Diseases (Grant 2R44 A134821-02).

Focusing on children and adolescents, this chapter discusses some strengths and limitations of interactive media in campaigns and other learning environments designed to encourage behavior change. It provides a brief overview of young people's responses to interactive media and describes features of these media that, when designed carefully, can stimulate interest and learning.

HIGHLY MOTIVATED AND INVOLVED USERS

Children and adolescents are avid users of interactive media, both in school and during leisure time. People born in the 1990s have been called "clickerati kids" (Harel, 1999), meaning that they have grown up in the digital age and are comfortable with interactive media. For them, change is the norm, and they thrive on it; they enjoy working on more than one task at a time; and they are comfortable with content that does not unfold linearly.

The computer, to this new generation, is not something to marvel at the way it is for their parents; it is simply a normal part of their everyday environment (Papert, 1996). E-mail, chat, and web pages are pervasive in many young people's lives. As television and the Internet converge, interactive TV formats are migrating from the desktop onto the TV screen and onto small wireless devices that can be carried anywhere. When today's children see a screen, it is not unusual for them to expect to be able to do something with it, not just look at it. Most young people like to control what is on the screen and to create new content themselves, and they enjoy being in contact with other people via that screen.

In interviews about media preferences (Lieberman & Brown, 1995), children and adolescents said they prefer to learn with video games, rather than with print media or video, because they enjoy the interactivity, feedback, and involvement that video games can provide. To them, video games "put the person in the environment," and with video games, "there's action, not just words" (p. 202). Also, "a book can explain, but you have the experience in a video game" and "a video game tells you if you're wrong, so you can learn" (p. 202).

Most U.S. children have access to interactive media technology at school or at home. In schools, the student-computer ratio is about 6 to 1, and the student-to-networked-computer ratio is 13 to 1; the number of computers in classrooms is increasing (Software & Information Industry Association, 1999). Approximately 70% of U.S. children have a computer in the home, and nearly 50% have home Internet access (Rideout, Foehr, Roberts, & Brodie, 1999). Youngsters who use computers at home spend about an hour and a half per day with them. Those ages 8 to 18 spend about one third of their computer time on-line and an additional one fourth of it playing interactive games. Also, 70% of U.S. children have a video game player at home and spend another hour and a quarter, on average, playing console video games.

When asked to pick the one form of media they would bring with them to a desert island, one third of a national sample of children picked "computer with

Internet access" and an additional 13% said "video games" (Rideout et al., 1999). Only 13% chose "television," which almost certainly would have been the overwhelming first choice a few years earlier, and only 8% picked "books or magazines." To reach young people during their leisure time, the best place to find them is via the interactive media they already use and prefer.

INTERACTIVE MEDIA FEATURES

The meaning of "interactive media" is constantly changing due to technological advances in delivery media, bandwidth, software capabilities, and interfaces. Basically, though, the way users experience these media does not change greatly, even in the face of technological progress. Table 30.1 presents some features of interactive media to help readers conceptualize fundamental aspects of human-computer interaction and to offer features for practitioners to consider when designing campaigns using interactive media.

Table 30.1 Interactive Media Features

Networks

> *Access to vast content:* Networks are powerful and convenient if desired content is easy to find, but they are overwhelming if the search process is difficult, time-consuming, or unproductive.

> *Content can be frequently added or updated at the source:* Users will be more likely to return to the content if they find useful updates, but they could be disappointed if desired content has changed or disappeared.

> *All users can send and receive content:* Networks create an open marketplace of ideas, but with few gatekeepers in place, the user must assess the content's quality, accuracy, authority, credibility, and timeliness. Hoaxes, software viruses, and invasion of privacy are serious potential problems.

Interactivity

> *Users receive messages and content based on their previous inputs:* The system is tirelessly responsive to the user's input and no other person needs to be present, but this is no substitute for face-to-face interaction when what is needed is a real person's ability to listen, care, reflect, counsel, and share emotions and experiences.

> *Interactive media bring extensive computational power and rote memory:* They can interact with users in ways that exceed human capacity, and this enables the creation of simulations, games, search engines, and other interactive environments that would otherwise be impossible to experience.

Personalized content

> *Targeted messages:* Content and messages can be automatically selected for the user based on the user's characteristics, on-line choices, and stated preferences. This can ensure that content is relevant to the user's needs, but it makes it difficult for the user to share the content with someone who has different characteristics.

Table 30.1 Continued

Format matched to user's abilities: The level of difficulty and the format of the presentation can be selected by a person or by the system to match the user. This capability is essential for users with special needs (children, disabled, etc.) and can increase interest and involvement if the difficulty level is adjusted to be challenging but not beyond reach.

User control

Content on demand: There is no need to wait for a broadcast or cablecast, no need to adjust one's personal schedule to acquire content, and a decreasing need to be tethered to a wire.

Customizing content: Users determine how content will be presented, for instance, by setting game options or by selecting the new topics that will consistently appear on a Home page, but it is advisable to offer a default version for users who are unable or unwilling to customize.

Managing and editing content: With the ability to save, scan, record, replay, edit, print, and send, the users can capture content, transform it, organize it, and apply it in various ways.

Communication

Real-time or asynchronous: People use interactive media to communicate using voice, video, or text in real time, or messages can be stored for later retrieval.

One-to-one or group communication: Communication can occur privately between individuals or from one person to many or among groups as in teleconferences; the user can create and disseminate content to targeted individuals or groups, or the user can make content available to everyone by posting it on the Internet.

Multiple presentation modes (video, audio, text, animation, etc.) and input modes

Juxtapose symbol systems: Experiencing a presentation in more than one mode can enhance comprehension and learning, as can matching the right mode to the learning task or to the user's learning style.

Save and display data from many sources: Users can enter music from a keyboard, game commands from a pressure-sensitive joystick, brush strokes from a digital paintbrush, their emotional state from the galvanic skin response recorded on the mouse, and blood glucose measurements from a drop of blood on a test strip.

Entertaining and fun: It is enjoyable to have choices, to experience a phenomenon in more than one way, and to attach an instrument to an interactive technology so that the user's input can be recorded, edited, organized, and shared.

Portability

Small, wireless devices allow continuous access: Users can access information or communicate with others from any place at any time, but occasionally a real-time message can be an unwelcome intrusion.

Puts media technology in a variety of educational, social, and leisure environments: Portability increases the variety of ways in which interactive media can support or enhance learning, information seeking, communication, and entertainment.

DESIGN RECOMMENDATIONS

Children select, attend to, and cognitively process media differently than do adults. They are a special user group, one that is ready for new media but that needs content and formats designed for their capabilities. From birth to age 18, children progress from concrete to abstract thinking; from an egocentric view of events to an ability to take the other's perspective; from holding very few to holding many mental models, or schemata, about the way events occur and how social and physical environments function; from low interest in learning rules and following them to high; from low reading skills and media literacy skills to high; from focusing on content regardless of its relevance to the main message to focusing almost entirely on content relevant to the main message; and from "centration" on one attribute in a presentation to perceiving multiple attributes simultaneously (Calvert, 1999; Clements, 1987; Doubleday & Droege, 1993). These and other developmental shifts should be addressed in campaign design decisions so that the material is appropriate for different target age groups.

Table 30.2 lists this chapter's nine recommendations for designing interactive campaigns for young people and highlights related themes discussed in the chapter.

Table 30.2 Recommendations for Designing Interactive Campaigns for Young People, With Related Themes

1. *Use young people's media and genres.* Themes: reduction of psychological distance; personal relevance; attention.

2. *Use characters that appeal to the age group.* Themes: role model; self-esteem; realistic consequences; social cognitive theory; social learning and observational learning.

3. *Support information searching.* Themes: user control; exploration of content; games that encourage information seeking.

4. *Incorporate challenges and goals.* Themes: challenge to reach a goal; motivation; flow; engagement, involvement, and immersion.

5. *Use learning-by-doing.* Themes: experiential learning; simulations and games; rule-based outcomes; repetition and rehearsal; individualized feedback; counterarguing; self-efficacy.

6. *Create functional learning environments.* Themes: personally meaningful activities; goal-driven activities; applying knowledge to real-world problems; sharing ideas and activities with others; success stories.

7. *Facilitate social interaction.* Themes: discussion of campaign issues; social support; on-line support groups; on-line chat, mailing lists, and bulletin boards; expert chat room moderators; games that link children to other people; realistic fictional stories and true stories.

8. *Allow user anonymity when appropriate.* Themes: alternative to face-to-face interaction when topic is sensitive; privacy.

9. *Involve young people in product design and testing.* Themes: participatory design; usability testing; field testing and beta testing.

Use Young People's Media and Genres

The medium used to present campaign messages, such as a pamphlet, poster, television program, popular song, or video game, affects the psychological distance between the message and a young audience or user group. For example, a text-based pamphlet about auto safety might not seem personally relevant to adolescents, but if they encountered the same content in a video game, they might perceive it as "their" medium and believe that the message is meant for them. Another way interactive campaigns, like other media, can remove psychological distance is through characters, settings, events, humor, artwork, music, and other stylistic features that appeal to an age group. These elements should be tested with young people to ensure that the material is appealing to the intended users. With psychological distance reduced, by the choice of medium and the nature of the content, young users who might not seek out a campaign's messages in other venues can become interested and involved (Parrott, 1995).

For example, preadolescents who do not pay attention to information about the health hazards of smoking might nonetheless be attracted to an action-adventure video game with a smoking prevention message—not for its content especially but for its interactive challenges and for the fact that a video game is "cool." In the process of playing the game, however, they would learn antismoking information as well. This occurred when children ages 10 to 12 were given a smoking prevention video game called *Rex Ronan* (*www.clickhealth.com*) to take home and play as much or as little as they wished. Many played the game enthusiastically, and in the course of doing so, they developed stronger antismoking attitudes, expressed stronger intentions not to start smoking, and became more aware of specific harmful effects of smoking on the body (Tingen, Grimling, Bennett, Gibson, & Renew, 1997).

Use Characters That Appeal to the Age Group

Young people pay close attention to characters that are similar to them; they feel validated when they see those characters in the media, and this can positively affect their self-esteem (McDermott & Greenberg, 1985). To engage them in exploring a campaign's content and message, the main characters or hosts should be appealing role model characters actively portraying the behaviors espoused by the campaign. If a simulation or game is used, the characters should appear in scenarios that involve the user in making decisions and performing skills intended by the campaign, and realistic consequences of those decisions should be depicted (Lieberman, 1997; Lieberman & Brown, 1995).

One CD-ROM series, *Choosing Success* (*www.ccclearn.com/products/successmaker*), uses simulations to help adolescents learn problem solving, critical thinking, and life skills. It presents very gritty, realistic videos of at-risk youth confronting personal problems on topics that include The Inner

You, Employability, Working Relationships, Family Circumstances, Peer Relationships, The Body-Mind Connection, Dating Pressures, and Community Advocacy. The main characters are real inner-city and suburban adolescents, not actors. These realistic, nonglamorous characters were highly appealing and credible to at-risk teens who took part in formative and summative evaluations of *Choosing Success* throughout the United States (Lieberman, 1993). The participants paid close attention to the characters and became involved in making decisions for them in the simulated interactive environment. The appeal of the role model characters helped attract and hold attention and stimulated group discussion about the life problems and solutions presented in the program.

Research on social cognitive theory has found that behaviors can be acquired from observing other people's actions and the consequences of those actions (Bandura, 1982, 1986, 1994). Through observational learning, also known as social learning, children and adults notice which actions tend to get rewarded and which have unpleasant outcomes. Those that are rewarded are the ones people may eventually repeat in their own lives, when the circumstances are right. Just as people learn when they observe others in real life, they also learn from characters in the media, in both video and animations (Bandura, 1994, 1997).

Children are more attentive to and will be more likely to emulate the behavior of those models who are demographically most similar to them. For children and adolescents, though, role model characters should be about 2 or 3 years older than the target group because they are anticipating how they might behave when they get a little older (Collins, 1983).

New research questions arise when role models appear in interactive media, in which the user is in control of the action. Although models may continue to attract the attention of certain users, to what extent does observational learning occur when a user can control the decisions and behaviors of a role model character? Does observational learning decrease, compared to traditional media, because users may discount the value of a decision they have made themselves? Does observational learning increase and is it retained longer because the user has made a thoughtful decision about the model's next step and has issued a command to make that event occur? Also, how about a boomerang effect, when a child makes the role model behave badly?

Support Information Searching

The Internet provides access to growing storehouses of information and interactive programs; more than 1,000 new web sites appear on the Internet every day. This can be an advantage when desired information is handy, but an unfulfilled search for information can lead to frustration and wasted time. To help children find the material they want, and to screen it for quality and age appropriateness, interactive campaign content could include a child-oriented search engine and clearly organized lists of links.

An example of this is *Ask Jeeves for Kids* (*www.ajkids.com*), a search engine that allows natural language inquiries. The child types a question, and the program parses it to identify topics to search. *Ask Jeeves for Kids* also provides Fun Tours, which are lists of links about interesting topics. Current topics in Fun Tours are earthquakes, pets, mythology, and games. There are also sections called Net-Mom Picks, Teachers, Today's World (news), and Brain Box TV (upcoming high-quality TV programs for children).

Interactive campaign materials can be designed specifically to spark children's interest in exploring campaign topics. For example, a campaign-related fact-hunting adventure game could ask children to find web sites that provide answers to questions. The adventure might involve solving a mystery, identifying a problem and deriving a possible solution, or finding information that helps complete a task. A powerful use of a simulation with novices (i.e., those who are unfamiliar with the rules and strategies of the simulation) is to let them try it and discover that there are gaps in their knowledge. At that point, they become highly motivated to seek information to improve their performance (Ambron & Hooper, 1990; Kozma, 1991; Lieberman & Linn, 1991).

Incorporate Challenges and Goals

Challenge to reach a goal is a key motivator in interactive activities (Malone & Lepper, 1987). If the process is entertaining and offers a challenge that is neither too easy nor too difficult, young people will try it repeatedly until they master it. There is evidence that skills learned in this way carry over to real-life decision making and behaviors (Brown et al., 1997; Lepper & Gurtner, 1989; Lieberman & Brown, 1995). Papert (1996) calls the appeal of challenging activities "hard fun."

Engaging in a challenging sequence of activities bounded by rules often brings a sense of pure enjoyment, or flow (Csikszentmihalyi, 1990). This outcome has been found in activities as diverse as reading, playing team sports, performing brain surgery, and playing video games. To achieve flow, the challenge ideally should match the person's abilities, and the experience should provide immediate feedback on performance. When people become engaged in a challenging activity such as this, they often lose their sense of time and place while they enjoy the concentrated effort. They are completely immersed. Youngsters, as much as adults, report having experienced this sense of immersion and enjoyment when playing a challenging but achievable video game (Lieberman, 1997). An interactive campaign could attract and engage children by capitalizing on their thirst for challenges, through the use of games, simulations, fact-hunting adventures, and other goal-oriented activities.

Use Learning-by-Doing

Children usually become very involved in experiential educational activities, such as simulations and games that involve them in active decision making (Austin, 1995; Larson, 1991; Lieberman & Linn, 1991). A simulation is a scenario in which users can change the conditions, or variables, and then observe rule-based outcomes in response to their choices. An example of a simulation on interactive media is the CD-ROM classic *SimCity* (*www.simcity.com*), which teaches about city planning, effects of pollution, and resources needed to keep the environment healthy. Users build a simulated city and observe the impact of various city-planning decisions. A major goal is to keep the city thriving; the city will lose its viability if poor planning decisions are made, much as happens to real cities.

Learning can occur with simulations and interactive games if the user has many chances for repetition and rehearsal; if the system provides immediate, individualized feedback on the consequences of the user's decisions; and if the content and feedback match the user's abilities (Bandura, 1986; Csikszentmihalyi, 1990; Lepper & Gurtner, 1989; McNeil & Nelson, 1991; Osman & Hannafin, 1993).

Learning-by-doing can also be integrated into consumer education campaigns by giving people a chance to formulate counterarguments to persuasive messages. Campaign researchers have experimented with interactive programs that support counterarguing against advertising slogans for unhealthful products, for example, by encouraging children to use a graphics program to paint graffiti over familiar cigarette ads. Creating and expressing antismoking arguments can make those thoughts salient to children who face a daily barrage of commercial messages to the contrary (Bandura, 1997).

According to social cognitive theory, when children or adults believe they are efficacious enough to be successful, they are more likely to try and to succeed (Bandura, 1994, 1997). *Self-efficacy,* a belief in one's own ability to carry out a specific task successfully, is predictive of future actions. Believing in your own capacity to perform is a bridge between knowing what to do and actually doing it. When self-efficacy is high, people are more likely to turn their knowledge into overt behavior. As interactive media users become successful while rehearsing a desirable but difficult activity, they are more likely to perceive themselves as efficacious enough to carry out that activity in real life. Also, as self-efficacy increases, so does their willingness to tackle more difficult challenges, which can increase self-efficacy even further.

People who have a strong sense of self-efficacy regarding health and self-care behaviors are more likely to have a healthy lifestyle, to seek and follow medical advice when ill, to avoid life crises, to cope with crises that do occur, and to establish closer personal ties so that social support is available to buffer against illness (Peterson & Stunkard, 1989). Conversely, those with low self-efficacy in this area think of themselves as helpless; they are more likely to become ill and to cope ineffectively with medical problems. There is strong evidence that interactive media can deliver interventions that improve users' self-efficacy for specific health behaviors so that they perform them more often or more appropriately and consequently experience improved health outcomes (Bandura, 1997; Brown et al., 1997).

A challenge to learn-by-doing is incorporated into a video game called *Packy & Marlon* (*www.clickhealth.com*), which teaches diabetes self-management skills to children and adolescents, ages 7 and older, who have insulin-dependent diabetes. The game includes a simulation of the diabetic main character's blood sugar levels, which fluctuate according to the player's choices of food and insulin for the character. If blood sugar stays in the normal zone, the character is robust enough to progress in the game; if blood sugar gets too high or too low, however, the character—and therefore the player—has to remedy the problem or lose the game.

A randomized field experiment with *Packy & Marlon* (Brown et al., 1997) found that diabetic children and adolescents who had the game at home for 6 months, to play as much or as little as they wished, improved in self-efficacy for diabetes self-management and also improved in self-management behaviors and health outcomes. They played the game an average of 1.5 hours per week. Their rehearsal of diabetes-related skills and behaviors in the game (e.g., monitoring blood glucose, taking insulin, and choosing a good balance of foods) predicted several improvements: increases in self-efficacy for diabetes self-management skills and behaviors, improvements in the behaviors in real life, and improved health outcomes in the form of a 77% decrease in players' emergency and urgent care visits related to diabetes. Study participants who were assigned to a control group and received a pinball video game with no health content also played their video game about 1.5 hours per week; they had no changes in diabetes-related self-efficacy, health behaviors, or health outcomes during the 6 months of the study.

Bronkie the Bronchiasaurus (*www.clickhealth.com*) is another game involving learning-by-doing for self-management of a chronic condition. It teaches asthma self-management to children and adolescents ages 7 and older. It incorporates a simulation of peak flow (breath strength) based on the main character's use of daily and emergency medications and on the character's avoidance or contact with asthma triggers in the environment (dust, pollen, smoke, furry animals, cold viruses, etc.). The child controls the main character's activities and self-care behaviors. Asthmatic children and adolescents who played the game improved in self-efficacy for asthma-related skills and were better able to keep their asthma under control (Lieberman, 1997, 1999).

Experiential learning is a unique and influential feature of interactive media, and there is clear research evidence demonstrating that learning-by-doing in this environment can lead to behavior change in a person's daily life. More research is needed to understand how, for whom, and under what conditions this process takes place.

Create Functional Learning Environments

Functional learning occurs when people are engaged in personally relevant activities that serve a useful purpose or function. Often, functional learning environments involve sharing information or working on problems with others; in these cases, there is a social component to the learning. People become motivated to learn when the learning will help them carry out a task or solve a problem that interests them or when they can share their ideas or discoveries with others (Repman, 1993; Riel, 1985, 1989).

Interactive media can provide opportunities for children to experience functional learning in goal-driven activities shared with others. This approach appears in the Earth Force (*www.earthforce.org*) web site, which helps youngsters implement solutions to environmental problems and offers success stories, community projects, and information. Envirolink (*www.envirolink. org*) is another environmental site targeted to youth, offering resources for improving the environment, information about environmental issues, on-line discussions, and a listing of Earth Day events. Not only do these sites provide on-line activities but also they use on-line communication and information to support off-line activities that involve young people in community projects.

A campaign can take advantage of the motivational, collaborative, and information-sharing aspects of functional learning by involving youngsters in interactive on-line campaign activities.

Facilitate Social Interaction

On-line activities stimulate discussion of a campaign with others, both face-to-face and on-line. This could help a young person see how campaign issues affect others, and it could influence personal decisions and behaviors. Interpersonal discussion has long been recognized as a key factor in the diffusion of ideas and behavior change (Rogers, 1987).

The InSite (*www.talkcity.com/theinsite*) web site offers information resources and moderated chat rooms about topics of interest to teens and young adults. Information on the site is organized into sections called Me, Myself, and I; Relationships Unlimited; Justice Now; and Spaceship Earth. The chat room moderators are experts at counseling adolescents. Presented on The InSite are fictional but realistic stories in the form of teens' journal entries, with new installments added regularly. Users are encouraged to respond to the life crises and personal dilemmas of the fictional characters through on-line discussions and bulletin board postings.

Another technique to focus youngsters on discussion of campaign topics is to post true stories about real children on a web site, as the U.S. Environmental Protection Agency has done in its Explorers' Club site (*www.epa.gov/kids*). The true stories demonstrate how some children have worked effectively to improve the environment, and additional on-line discussion is encouraged. This highly interactive site offers—in addition to true stories—contests, games, art, comic books, interactive fiction, pictures, science, and experiments.

Social support is an important factor in behavioral health interventions and campaigns. Without social interaction and support, people are less likely to remain healthy or to cope effectively when health problems occur (Peterson & Stunkard, 1989). Interactive campaigns can foster social support by providing multimedia activities for groups to do together as a way to stimulate interpersonal interaction. They can also help people find others who share their interests and concerns and allow them to communicate with each other. One example is Starbright World (*www.starbright.org*), a network that enables seriously ill children throughout the United States to communicate with other hospitalized children who are experiencing similar life-threatening problems.

Beginning at about 7 or 8, children enjoy communicating with others when they use computers, video games, and the Internet. They do this on-line with e-mail, bulletin boards, real-time chat, and on-line games (Rideout et al., 1999), and they also get together to play video games with friends (Lieberman, 1997). Both communication via interactive media and face-to-face sharing of interactive media have the potential to encourage and support children's discussions of campaign issues and activities.

Allow User Anonymity When Appropriate

The privacy and anonymity of interactive media can be an attractive alternative to interacting with people face-to-face when users have reason to keep their questions confidential. The benefits of anonymous interaction were documented in a study of the *Body Awareness Resource Network,* a database of information that was available to adolescents in a private setting and that concerned highly sensitive topics, such as alcohol and other drugs, human sexuality, smoking prevention and cessation, stress management, and diet. When allowed to access the system anonymously, many adolescents used it to find out about their own high-risk health behaviors. Normally, this group would be most unlikely to seek such information face-to-face from parents, teachers, or health professionals. Interactive media provided an acceptable way to explore personal questions and concerns (Gustafson, Bosworth, Chewning, & Hawkins, 1987).

Involve Young People in Product Design and Testing

One way to ensure the target group will be attracted to the campaign format is to include members of that group in the design and planning process (Druin et al., 1999; Druin & Solomon, 1996; Kafai, 1995; Kafai & Resnick, 1996; Scaife & Rogers, 1999). Participatory design groups involving both children and adults can develop novel and creative ideas about formats and content of interactive media that would appeal to young media users. In addition to initial design ideas, children should have opportunities for input throughout the development of an interactive campaign. Campaign designers should test early prototypes with target users to ensure they understand the content and format, they see how to navigate through it, and they consider the material engaging and appealing (Hanna, Risden, Czerwinski, & Alexander, 1999; Lieberman, 1999; see Chapter 7, this volume).

When campaign media are fully operational, youngsters could participate in a field test, or beta test, using the campaign media in the intended settings for several days or weeks. Campaign designers could observe patterns of use and gather evaluative feedback from the children and their families, teachers, and friends. This would help them identify the campaign's strengths and weaknesses so that immediate adjustments could be made and future revisions planned.

CONCLUSION

Interactive media provide a rich and unprecedented environment for experiential communication campaigns geared to young people. These media are attractive to children and adolescents. When designed well, they offer participation, interactivity, and choice, with messages individualized to the user's input. They combine human-computer interaction with mediated interpersonal communication; each mode can enhance the other.

There have not been many studies of interactive campaigns, but research and theory in related areas offer guideposts. Mass media and interactive media research, studies of traditional mass media campaigns, and studies of communication and children are all relevant. Old questions should be retested in the new interactive campaign environment, however, and many new questions about human-computer interaction and mediated interpersonal communication should be investigated. We need novel conceptualizations of users and of the many facets of mediated interactive communication. Also, we need to study and understand the limitations of interactive campaigns; not every campaign goal is amenable to this approach. Successes to date suggest, however, that much more can be done using this versatile communication resource (see also Rice & Katz, 2001).

REFERENCES

Ambron, S., & Hooper, K. (Eds.). (1990). *Learning with interactive multimedia.* Redmond, WA: Microsoft Press.

Austin, E. W. (1995). Reaching young audiences: Developmental considerations in designing health messages. In E. W. Maibach & R. L. Parrott (Eds.), *Designing health messages: Approaches from communication theory and public health practice* (pp. 114-144). Thousand Oaks, CA: Sage.

Bandura, A. (1982). Self-efficacy mechanism in human agency. *American Psychologist, 37*, 122-147.

Bandura, A. (1986). *Social foundations of thought and action: A social cognitive theory.* Englewood Cliffs, NJ: Prentice Hall.

Bandura, A. (1994). Social cognitive theory of mass communication. In J. Bryant & D. Zillmann (Eds.), *Media effects: Advances in theory and research* (pp. 61-90). Hillsdale, NJ: Lawrence Erlbaum.

Bandura, A. (1997). *Self-efficacy: The exercise of control.* New York: Freeman.

Brown, S. J., Lieberman, D. A., Gemeny, B. A., Fan, Y. C., Wilson, D. M., & Pasta, D. J. (1997). Educational video game for juvenile diabetes: Results of a controlled trial. *Medical Informatics, 22*(1), 77-89.

Calvert, S. (1999). *Children's journeys through the information age.* Boston: McGraw-Hill.

Clements, D. (1987). Computers and young children: A review of research. *Young Children, 43*(1), 34-43.

Collins, W. A. (1983). Interpretation and inference in children's television viewing. In J. Bryant & D. Anderson (Eds.), *Children's understanding of television: Research on attention and comprehension* (pp. 125-179). New York: Academic Press.

Csikszentmihalyi, M. (1990). *Flow: The psychology of optimal experience.* New York: Harper & Row.

Doubleday, C. N., & Droege, K. L. (1993). Cognitive developmental influences on children's understanding of television. In G. L. Berry & J. K. Asamen (Eds.), *Children & television: Images in a changing sociocultural world* (pp. 23-37). Newbury Park, CA: Sage.

Druin, A., Bederson, B., Boltman, A., Miura, A., Knotts-Callahan, D., & Platt, M. (1999). Children as our technology design partners. In A. Druin (Ed.), *The design of children's technology* (pp. 51-72). San Francisco: Morgan Kaufmann.

Druin, A., & Solomon, C. (1996). *Designing multimedia environments for children: Computers, creativity, and kids.* New York: Wiley.

Gustafson, D. H., Bosworth, K., Chewning, B., & Hawkins, R. P. (1987). Computer-based health promotion: Combining technological advances with problem-solving techniques to effect successful health behavior changes. *Annual Review of Public Health, 8*, 387-415.

Hanna, L., Risden, K., Czerwinski, M., & Alexander, K. J. (1999). The role of usability research in designing children's computer products. In A. Druin (Ed.), *The design of children's technology* (pp. 3-26). San Francisco: Morgan Kaufmann.

Harel, E. (1999). *Clickerati kids: Who are they?* [On-line]. Available: *www.mamamedia. com.*

Kafai, Y. B. (1995). *Minds in play: Computer game design as a context for children's learning.* Hillsdale, NJ: Lawrence Erlbaum.

Kafai, Y. B., & Resnick, M. (Eds.). (1996). *Constructionism in practice: Designing, thinking, and learning in a digital world.* Mahwah, NJ: Lawrence Erlbaum.

Kozma, R. B. (1991). Learning with media. *Review of Educational Research, 61*(2), 179-211.

Larson, M. S. (1991). Health-related messages embedded in prime-time television entertainment. *Health Communication, 3*, 175-184.

Lepper, M. R., & Gurtner, J. (1989). Children and computers: Approaching the twenty-first century. *American Psychologist, 44*(2), 170-178.

Lieberman, D. A. (1993). *Field test of Choosing Success with at-risk teens: Usage, outcomes, and recommended design revisions.* Unpublished report. Sunnyvale, CA: Computer Curriculum Corporation.

Lieberman, D. A. (1997). Interactive video games for health promotion: Effects on knowledge, self-efficacy, social support, and health. In R. L. Street, W. R. Gold, & T. Manning (Eds.), *Health promotion and interactive technology: Theoretical applications and future directions* (pp. 103-120). Mahwah, NJ: Lawrence Erlbaum.

Lieberman, D. A. (1999). The researcher's role in the design of children's media and technology. In A. Druin (Ed.), *The design of children's technology* (pp. 73-97). San Francisco: Morgan Kaufmann.

Lieberman, D. A., & Brown, S. J. (1995). Designing interactive video games for children's health education. In K. Morgan, R. Sativa, H. Sieburg, R. Mattheus, & J. Christensen (Eds.), *Interactive technology and the new paradigm for healthcare* (pp. 201-210). Amsterdam: IOS Press.

Lieberman, D. A., & Linn, M. C. (1991). Learning to learn revisited: Computers and the development of self-directed learning skills. *Journal of Research on Computing in Education, 23*(3), 373-395.

Malone, T. W., & Lepper, M. R. (1987). Making learning fun: A taxonomy of intrinsic motivations for learning. In R. E. Snow & M. J. Farr (Eds.), *Aptitude, learning and instruction III. Conative and affective process analyses* (pp. 223-253). Hillsdale, NJ: Lawrence Erlbaum.

McDermott, S., & Greenberg, B. (1985). Parents, peers, and television as determinants of black children's esteem. *Communication Yearbook, 8,* 164-177.

McNeil, B. J., & Nelson, K. R. (1991). Meta-analysis of interactive video instruction: A 10 year review of achievement effects. *Journal of Computer-Based Instruction, 18*(1), 1-6.

Osman, M. E., & Hannafin, M. J. (1993). Metacognition research and theory: Analysis and implications for instructional design. *Educational Technology Research and Development, 40*(2), 83-99.

Papert, S. (1996). *The connected family: Bridging the digital generation gap.* Atlanta: Longstreet.

Parrott, R. L. (1995). Motivation to attend to health messages: Presentation of content and linguistic considerations. In E. W. Maibach & R. L. Parrott (Eds.), *Designing health messages: Approaches from communication theory and public health practice* (pp. 2-23). Thousand Oaks, CA: Sage.

Peterson, C., & Stunkard, A. J. (1989). Personal control and health promotion. *Social Science and Medicine, 28,* 819-828.

Repman, J. (1993). Collaborative, computer-based learning: Cognitive and affective outcomes. *Journal of Educational Computing Research, 9*(2), 149-163.

Rice, R. E., & Katz, J. (Eds.) (2001). *The Internet and health communication.* Thousand Oaks, CA: Sage.

Rideout, V. J., Foehr, U. G., Roberts, D. F., & Brodie, M. (1999). *Kids & media @ the new millennium: A comprehensive national analysis of children's media use.* Menlo Park, CA: Henry J. Kaiser Family Foundation.

Riel, M. (1985). The Computer Chronicles Newswire: A functional learning environment for acquiring literacy skills. *Journal of Educational Computing Research, 1,* 317-337.

Riel, M. (1989). The impact of computers in classrooms. *Journal of Research on Computing in Education, 22,* 180-190.

Rogers, E. M. (1987). Progress, problems, and prospects for network research: Investigating relationships in the age of electronic communication technologies. *Social Networks, 9,* 285-310.

Scaife, M., & Rogers, Y. (1999). Kids as informants: Telling us what we didn't know or confirming what we knew already? In A. Druin (Ed.), *The design of children's technology* (pp. 27-50). San Francisco: Morgan Kaufmann.

Software & Information Industry Association. (1999). *Consumer market and education market survey report.* Washington, DC: Author.

Tingen, M. S., Grimling, L. F., Bennett, G., Gibson, E. M., & Renew, M. M. (1997). A pilot study of preadolescents to evaluate a video game-based smoking prevention strategy. *Journal of Addictions Nursing, 9*(3), 118-124.

31

Putting Policy Into Health Communication[1]

The Role of Media Advocacy

Lawrence Wallack
Lori Dorfman

Public communication campaigns are very seductive. They provide the promise of knowledge as ultimate power. Those at risk for a wide range of health problems simply need to get the right information. Once the targets of the campaign have acquired this information, whether it be about how many fruits and vegetables they should eat to avoid cancer or that it is necessary to "think when you drink," they should be able to act appropriately and avoid health problems. The strategy systematically ignores the wide range of social forces that influence health and focuses on personal choice. Thus, flaws are defined and remedied at the individual level, leaving important contributory social and economic factors unchanged.

The purpose of this chapter is to argue that this strategy is misdirected because it is fundamentally inconsistent with the mission and goals of public health. Health communication campaigns evolve out of a desire to ensure that people have the right information about their health. Although information is important, traditional campaign approaches have been poor tools for improving health status. This chapter suggests some of the reasons for the lack of success of these approaches in improving the health status of populations and argues that media advocacy, a more policy-oriented approach, is necessary.

HEALTH COMMUNICATION CAMPAIGNS

The use of mass media to improve public health has become increasingly sophisticated in the past generation (see Chapter 3, this volume). The careful application of behavior change theories and social marketing techniques has increased the potential of large-scale public education campaigns to achieve their goals. In addition, the use of paid rather than public service advertising, particularly in the area of tobacco and illicit drugs, has become more common (see Chapter 12, this volume). This helps to ensure repeated exposures to the desired message. Nonetheless, there is continuing concern as to whether such campaigns do, in fact, change behavior and contribute to improved population health status.

Public education campaigns are largely governed by the idea that people need more and better personal information to navigate a hazardous health environment. This may seem intuitively reasonable, and the history of media campaigns demonstrates a primary focus on increasing personal knowledge and not promoting collective action or policy change. These campaigns provide individuals with knowledge about risks such as alcohol, tobacco, sedentary lifestyles, diet, and unsafe sex in the hope that they will change the way in which they act.

Mass-mediated health communication efforts generally flow from a pragmatic logic that assumes an information gap in individuals: If people just knew and understood that certain behaviors were bad for them and others good, then these people would change to the behaviors that benefited their health. Filling the information gap becomes the purpose of the campaign; if enough people changed their behavior, then this would lead to a healthier society. The problem is operationally defined as people just not knowing any better. The goal, then, is to warn and inform people so they can change. To make this happen, campaigns focus on developing the right message to deliver to the largest number of people through the mass media. Finding the right message is central to the campaign and extremely important. The message, however, is almost always about personal change rather than social change, institutional accountability, or collective action.

Although there are many ways in which a well-designed campaign can increase the potential for success, meaningful success has been elusive. In a comprehensive review of communication campaigns, Rogers and Storey (1987) noted, "The literature of campaign research is filled with failures, along with qualified successes—evidence that campaigns *can* be effective under certain conditions" (p. 817). This review, more optimistic than some and slightly more pessimistic than others, generally echoed previous reviews (Alcalay, 1983; Atkin, 1981; McGuire, 1986; Wallack, 1981, 1984) and anticipated later reviews (Brown & Walsh-Childers, 1994; DeJong & Winsten, 1998; Salmon, 1989; Wallack & DeJong, 1995; see Chapter 10, this volume).

Better health communication campaigns are characterized by at least three important factors. First, these campaigns are more likely to use mass communication and behavior change theory as a basis for campaign design. This means using a variety of mass communication channels, ensuring that the audience is exposed to the message, reducing barriers to change, and providing a clear and specific action for the individual to take. Second, they are more likely to use formative research such as focus groups to develop messages and inform campaign strategy. Many better designed interventions also include various social marketing strategies, such as market segmentation, channel analysis, and message pretesting (Lefebvre & Flora, 1988; see Chapter 7, this volume). Third, they are more likely to link media strategies with community programs, thus reinforcing the media message and providing local support for desired behavior changes (Wallack & DeJong, 1995; see Chapter 27, this volume). These three factors improve the traditional approach, but they do not remedy the fundamental problem of the focus on personal behavior change. Approaches that change the environment in which people make their health decisions have a better chance of improving health status across broad populations over the long term. Without this orientation, the potential of health communication campaigns will always be limited.

LIMITS OF HEALTH COMMUNICATION CAMPAIGNS

Much of the reason for the lack of clear, consistent effects of mass media campaigns may be that they are just not comprehensive enough to affect public health problems. Such campaigns may fall short in at least three areas.

First, many media campaigns are based on "risk factorology" (McKinlay & Marceau, 2000) and focus primarily on changing individual behavior. Even when the body of risk factors for specific diseases is aggregated, however, seldom is more than 50% of the variance explained. Lomas (1998) argues that individual risk factor modification, an approach at the core of most mass media campaigns, has been "spectacularly unsuccessful" (p. 1183). Even if campaigns are successful in changing risk factor behaviors in some, they are unlikely to be effective in improving health status across populations.

Second, the lessons from prototypical public education campaigns such as the Stanford Heart Disease Prevention Program clearly indicate that to be successful, campaigns must be linked to broader community action (see Chapters 11 and 27, this volume), but this is seldom the case. For example, the recent $2 billion antidrug campaign by the federal Office on Narcotics and Drug Control Policy uses extensive paid advertising but has weak links to community participation (see Chapter 12, this volume). The expectation is that local people will be motivated by the campaign to "get involved" in preventing drug use, but no resources are allocated to ensure that this happens (DeJong & Wallack, 1999).

Third, the mission of public health is to ensure "conditions in which people can be healthy" (Institute of Medicine, 1998, p. 140). Public policy to change the conditions that give rise to and sustain public health problems is fundamental to improving population health (Beauchamp, 1976). Few campaigns, however, move out of the behavioral context to the larger issue of policies that create the environment that determines the range of personal and behavioral choices available to individuals (see Chapter 8, this volume). Motivating people to jog in neighborhoods riddled by violence or encouraging consumption of fresh fruits and vegetables where none is available, even if somehow successful in getting people's attention and motivating them to change, will do little to improve their overall life chances.

Certainly, there is a need for clear health-related information, well-produced and widely distributed. Often, however, it is not an appropriate starting point for health promotion. For example, 5-a-Day campaigns have as their goal improving health status by increasing consumption of fruit and vegetables. This worthy goal will remain unattainable, despite the most persuasive communications campaign, if fruit and vegetables are not easily available and affordable. One local group in California wanted to initiate a local 5-a-Day campaign to improve the outcomes of teen pregnancies. When they sought our advice on administering a 5-a-Day campaign, we asked, "Where will the young women get the fruit and vegetables?" The major supermarkets had abandoned the inner-city neighborhoods that were home to the teens they wanted to reach, leaving nothing but corner liquor stores that stocked old and expensive fruit and vegetables, if they stocked them at all. We suggested they frame this from an economic development perspective and involve the teens in a campaign to demand the return of the grocers, to initiate a community garden, or other effort to create an environment in which they could make healthy choices for themselves and their families. In this example, a 5-a-Day social marketing campaign would make sense only after a campaign had been carried out to ensure the local availability of fruits and vegetables.

It is particularly important that the mission of public health emphasizes the need to focus on public policy and not just personal habits. This means that populations, rather than individuals, are the primary focus (Rose, 1992) and points to the importance of addressing the rules that shape the social and physical environments that largely determine health. When policy is understood as central to the mission of public health, then our understanding of media campaigns will shift. For example, the role of the news media in setting the public and policy agenda and framing public debate becomes critical.

If media campaigns are to move beyond a risk factor focus, if they are to connect people to community action and attend to the policies that create unhealthy conditions, then people need skills to better participate in the public policy process to make the environment less hazardous. Health communication campaigns can contribute to this skill development if the audience is thought of as potential participants in the social change process rather than simply being viewed as vehicles for personal behavior change (see Chapters 7 and 13, this volume).

SOME UNINTENDED ADVERSE CONSEQUENCES OF CAMPAIGNS

Overreliance on public education campaigns, even the better designed ones, may actually be a barrier to the accomplishment of public health goals for three reasons. First, such an emphasis conflicts with the social justice ethic of public health that calls for a fair sharing of the burden for prevention (Beauchamp, 1976). At worst, such campaigns may contribute to the problem they seek to address. This happens when the narrow behavioral focus of the campaign deflects attention away from social and structural determinants of health by focusing exclusively on the behavior of individuals—in effect blaming the victim for the problem and placing the sole burden for change on him or her (Dorfman & Wallack, 1993; Ryan, 1976; Wallack, 1989, 1990).

Second, participation in collective action and policy change is generally not advanced by most of these campaigns because they tend to focus on personal behaviors that individuals can take on their own behalf to improve their health. Public policy or social action is seldom, if ever, a focus of public health media campaigns because these campaigns are usually supported with public money that makes advocacy for specific policies problematic. Also, many media outlets will not accept public service announcements or even paid advertisements that are considered controversial—and policy issues that inevitably confront corporate interests are inherently controversial (see Chapter 25, this volume).

Third, it is not logical or effective to define a problem at the community or societal level and then focus primarily on solutions at the personal or individual level. There are many definitions of public health, but one clear thread running through these is the fundamental idea that the primary focus must be on the health and well-being of communities or populations, not individuals (Mann, 1997; Rose, 1985, 1992).

The crucial issue, then, is what kinds of media approaches can increase the capacity of groups, and broader communities, to act on matters related to public health that potentially benefit the entire society? Media advocacy is one approach that provides a framework and a set of skills for shifting the focus to policy issues addressing population health.

MEDIA ADVOCACY

Media advocacy is the strategic use of mass media in combination with community organizing to advance healthy public policies. The primary focus is on the role of news media, with secondary attention to the use of paid advertising (Chapman & Lupton, 1994; U.S. Department of Health and Human Services, 1988; Wallack, 1994; Wallack & Dorfman, 1996; Wallack, Dorfman, Jernigan,

& Themba, 1993; Wallack & Sciandra, 1990-1991; Wallack, Woodruff, Dorfman, & Diaz, 1999; Winett & Wallack, 1996). Media advocacy seeks to raise the volume of voices for social change and shape the sound so that it resonates with the social justice values that are the presumed basis of public health (Beauchamp, 1976; Mann, 1997). It has been used by a wide range of grassroots community groups, public health leadership groups, public health and social advocates, and public health researchers (Wallack et al., 1993, 1999).

The practical origins of media advocacy can be traced to the late 1980s. It grew from a collaboration of public health groups working on tobacco and alcohol issues with public interest and consumer groups also working on these or similar issues. The public interest and consumer groups brought a new array of strategies and tactics that were more common in political campaigns than in public health efforts. The public health perspective provided a clearer understanding of the substantive scientific issues and the importance of theory in creating change. The result has been an approach that blends science, politics, and advocacy to advance public health goals.

From a theoretical perspective, media advocacy borrows from mass communication, political science, sociology, and political psychology to understand the role of news in policy making and to develop strategy. Central to media advocacy is the concept of agenda-setting (Dearing & Rogers, 1997; McCombs & Shaw, 1972) and framing (Gamson, 1989; Iyengar, 1991; Ryan, 1991). Agenda-setting research encourages the media advocacy approaches to focus attention on specific public health issues. Lessons from "framing" studies help shape the debate to reflect a public health perspective. Media advocacy also borrows from community organizing, key elements of formative research (i.e., focus groups and polling), and political campaign strategy (e.g., application of selective pressure on key groups or individuals) (Wallack et al., 1993). Blending theory with practice provides an overall framework for advocacy and social change.

Media advocacy differs in many ways from traditional public health campaigns. It is most marked by an emphasis on

1. Linking public health and social problems to inequities in social arrangements rather than to flaws in the individual

2. Changing public policy rather than personal health behavior

3. Focusing primarily on reaching opinion leaders and policymakers rather than those who have the problem (the traditional audience of public health communication campaigns)

4. Working with groups to increase participation and amplify their voices rather than providing health behavior change messages

5. Having a primary goal of reducing the power gap rather than just filling the information gap

Media advocacy is generally viewed as a part of a broader strategy rather than as a strategy per se. One of the fundamental rules of media advocacy is that it is not possible to have a media strategy without an overall strategy. Media advocacy is part of the overall plan, but it is not the plan, for achieving policy change. For example, a group in Oakland, California, effectively used media advocacy to advance a city ordinance to place a tax on liquor stores and institute a 1-year moratorium on new licenses in the city (Seevak, 1997). The effort took 4 years to implement, starting at the local zoning commission and ending at the California State Supreme Court. During this period, the group used media advocacy to provide legitimacy to the issue, to increase the credibility of their position and add urgency to the problem, and to let politicians know that the community was very involved in the issue and would be following all votes. To achieve this, they used a variety of tactics to generate news coverage and discussion on the editorial pages. This increased the effectiveness of the grassroots coalition advancing the policy but would have made little difference if the coalition did not have strong community support for the issue (resulting in large turnouts at key meetings and hearings and also visits and calls to politicians), a clear and reasonable policy goal, research to support their claims, and a media strategy to advance the policy and support community organizing. Media advocacy helped amplify and accelerate their efforts; the news coverage provided a sense of urgency to their demands, increased legitimacy and credibility of the policy they were advancing, and attracted new supporters while reinforcing the commitment of the original supporters.

Overall Strategy Development

Media advocacy focuses on four primary activities in support of community organizing, policy development, and advancing policy.

Media advocacy uses critical thinking to understand and respond to problems as social issues rather than personal problems. With this problem definition, the focus of the strategy is on elaborating policy options; identifying the person, group, or organization that has the power to create the necessary change; and identifying organizations that can apply pressure to advance the policy and create change (e.g., in the Oakland example discussed previously, various elements of the community were organized to apply pressure on the zoning commission, the mayor's office, city council, and state legislature, which were all targets at various points in the campaign). Finally, various messages for the different targets of the campaign are developed. Again, in media advocacy, the target is the policymaker, organization, or legislative body that has the power to make the desired policy change rather than the individuals with the problem.

Setting the Agenda

Getting an issue in the media can help set the agenda and provide legitimacy and credibility to the issue and group. Media advocacy involves understanding how journalism works so that access to the news media can be increased. This includes maintaining a media list, monitoring the news media, understanding the elements of newsworthiness, pitching stories, organizing news events, and developing editorial page strategies for reaching key opinion leaders.

Shaping the Debate

The news media generally focus on the plight of the victim, whereas policy advocates emphasize social conditions that create victims. Media advocates frame policy issues using public health values that resonate with broad audiences. Some of the steps include "translat[ing] personal troubles into public issues" (Mills, 1959, p. 187); emphasizing social accountability as well as personal responsibility; identifying individuals and organizations that must assume a greater burden for addressing the problem; presenting a clear and concise policy solution; and packaging the story by combining key elements such as visuals, expert voices, authentic voices (those with experience of the problem), media bites, social math (creating a context for large numbers that is interesting to the press and understandable to the public), research summaries, fact sheets, policy papers, and so on. The challenge is to provide journalists with varied story elements that make it easier for them to tell the story from the population and policy perspective rather than just the individual or personal angle.

Advancing the Policy

Policy battles are often long and contentious, and it is important to make effective use of the media to keep the issue on the media agenda. The Oakland effort took 4 years, and now it must focus media attention to ensure that the policy is properly implemented. Thus, it is important to develop strategies to maintain the media spotlight on the policy issue on a continuing basis. This means identifying opportunities to reintroduce the issue to the media, such as key anniversaries of relevant dates, publication of new reports, significant meetings or hearings, and linking the policy solution to breaking news.

Media advocacy has been applied to many public health and social issues, including affirmative action, child care, alcohol, tobacco, childhood lead poisoning, health promotion, nutrition, exercise, violence, handgun control, and suicide prevention. This approach grew out of the tobacco control movement's goal to change the way Americans thought about smoking and its sequelae. During the past 30 years, tobacco control advocates have used media advocacy approaches in efforts to increase the excise tax on tobacco, remove billboards and other advertising, outlaw vending machines, and give the Food and Drug Administration jurisdiction over tobacco, in addition to other policies. In each of these efforts, the target has been the legislator, legislative body, or executive that had the power to enact the policy being sought. Although the specific target changed based on local circumstances, the overall framing has focused on the tobacco industry and the government body that regulates it rather than just the smoker.

Media advocacy has since moved beyond tobacco control. Children's health advocates have used media advocacy to pressure policymakers to include prevention measures for childhood lead poisoning in national legislation. Disability rights advocates used media advocacy to fight for accessible public transportation and federal support for home attendant care (Hartman & Johnson, 1993). In New Zealand, alcohol control advocates used media advocacy to frame alcohol problems in terms of easy availability and to increase support for alcohol policies (Stewart & Casswell, 1993). In the United States, alcohol control advocates used media advocacy to reframe the problem as one of public safety and quality of community life and helped pass policy to reduce access to alcohol (Seevak, 1997). Violence prevention advocates are using media advocacy to advocate for policies to reduce morbidity and mortality from firearms (Wallack, 1999). Housing activists used media advocacy to pressure a local housing authority to make repairs and improve conditions (University Research Corporation, 1996). These examples are emblematic of efforts that are using the mass media in its most powerful form to change policy.

Common to all these media advocacy campaigns is a focus on policies that change the environment in which people live and make their health decisions. Some efforts focus on a single business or government institution, such as the local housing authority; some are a series of local efforts that creates momentum for statewide policy. For example, local efforts to ban Saturday night specials (poorly made, easily concealable handguns frequently used in crime) in cities and counties throughout California eventually led to a statewide ban; media advocacy was a key strategy used by groups at both the local and statewide levels (Wallack, 1999). Other efforts are national. In each case, the policy chosen is usually an incremental step in a long-term process in which the choice is dictated by the proximate circumstances. The disability rights community, for example, used media advocacy to advocate for access to public transportation, which, because of this community's efforts, was included in the Americans with Disabilities Act of 1990. After this success, they used media advocacy to focus attention on shifting 25% of the Medicare budget from nursing homes to attendant care. Ultimately, whether media advocacy strategies are used is determined by the overall strategy and the community organizing and policy advocacy under way.

To date, most evaluations of media advocacy have been case studies (Chapman & Lupton, 1994; DeJong, 1996; Jernigan & Wright, 1996; Wallack & Dorfman, 1996; Wallack et al., 1993, 1999; Woodruff, 1996). These case studies have shown that community groups trained in media advocacy can effectively gain access to the news media and enhance their participation in the process of public policy making. In California, for example, media advocacy training, follow-up, and support were provided to hundreds of community activists, researchers, service providers, and others working on violence prevention. These skills were used in the process of passing more than 40 local ordinances throughout the state limiting the availability of firearms and ultimately passing statewide legislation banning the manufacture and sale of Saturday night specials or junk guns (Wallack, 1997, 1999). Given such issues, media advocacy can be controversial, and there are risks to the organizations that use it as part of their strategy (DeJong, 1996).

In a more systematic evaluation of the role of media advocacy in a controlled study designed to advance community policies to reduce drinking and driving, Holder and Treno (1997) concluded that media advocacy was effective in several areas and "an important tool for community prevention" (p. S198). For example, local people trained in media advocacy were able to increase local news coverage in television and newspapers and presumably frame it around policy issues. They suggest that results of the media advocacy component of the intervention "can focus public and leader attention on specific issues and approaches to local policies of relevance to reducing alcohol-involved injuries" (p. S198). Another evaluation examined the effects of media advocacy in the Stanford Five-City Heart Disease Prevention Project (Schooler, Sundar, & Flora, 1996; see Chapter 11, this volume). Dependent variables included coverage of the issue, prominence of the article, framing of the article (e.g., prevention vs. treatment), and the impact on the media agenda (i.e., ratio of locally generated articles on heart disease vs. other health issues). The study concluded that "media advocacy efforts can be successful" (p. 361) but found that maintenance of the effects was weak. In both of these evaluation studies (particularly Schooler et al., 1996), it was unclear whether there was a focus on advancing public policies or whether, as in many media efforts, the focus was related more to increasing awareness. Also, it was unclear as to whether a comprehensive media advocacy approach was implemented, as was found in the case studies on limiting alcohol outlets in Oakland and banning junk guns in California.

CONCLUSION

Public education campaigns, even if successful in changing some individual behavior, are not sufficient to address significant public health problems. These problems are rooted in our social structure and linked primarily to how we make policy decisions as a society, not personal health decisions as individuals. Media advocacy approaches designed to change policy must be integrated into public health interventions. Such approaches can make traditional health communication campaigns more comprehensive and more consistent with the mission and goals of public health.

As a society, we exalt the person who can "beat the odds" and succeed against adversity (Shorr, 1988). This "triumphant individual" story, in fact, is one of the dominant parables that guides political thought, rhetoric, and policy development in our society (Reich, 1988). Public health is a profession that should work to reduce the odds so that more people can succeed, and not a profession that simply provides information, services, and encouragement to people so they might be among the lucky ones to beat the odds. In considering media approaches, we must include the kinds of strategies that have the long-range potential to change the odds.

NOTE

1. This chapter draws extensively on Wallack (2000).

REFERENCES

Alcalay, R. (1983). The impact of mass communication campaigns in the health field. *Social Science Medicine, 17,* 87-794.

Atkin, C. K. (1981). Mass media information campaign effectiveness. In R. E. Rice & W. Paisley (Eds.), *Public communication campaigns* (pp. 265-279). Beverly Hills, CA: Sage.

Beauchamp, D. (1976). Public health as social justice. *Inquiry, 8,* 3-14.

Brown, J. B., & Walsh-Childers, K. (1994). Effects of media on personal and public health. In J. Bryant & D. Zillmann (Eds.), *Media effects: Advances in theory and research* (pp. 389-416). Hillsdale, NJ: Lawrence Erlbaum.

Chapman, S., & Lupton, D. (1984). *The fight for public health: Principles and practice of media advocacy.* London: BMJ.

Dearing, J. W., & Rogers, E. M. (1997). *Agenda-setting.* Thousand Oaks, CA: Sage.

DeJong, W. (1996). MADD Massachusetts versus Senator Burke: A media advocacy case study. *Health Education Quarterly, 23*(3), 318-329.

DeJong, W., & Wallack, L. A. (1999). Critical perspective on the Drug Czar's antidrug media campaign. *Journal of Health Communication, 5,* 155-160.

DeJong, W., & Winsten, J. A. (1998). *The media and the message.* Washington, DC: The National Campaign to Prevent Teen Pregnancy.

Dorfman, L., & Wallack, L. (1993). Advertising health: The case for counter-ads. *Public Health Reports, 108*(6), 716-726.

Gamson, W. A. (1989). News as framing: Comments on Graber. *American Behavioral Scientist, 33*(2), 157-162.

Hartman, T., & Johnson, M. (1993). *Making news: How to get news coverage for disability rights issues.* Avocado Press.

Holder, H. D., & Treno, A. J. (1997). Media advocacy in community prevention: News as a means to advance policy change. *Addiction, 92*(Suppl. 2), S189-S199.

Institute of Medicine. (1998). *The future of public health*. Washington, DC: National Academy Press.

Iyengar, S. (1991). *Is anyone responsible?* Chicago: University of Chicago Press.

Jernigan, D. H., & Wright, P. A. (1996). Media advocacy: Lessons from community experiences. *Journal of Public Health Policy, 17*(3), 306-330.

Lefebvre, C., & Flora, J. (1988). Social marketing and public health intervention. *Health Education Quarterly, 15*(3), 299-315.

Lomas, J. (1998). Social capital and health: Implications for public health and epidemiology. *Social Science Medicine, 47*(9), 1181-1188.

Mann, J. M. (1997). Medicine and public health, ethics and human rights. *Hastings Center Report, 27*(3), 6-13.

McCombs, M., & Shaw, D. (1972). The agenda-setting function of mass media. *Public Opinion Quarterly, 36*, 176-187.

McGuire, W. J. (1986). The myth of massive media impact: Savaging and salvagings. In G. Comstock (Ed.), *Public communication and behavior* (Vol. 1, pp. 173-257). New York: Academic Press.

McKinlay, J. B., & Marceau, L. D. (2000). To boldly go. . . . *American Journal of Public Health, 90*(1), 25.

Mills, C. W. (1959). *The sociological imagination*. New York: Oxford University Press.

Reich, R. B. (1988). *Tales of a new America: The anxious liberal's guide to the future*. New York: Vintage.

Rogers, E. M., & Storey, J. D. (1987). Communication campaigns. In C. R. Berger & S. H. Chaffee (Eds.), *Handbook of communication science* (pp. 817-846). Newbury Park, CA: Sage.

Rose, G. (1985). Sick individuals and sick populations. *International Journal of Epidemiology, 14*(1), 32-38.

Rose, G. (1992). *The strategy of preventive medicine*. New York: Oxford University Press.

Ryan, C. (1976). *Blaming the victim*. New York: Vintage.

Ryan, C. (1991). *Prime time activism*. Boston: South End Press.

Salmon, C. (Ed.) (1989). *Information campaigns: Balancing social values and social change*. Newbury Park, CA: Sage.

Schooler, C., Sundar, S. S., & Flora, J. (1996). Effects of the Stanford five-city project media advocacy program. *Health Education Quarterly, 23*(3), 346-364.

Seevak, A. (1997, December 7). Oakland shows the way: The coalition on alcohol outlet issues and media advocacy as a tool for policy change. *Berkeley Media Studies Group, 3*.

Shorr, L. (1988). *Within our reach*. New York: Anchor/Doubleday.

Stewart, E., & Casswell, S. (1993). Media advocacy for alcohol policy support: Results from the New Zealand Community Action Project. *Health Promotion International, 8*(3), 165-175.

U.S. Department of Health and Human Services. (1988, January). *Media strategies for smoking control*. Washington, DC: Government Printing Office.

University Research Corporation. (1996, August 14). *Henry Horner Mothers Guild: Tenants go public on public housing*. Submitted to U.S. Office of Personnel Management and the Center for Substance Abuse Prevention under OPM Contract No. 91-2960.

Wallack, L. (1981). Mass media campaigns: The odds against finding behavior change. *Health Education Quarterly, 8*(3), 209-260.

Wallack, L. (1984). Drinking and driving: Toward a broader understanding of the role of mass media. *Journal of Public Health Policy, 5*(4), 471-498.

Wallack, L. (1989). Mass communication and health promotion: A critical perspective. In R. E. Rice & C. K. Atkin (Eds.), *Public communication campaigns* (2nd ed., pp. 353-367). Newbury Park, CA: Sage.

Wallack, L. (1990). Improving health promotion: Media advocacy and social marketing approaches. In C. Atkin & L. Wallack (Eds.), *Mass communication and public health: Complexities and conflicts* (pp. 147-163). Newbury Park, CA: Sage.

Wallack, L. (1994). Media advocacy: A strategy for empowering people and communities. *Journal of Public Health Policy, 15*(4), 420-436.

Wallack, L. (1997). Strategies for reducing youth violence: Media, community and policy. *University of California/the California Wellness Foundation, 1997 Wellness Lectures* (pp. 37-69). Berkeley: The Regents of the University of California.

Wallack, L. (1999). The California violence prevention initiative: Advancing policy to ban Saturday night specials. *Health Education and Behavior, 26*(6), 841-857.

Wallack, L. (2000). The role of mass media in creating social capital: A new direction for public health. In B. D. Smedley & S. L. Syme (Eds.), *Promoting health: Intervention strategies from social and behavioral research* (pp. 260-283). Washington, DC: National Academy Press.

Wallack, L., & DeJong, W. (1995). Mass media and public health. In U.S. Department of Health and Human Services (Ed.), *The effects of mass media on the use and abuse of alcohol* (pp. 253-268). Bethesda, MD: National Institute of Health.

Wallack, L., & Dorfman, L. (1996). Media advocacy: A strategy for advancing policy and promoting health. *Health Education Quarterly, 23*(3), 293-317.

Wallack, L., Dorfman, L., Jernigan, D., & Themba, M. (1993). *Media advocacy and public health: Power for prevention*. Newbury Park, CA: Sage.

Wallack, L., & Sciandra, R. (1990-1991). Media advocacy and public education in the community trial to reduce heavy smoking. *International Quarterly of Community Health Education, 11*, 205-222.

Wallack, L., Woodruff, K., Dorfman, L., & Diaz, I. (1999). *News for a change: An advocate's guide to working with the media*. Thousand Oaks, CA: Sage.

Winett, L., & Wallack, L. (1996). Advancing public health goals through the mass media. *Journal of Health Communication, 1*(2), 173-196.

Woodruff, K. (1996). Alcohol advertising and violence against women: A media advocacy case study. *Health Education Quarterly, 23*(3), 330-345.

Related References

Clearly, since the first edition in 1981, when there were essentially no other books on the topic, the range of books has expanded tremendously, as the following listing indicates. On one hand, this may indicate greater competition in the marketplace for textbooks on public communication campaigns. On the other hand, it is evidence of the growing need for, and importance of, good research and implementation materials about campaigns.

Atkin, C., & Wallack, L. (Eds.). (1990). *Mass communication and public health: Complexities and conflicts.* Newbury Park, CA: Sage.

Backer, T., & Rogers, E. (1993). *Organizational aspects of health communication campaigns: What works?* Newbury Park, CA: Sage.

Backer, T., Rogers, E. M., & Sopory, P. (1992). *Designing health communication campaigns: What works?* Newbury Park, CA: Sage.

Bogart, L. (1984). *Strategy in advertising: Matching media and messages to markets and motivations.* Chicago: Crain.

Bracht, N. (Ed.). (1999). *Health promotion at the community level: New advances* (2nd ed.). Thousand Oaks, CA: Sage.

Brawley, E. (1983). *Mass media and human services.* Beverly Hills, CA: Sage.

Brennan, P. F., Schneider, S., & Tornquist, E. (1997). *Information networks for community health (Computers in health care).* New York: Springer.

Dearing, J. W., & Rogers, E. M. (1996). *Agenda-setting.* Thousand Oaks, CA: Sage.

Dignan, M., & Carr, P. (1986). *Program planning for health education and health promotion.* Philadelphia: Lea & Febiger.

Donohew, L., Sypher, H., & Bukoski, W. (Eds.). (1991). *Persuasive communication and drug abuse prevention.* Hillsdale, NJ: Lawrence Erlbaum.

Dozier, D., Grunig, L., & Grunig, J. (1995). *Manager's guide to excellence in public relations and communication management.* Mahwah, NJ: Lawrence Erlbaum.

Edgar, T., Fitzpatrick, M. A., & Freimuth, V. S. (Eds.). (1992). *AIDS: A communication perspective.* Hillsdale, NJ: Lawrence Erlbaum.

Fine, S. (1981). *The marketing of ideas and social issues.* New York: Praeger.

Frederiksen, L., Solomon, L., & Brehony, K. (1984). *Marketing health behavior: Principles, techniques, and applications.* New York: Plenum.

Freimuth, V. S., Stein, J., & Kean, T. (1989). *Searching for health information: The Cancer Information Service model.* Philadelphia: University of Pennsylvania Press.

Galbally, R. (1997). *A firm foundation for health promotion: An organisational approach.* Melbourne, Australia: VicHealth.

Glanz, K., Lewis, F., & Rimer, B. (Eds.). (1990). *Health behavior and health education: Theory, research, and practice.* San Francisco: Jossey-Bass.

Glasser, T., & Salmon, C. T. (Eds.). (1995). *Public opinion and the communication of consent.* New York: Guilford.

Goldberg, M., Fishbein, M., & Middlestadt, S. (Eds.). (1997). *Social marketing: Theoretical and practical perspectives.* Mahwah, NJ: Lawrence Erlbaum.

Green, L., & Kreuter, M. (1991). *Health promotion planning: An educational and environmental approach* (2nd ed.). Mountain View, CA: Mayfield.

Green, L., & Lewis, F. (1986). *Measurement and evaluation in health education and health promotion.* Palo Alto, CA: Mayfield.

Grunig, J., Dozier, D., & Grunig, L. (Eds.). (1992). *Excellence in public relations and communication management.* Hillsdale, NJ: Lawrence Erlbaum.

Grunig, J., & Hunt, T. (1984). *Managing public relations.* New York: Holt, Rinehart & Winston.

Harris, L. (Ed.). (1995). *Health and the new media: Technologies transforming personal and public health.* Mahwah, NJ: Lawrence Erlbaum.

Hastings House. (1977). *Controversy advertising: How advertisers present points of view in public affairs.* New York: Author.

Hornik, R. C. (1988). *Development communication: Information, agriculture, and nutrition in the Third World.* New York: Longman.

Kotler, P. (1982). *Marketing for non-profit organizations.* Englewood Cliffs, NJ: Prentice Hall.

Kotler, P. (1987). *Marketing for health care organizations.* Englewood Cliffs, NJ: Prentice Hall.

Kotler, P., & Roberto, E. (1989). *Social marketing: Strategies for changing public behavior.* New York: Free Press.

Lasswell, H., Lerner, D., & Speier, H. (Eds.). (1979). *Propaganda and communication in world history: Vol. 1. The symbolic instrument in early times.* Honolulu: University Press of Hawaii.

Lasswell, H., Lerner, D., & Speier, H. (Eds.). (1980). *Propaganda and communication in world history: Vol. 2. Emergence of public opinion in the West.* Honolulu: University Press of Hawaii.

Leathar, D., Hastings, G., & Davies, J. (Eds.). (1981). *Health education and the media.* Oxford, UK: Pergamon.

Leathar, D., Hastings, G., O'Reilly, K., & Davies, J. (Eds.). (1986). *Health education and the media, II.* Oxford, UK: Pergamon.

Maibach, E., & Parrott, R. (Eds.). (1995). *Designing health messages: Approaches from communication theory and public health practice.* Thousand Oaks, CA: Sage.

Manoff, R. K. (1985). *Social marketing: New imperative for public health.* New York: Praeger.

Matarazzo, J., Weiss, S., Herd, J., Miller, N., & Weiss, S. (Eds.). (1984). *Behavioral health: A handbook of health enhancement and disease prevention.* New York: Wiley.

Matera, F., & Artigue, R. (1999). *Public relations campaigns and techniques: Building bridges into the 21st century.* Boston: Allyn & Bacon. (See chapter, "The Information Campaign: Does Smokey Bear Practice Safe Sex?")

Mcycr, M. (Ed.). (1981). *Health education by television and radio.* Munich: K. G. Saur Verlag. (Reprinted in German and French versions in 1982 and 1983, respectively)

Paletz, D. (1977). *Politics in public service advertising on television.* New York: Praeger.

Pfau, M., & Parrott, R. (1992). *Persuasive communication campaigns.* Boston: Allyn & Bacon.

Piotrow, P. T., Kincaid, D. L., Rimon, J., Jr., & Rinehart, W. (1997). *Health communication: Lessons from family planning and reproductive health.* Westport, CT: Praeger.

Proctor, R. (1995). *Cancer wars: How politics shapes what you know and don't know about cancer.* New York: Basic Books.

Ratzan, S. (Ed.). (1993). *AIDS: Effective health communication for the 90s.* Washington, DC: Taylor & Francis.

Rogers, E. M. (1993). *Diffusion of innovations* (4th ed.). New York: Free Press.

Rothman, J., Teresa, J., Kay, T., & Morningstar, G. (1983). *Marketing human service innovations.* Beverly Hills, CA: Sage.

Salmon, C. T. (Ed.). (1989). *Information campaigns: Balancing social values and social change.* Newbury Park, CA: Sage.

Schultz, D. (1984). *Strategic advertising campaigns.* Chicago: Crain.

Sechrest, L., Backer, T., Rogers, E. M., Campbell, T. F., & Grady, M. L. (Eds.). (1994). *Effective dissemination of clinical and health information* (Agency for Health Care Policy and Research Conference Summary, Publication No. 95-0015). Rockville, MD: Agency for Health Care Policy and Research, Public Health Service.

Seedhouse, D. (1997). *Health promotion: Philosophy, prejudice and practice.* Chichester, UK: Wiley.

Selnow, G., & Crano, W. (1987). *Planning, implementing, and evaluating targeted communication programs: A manual for business communicators.* New York: Quorum.

Shoemaker, P. (Ed.). (1989). *Communication campaigns about drugs: Government, media, and the public.* Hillsdale, NJ: Lawrence Erlbaum.

Siegel, M., & Doner, L. (1998). *Marketing public health: Strategies to promote social change.* Gaithersburg, MD: Aspen.

Singhal, A., & Rogers, E. M. (1999). *Entertainment-education: A communication strategy for social change.* Mahwah, NJ: Lawrence Erlbaum.

Street, R. L., Gold, W., & Manning, T. (Eds.). (1997). *Health promotion and interactive technology: Theoretical applications and future directions.* Mahwah, NJ: Lawrence Erlbaum.

Valente, T. (1995). *Network models of the diffusion of innovations.* Cresskill, NJ: Hampton.

Wallack, L., Dorfman, L., Jernigan, D., & Themba, M. (1993). *Media advocacy and public health: Power for prevention.* Newbury Park, CA: Sage.

Windsor, R., Baranowski, T., Clark, N., & Cutter, G. (1984). *Evaluation of health promotion and education programs.* Palo Alto, CA: Mayfield.

Winett, R. (1986). *Information and behavior: Systems of influence.* Hillsdale, NJ: Lawrence Erlbaum.

Winston, W. (1986). *Advertising handbook for health care services.* New York: Haworth.

Index

About the Authors

Ronny Adhikarya, PhD, works for the Agricultural Extension Service, Food and Agricultural Organization, United Nations, in Rome.

R. Kirkland Ahern is a doctoral student at the University of Pennsylvania's Annenberg School for Communication. Her research interests are the neurological and psychological processes of cognition and affect that give rise to message effects, such as how health messages are processed and how the Internet affects information perception.

Charles K. Atkin, PhD, is Professor in the Departments of Communication and Telecommunication at Michigan State University. His research has focused on the effects of TV advertising and public service messages on youthful audiences, and he is recognized as one of the nation's leading experts on alcohol advertising campaigns. He conducted the first major study of adolescents and alcohol advertising in 1980. He has testified to the U.S. Senate and House committees on alcohol advertising issues and served as a consultant to Surgeon General Koop on the role of advertising in drunk driving. Among his numerous publications on this subject, he wrote the key chapter reviewing survey and experimental evidence for the 1995 NIAAA monograph on alcohol advertising. He is currently conducting a large grant project on liquor advertising for the Robert Wood Johnson Foundation. He has carried out many grants from state and federal agencies to examine the role of television in preventing alcohol use and abuse, especially with teenagers. He is co-editor of *Public Communication Campaigns* and *Mass Communication and Public Health.*

Bryan Ax is Multimedia Programmer in the Division of Biomedical Communications at the University of Arizona.

Sherry L. Barr, PsyD, is Director of the New Jersey Teen Prevention Education Program, Princeton University. She is actively involved in prevention programming and evaluation addressing body image, eating disorders, alcohol use, violence, and sexual health.

Ron Borland is Deputy Director of the Centre for Behavioural Research in Cancer at the Anti-Cancer Council of Victoria, Australia.

Neil Bracht, MPH, is Professor Emeritus in the School of Public Health and School of Social Work at the University of Minnesota and is also an independent community health consultant. He is editor of *Health Promotion at the Community Level: New Advances* (2nd ed.) (1999).

Melissa Brown is an Instructional Design Specialist in the Center for Behavioral Research at the AMC Cancer Research Center.

David B. Buller is Senior Scientist in the Center for Behavioral Research at the AMC Cancer Research Center. He is the principal investigator on the Comparison of Community Channels for Family Sun Safety, Sunny Days, Healthy Ways Grades 6-8 Sun Safety Curricula, and Arresting Smoking Uptake With Interactive Multimedia projects.

Matilda Butler, PhD, conducted research on health and education issues at Stanford University; managed health and education outreach programs at Far West Laboratory; and cofounded an electronic publishing company, Knowledge Access International. She is coauthor of *Women and the Mass Media* and coeditor of *Knowledge Utilization Systems in Education.*

Joseph N. Cappella, PhD, is Professor of Communication and holds the Gerald R. Miller Chair at the Annenberg School for Communication at the University of Pennsylvania. His research has focused on social interaction, interpersonal communication, political communication, nonverbal behavior, media effects, and statistical methods. He is author of *Spiral of Cynicism, Multivariate Techniques in Human Communication Research,* and *Sequence and Pattern in Communicative Behavior.* He is a Fellow of the ICA, recipient of the B. Aubrey Fisher Mentorship Award, and President of the International Communication Association.

Robert B. Cialdini, PhD, is Regents' Professor of Psychology and Distinguished Graduate Research Professor at Arizona State University. He has been elected president of the Society of Personality and Social Psychology and of the Personality and Social Psychology Division of the American Psychological Association. His research interests include the social influence process and strategies of self-presentation.

James W. Dearing, PhD, is a Professor in the Department of Communication at Michigan State University. He teaches courses in diffusion of innovations and evaluation of communication programs. He is author of *Growing a Japanese Science City: Communication in Scientific Research* and coauthor of *Agenda-Setting.*

William DeJong, PhD, is Lecturer on health communication, Department of Health and Social Behavior, Director of The Higher Education Center for Alcohol and Other Drug Prevention, and Director of Communications for the Harvard Center for Cancer Prevention at Harvard University. He focuses on research synthesis and technology transfer, policy analysis and development, intervention design and evaluation, and the application of health communication strategies, especially using the mass media. He is a governing member of the Oversight Council for the Massachusetts Tobacco Control Program, serves on the executive board of the Harvard Center for Cancer Prevention, and serves on the national board of directors for Mothers Against Drunk Driving.

Brenda Dervin, PhD, is Professor in the School of Journalism and Communications at Ohio State University. Her research and teaching focus on the philosophy of communication, qualitative and quantitative interpretive research methodologies, and applied communication theory focusing specifically on democratic and responsive design, including the design of interactive systems, communication education programs, and information and communication structures. She is coauthoring books tentatively titled *The Phone in the Eye of the Beholder: The Missing User in Telecommunication Research* and *Sense-Making as Methodology Between the Cracks.*

Lewis Donohew, PhD, is Professor Emeritus in the Department of Communication at the University of Kentucky. He has focused on human attention processes and the science of persuasive message design. He is author of *Persuasive Communication and Drug Abuse Prevention* and *Communication and Health: Systems and Applications.*

Lori Dorfman is Director of the Berkeley Media Studies Group (BMSG), a project of the Public Health Institute, where she directs BMSG's work with community groups, journalists, and public health professionals. Her current research examines how local television news and newspapers portray youth and violence. She has published articles on public health and mass communication issues, coauthored *Public Health and Media Advocacy: Power for Prevention* and *News for a Change: An Advocate's Guide to Working With the Media,* and is completing a book on how television reports on health.

David M. Dozier, PhD, is Professor of Public Relations and Communication Management in the School of Journalism at San Diego State University. He is coauthor of *Using Research in Public Relations: Applications to Program Management* and *Manager's Guide to Excellence in Public Relations and Communication Management.* He is a principal in Lauzen & Dozier Associates, a communication research and planning consulting firm in San Diego.

Martin Fishbein, PhD, is the Harry C. Coles, Jr. Distinguished Professor of Communication in the Public Policy Center of the Annenberg School for Communication at the University of Pennsylvania. He was appointed a Guggenheim Fellow, was 1 of the 10 initial inductees in the American Marketing Association's Attitude Research Hall of Fame in 1981, and received CDC's Charles C. Shepard Science Award in 1999 for scientific excellence. In addition to contributing many articles and chapters to professional books and journals, he has authored or edited six books.

June A. Flora, PhD, is Senior Research Scholar in the Stanford Center for Research in Disease Prevention at the Stanford University Medical School. She has authored or coauthored many peer-reviewed journal articles and book chapters in the area of health communication and social marketing, particularly mass media campaign effects, message design, audience analysis, and the design of anti-tobacco messages and campaigns. She is writing a book on the lessons learned from the Stanford Five-City media campaigns. She also consults regularly, reviews grants, and serves on national and state health advisory boards.

Dennis R. Foote, PhD, is Vice President and Director of Global Communications and Distance Learning Systems at the Academy for Educational Development. He concentrates on evaluating the impact of social programs, both in the United States and abroad.

Vicki S. Freimuth, PhD, is Associate Director for Communication at the Centers for Disease Control and Prevention. Her research focuses on the role of communication in health promotion and disease prevention. She is editor of *AIDS: A Communication Perspective* and author of *Searching for Health Information.*

Micheline Frenette, MSc, MPs, is Associate Professor in the Department of Communication at the University of Montreal. Her research and teaching focus on media theory and applied communication, the design and evaluation of health campaigns and of educational technology, the integration of communication technologies in family and school settings, and qualitative and quantitative research methodologies. She has authored a book on adolescents and television.

Walter Gantz, PhD, is Chair of the Department of Telecommunication at Indiana University.

Fern Walter Goodhart, MSPH, CHES, is Director of Health Education in the Rutgers University Health Services and Lecturer in the University of Medicine and Dentistry of New Jersey School of Public Health. Her interests focus on adolescent health and sexual education and on public health education and advocacy.

Bradley S. Greenberg, PhD, is University Distinguished Professor of Communication and Telecommunication at Michigan State University. He has investigated the content and effects of televised portrayals of sex, ethnicity, social roles, and substance use. Currently, he is studying awareness and the impact of the new television program ratings system. He is coauthor of *Media, Sex and the Adolescent* and *The Alphabet Soup of Television Program Ratings.*

James E. Grunig, PhD, is Professor of Public Relations in the Department of Journalism at the University of Maryland. He is coauthor of *Managing Public Relations, Public Relations Techniques,* and *Manager's Guide to Excellence in Public Relations and Communication Management.* He is editor of *Excellence in Public Relations and Communication Management.*

Larissa A. Grunig, PhD, is Associate Professor in the Department of Journalism at the University of Maryland. She teaches and conducts research on public relations, development communication, communication theory, gender issues, organizational response to activism, organizational power and structure, and scientific and technical writing. She is founding coeditor of the *Journal of Public Relations Research* and is author of *Manager's Guide to Excellence in Public Relations and Communication Management* and *Women in Public Relations.*

John R. Hall is Associate Director of the Division of Biomedical Communications at the University of Arizona.

Nancy Grant Harrington, PhD, is Chair of the Department of Communication at the University of Kentucky. She conducts research on persuasive message design and evaluation, with an emphasis on adolescent and young adult health promotion and disease prevention.

Joan Marquardt Hines, MPH, is Senior Project Manager of the Center for Health Communication at the AMC Cancer Research Center.

Robert Hornik, PhD, is Professor in the Annenberg School for Communication at the University of Pennsylvania. He holds the Wilbur Schramm Chair in Communication and Health Policy and is affiliated with the Health Communication Group of the Annenberg Public Policy Center. He is currently coprincipal investigator and scientific director for the evaluation of the National Youth Anti-Drug Media Campaign and principal investigator on two evaluations of domestic violence prevention projects. He is currently writing *Public Health Communication: Evidence for Behavior Change.*

D. Lawrence Kincaid, PhD, is a faculty member of Social and Behavioral Sciences, Department of Health Policy and Management, in the School of Public Health and also Senior Advisor in the Center for Communication Programs at Johns Hopkins University. His research interests include the evaluation of the impact of health communication programs, communication networks and social influence, and cognitive image mapping. He is coauthor of *Communication Networks: Toward a New Paradigm for Research.*

Lisa Laitman, MEd, is Director of the Alcohol and Other Drug Assistance Program for Students in the Rutgers University Health Services at Rutgers University and is a Certified Alcohol and Drug Counselor.

Linda C. Lederman, PhD, is Professor and a director of the CHI—the Communication and Health Issues Partnership for Education and Research in the School of Communication and Information Studies at Rutgers University. She specializes in interpersonal and instructional communication, with an emphasis on qualitative research methods. Her simulation of drinking-related decisions for college students called *Imagine That!* is currently in use at more than 250 colleges and universities in the United States and Canada.

Debra A. Lieberman, PhD, is Senior Researcher at the Institute for Social, Behavioral, and Economic Research at the University of California, Santa Barbara. She is also a research, evaluation, and instructional design consultant in the software industry. She specializes in interactive media learning.

Alan P. L. Liu, PhD, is Professor of Political Science, University of California, Santa Barbara. His current research deals with comparative modernizations in the People's Republic of China, the Republic of China (Taiwan), and the Pacific Basin area. He is the author of *Communications and National Integration in Communist China, Political Culture and Group Conflict in Communist China, How China is Ruled, Phoenix and the Lame Lion, Modernization in Taiwan and Mainland China 1950-80,* and *Mass Politics in the People's Republic.*

William J. McGuire, PhD, is Professor Emeritus in the Department of Psychology at Yale University. His research has focused on attitude change, the self-concept, and the structure of thought systems. His most recent book is *Constructing Social Psychology: Creative and Critical Processes.*

Lisa Murray-Johnson, PhD, is Professor in the Department of Communication at Michigan State University. She focuses her research and teaching in the areas of health, cognition and affect, interpersonal communication, communication theories, and research design and evaluation. Other projects concern inter-cultural health communication, occupational safety and health, risk communication, cognitive load and affect in interpersonal deception, and mother-daughter communication.

Garrett J. O'Keefe, PhD, is Professor of Life Sciences Communication and Environmental Studies at the University of Wisconsin-Madison. He has written extensively on the uses and effects of public information campaigns pertaining to environment, health, and public safety, as well as on public opinion and media effects.

William J. Paisley, PhD, was coeditor of the first edition of this volume (1981) and taught in the Stanford University Communication Department from 1965 to 1985. He since has cofounded and codirected Knowledge Access, Inc., an electronic publishing company. His research and writing continue to focus on American public knowledge in its social-historical context.

Philip Palmgreen, PhD, is Professor in the Department of Communication at the University of Kentucky. He is known for his research on media drug abuse prevention campaigns and for his work on audience uses of the mass media. He is a member of the Behavior Change Expert Panel guiding the Office of National Drug Control Policy's $2 billion National Youth Anti-Drug Media Campaign.

Phyllis Tilson Piotrow, PhD, is Director of the Center for Communication Programs and Professor in the Department of Population and Family Health Sciences at Johns Hopkins University. She is coauthor of *Health Communication: Lessons From Family Planning and Reproductive Health* and author of *World Population Crisis: The United States Response.*

Richard L. Powell, MPA, is Instructor/Coordinator of Alcohol and Other Drug Education Program for Training in the Department of Health Education at Rutgers University. His interest is in high-risk student behaviors.

Robert Proctor, PhD, is Professor of the History of Science in the Department of History and Religious Studies at Pennsylvania State University. He specializes in the political history and philosophy of science and the social construction of ignorance and impotence. Recent books include *Racial Hygiene: Medicine Under the Nazis; Value-Free Science? Purity and Power in Modern Knowledge; Cancer Wars: How Politics Shapes What We Know and Don't Know About Cancer;* and *The Nazi War on Cancer.*

Kathaleen Reid-Martinez, PhD, is Dean of the Center for Leadership Studies at Regent University. She has worked extensively on rhetorical analysis of information campaigns, and she currently focuses on leadership and management styles and strategies.

Ronald E. Rice, PhD, is Professor in the School of Communication, Information and Library Studies at Rutgers University. He has coauthored or coedited *Public Communication Campaigns; The New Media: Communication, Research and Technology; Managing Organizational Innovation; Research Methods and the New Media;* and *The Internet and Health Communication.* He has conducted research and published widely in communication science, public communication campaigns, computer-mediated communication systems, methodology, organizational and management theory, information systems, information science and bibliometrics, and social networks. He is currently on the ICA Publications Board and is on the editorial board of six communication, management, information science, and information systems journals.

Everett M. Rogers is Regents' Professor in the Department of Communication and Journalism at the University of New Mexico. He is most widely known for his book *Diffusion of Innovations* (4th ed.). He has been teaching and conducting research on the diffusion of innovations for the past 40 years. He was co-principal investigator of the Stanford Heart Disease Prevention Program. Rogers has also authored or coauthored books on the history of communication study, organizational aspects of health communication campaigns, intercultural communication, development communication, Silicon Valley, and agenda-setting, and he is coauthor of *Entertainment-Education: A Communication Strategy for Social Change.*

Charles T. Salmon, PhD, is Associate Dean for Graduate Education and Research and the Ellis N. Brandt Professor of Public Relations in the College of Communication Arts and Sciences at Michigan State University. He is editor of *Information Campaigns: Balancing Social Values and Social Change* and coeditor of *Public Opinion and the Communication of Consent.* He has evaluated campaigns for the Minnesota Heart Health Program and served as a visiting scientist with the Centers for Disease Control and Prevention, where he conducted communication research for the National AIDS Information and Education Program and the Division of Diabetes Translation.

Sarah Sayeed, PhD, is a post-doctoral researcher at the Annenberg School for Communication at the University of Pennsylvania. She is engaged in research about antidrug media campaigns, especially on the interplay of interpersonal and mass communication processes in determining health outcomes.

Arvind Singhal, PhD, is Professor in the College of Communication at Ohio University. He teaches and conducts research in the areas of diffusion of innovations, organizing for change, design and implementation of strategic communication campaigns, and the entertainment-education communication strategy. He is coauthor of *India's Information Revolution* and *Entertainment-Education: A Communication Strategy for Social Change.*

Leslie B. Snyder, PhD, is Professor in the Department of Communication Sciences at the University of Connecticut. She studies the effectiveness of health, environment, and advertising campaigns, domestically and abroad, and how people process news. She is currently examining the effects of liquor advertising on youth, and she is coprincipal investigator on a U.S. Department of Agriculture contract conducting and evaluating the Eight-Mile River campaign.

Michael T. Stephenson, PhD, is Assistant Professor in the Department of Communication at the University of Missouri-Columbia. His research focuses on illicit substance use and prevention, message processing, persuasion, and mass media health campaigns.

Lea P. Stewart, PhD, is Professor in the Department of Communication at Rutgers University and a director of CHI—the Communication and Health Issues Partnership for Education and Research at the School of Communication and Information Studies at Rutgers University. She specializes in communication, gender issues, and experience-based learning. She has written extensively about media campaigns and gender bias.

Thomas W. Valente, PhD, is Director of the MPH Program of the School of Medicine, UCLA. He teaches and conducts research on evaluation of communication programs to promote health-related behaviors. He is author of *Network Models of the Diffusion of Innovations* and *Methods for Communication Campaign Evaluation.*

Lawrence Wallack, PhD, is Professor of Public Health, Division of Health Policy and Administration, at the University of California, Berkeley; Codirector of the Berkeley Media Studies Group; and Professor in the School of Community Health, College of Urban and Public Affairs, Portland State University. His research interests include media advocacy for violence prevention, case studies in media advocacy, and the role of mass communication to address public health problems. He is the principal author of *Media Advocacy and Public Health* and coeditor of *Mass Media and Public Health: Complexities and Conflicts.*

Jay A. Winsten, PhD, is Associate Dean for Public and Community Affairs, Frank Stanton Director of the Center for Health Communication, and a faculty member in the School of Public Health at Harvard University. He has written a variety of articles on health policy and scientific research for both the popular press and academic journals. He is coeditor (with Nobel laureate James Watson and Howard Hiatt) of *Origins of Human Cancer.*

Kim Witte, PhD, is Assistant Professor in the Department of Communication at Michigan State University. She conducts research on the development of effective health risk messages for members of diverse cultures. She serves on 11 editorial boards and has served as expert consultant to several government agencies.

W. Gill Woodall is Associate Professor in the Department of Communication and Journalism and in the Department of Internal Medicine and is also Director of Prevention Research at the Center on Alcohol, Substance Abuse, and Addiction at the University of New Mexico.